ANONYMOUS NOISE

Ryoko Fukuyama

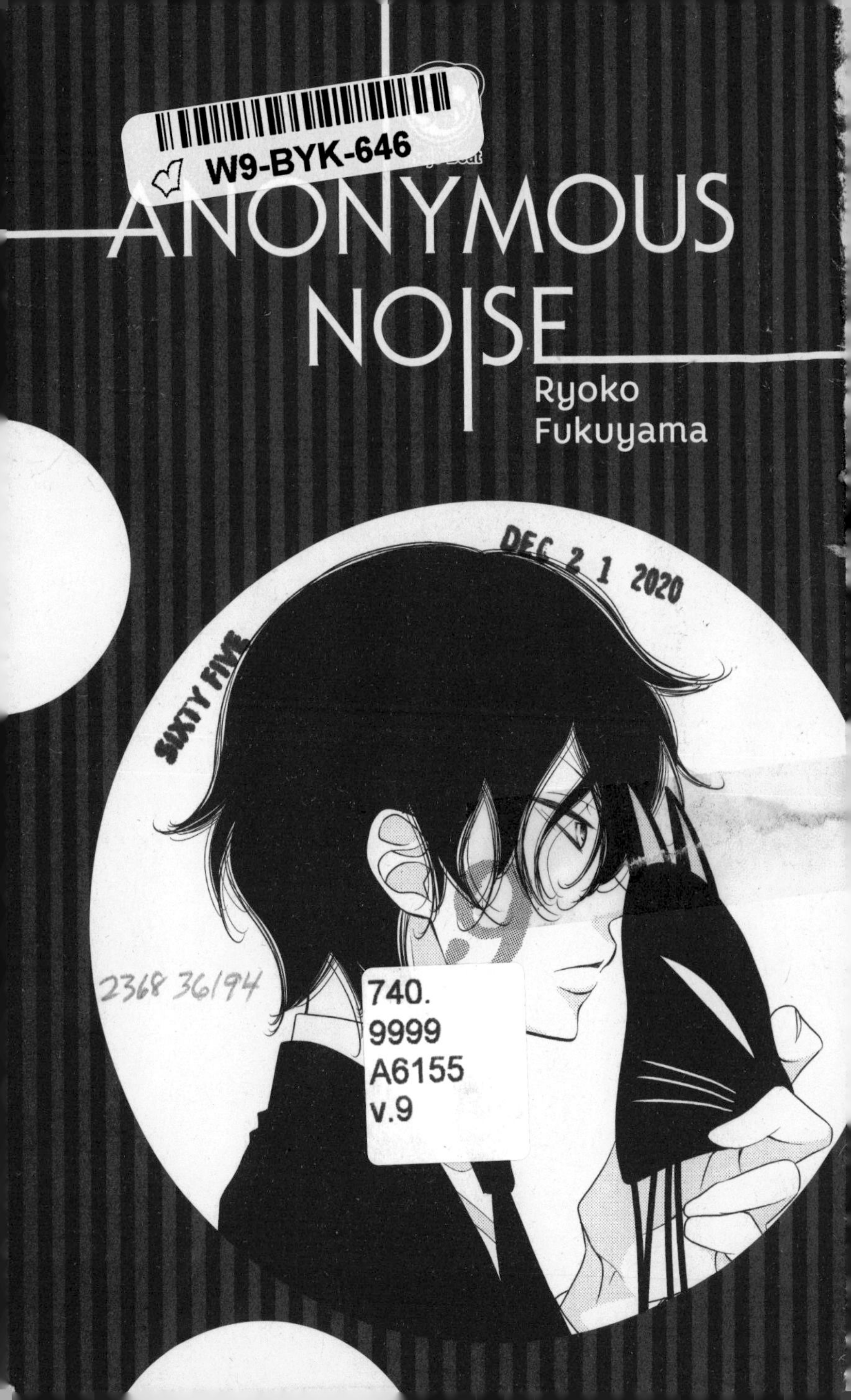

Characters

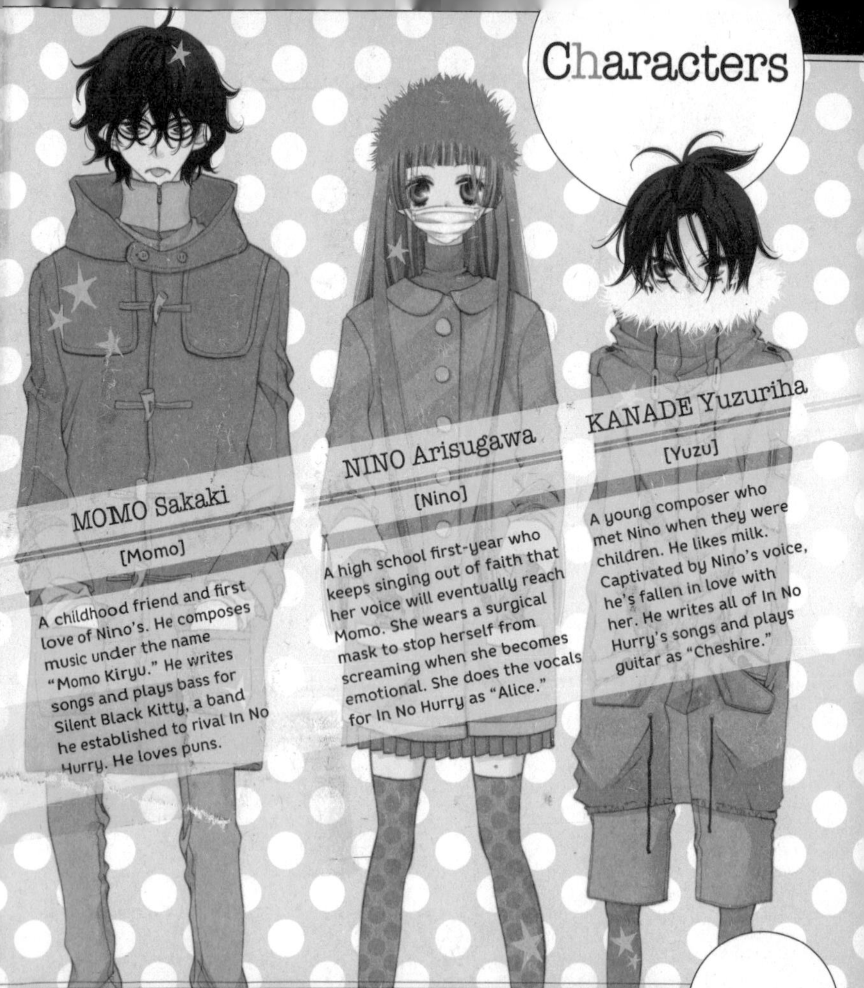

MOMO Sakaki
[Momo]

A childhood friend and first love of Nino's. He composes music under the name "Momo Kiryu." He writes songs and plays bass for Silent Black Kitty, a band he established to rival In No Hurry. He loves puns.

NINO Arisugawa
[Nino]

A high school first-year who keeps singing out of faith that her voice will eventually reach Momo. She wears a surgical mask to stop herself from screaming when she becomes emotional. She does the vocals for In No Hurry as "Alice."

KANADE Yuzuriha
[Yuzu]

A young composer who met Nino when they were children. He likes milk. Captivated by Nino's voice, he's fallen in love with her. He writes all of In No Hurry's songs and plays guitar as "Cheshire."

Story

★ Music-loving Nino was abandoned twice in her youth—first by her girlhood crush Momo and then by the young composer Yuzu. Believing both their promises that they will find her again through her voice, Nino keeps singing. Later, in high school, she reunites with Yuzu, who invites her to become In No Hurry's new singer. Once again having a reason to sing, Nino throws herself into her vocal training.

★ Meanwhile, Momo becomes a rival to Yuzu and forms his own masked alternative rock band called "Silent Black Kitty." The two bands face off against each other in spectacular performances at the Rock Horizon festival, but after his set, Momo disappears.

★ Striving to reach new heights, In No Hurry is embarking upon its first national tour. As the members complete their preparations, they're informed of two shocking developments: Momo has been found, and the band will be playing a double bill with Silent Black Kitty in the last show of the tour.

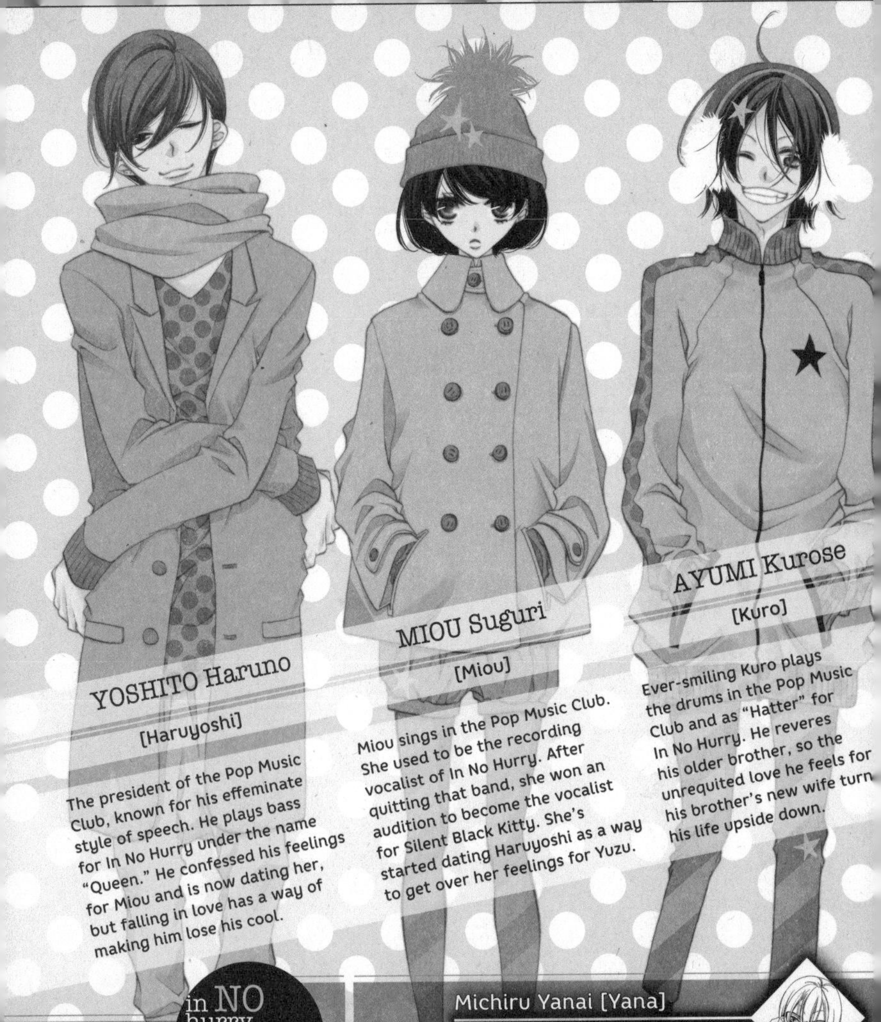

YOSHITO Haruno
[Haruyoshi]

The president of the Pop Music Club, known for his effeminate style of speech. He plays bass for In No Hurry under the name "Queen." He confessed his feelings for Miou and is now dating her, but falling in love has a way of making him lose his cool.

MIOU Suguri
[Miou]

Miou sings in the Pop Music Club. She used to be the recording vocalist of In No Hurry. After quitting that band, she won an audition to become the vocalist for Silent Black Kitty. She's started dating Haruyoshi as a way to get over her feelings for Yuzu.

AYUMI Kurose
[Kuro]

Ever-smiling Kuro plays the drums in the Pop Music Club and as "Hatter" for In No Hurry. He reveres his older brother, so the unrequited love he feels for his brother's new wife turn his life upside down.

in NO hurry to shout;

In No Hurry to Shout

A popular rock band whose members hide their identities with masks and eye patches.
Vocals: Alice
Guitar: Cheshire
Bass: Queen
Drums: Hatter

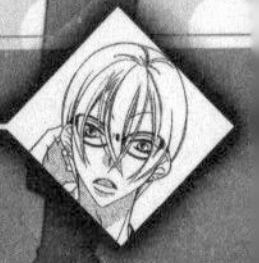

Michiru Yanai [Yana]

In No Hurry's business manager.
A heavy smoker.

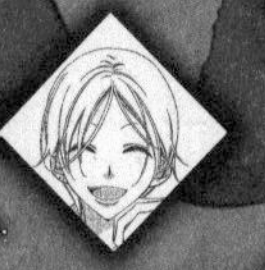

Tsukika Kuze

Momo's manager who acts as something of a foster mother to him.

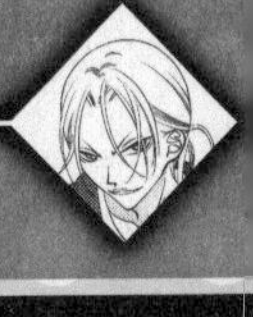

Ayame Hojo

Silent Black Kitty's drummer.

Anonymous Noise
Volume 9

CONTENTS

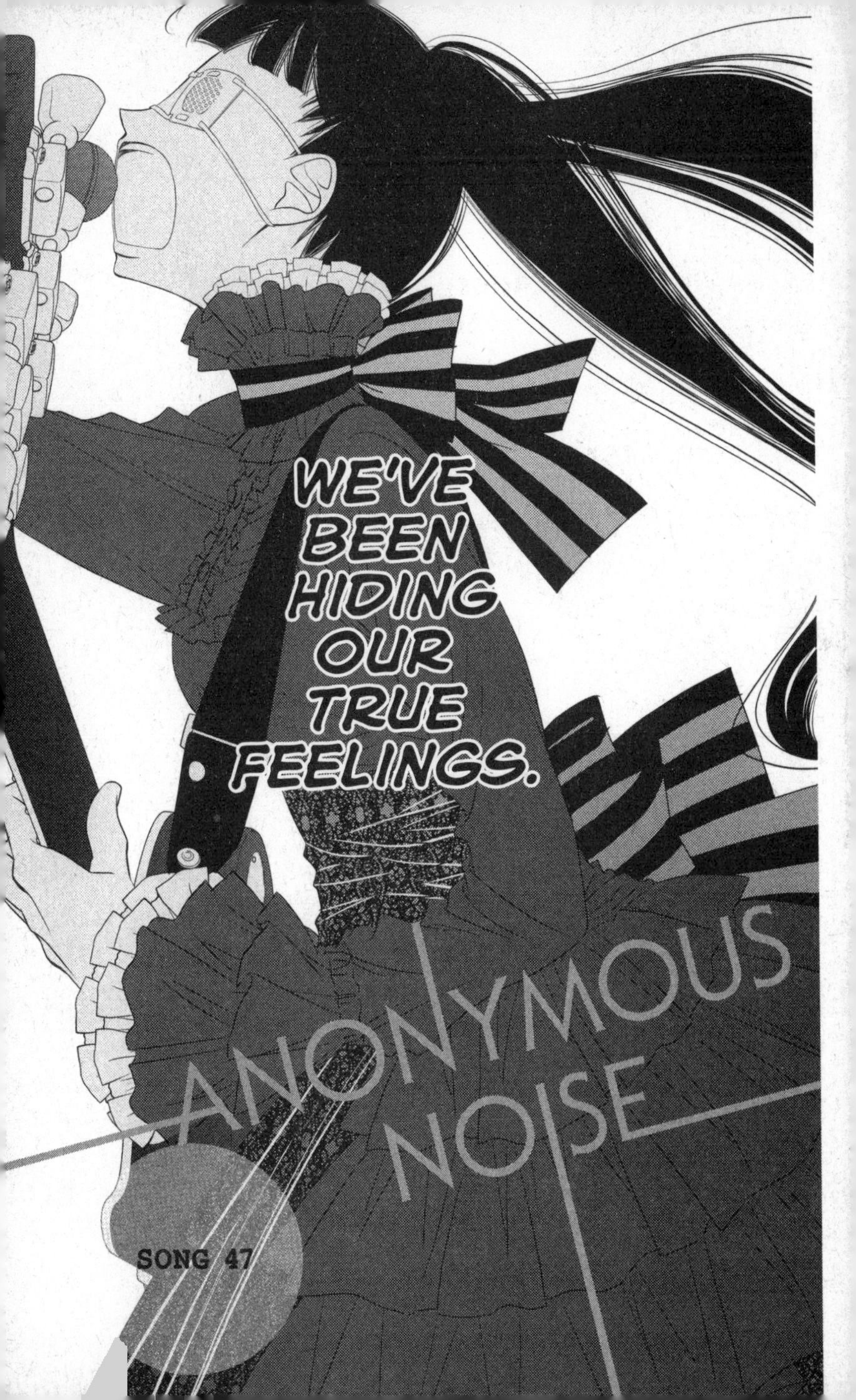
WE'VE BEEN HIDING OUR TRUE FEELINGS.
ANONYMOUS NOISE
SONG 47

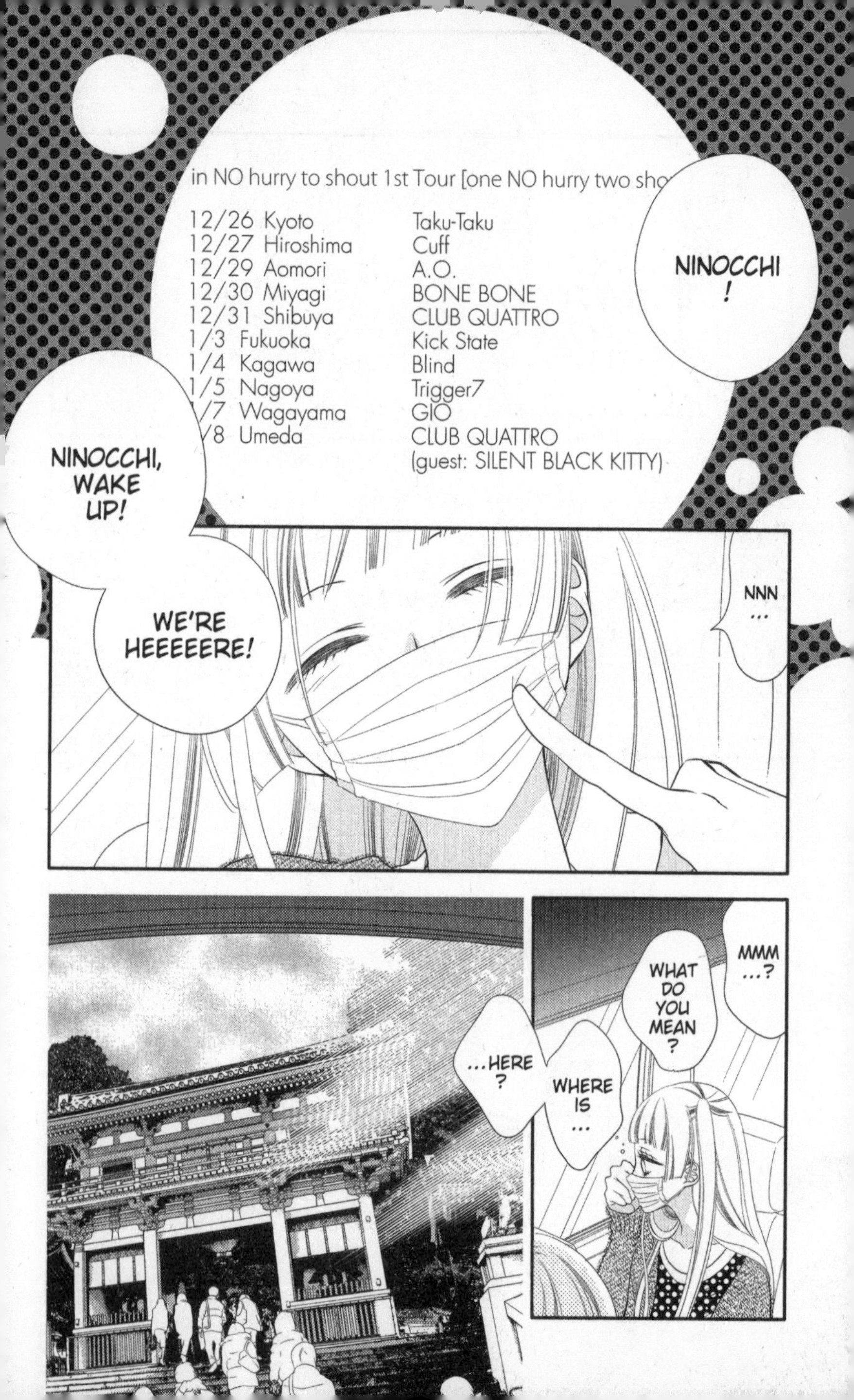
in NO hurry to shout 1st Tour [one NO hurry two sho
12/26 Kyoto Taku-Taku
12/27 Hiroshima Cuff
12/29 Aomori A.O.
12/30 Miyagi BONE BONE
12/31 Shibuya CLUB QUATTRO
1/3 Fukuoka Kick State
1/4 Kagawa Blind
1/5 Nagoya Trigger7
/7 Wagayama GIO
/8 Umeda CLUB QUATTRO
(guest: SILENT BLACK KITTY)
NINOCCHI!
NINOCCHI, WAKE UP!
WE'RE HEEEEEERE!
NNN...
MMM...?
WHAT DO YOU MEAN?
WHERE IS...
...HERE?

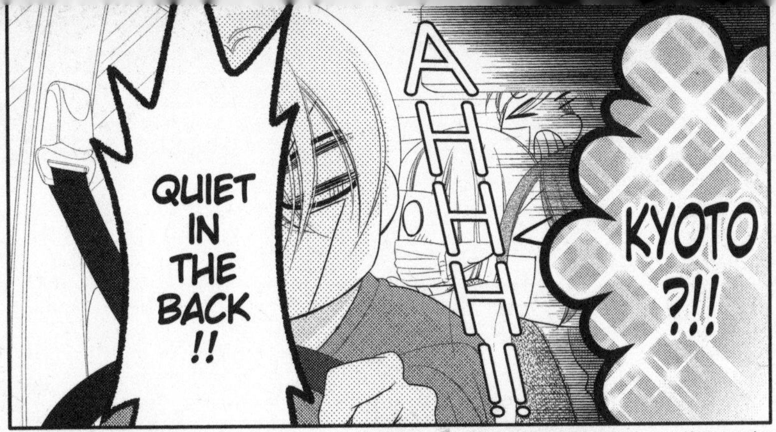
KYOTO ?!!
AHHHH!!
QUIET IN THE BACK !!

*A meditative Buddhist practice associated with some Kyoto temples

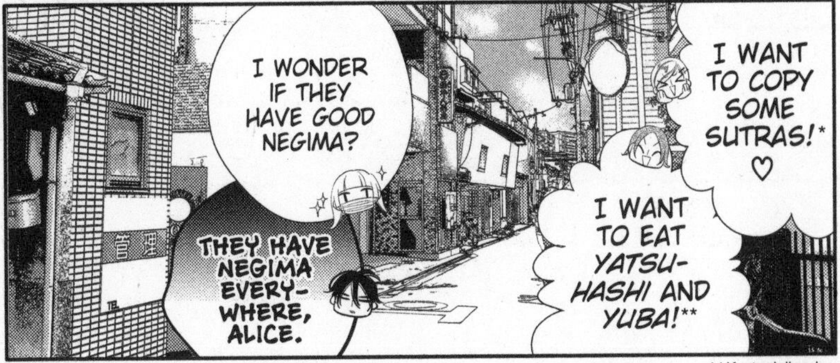
I WANT TO COPY SOME SUTRAS!* ♡
I WANT TO EAT YATSU-HASHI AND YUBA!**
I WONDER IF THEY HAVE GOOD NEGIMA?
THEY HAVE NEGIMA EVERY-WHERE, ALICE.

**Kyoto delicacies

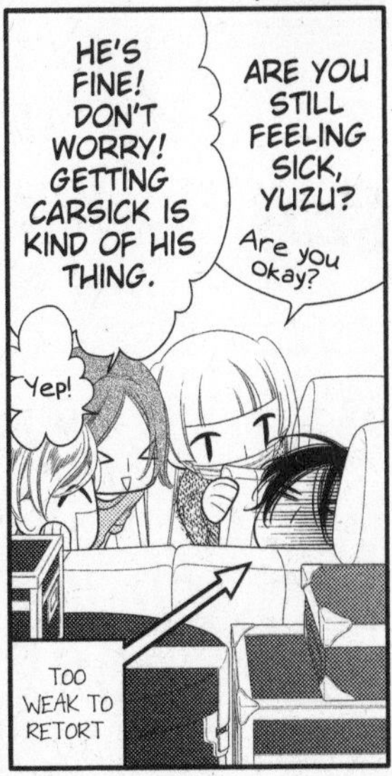
ARE YOU STILL FEELING SICK, YUZU?
Are you okay?
HE'S FINE! DON'T WORRY! GETTING CARSICK IS KIND OF HIS THING.
Yep!
TOO WEAK TO RETORT

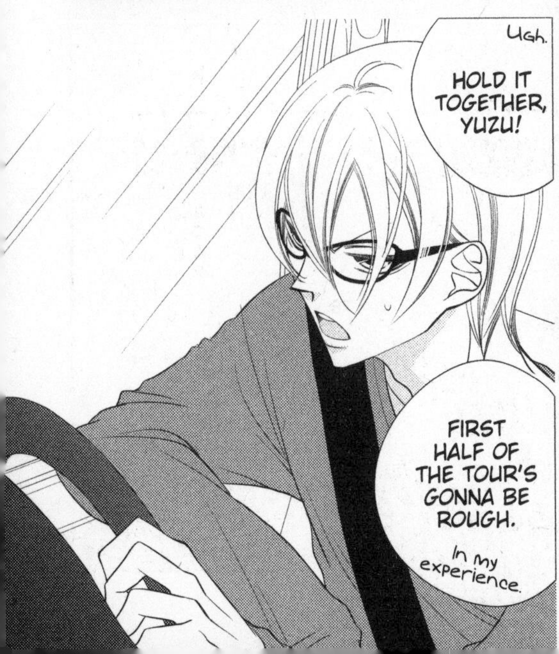
Ugh.
HOLD IT TOGETHER, YUZU!
FIRST HALF OF THE TOUR'S GONNA BE ROUGH.
In my experience.

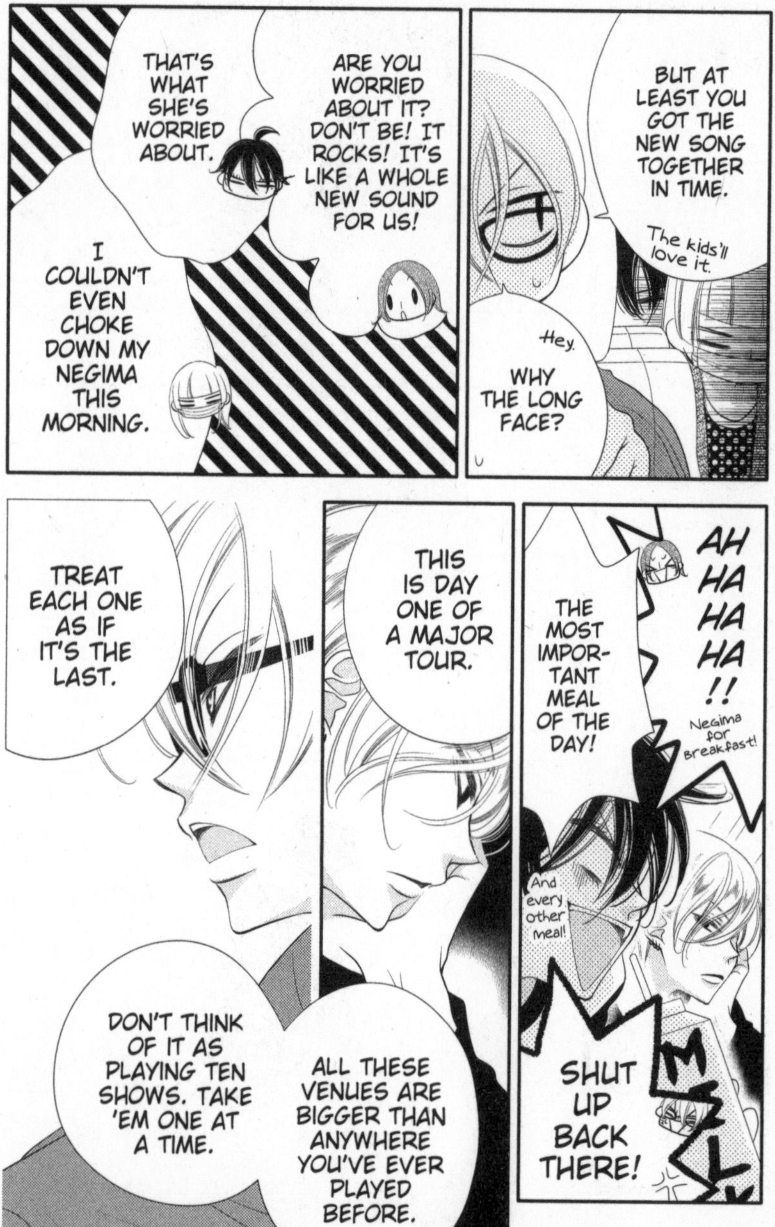
BUT AT LEAST YOU GOT THE NEW SONG TOGETHER IN TIME.
The kids'll love it.
Hey.
WHY THE LONG FACE?
ARE YOU WORRIED ABOUT IT? DON'T BE! IT ROCKS! IT'S LIKE A WHOLE NEW SOUND FOR US!
THAT'S WHAT SHE'S WORRIED ABOUT.
I COULDN'T EVEN CHOKE DOWN MY NEGIMA THIS MORNING.
AH HA HA HA!!
Negima for Breakfast!
THE MOST IMPORTANT MEAL OF THE DAY!
And every other meal!
SHUT UP BACK THERE!
THIS IS DAY ONE OF A MAJOR TOUR.
ALL THESE VENUES ARE BIGGER THAN ANYWHERE YOU'VE EVER PLAYED BEFORE.
TREAT EACH ONE AS IF IT'S THE LAST.
DON'T THINK OF IT AS PLAYING TEN SHOWS. TAKE 'EM ONE AT A TIME.

RIGHT !!!

QUIET DOWN! WE'RE HERE!

I need a smoke.

Sign: Taku-Taku

FILE TRANSFER COMPLETE

DING!

...

...IT'S DONE.

AND...

= MOMO WEARS A JACKET IN RESTAURANTS BECAUSE HE RUNS COLD.

1

Greetings! Ryoko Fukuyama here.

Thank you for picking up volume 9 of Anonymous Noise. Volume 9, huh? Momo, huh? Momo doesn't appear in the manga all that often, so it's a lot of fun to get to draw him. Momoooo!

I had to change the color scheme on the bass he's holding for certain reasons, but in reality it's red. Anyway, I hope you enjoy volume 9!

Now, I have an announcement! But I'll save that for the next column.

LATELY...

I'VE WANTED TO LEARN HOW TO PLAY BASS.

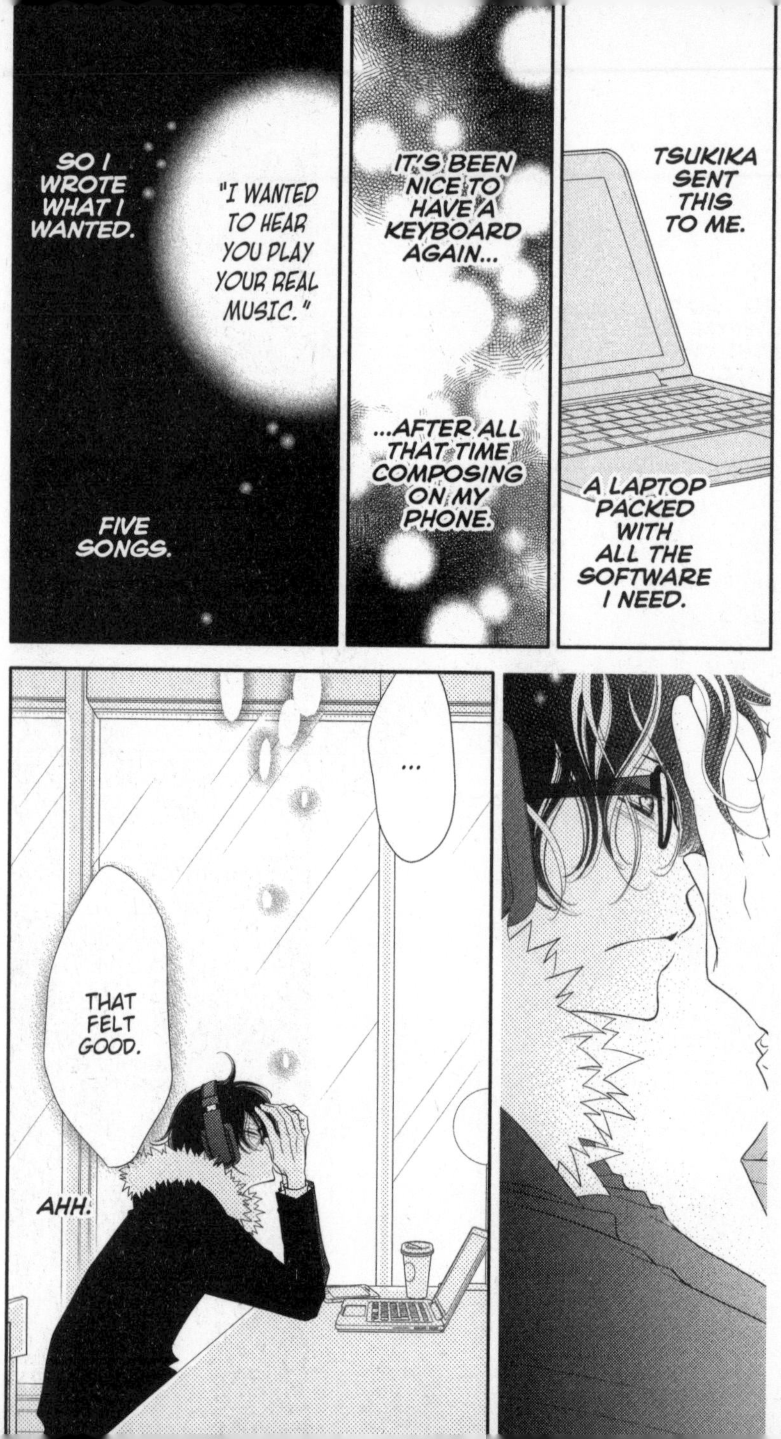
TSUKIKA SENT THIS TO ME.
A LAPTOP PACKED WITH ALL THE SOFTWARE I NEED.
IT'S BEEN NICE TO HAVE A KEYBOARD AGAIN...
...AFTER ALL THAT TIME COMPOSING ON MY PHONE.
"I WANTED TO HEAR YOU PLAY YOUR REAL MUSIC."
SO I WROTE WHAT I WANTED.
FIVE SONGS.
...
THAT FELT GOOD.
AHH.

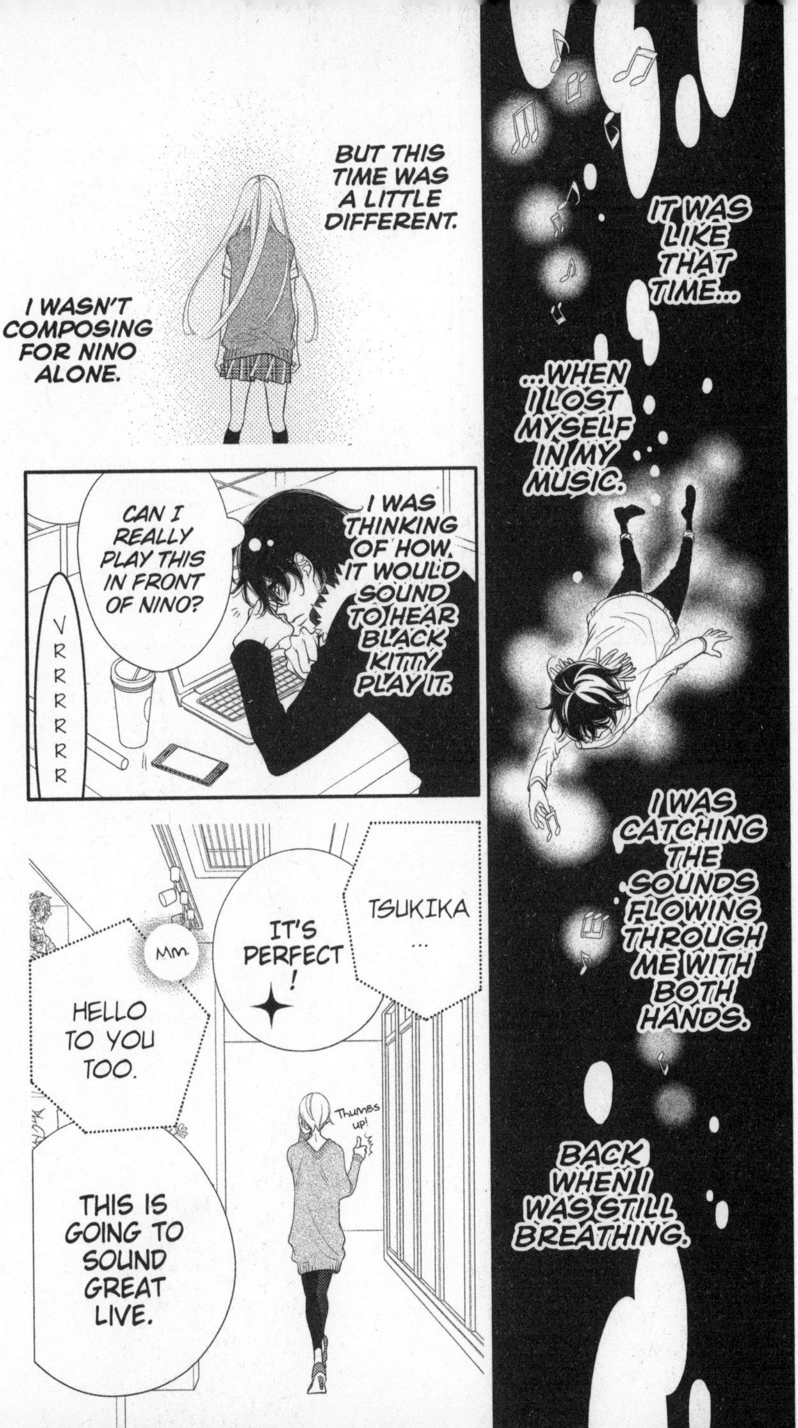
IT WAS LIKE THAT TIME...
...WHEN I LOST MYSELF IN MY MUSIC.
I WAS CATCHING THE SOUNDS FLOWING THROUGH ME WITH BOTH HANDS.
BACK WHEN I WAS STILL BREATHING.
BUT THIS TIME WAS A LITTLE DIFFERENT.
I WASN'T COMPOSING FOR NINO ALONE.
I WAS THINKING OF HOW IT WOULD SOUND TO HEAR BLACK KITTY PLAY IT.
CAN I REALLY PLAY THIS IN FRONT OF NINO?
VRRRRRRR
TSUKIKA...
IT'S PERFECT!
Mm.
HELLO TO YOU TOO.
Thumbs up!
THIS IS GOING TO SOUND GREAT LIVE.

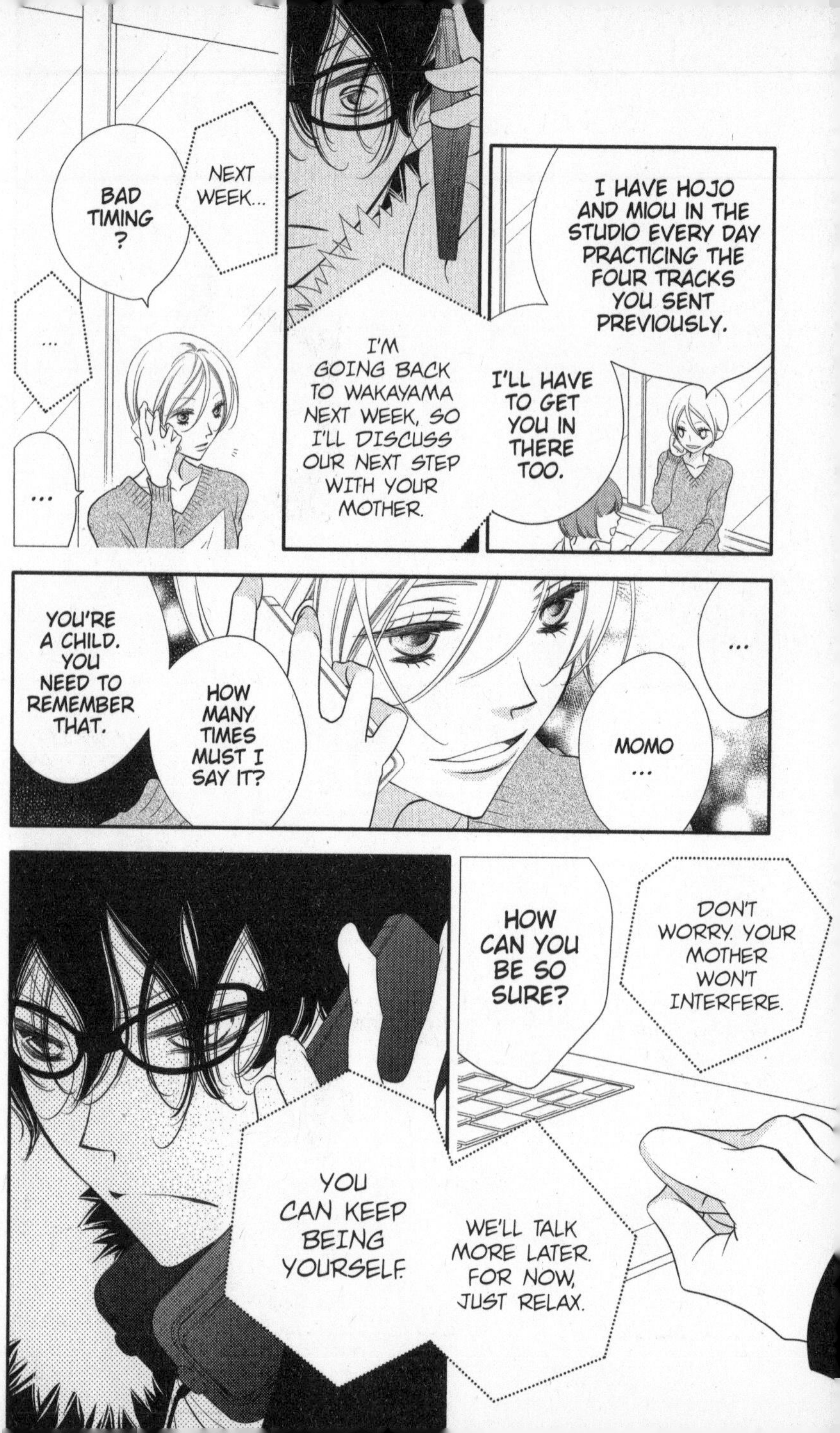
I HAVE HOJO AND MIOU IN THE STUDIO EVERY DAY PRACTICING THE FOUR TRACKS YOU SENT PREVIOUSLY.
I'LL HAVE TO GET YOU IN THERE TOO.
I'M GOING BACK TO WAKAYAMA NEXT WEEK, SO I'LL DISCUSS OUR NEXT STEP WITH YOUR MOTHER.
NEXT WEEK...
BAD TIMING?
...
...
...
MOMO...
HOW MANY TIMES MUST I SAY IT?
YOU'RE A CHILD. YOU NEED TO REMEMBER THAT.
DON'T WORRY. YOUR MOTHER WON'T INTERFERE.
HOW CAN YOU BE SO SURE?
WE'LL TALK MORE LATER. FOR NOW, JUST RELAX.
YOU CAN KEEP BEING YOURSELF.

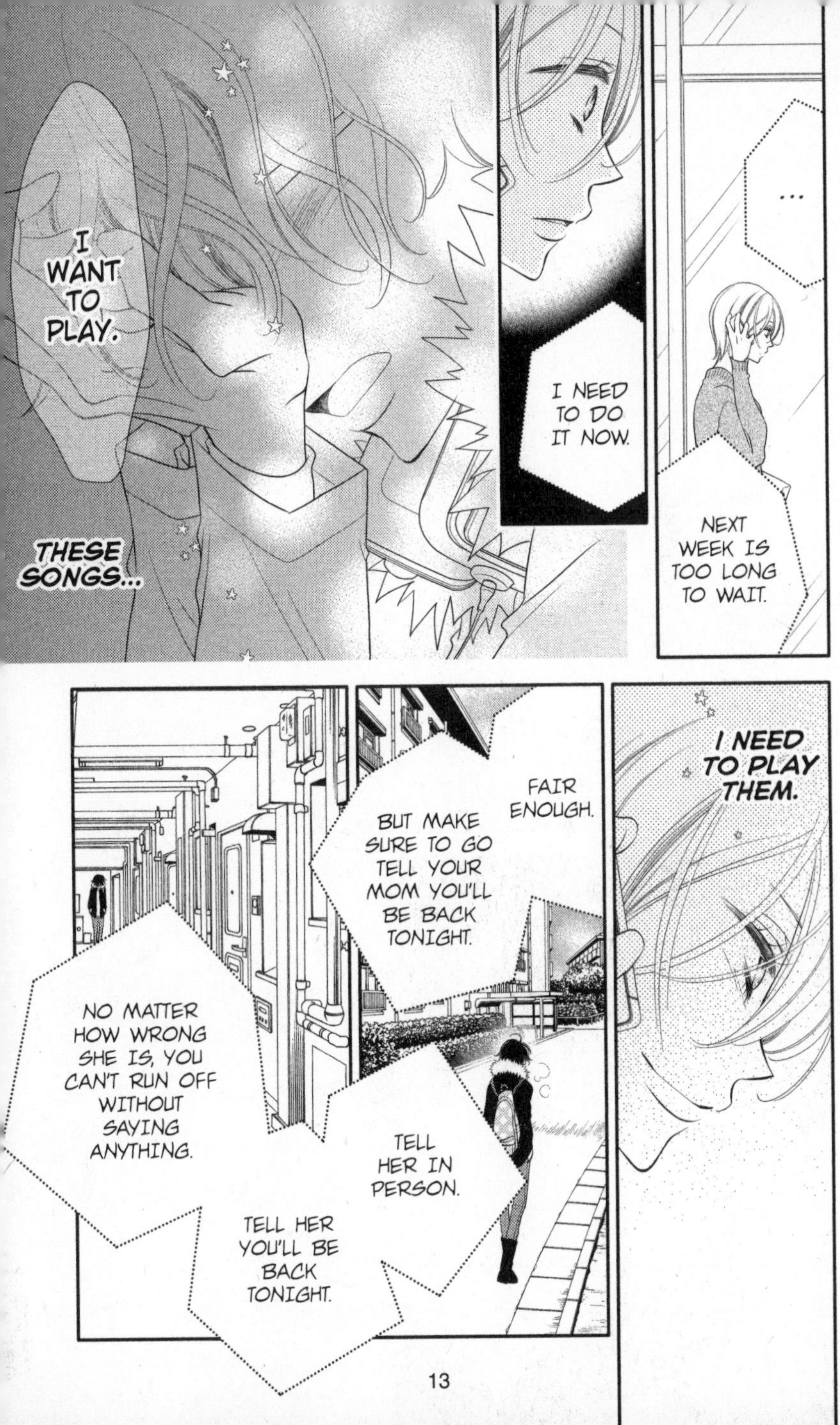
...
NEXT WEEK IS TOO LONG TO WAIT.
I NEED TO DO IT NOW.
I WANT TO PLAY.
THESE SONGS...
I NEED TO PLAY THEM.
FAIR ENOUGH.
BUT MAKE SURE TO GO TELL YOUR MOM YOU'LL BE BACK TONIGHT.
NO MATTER HOW WRONG SHE IS, YOU CAN'T RUN OFF WITHOUT SAYING ANYTHING.
TELL HER IN PERSON.
TELL HER YOU'LL BE BACK TONIGHT.

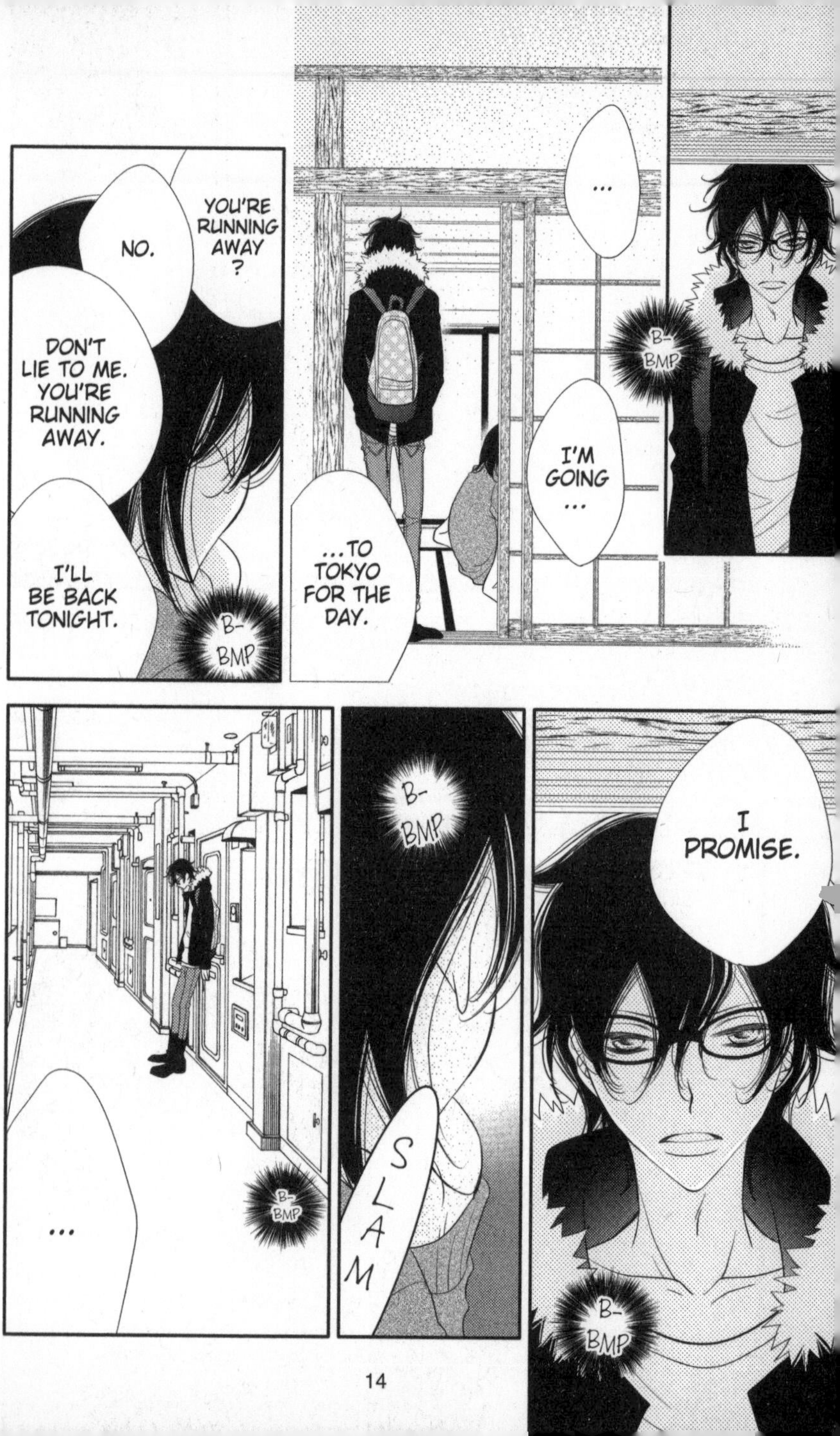
...
B-BMP
I'M GOING ...
...TO TOKYO FOR THE DAY.
YOU'RE RUNNING AWAY?
NO.
DON'T LIE TO ME. YOU'RE RUNNING AWAY.
I'LL BE BACK TONIGHT.
B-BMP
I PROMISE.
B-BMP
B-BMP
SLAM
B-BMP
...

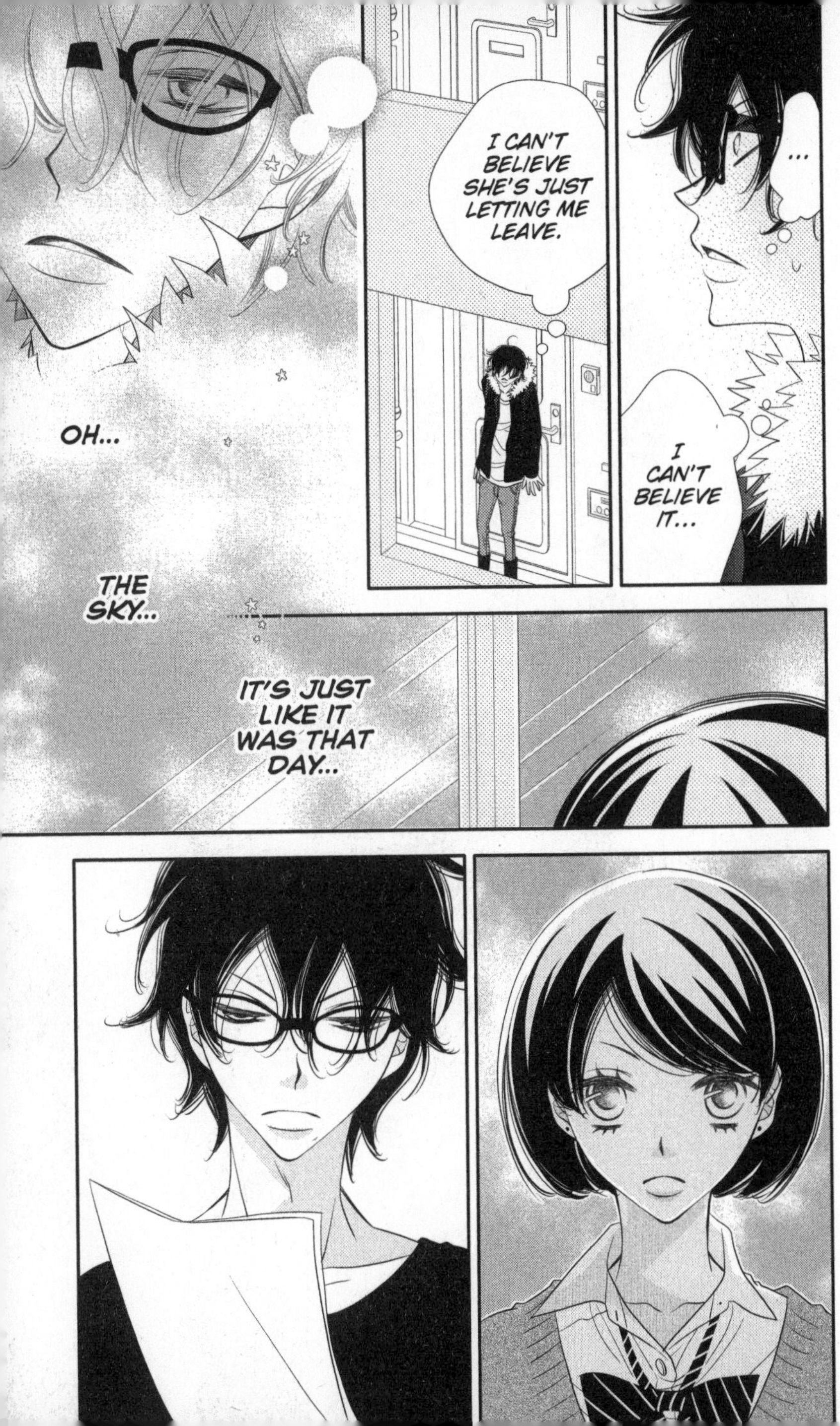
...
I CAN'T BELIEVE IT...
I CAN'T BELIEVE SHE'S JUST LETTING ME LEAVE.
OH...
THE SKY...
IT'S JUST LIKE IT WAS THAT DAY...

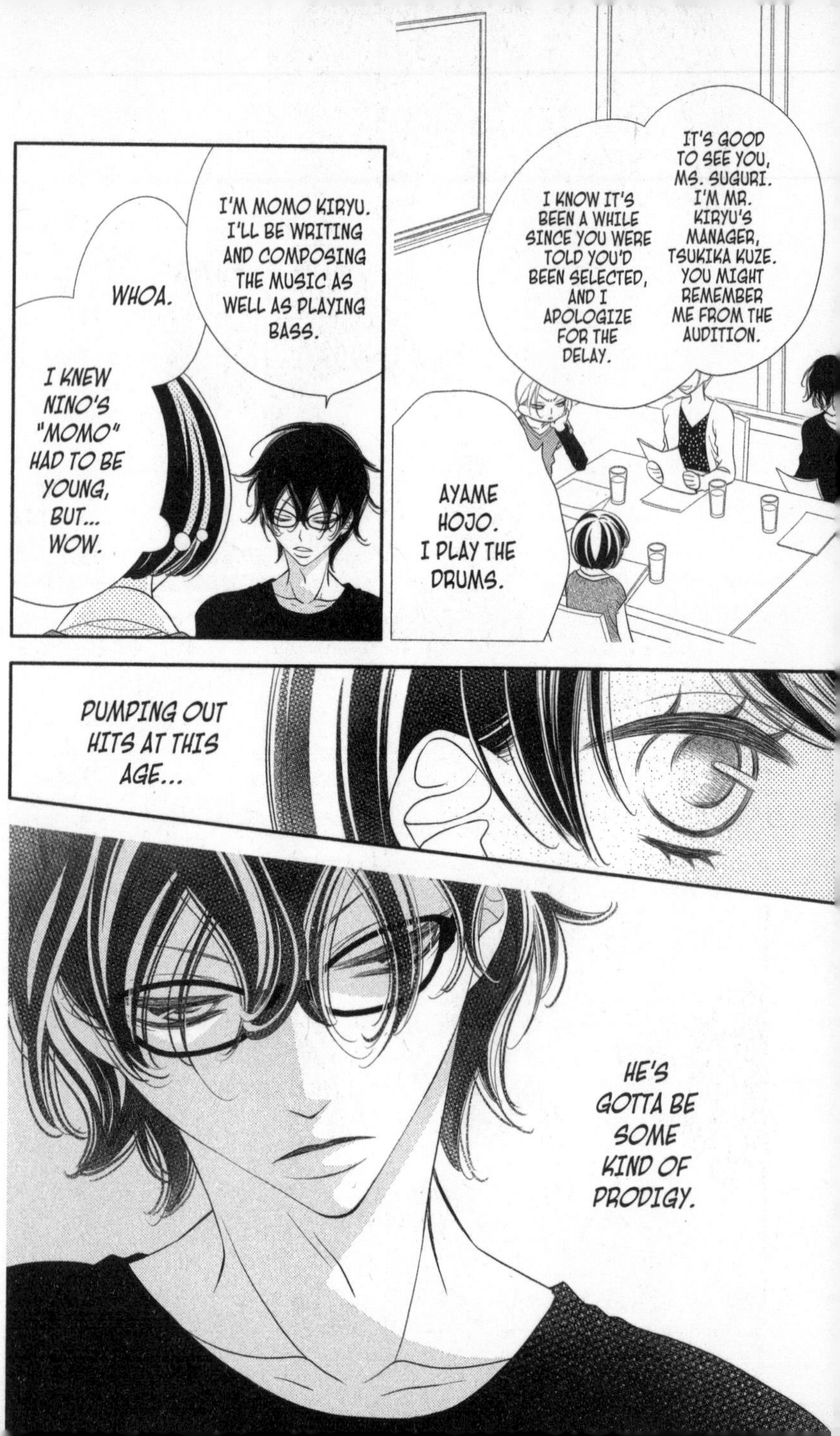
IT'S GOOD TO SEE YOU, MS. SUGURI. I'M MR. KIRYU'S MANAGER, TSUKIKA KUZE. YOU MIGHT REMEMBER ME FROM THE AUDITION.
I KNOW IT'S BEEN A WHILE SINCE YOU WERE TOLD YOU'D BEEN SELECTED, AND I APOLOGIZE FOR THE DELAY.
AYAME HOJO. I PLAY THE DRUMS.
I'M MOMO KIRYU. I'LL BE WRITING AND COMPOSING THE MUSIC AS WELL AS PLAYING BASS.
WHOA.
I KNEW NINO'S "MOMO" HAD TO BE YOUNG, BUT... WOW.
PUMPING OUT HITS AT THIS AGE...
HE'S GOTTA BE SOME KIND OF PRODIGY.

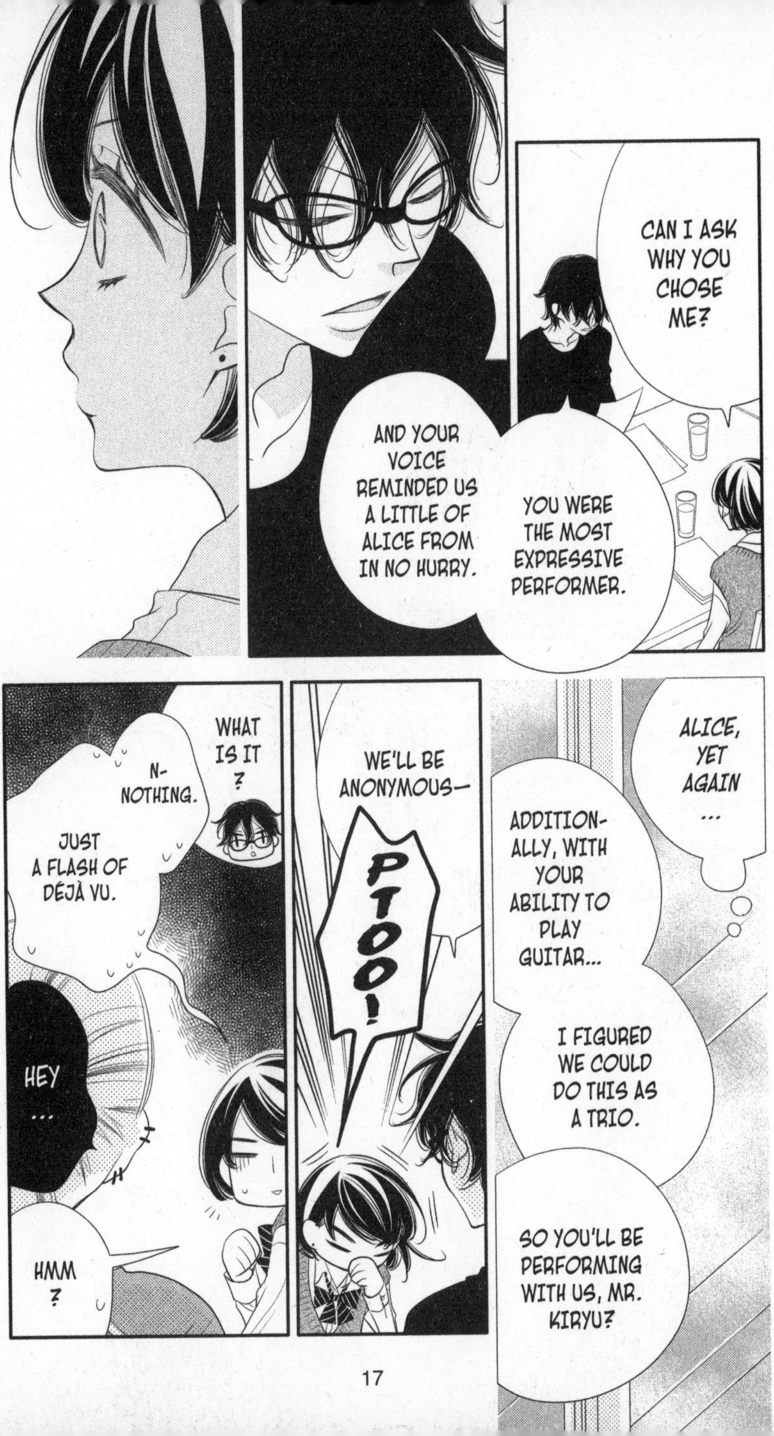
CAN I ASK WHY YOU CHOSE ME?
YOU WERE THE MOST EXPRESSIVE PERFORMER.
AND YOUR VOICE REMINDED US A LITTLE OF ALICE FROM IN NO HURRY.
ALICE, YET AGAIN...
ADDITION-ALLY, WITH YOUR ABILITY TO PLAY GUITAR...
I FIGURED WE COULD DO THIS AS A TRIO.
SO YOU'LL BE PERFORMING WITH US, MR. KIRYU?
WE'LL BE ANONYMOUS—
PTOO!
WHAT IS IT?
N-NOTHING.
JUST A FLASH OF DÉJÀ VU.
HEY...
HMM?

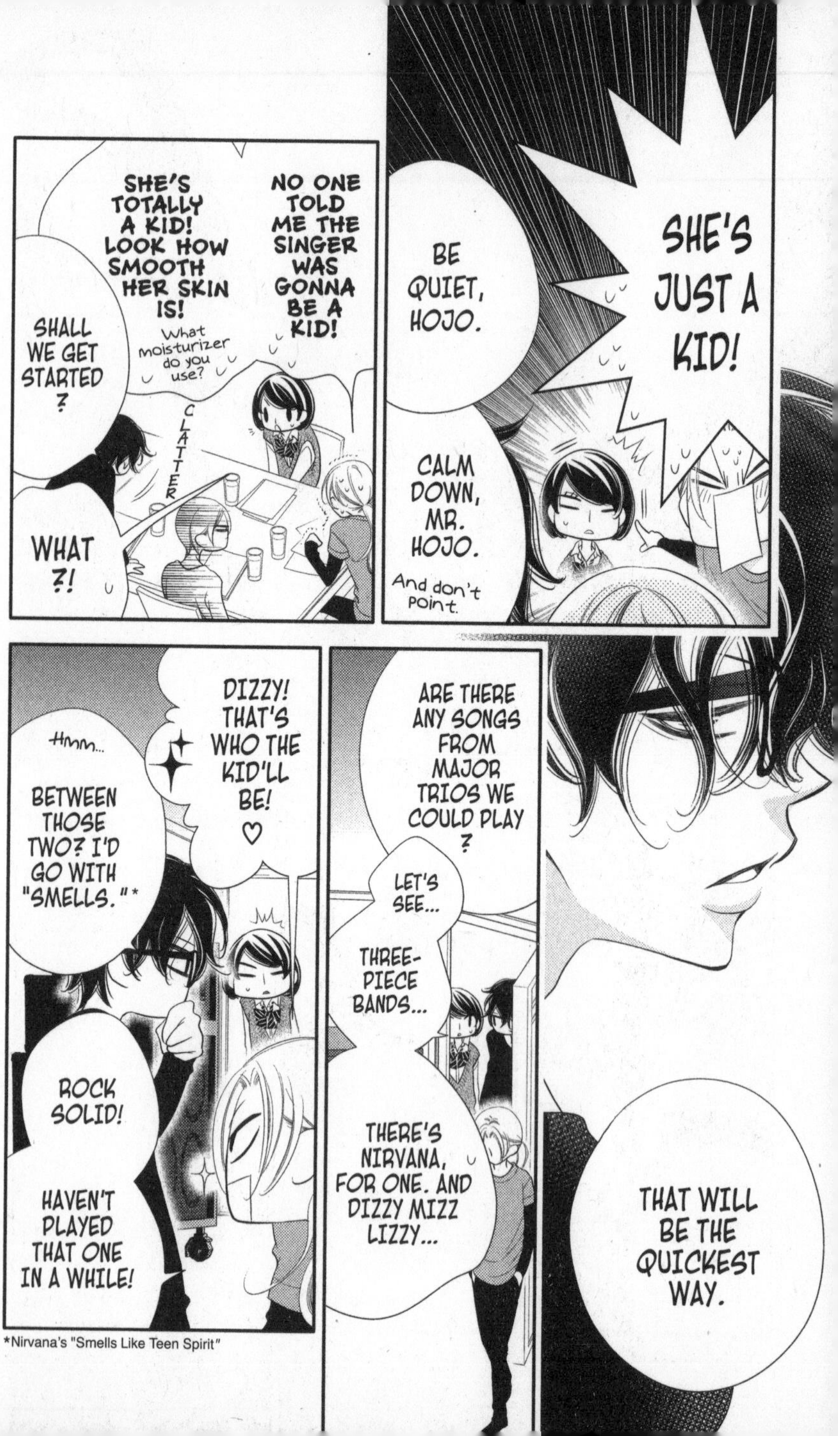
SHE'S JUST A KID!
BE QUIET, HOJO.
CALM DOWN, MR. HOJO.
And don't point.
NO ONE TOLD ME THE SINGER WAS GONNA BE A KID!
SHE'S TOTALLY A KID! LOOK HOW SMOOTH HER SKIN IS!
What moisturizer do you use?
SHALL WE GET STARTED?
CLATTER
WHAT?!
THAT WILL BE THE QUICKEST WAY.
ARE THERE ANY SONGS FROM MAJOR TRIOS WE COULD PLAY?
LET'S SEE...
THREE-PIECE BANDS...
THERE'S NIRVANA, FOR ONE. AND DIZZY MIZZ LIZZY...
DIZZY! THAT'S WHO THE KID'LL BE! ♡
Hmm...
BETWEEN THOSE TWO? I'D GO WITH "SMELLS."*
ROCK SOLID!
HAVEN'T PLAYED THAT ONE IN A WHILE!

*Nirvana's "Smells Like Teen Spirit"

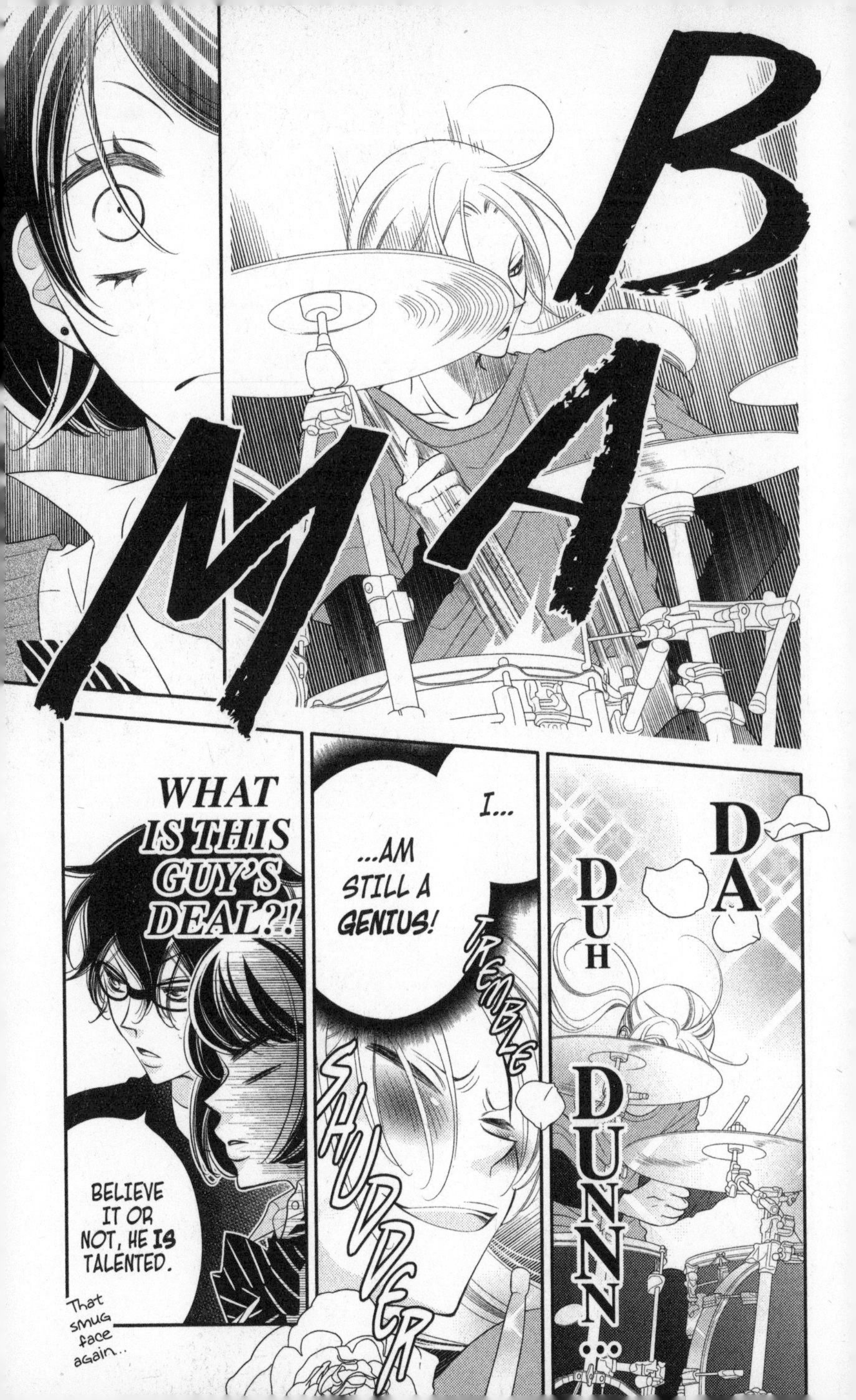
BAM
DA
DUH
DUNN...
I...
...AM STILL A GENIUS!
TREMBLE
SHUDDER
WHAT IS THIS GUY'S DEAL?!
BELIEVE IT OR NOT, HE IS TALENTED.
That smug face again...

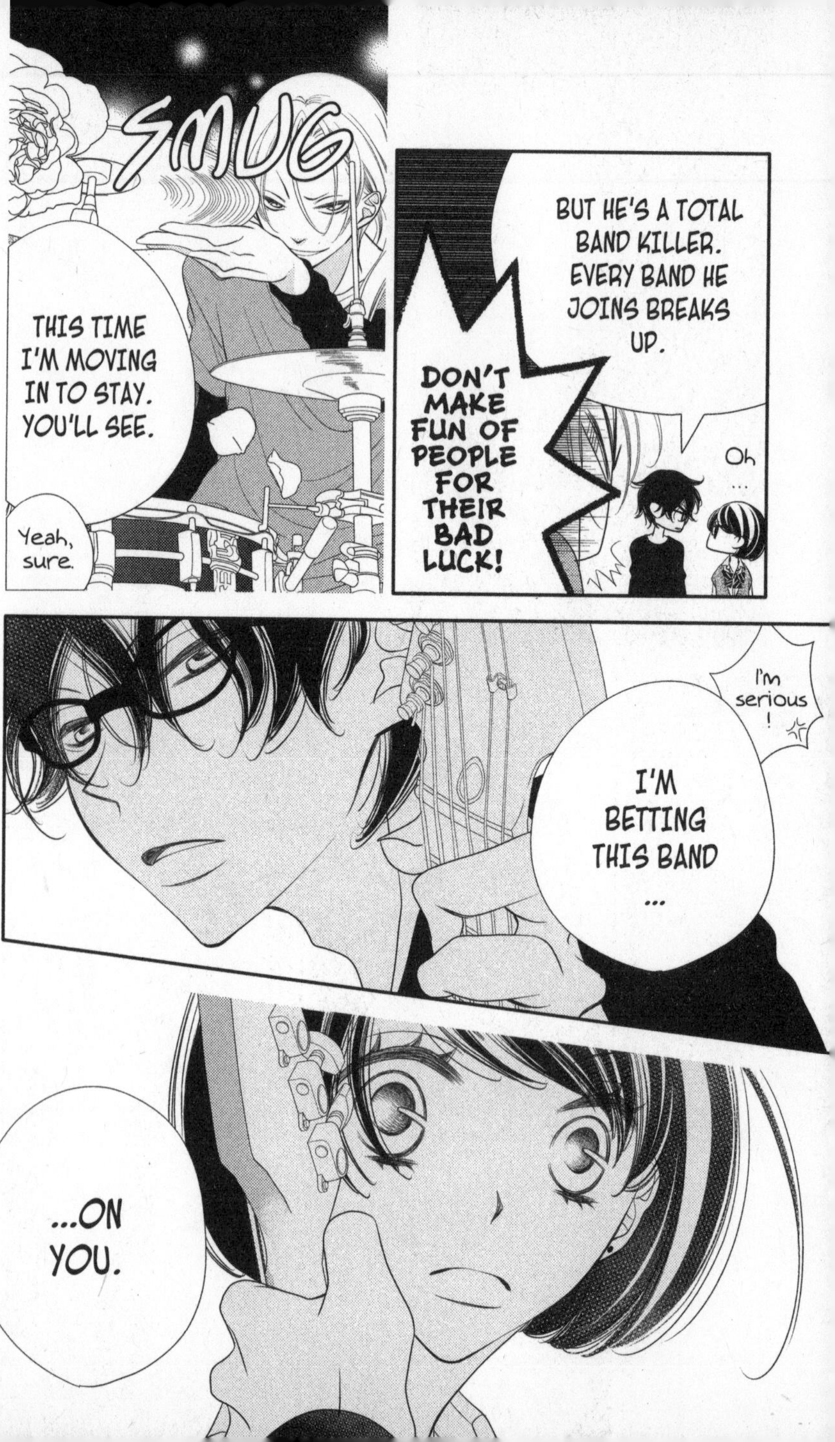
BUT HE'S A TOTAL BAND KILLER. EVERY BAND HE JOINS BREAKS UP.
DON'T MAKE FUN OF PEOPLE FOR THEIR BAD LUCK!
Oh ...
SMUG
THIS TIME I'M MOVING IN TO STAY. YOU'LL SEE.
Yeah, sure.
I'm serious!
I'M BETTING THIS BAND ...
...ON YOU.

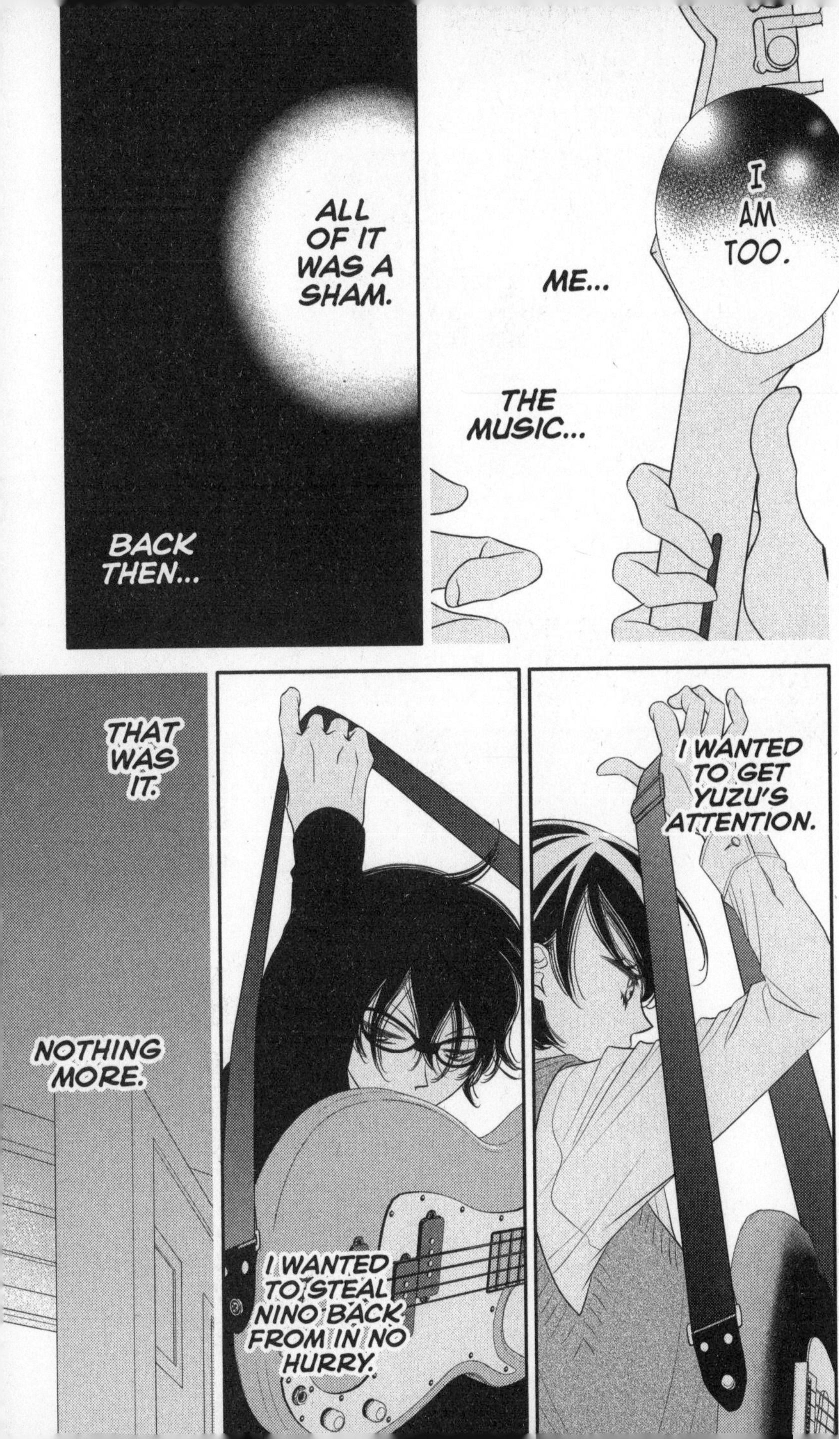
I AM TOO.
ME...
THE MUSIC...
ALL OF IT WAS A SHAM.
BACK THEN...
I WANTED TO GET YUZU'S ATTENTION.
I WANTED TO STEAL NINO BACK FROM IN NO HURRY.
THAT WAS IT.
NOTHING MORE.

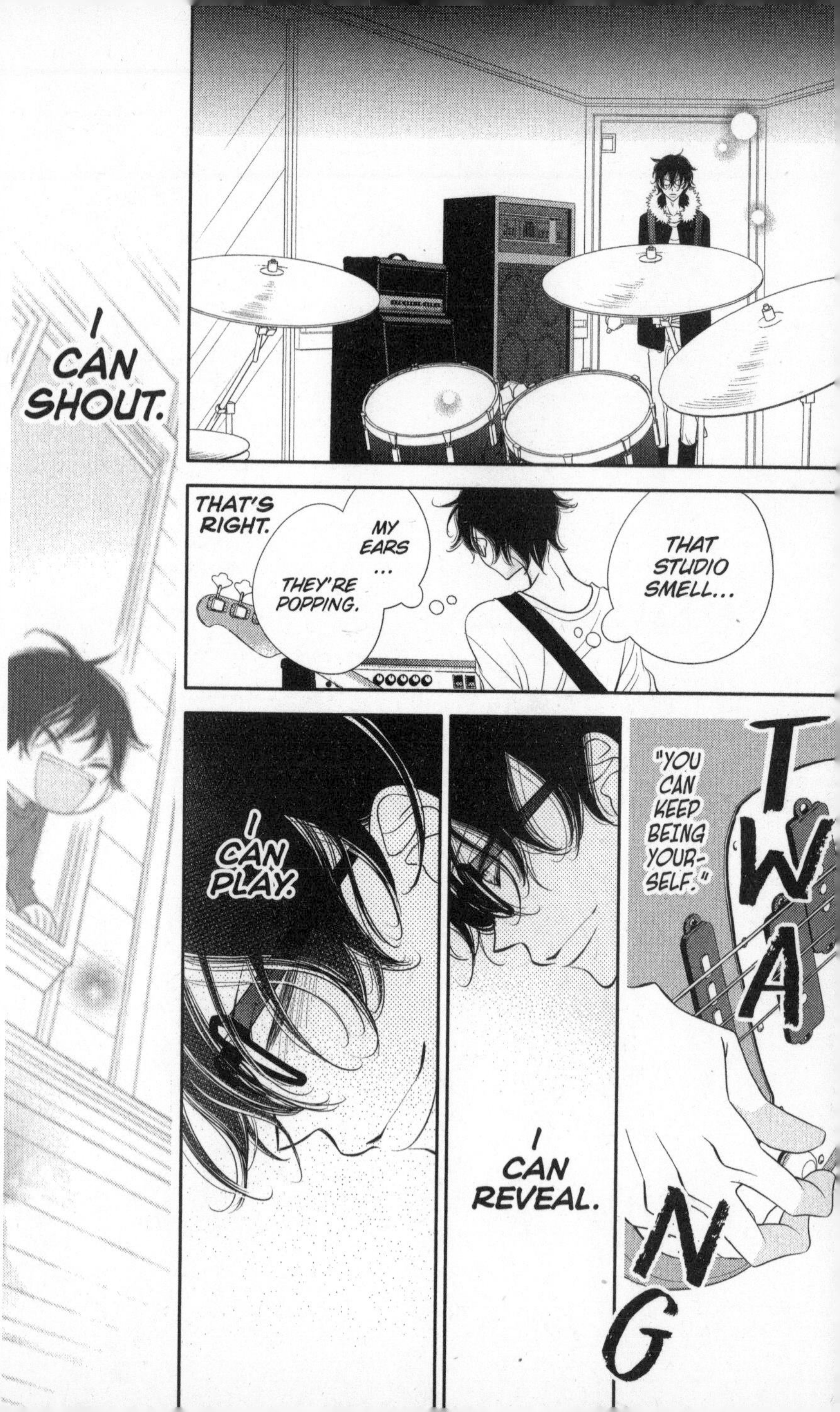
THAT STUDIO SMELL...
MY EARS...
THEY'RE POPPING.
THAT'S RIGHT.
TWANG
"YOU CAN KEEP BEING YOURSELF."
I CAN REVEAL.
I CAN PLAY.
I CAN SHOUT.

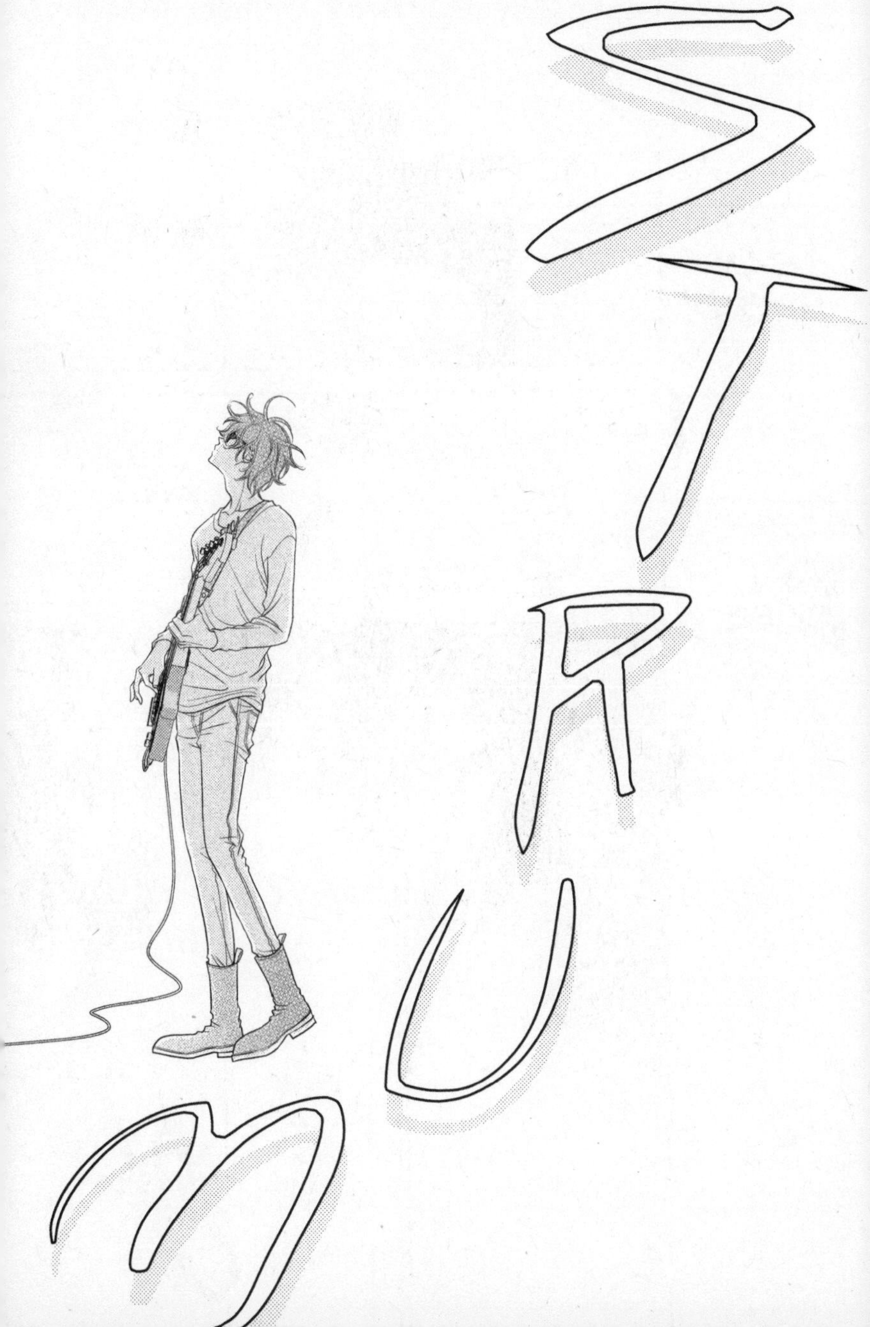
STRUM

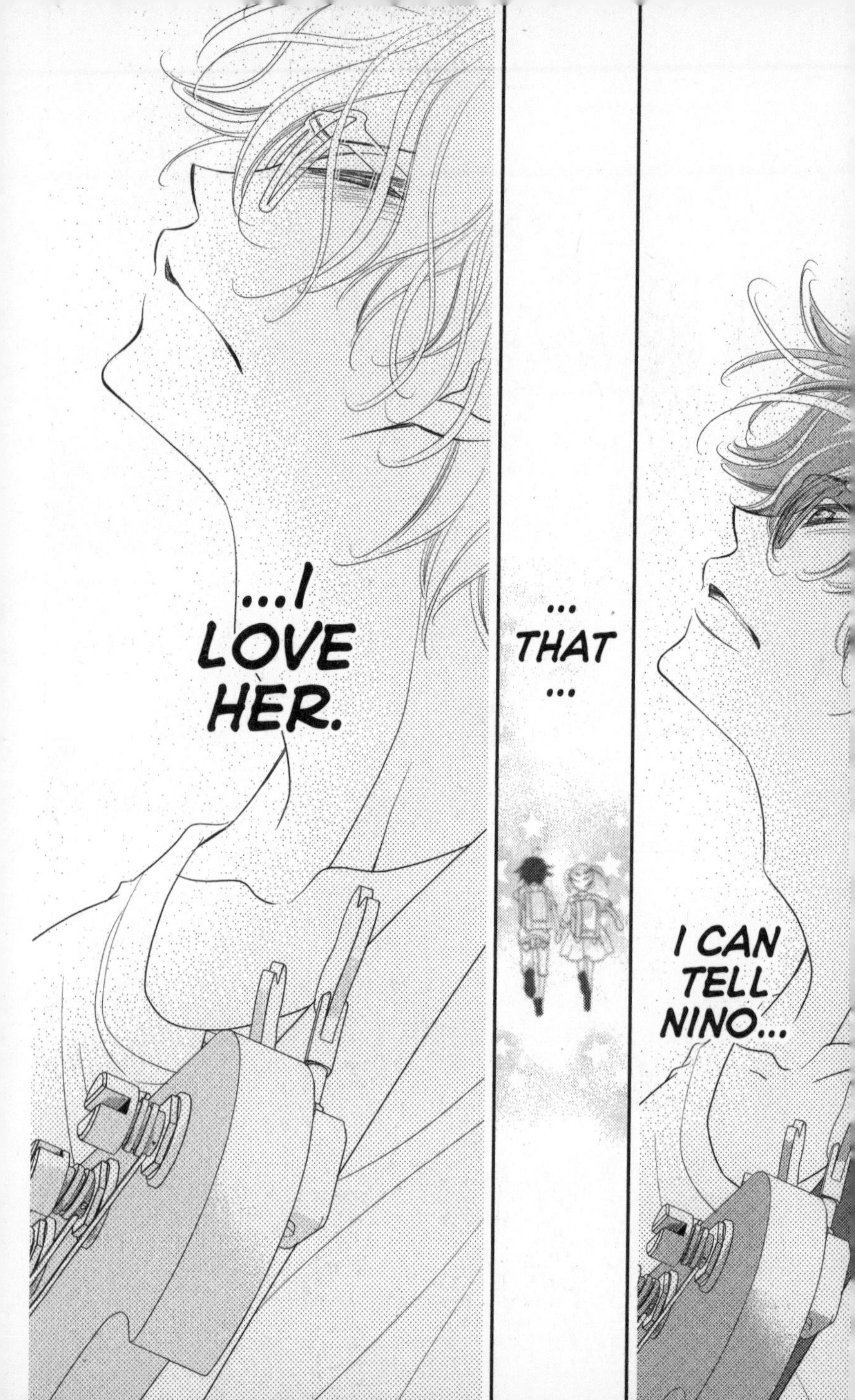
I CAN TELL NINO...
... THAT ...
...I LOVE HER.

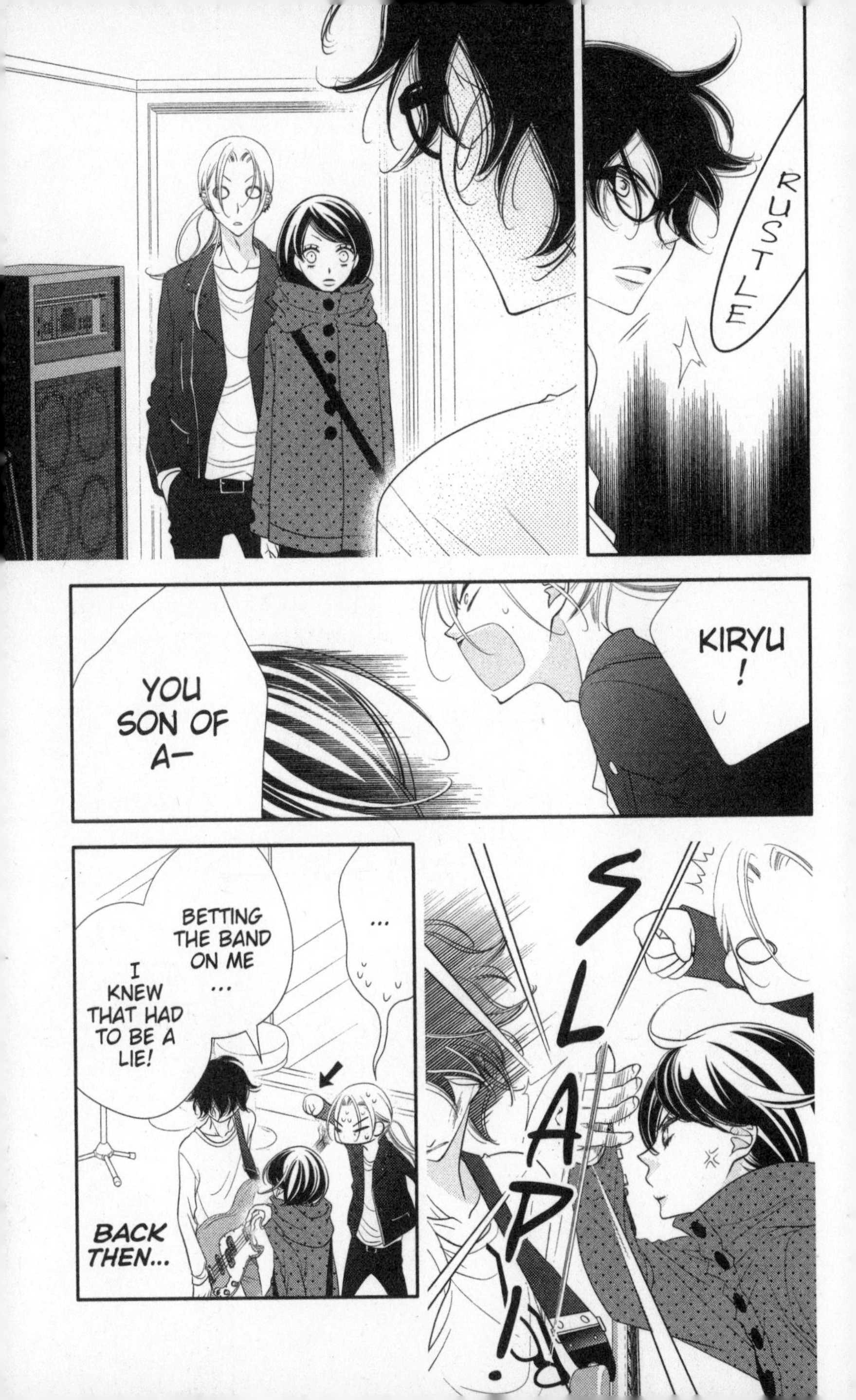
RUSTLE
KIRYU!
YOU SON OF A—
SLAP!!
...
BETTING THE BAND ON ME...
I KNEW THAT HAD TO BE A LIE!
BACK THEN...

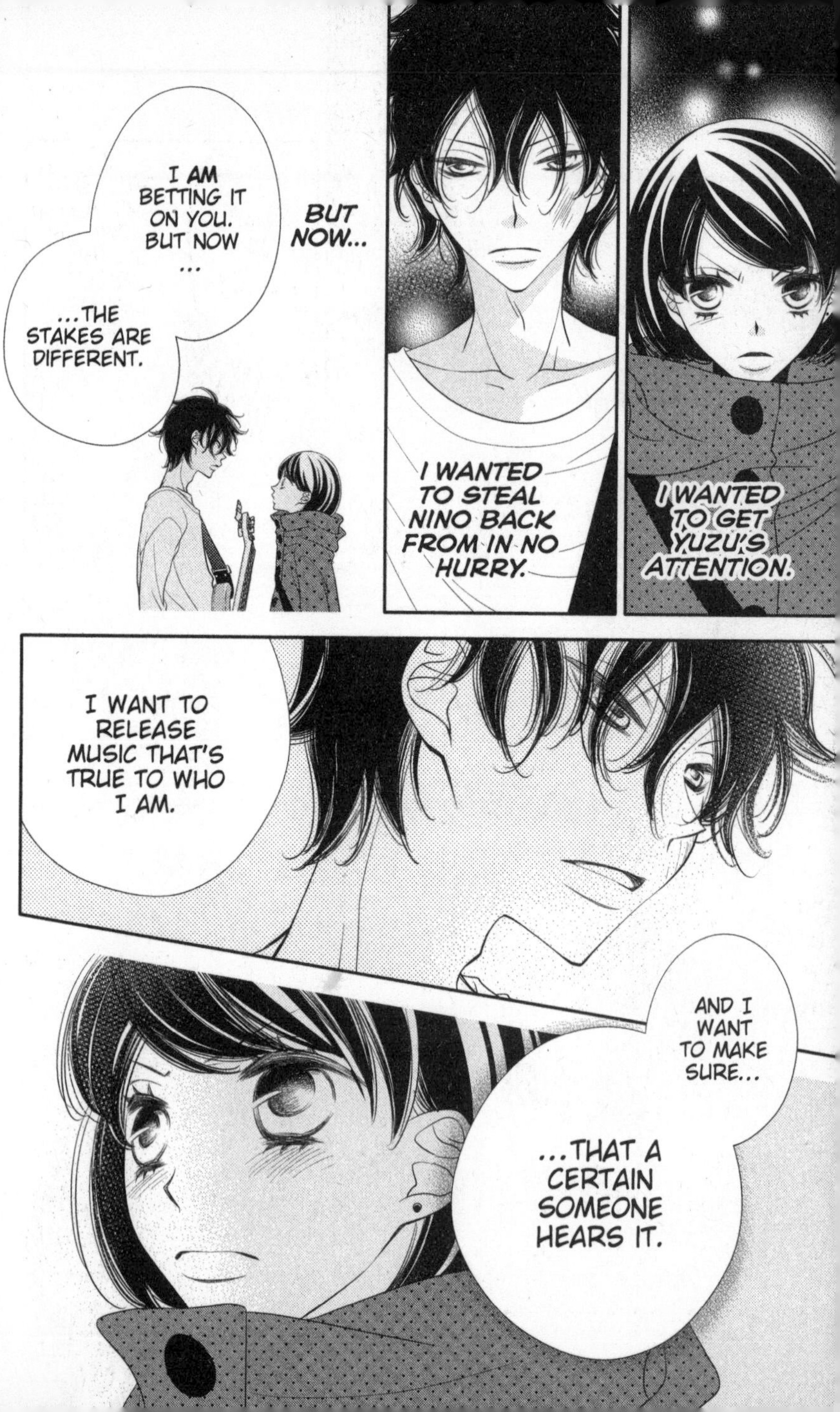
I WANTED TO GET YUZU'S ATTENTION.
I WANTED TO STEAL NINO BACK FROM IN NO HURRY.
BUT NOW...
I AM BETTING IT ON YOU. BUT NOW ...
...THE STAKES ARE DIFFERENT.
I WANT TO RELEASE MUSIC THAT'S TRUE TO WHO I AM.
AND I WANT TO MAKE SURE...
...THAT A CERTAIN SOMEONE HEARS IT.

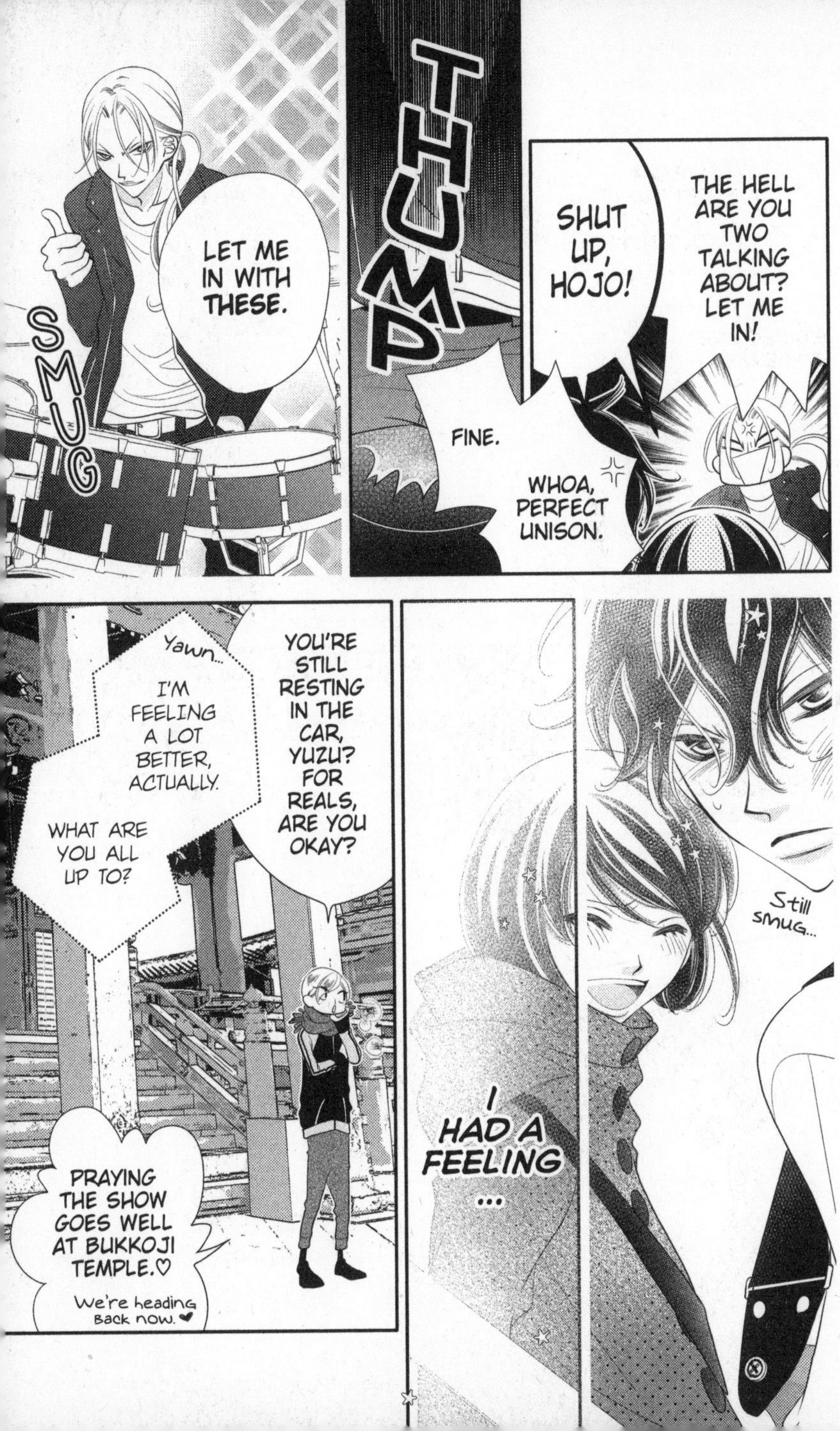
THE HELL ARE YOU TWO TALKING ABOUT? LET ME IN!
SHUT UP, HOJO!
THUMP
WHOA, PERFECT UNISON.
FINE.
LET ME IN WITH THESE.
SMUG
Still smug...
I HAD A FEELING ...
YOU'RE STILL RESTING IN THE CAR, YUZU? FOR REALS, ARE YOU OKAY?
Yawn...
I'M FEELING A LOT BETTER, ACTUALLY.
WHAT ARE YOU ALL UP TO?
PRAYING THE SHOW GOES WELL AT BUKKOJI TEMPLE.♡
We're heading back now.♥

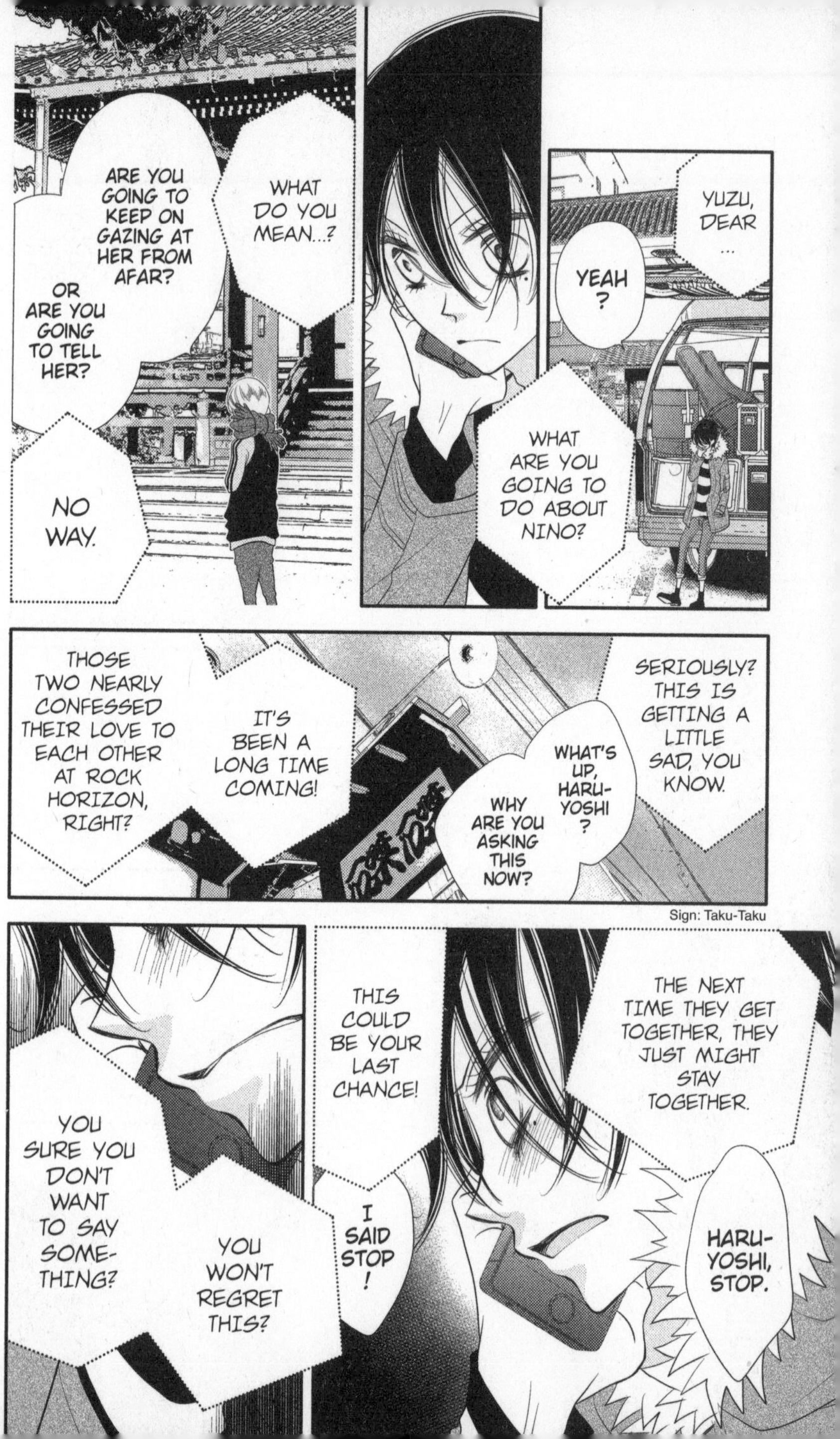
YUZU, DEAR ...
YEAH?
WHAT ARE YOU GOING TO DO ABOUT NINO?
WHAT DO YOU MEAN...?
ARE YOU GOING TO KEEP ON GAZING AT HER FROM AFAR?
OR ARE YOU GOING TO TELL HER?
NO WAY.
SERIOUSLY? THIS IS GETTING A LITTLE SAD, YOU KNOW.
WHAT'S UP, HARU-YOSHI?
WHY ARE YOU ASKING THIS NOW?
IT'S BEEN A LONG TIME COMING!
THOSE TWO NEARLY CONFESSED THEIR LOVE TO EACH OTHER AT ROCK HORIZON, RIGHT?
THE NEXT TIME THEY GET TOGETHER, THEY JUST MIGHT STAY TOGETHER.
HARU-YOSHI, STOP.
THIS COULD BE YOUR LAST CHANCE!
I SAID STOP!
YOU SURE YOU DON'T WANT TO SAY SOME-THING?
YOU WON'T REGRET THIS?
Sign: Taku-Taku

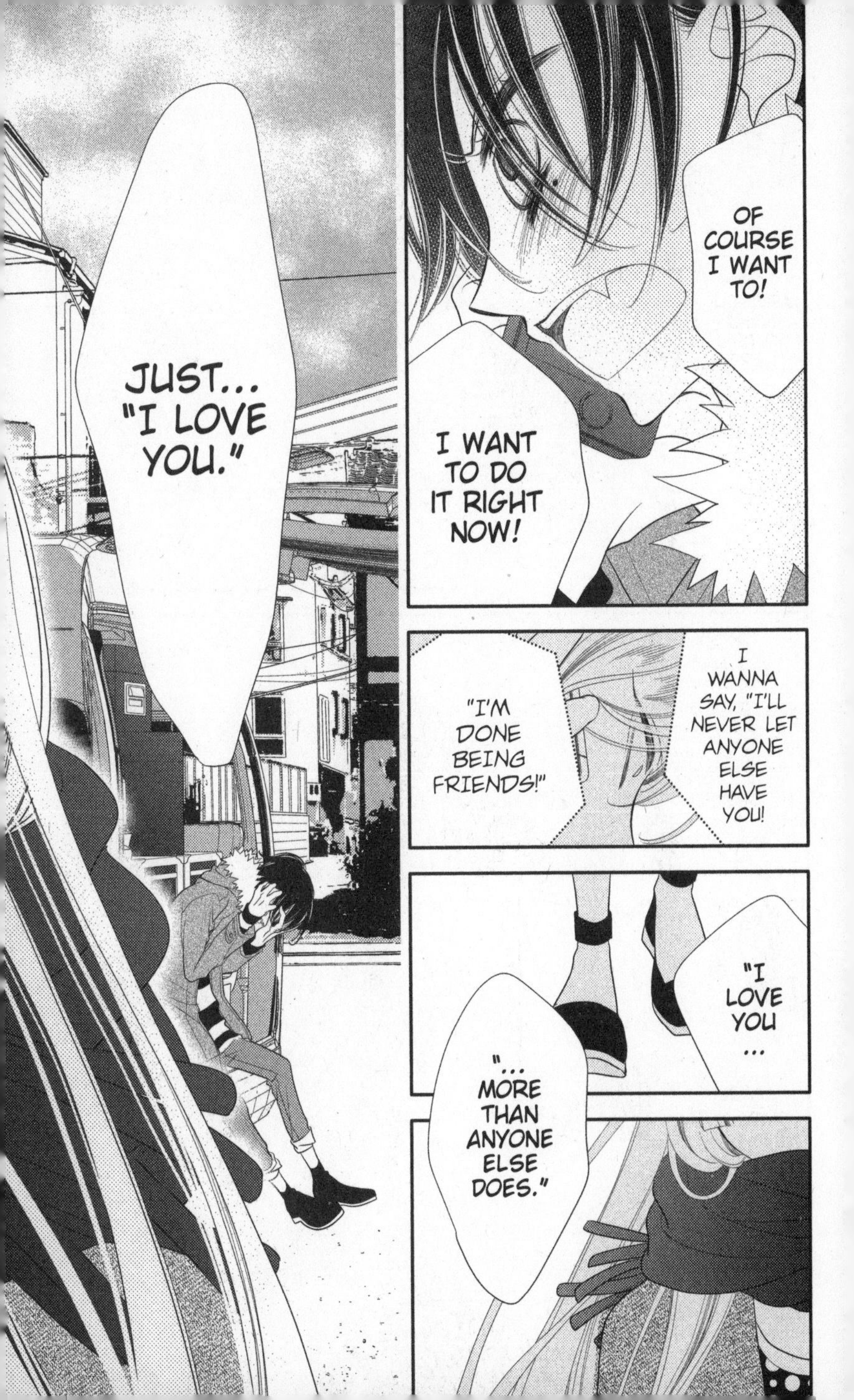
OF COURSE I WANT TO!
I WANT TO DO IT RIGHT NOW!
I WANNA SAY, "I'LL NEVER LET ANYONE ELSE HAVE YOU!
"I'M DONE BEING FRIENDS!"
"I LOVE YOU ...
"... MORE THAN ANYONE ELSE DOES."
JUST... "I LOVE YOU."

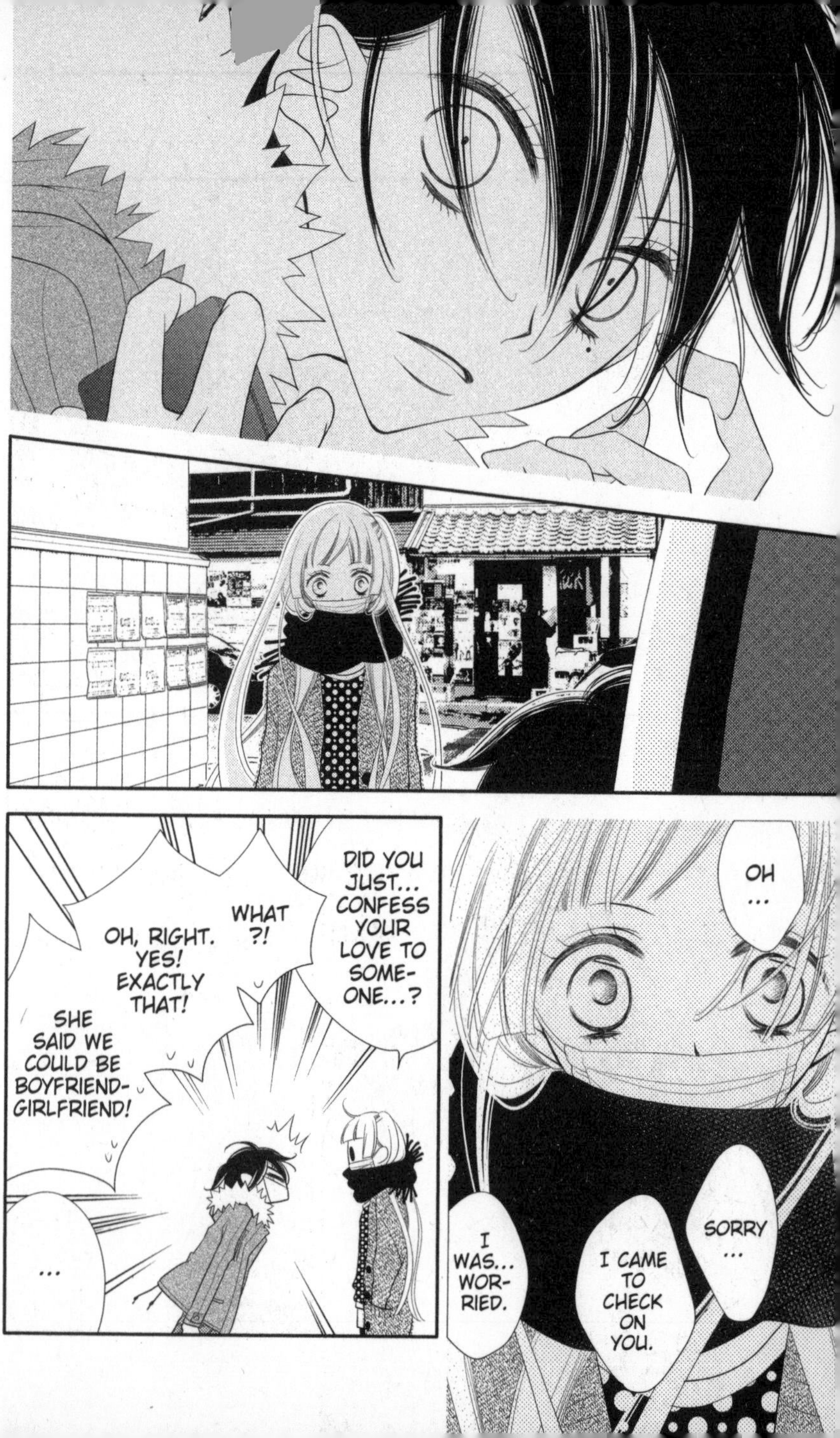
OH ...
SORRY ...
I CAME TO CHECK ON YOU.
I WAS... WORRIED.
DID YOU JUST... CONFESS YOUR LOVE TO SOMEONE...?
WHAT ?!
OH, RIGHT. YES! EXACTLY THAT!
SHE SAID WE COULD BE BOYFRIEND-GIRLFRIEND!
...

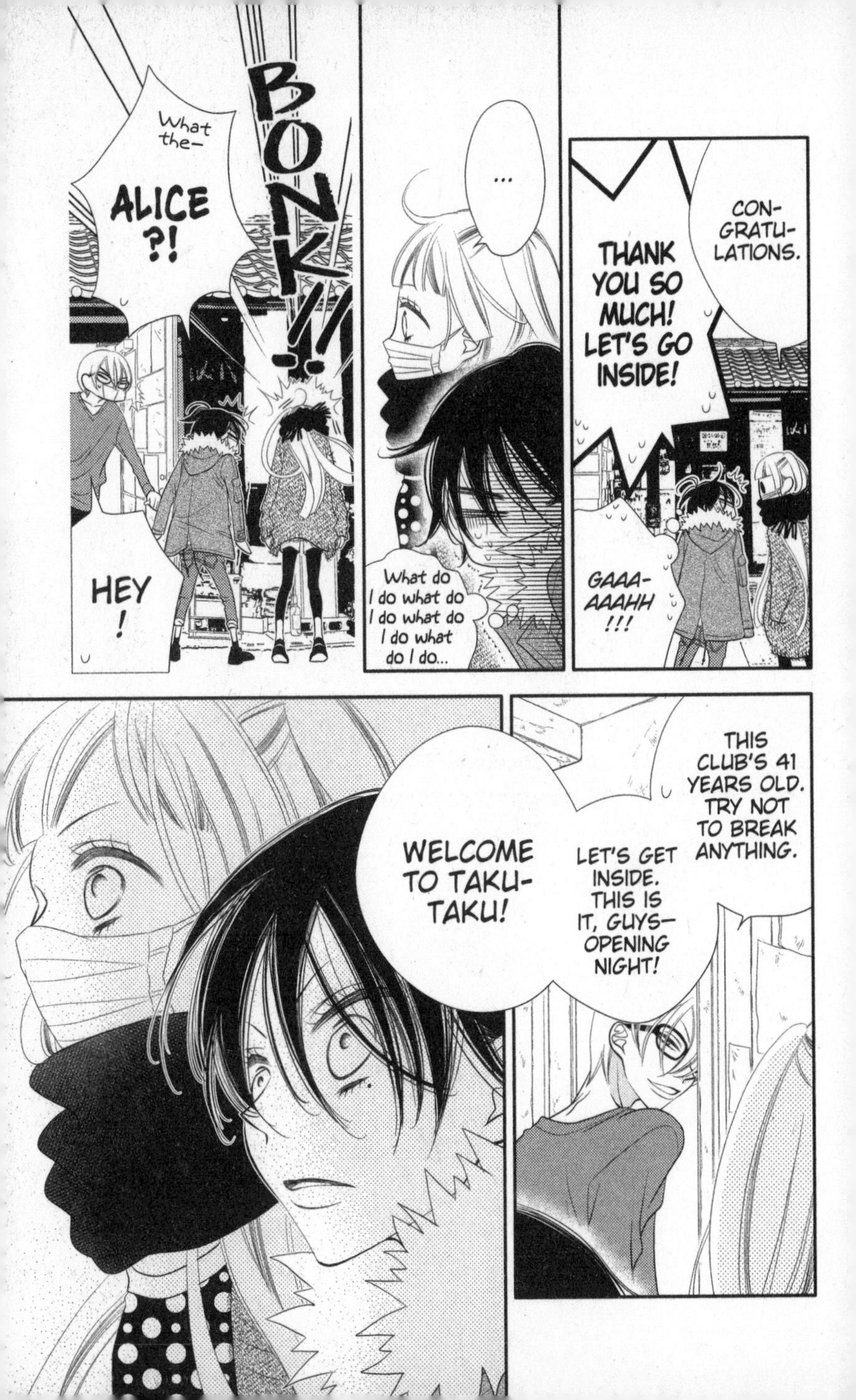
CON-GRATU-LATIONS.
THANK YOU SO MUCH! LET'S GO INSIDE!
GAAA-AAAHH!!!
...
What do I do what do I do what do I do what do I do...
What the-
ALICE?!
BONK!!
HEY!
THIS CLUB'S 41 YEARS OLD. TRY NOT TO BREAK ANYTHING.
LET'S GET INSIDE. THIS IS IT, GUYS—OPENING NIGHT!
WELCOME TO TAKU-TAKU!

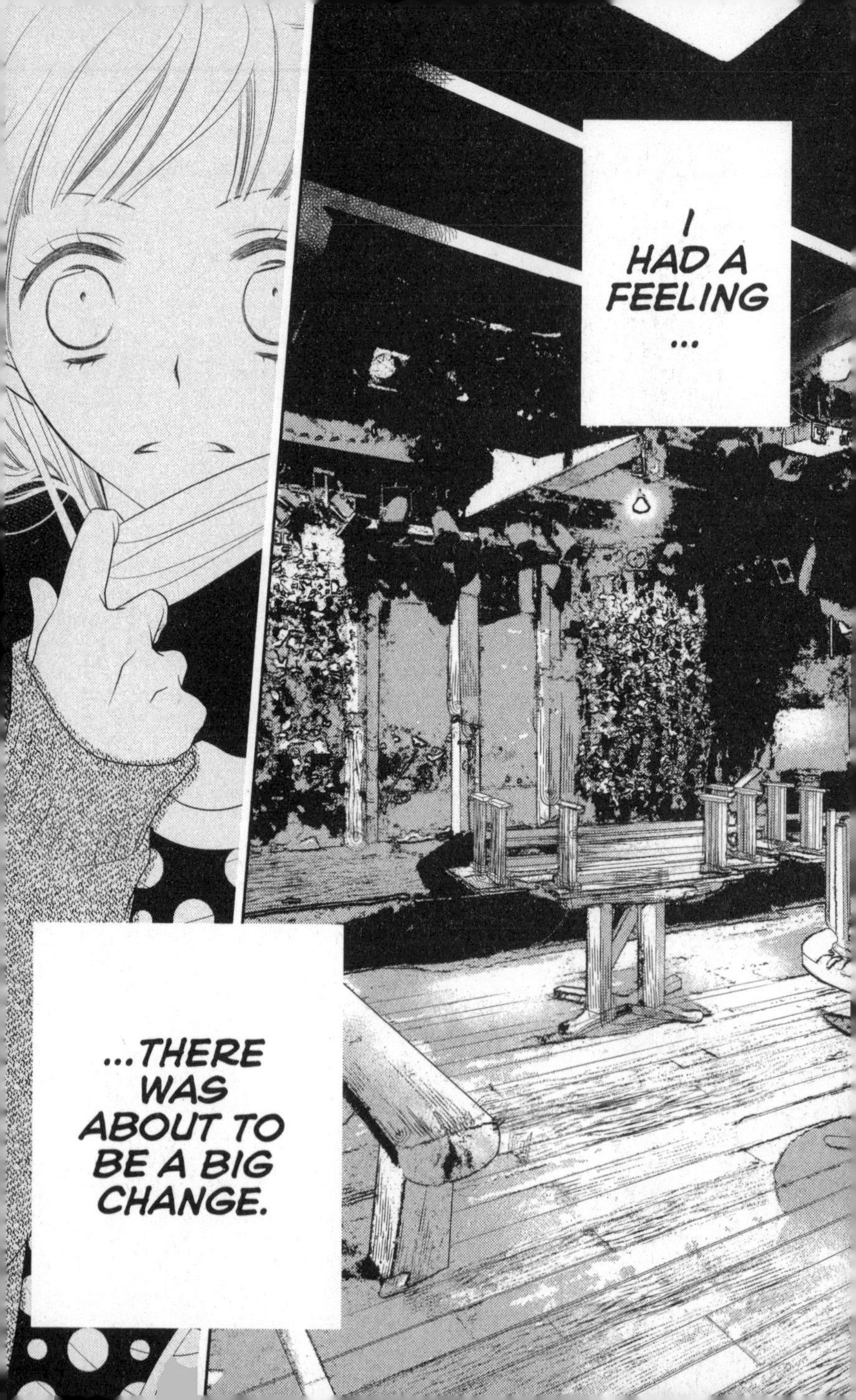
I HAD A FEELING ...
...THERE WAS ABOUT TO BE A BIG CHANGE.

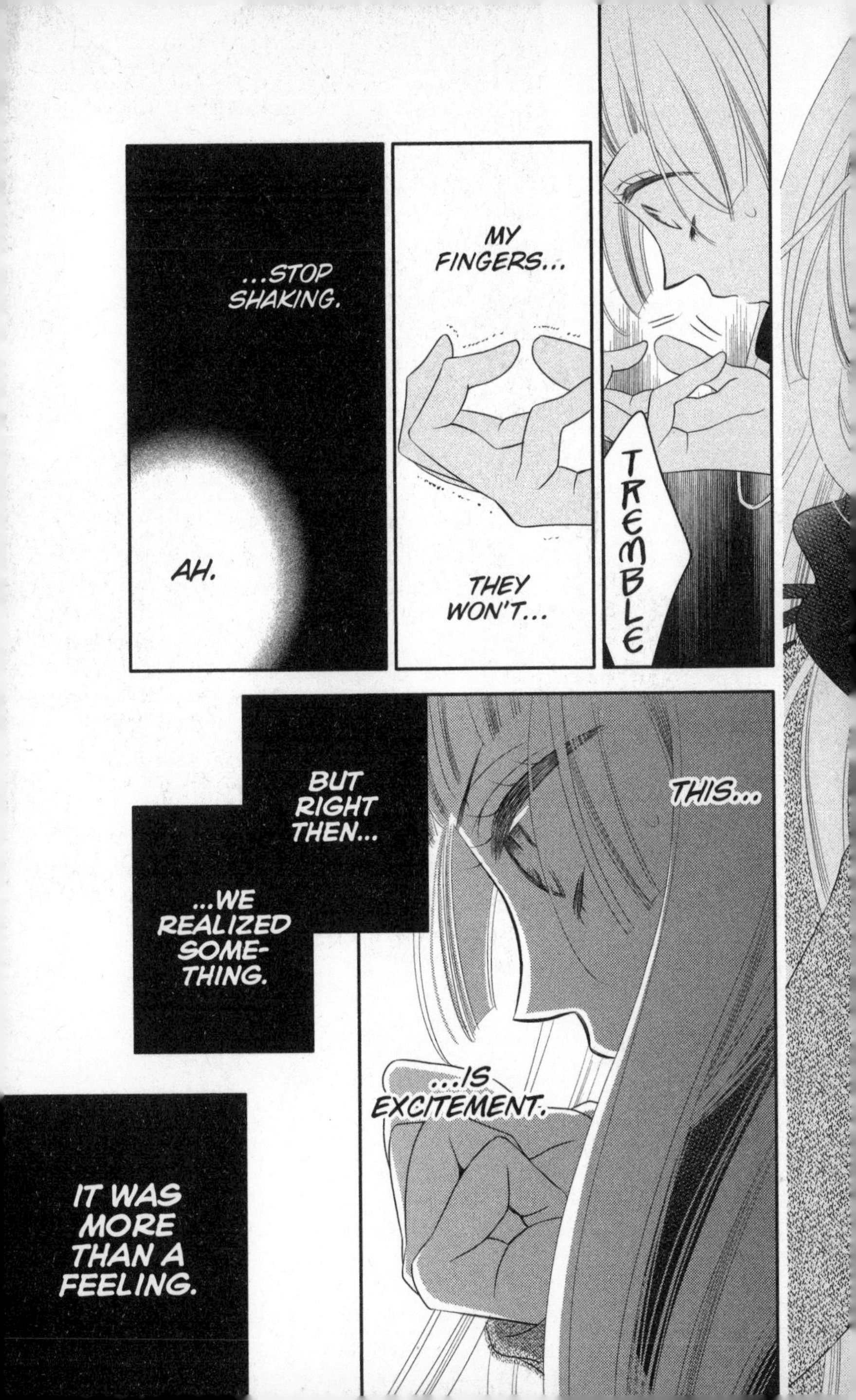
TREMBLE
MY FINGERS...
THEY WON'T...
...STOP SHAKING.
AH.
THIS...
BUT RIGHT THEN...
...WE REALIZED SOMETHING.
...IS EXCITEMENT.
IT WAS MORE THAN A FEELING.

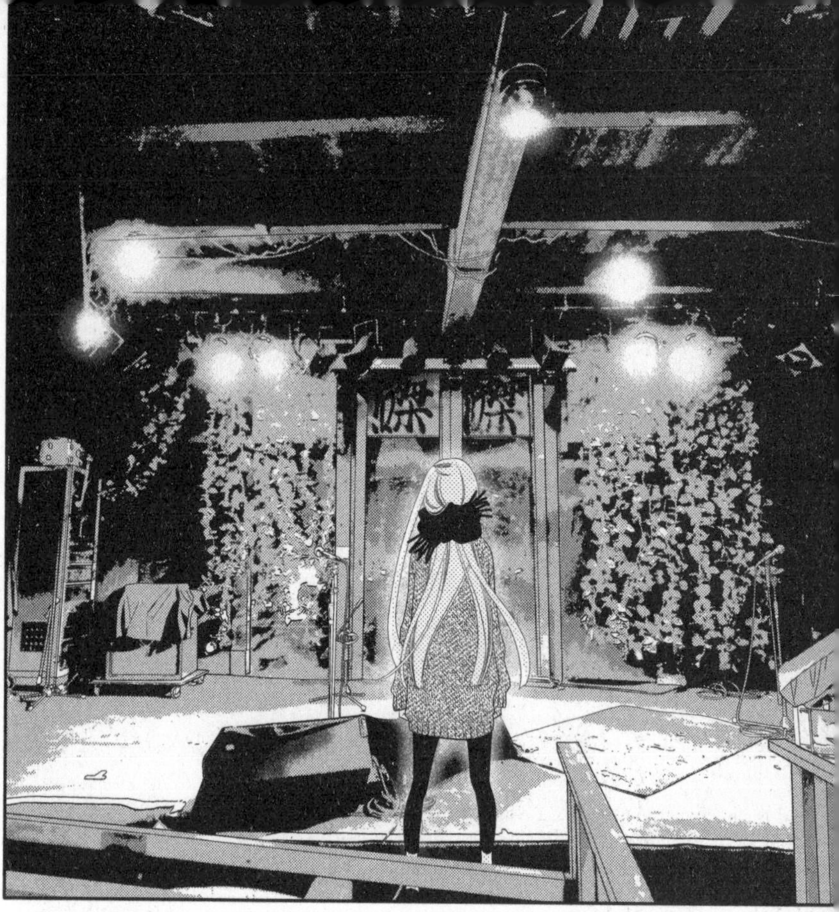

IT WAS A CERTAINTY.

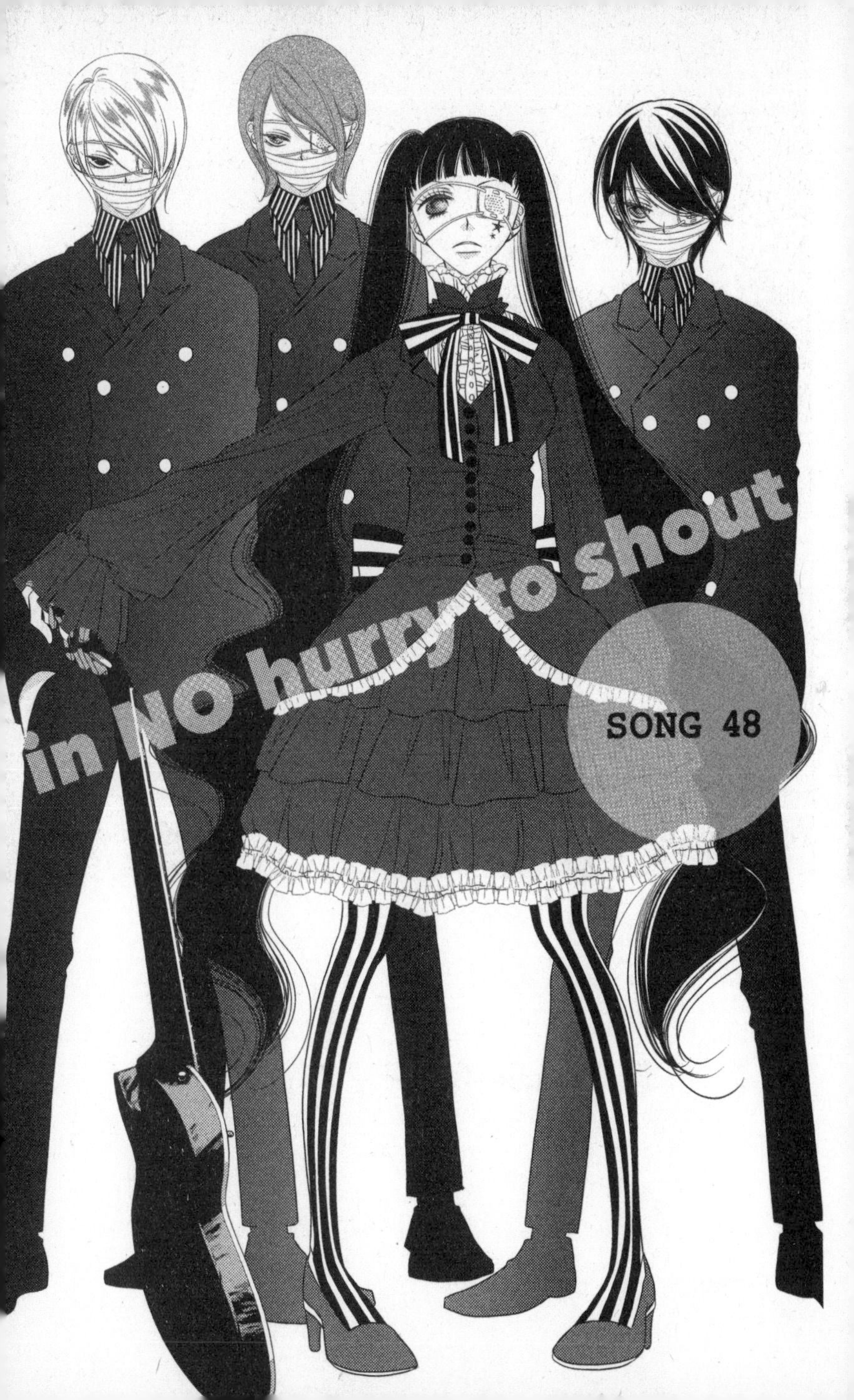
in NO hurry to shout
SONG 48

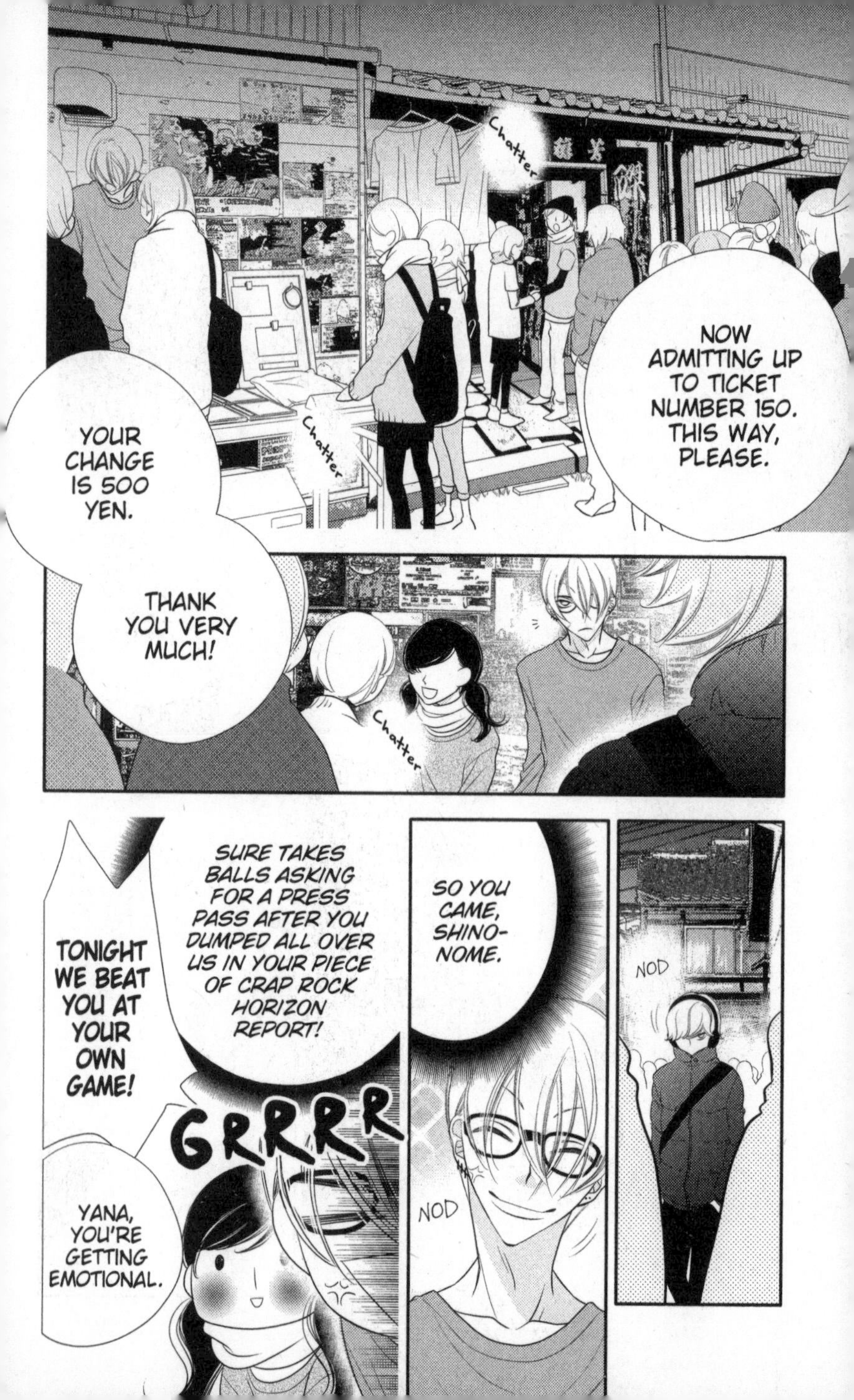

Chatter
NOW ADMITTING UP TO TICKET NUMBER 150. THIS WAY, PLEASE.
YOUR CHANGE IS 500 YEN.
Chatter
THANK YOU VERY MUCH!
Chatter
NOD
SO YOU CAME, SHINO-NOME.
NOD
SURE TAKES BALLS ASKING FOR A PRESS PASS AFTER YOU DUMPED ALL OVER US IN YOUR PIECE OF CRAP ROCK HORIZON REPORT!
TONIGHT WE BEAT YOU AT YOUR OWN GAME!
GRRRR
YANA, YOU'RE GETTING EMOTIONAL.

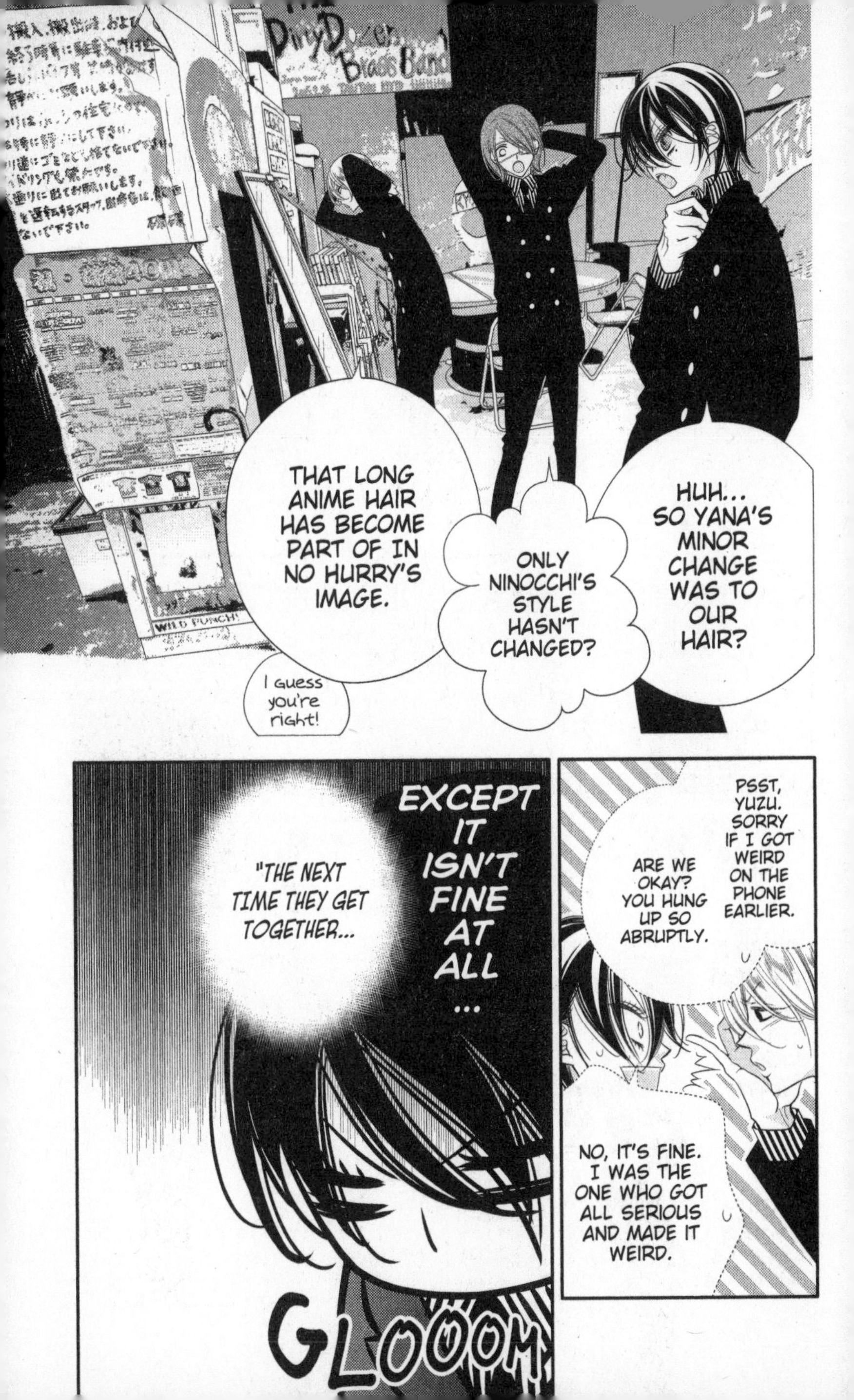
HUH... SO YANA'S MINOR CHANGE WAS TO OUR HAIR?
ONLY NINOCCHI'S STYLE HASN'T CHANGED?
THAT LONG ANIME HAIR HAS BECOME PART OF IN NO HURRY'S IMAGE.
I guess you're right!
PSST, YUZU. SORRY IF I GOT WEIRD ON THE PHONE EARLIER.
ARE WE OKAY? YOU HUNG UP SO ABRUPTLY.
NO, IT'S FINE. I WAS THE ONE WHO GOT ALL SERIOUS AND MADE IT WEIRD.
EXCEPT IT ISN'T FINE AT ALL...
"THE NEXT TIME THEY GET TOGETHER...
GLOOOM

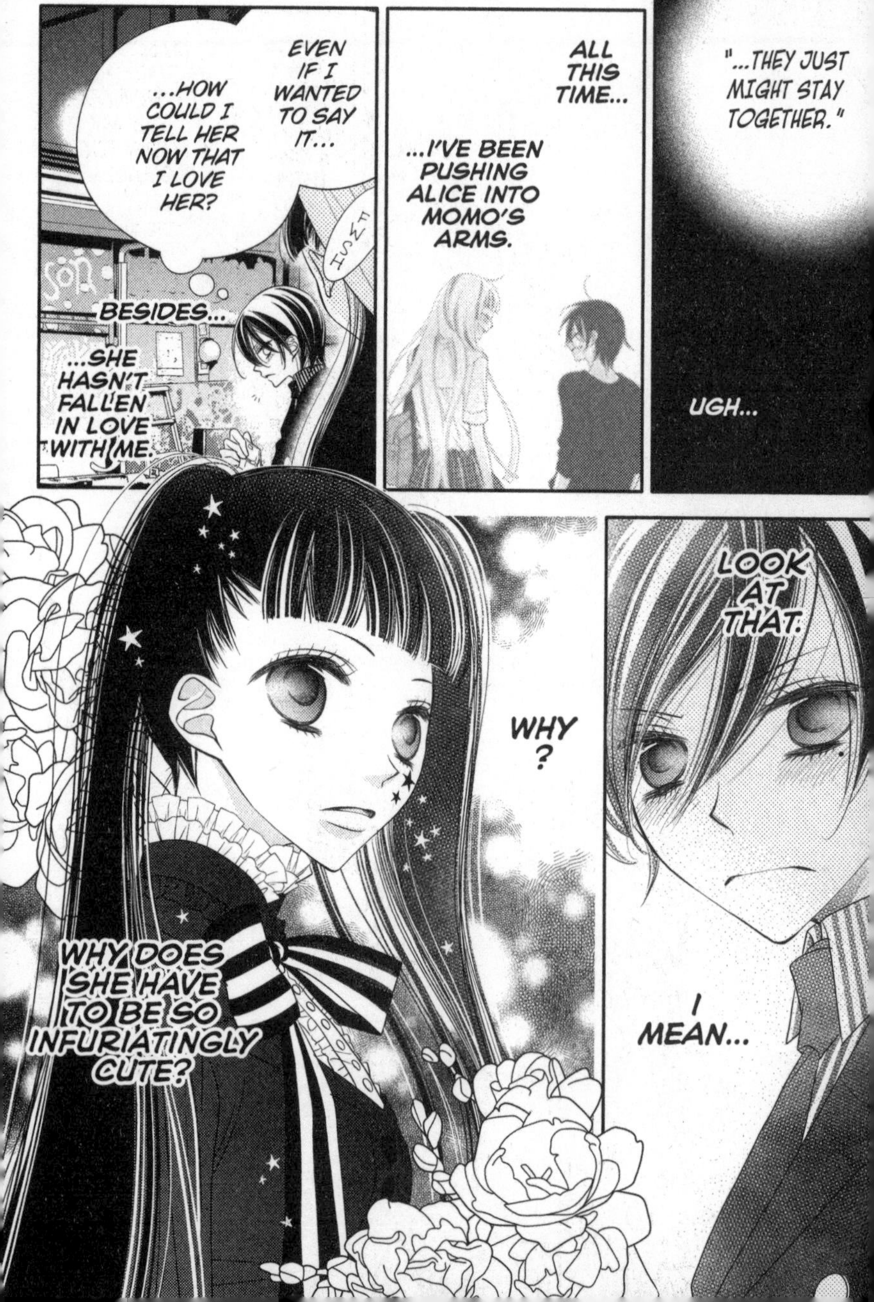
"...THEY JUST MIGHT STAY TOGETHER."
UGH...
ALL THIS TIME...
...I'VE BEEN PUSHING ALICE INTO MOMO'S ARMS.
EVEN IF I WANTED TO SAY IT...
...HOW COULD I TELL HER NOW THAT I LOVE HER?
FWSH
BESIDES...
...SHE HASN'T FALLEN IN LOVE WITH ME.
LOOK AT THAT.
I MEAN...
WHY?
WHY DOES SHE HAVE TO BE SO INFURIATINGLY CUTE?

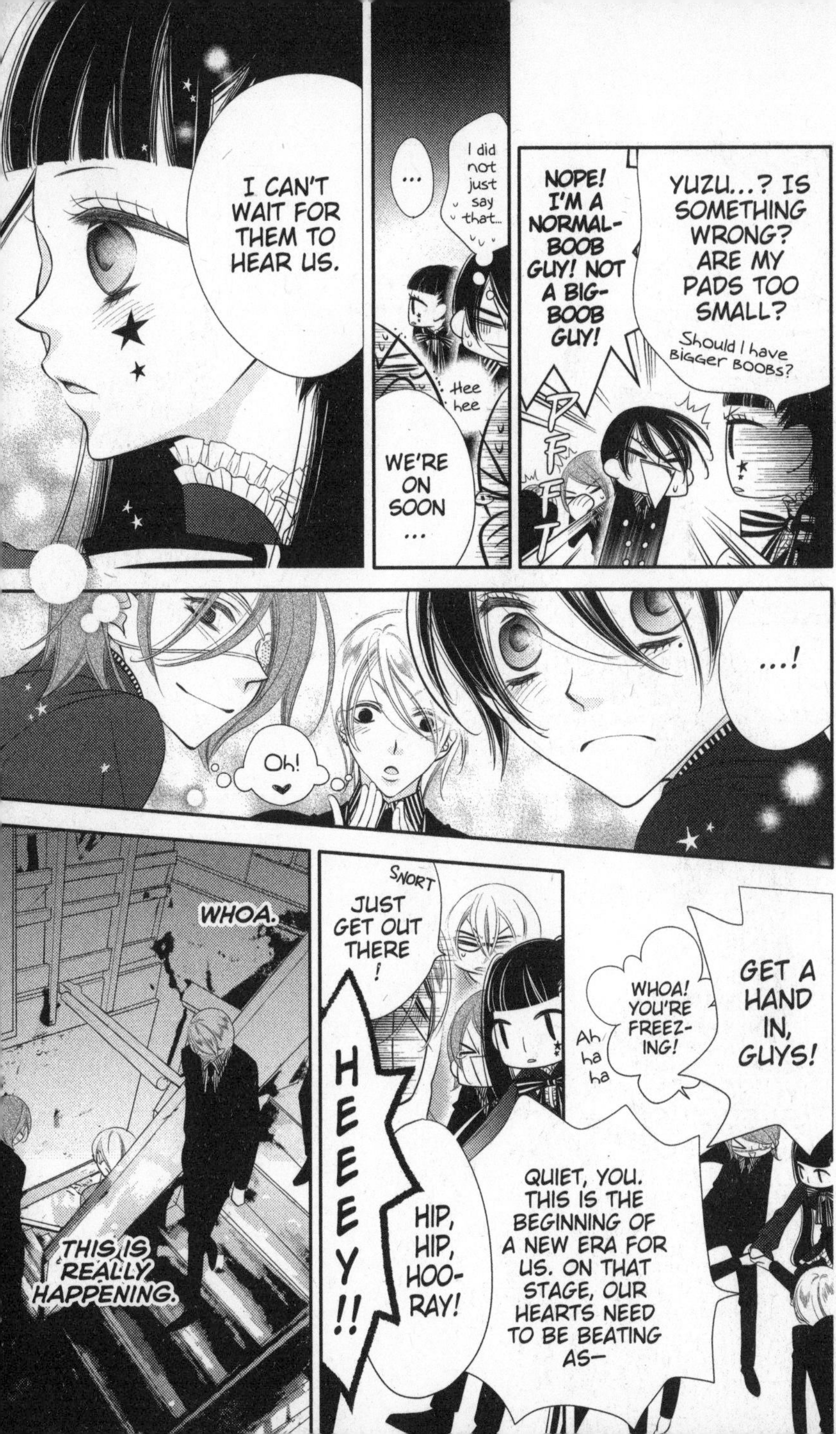
YUZU...? IS SOMETHING WRONG? ARE MY PADS TOO SMALL?
Should I have bigger boobs?
NOPE! I'M A NORMAL-BOOB GUY! NOT A BIG-BOOB GUY!
PFFT
I did not just say that...
...
Hee hee
WE'RE ON SOON...
I CAN'T WAIT FOR THEM TO HEAR US.
...!
Oh!
GET A HAND IN, GUYS!
WHOA! YOU'RE FREEZ-ING!
Ah ha ha
SNORT
JUST GET OUT THERE!
QUIET, YOU. THIS IS THE BEGINNING OF A NEW ERA FOR US. ON THAT STAGE, OUR HEARTS NEED TO BE BEATING AS—
HIP, HIP, HOO-RAY!
HEEEEY!!
WHOA.
THIS IS REALLY HAPPENING.

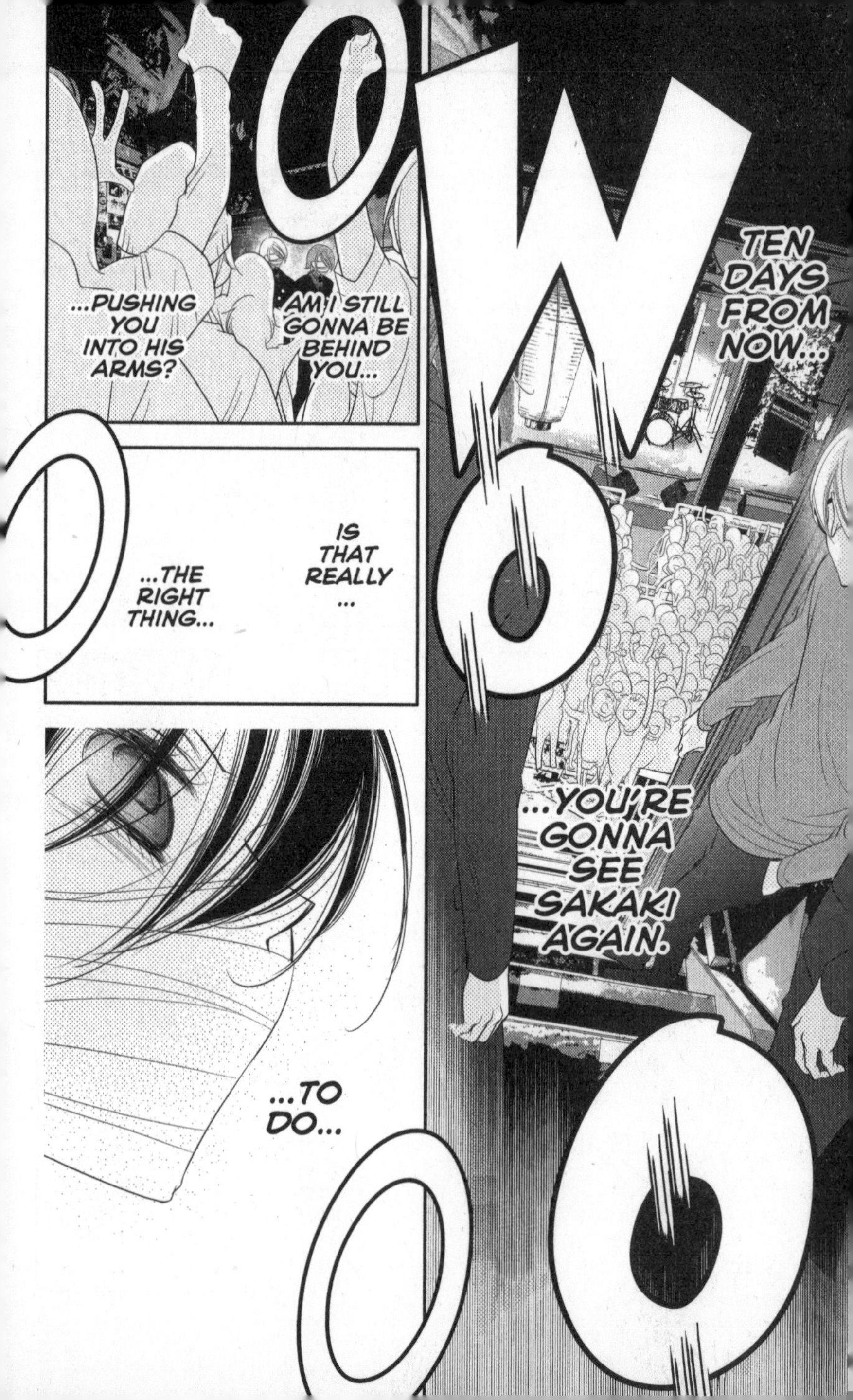

TEN DAYS FROM NOW...
...YOU'RE GONNA SEE SAKAKI AGAIN.
AM I STILL GONNA BE BEHIND YOU...
...PUSHING YOU INTO HIS ARMS?
IS THAT REALLY...
...THE RIGHT THING...
...TO DO...

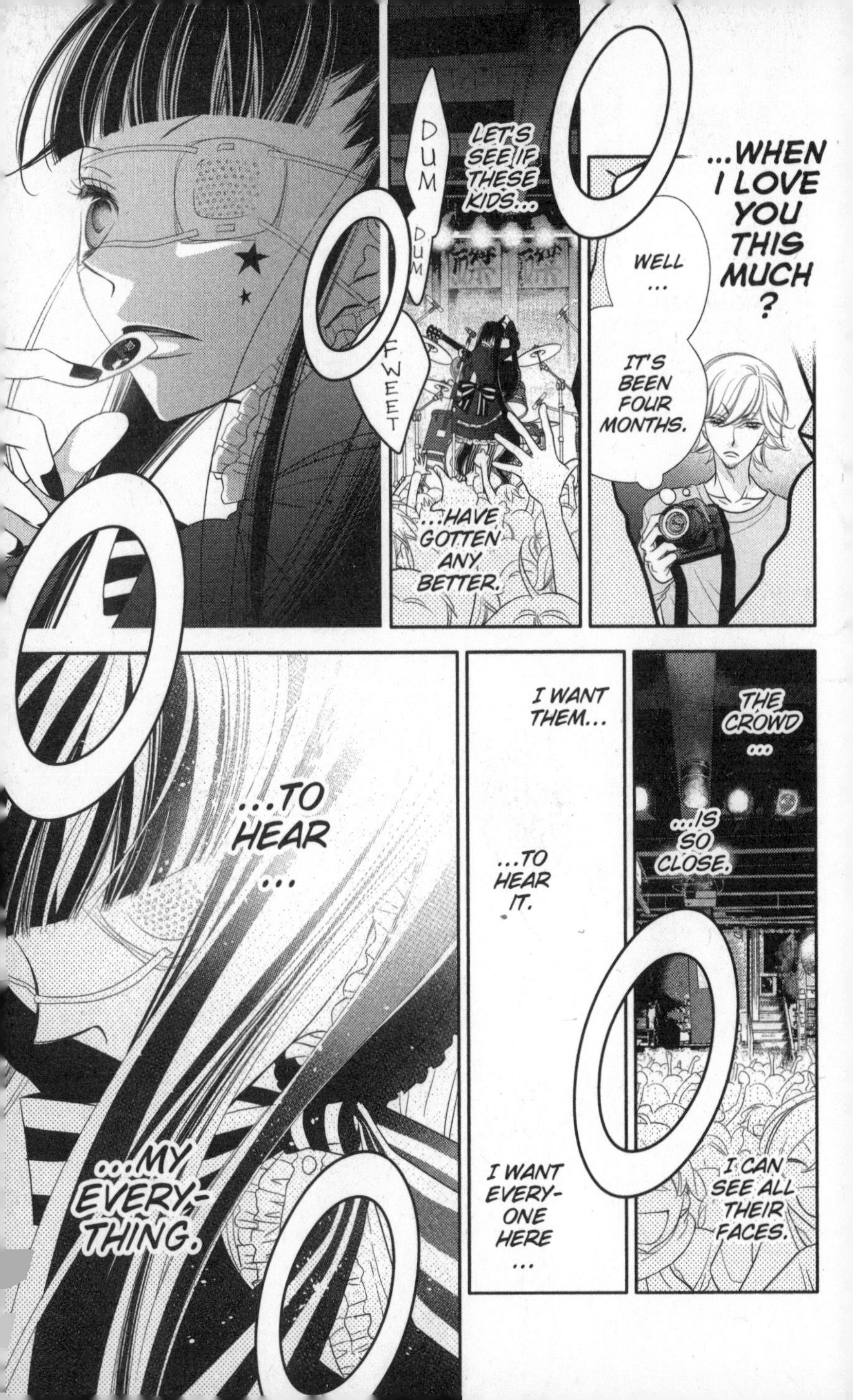
...WHEN I LOVE YOU THIS MUCH?
WELL ...
IT'S BEEN FOUR MONTHS.
LET'S SEE IF THESE KIDS...
DUM
DUM
FWEET
...HAVE GOTTEN ANY BETTER.
THE CROWD ...
...IS SO CLOSE.
I CAN SEE ALL THEIR FACES.
I WANT THEM...
...TO HEAR IT.
I WANT EVERY-ONE HERE ...
...TO HEAR ...
...MY EVERY-THING.

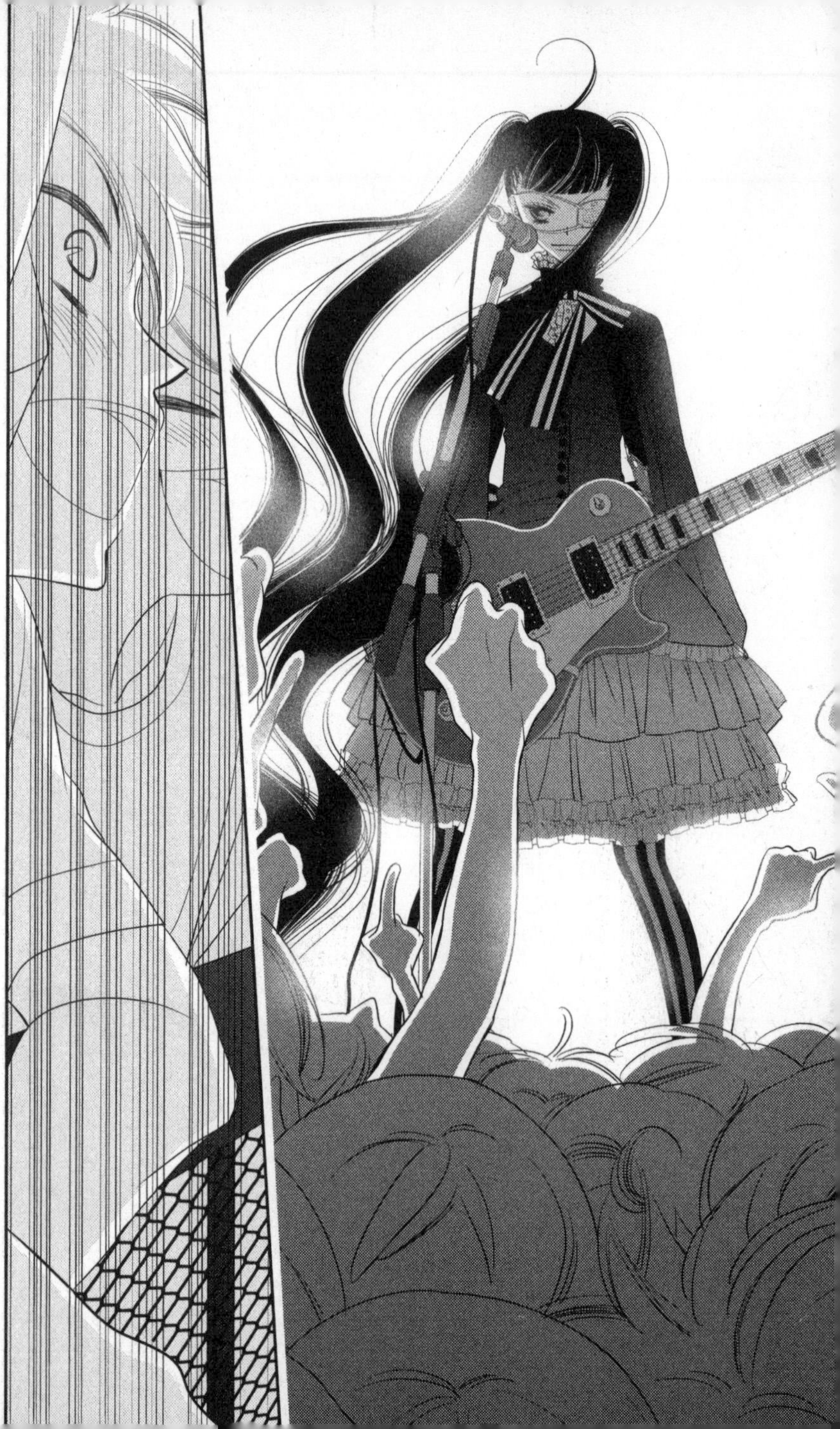

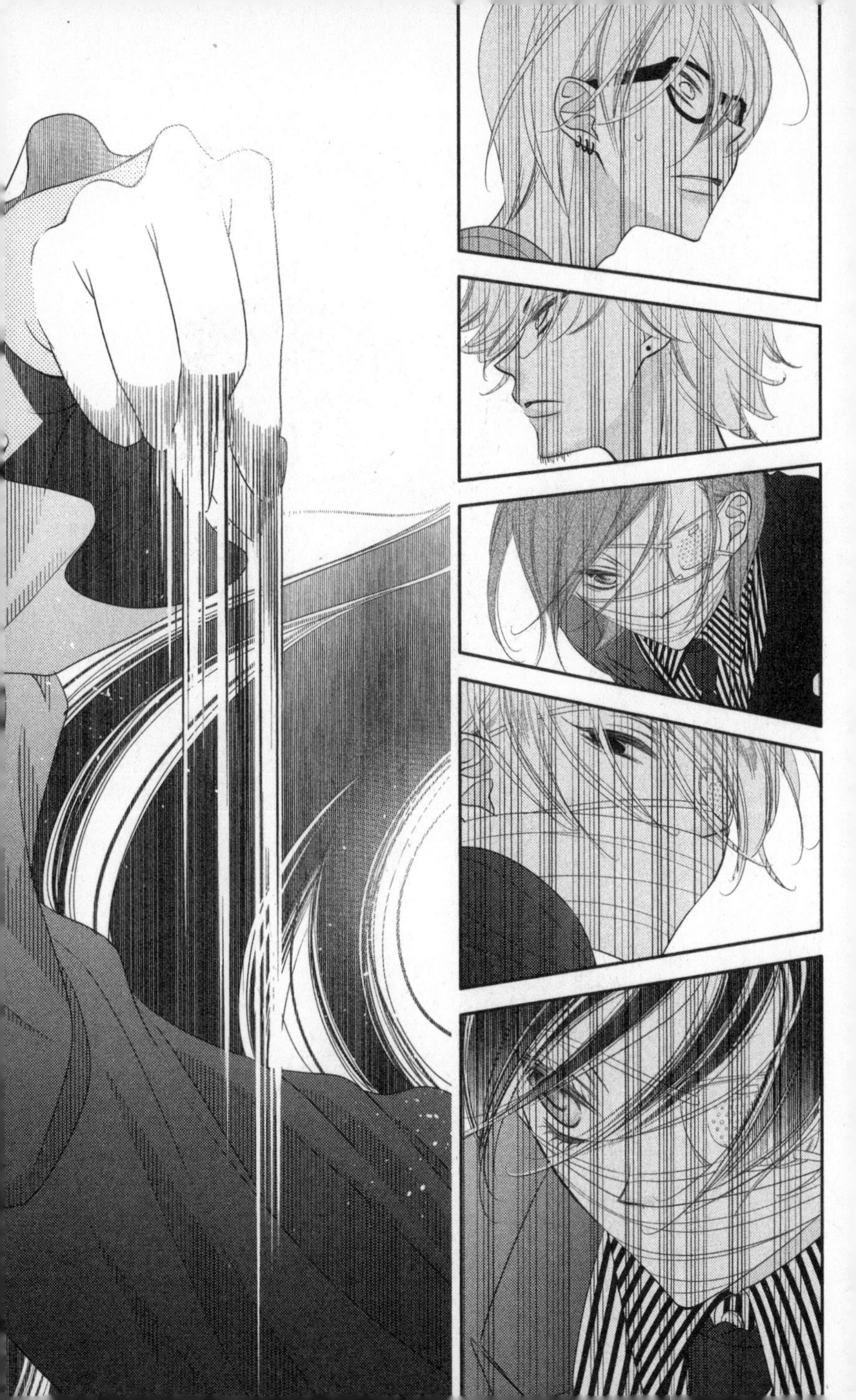

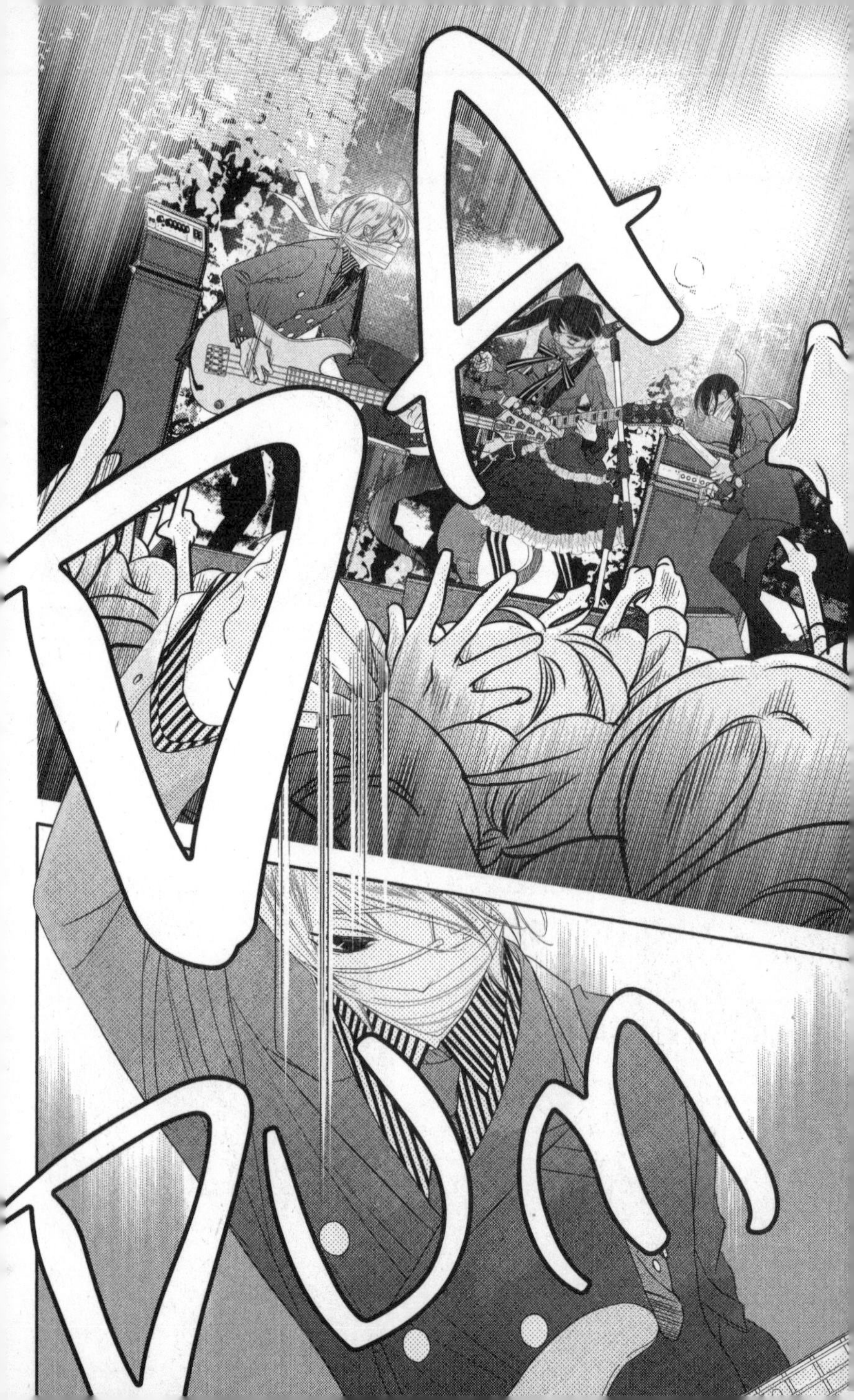

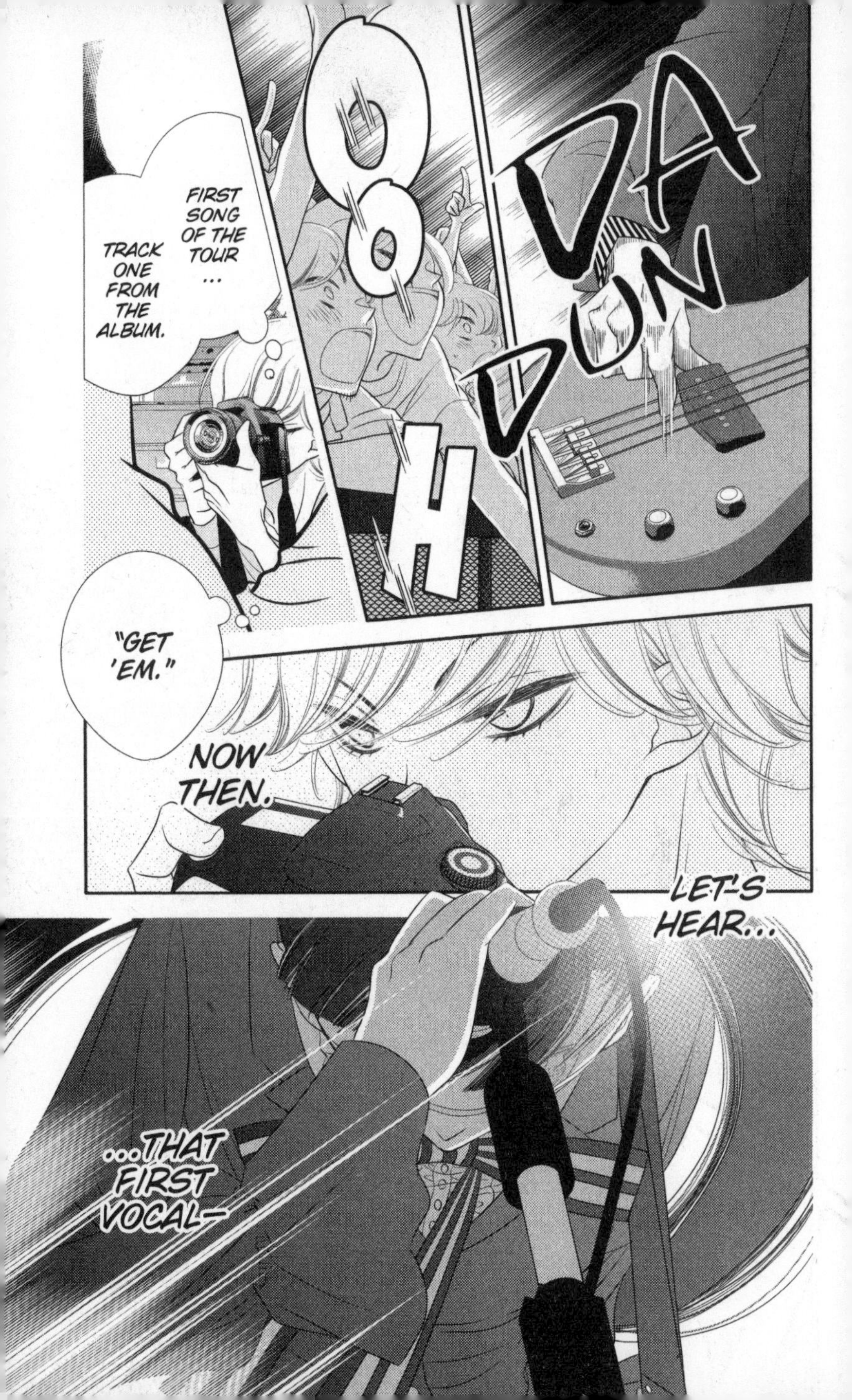
DA DUN
OOOH
FIRST SONG OF THE TOUR...
TRACK ONE FROM THE ALBUM.
"GET 'EM."
NOW THEN.
LET'S HEAR...
...THAT FIRST VOCAL—

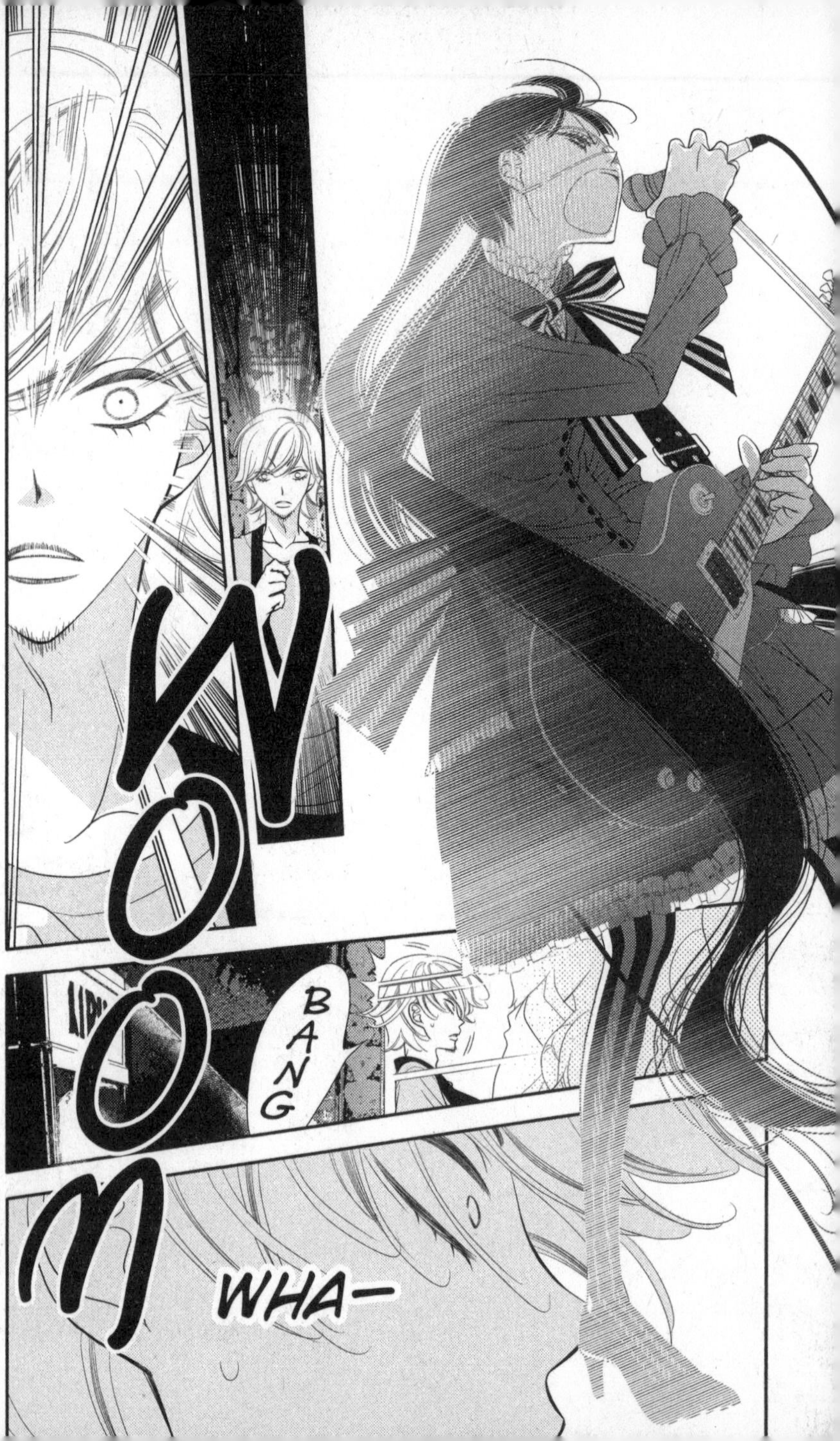
WOOM
BANG
WHA-

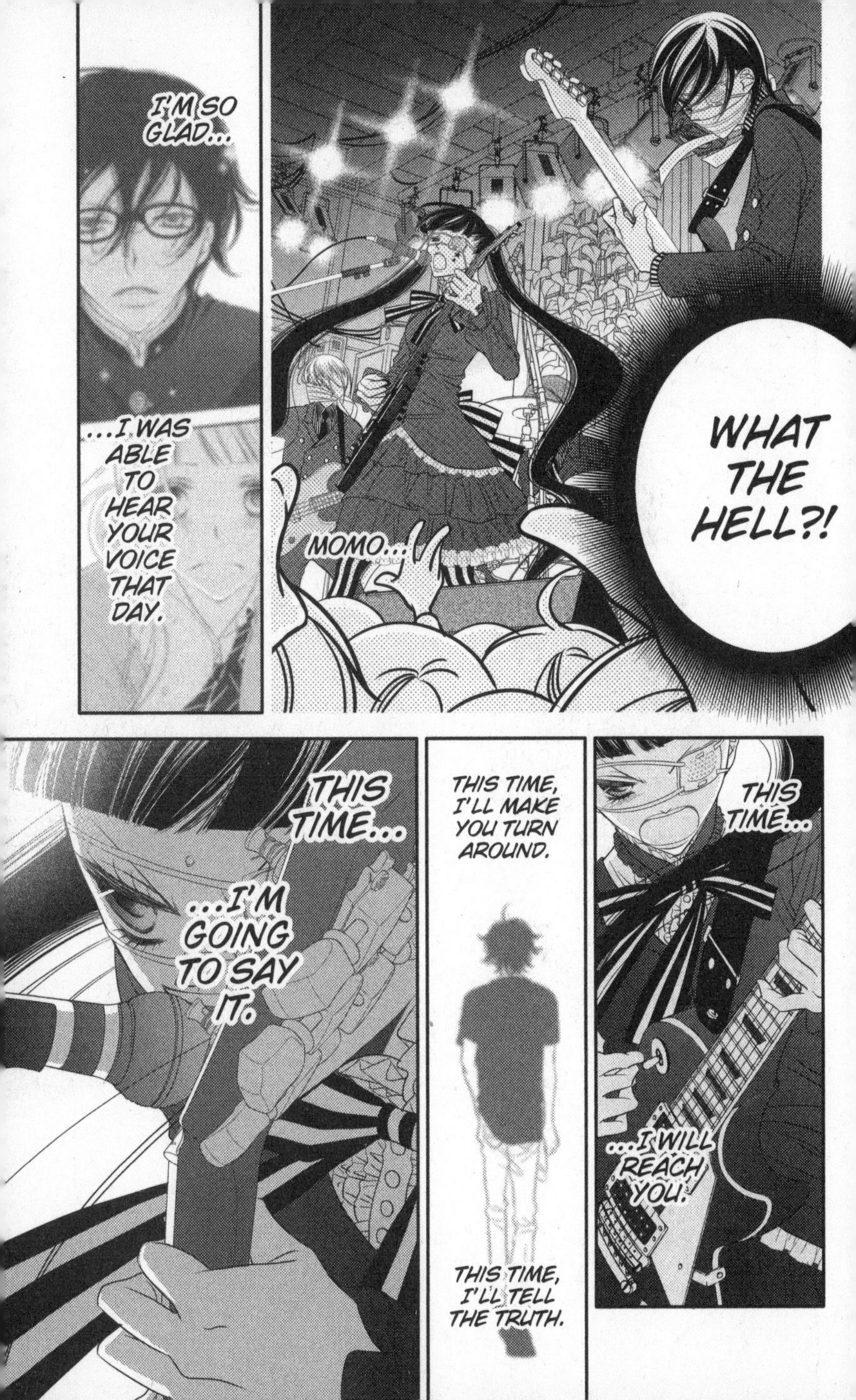
WHAT THE HELL?!
MOMO...
I'M SO GLAD...
...I WAS ABLE TO HEAR YOUR VOICE THAT DAY.
THIS TIME...
...I WILL REACH YOU.
THIS TIME, I'LL MAKE YOU TURN AROUND.
THIS TIME, I'LL TELL THE TRUTH.
THIS TIME...
...I'M GOING TO SAY IT.

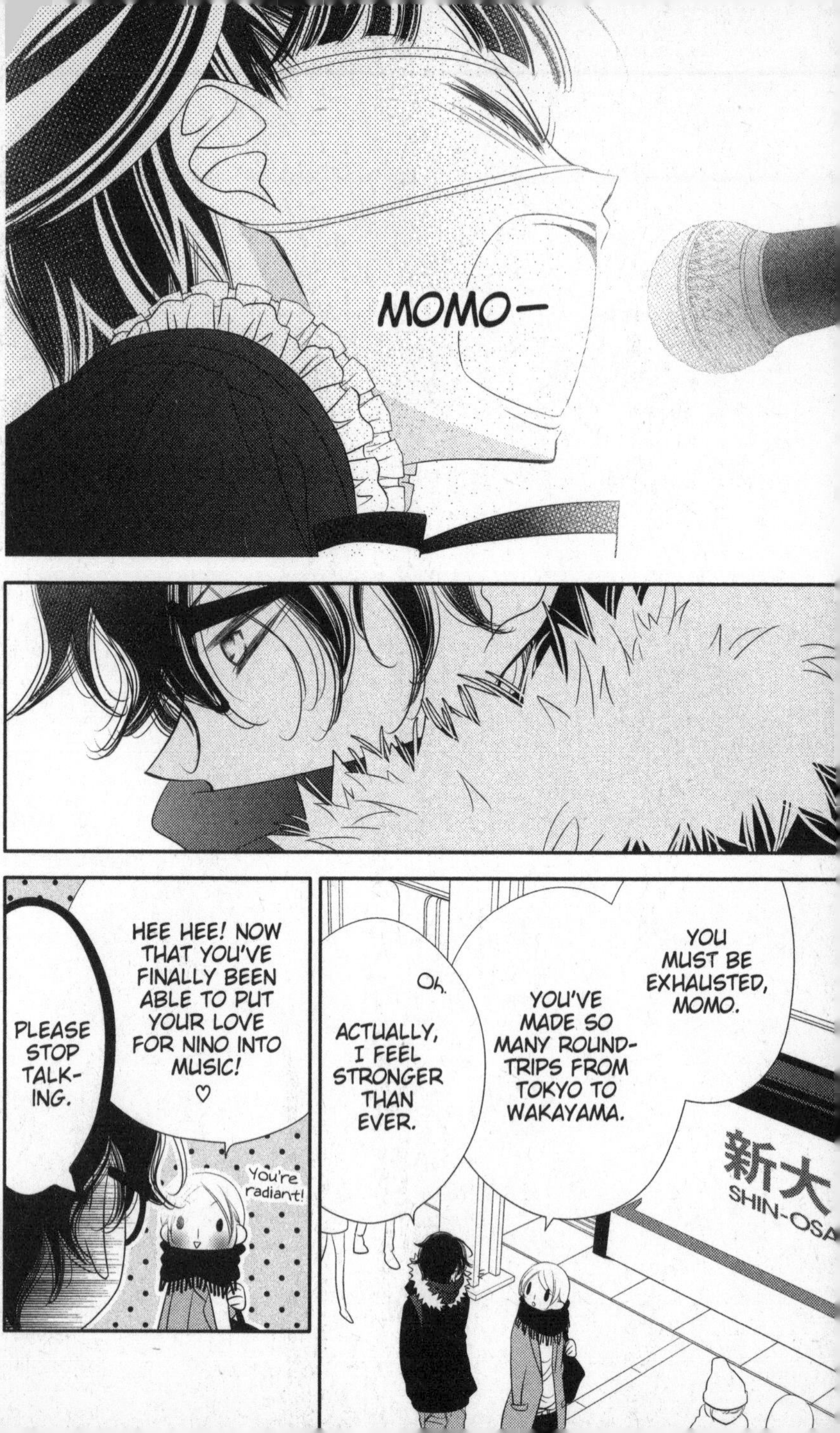
MOMO—
YOU MUST BE EXHAUSTED, MOMO.
YOU'VE MADE SO MANY ROUND-TRIPS FROM TOKYO TO WAKAYAMA.
Oh.
ACTUALLY, I FEEL STRONGER THAN EVER.
新大
SHIN-OSA
HEE HEE! NOW THAT YOU'VE FINALLY BEEN ABLE TO PUT YOUR LOVE FOR NINO INTO MUSIC! ♡
PLEASE STOP TALK-ING.
You're radiant!

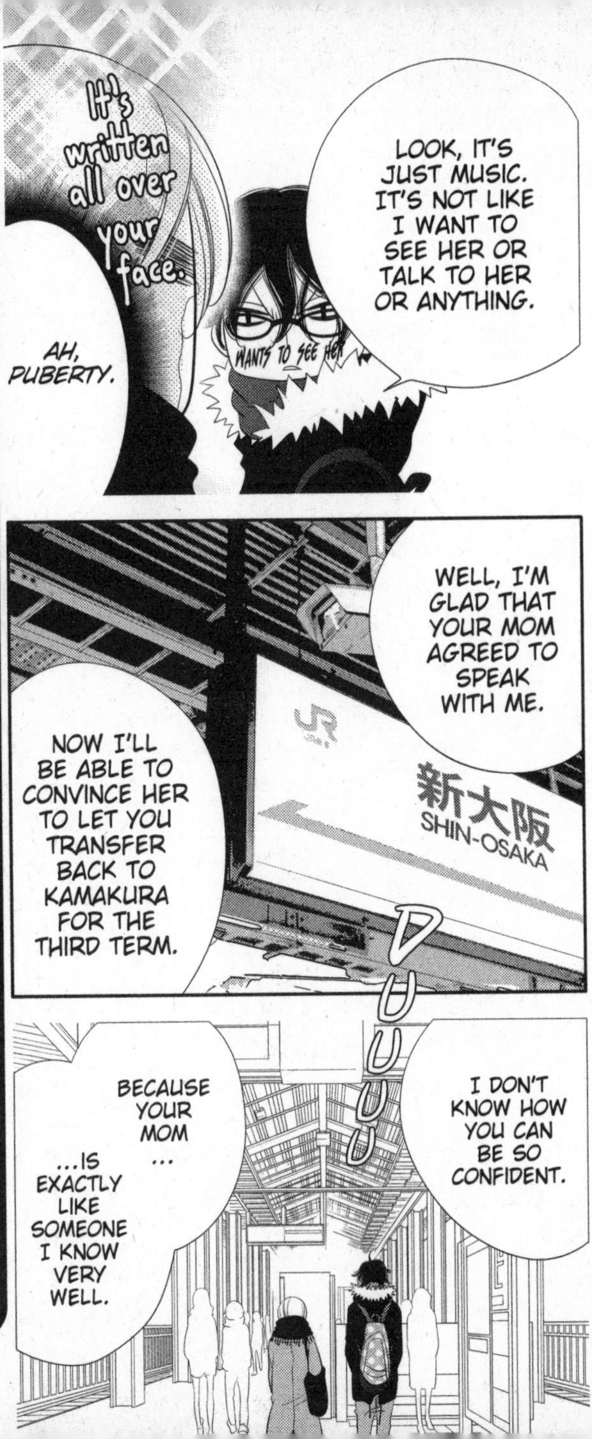
LOOK, IT'S JUST MUSIC. IT'S NOT LIKE I WANT TO SEE HER OR TALK TO HER OR ANYTHING.
It's written all over your face.
WANTS TO SEE HER
AH, PUBERTY.
WELL, I'M GLAD THAT YOUR MOM AGREED TO SPEAK WITH ME.
新大阪
SHIN-OSAKA
NOW I'LL BE ABLE TO CONVINCE HER TO LET YOU TRANSFER BACK TO KAMAKURA FOR THE THIRD TERM.
I DON'T KNOW HOW YOU CAN BE SO CONFIDENT.
BECAUSE YOUR MOM ...
...IS EXACTLY LIKE SOMEONE I KNOW VERY WELL.

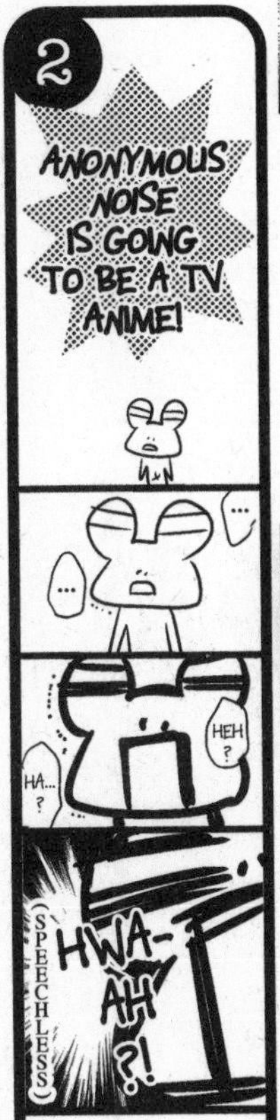
2
ANONYMOUS NOISE IS GOING TO BE A TV ANIME!
...
...
HEH?
HA...?
(SPEECHLESS)
HWA-AH?!

This never would have happened without you, my faithful readers. Thank you so much for supporting my work!!

SO THANKFUL!!

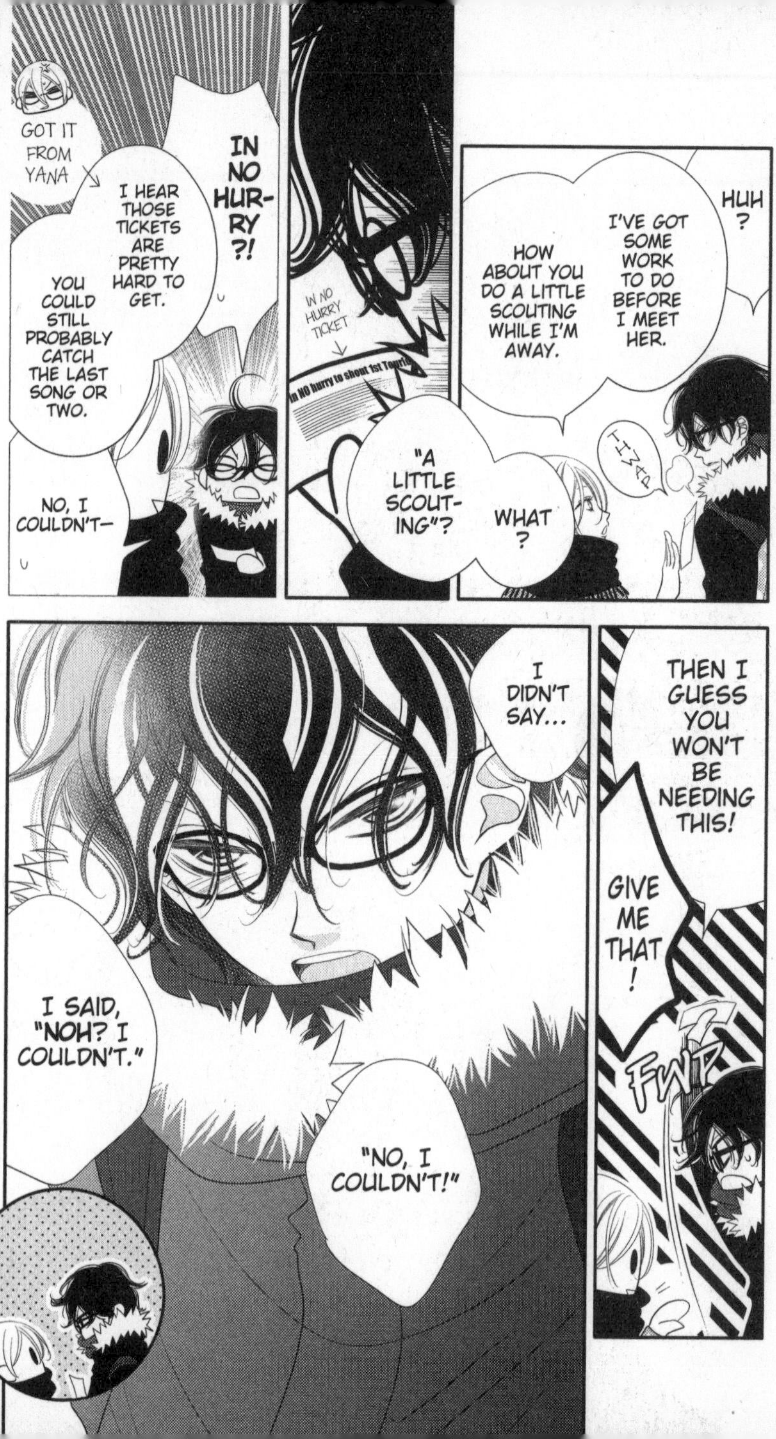
HUH?
I'VE GOT SOME WORK TO DO BEFORE I MEET HER.
HOW ABOUT YOU DO A LITTLE SCOUTING WHILE I'M AWAY.
WHAT?
"A LITTLE SCOUTING"?
IN NO HURRY TICKET
IN NO HURRY?!
I HEAR THOSE TICKETS ARE PRETTY HARD TO GET.
GOT IT FROM YANA
YOU COULD STILL PROBABLY CATCH THE LAST SONG OR TWO.
NO, I COULDN'T—
THEN I GUESS YOU WON'T BE NEEDING THIS!
GIVE ME THAT!
FWP
I DIDN'T SAY...
I SAID, "NOH? I COULDN'T."
"NO, I COULDN'T!"

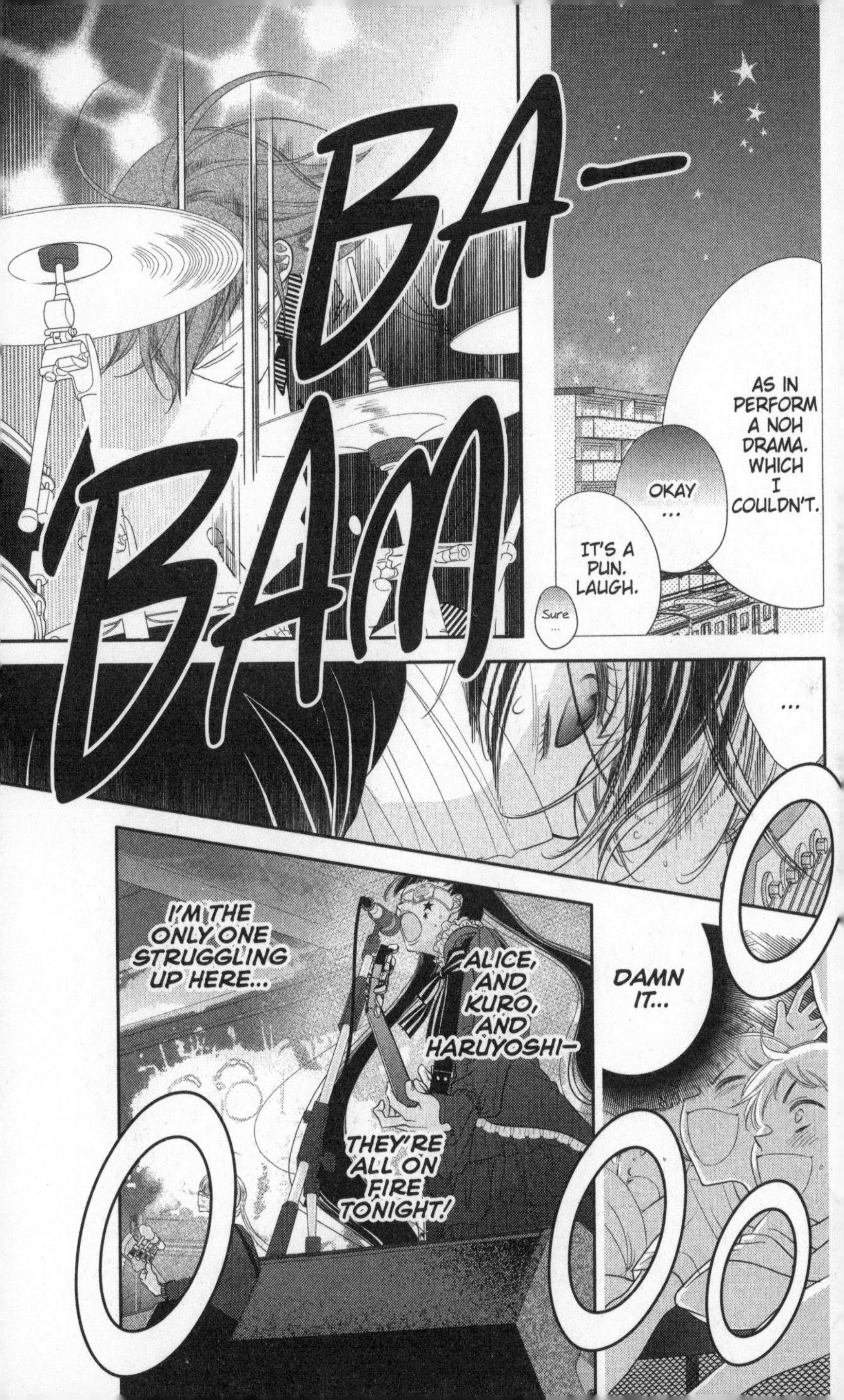
AS IN PERFORM A NOH DRAMA. WHICH I COULDN'T.
OKAY...
IT'S A PUN. LAUGH.
Sure...
BA-BAM
...
DAMN IT...
I'M THE ONLY ONE STRUGGLING UP HERE...
ALICE, AND KURO, AND HARUYOSHI—
THEY'RE ALL ON FIRE TONIGHT!

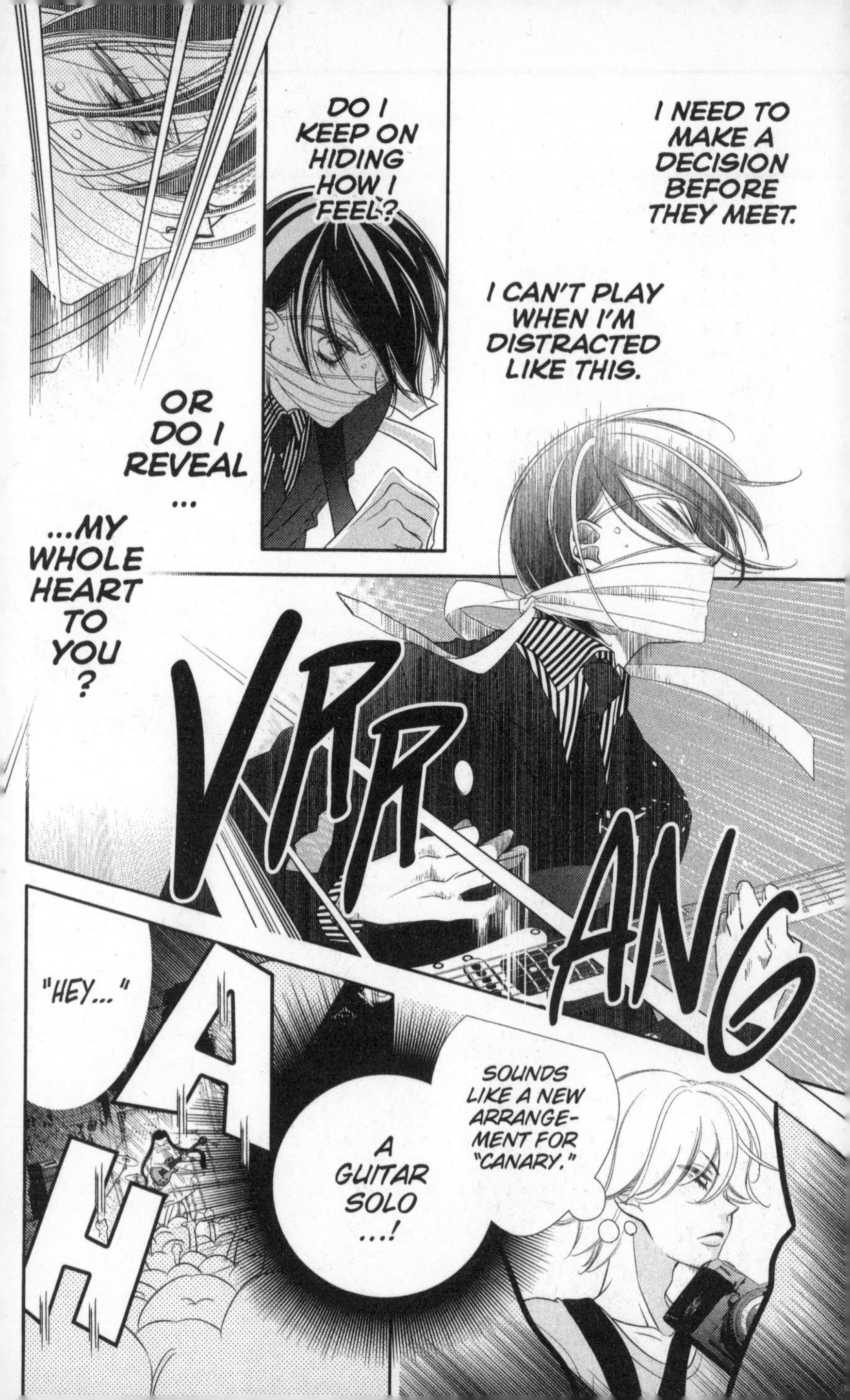
I NEED TO MAKE A DECISION BEFORE THEY MEET.
I CAN'T PLAY WHEN I'M DISTRACTED LIKE THIS.
DO I KEEP ON HIDING HOW I FEEL?
OR DO I REVEAL ...
...MY WHOLE HEART TO YOU?
VRR ANG
SOUNDS LIKE A NEW ARRANGE-MENT FOR "CANARY."
A GUITAR SOLO ...!
"HEY..."
AH

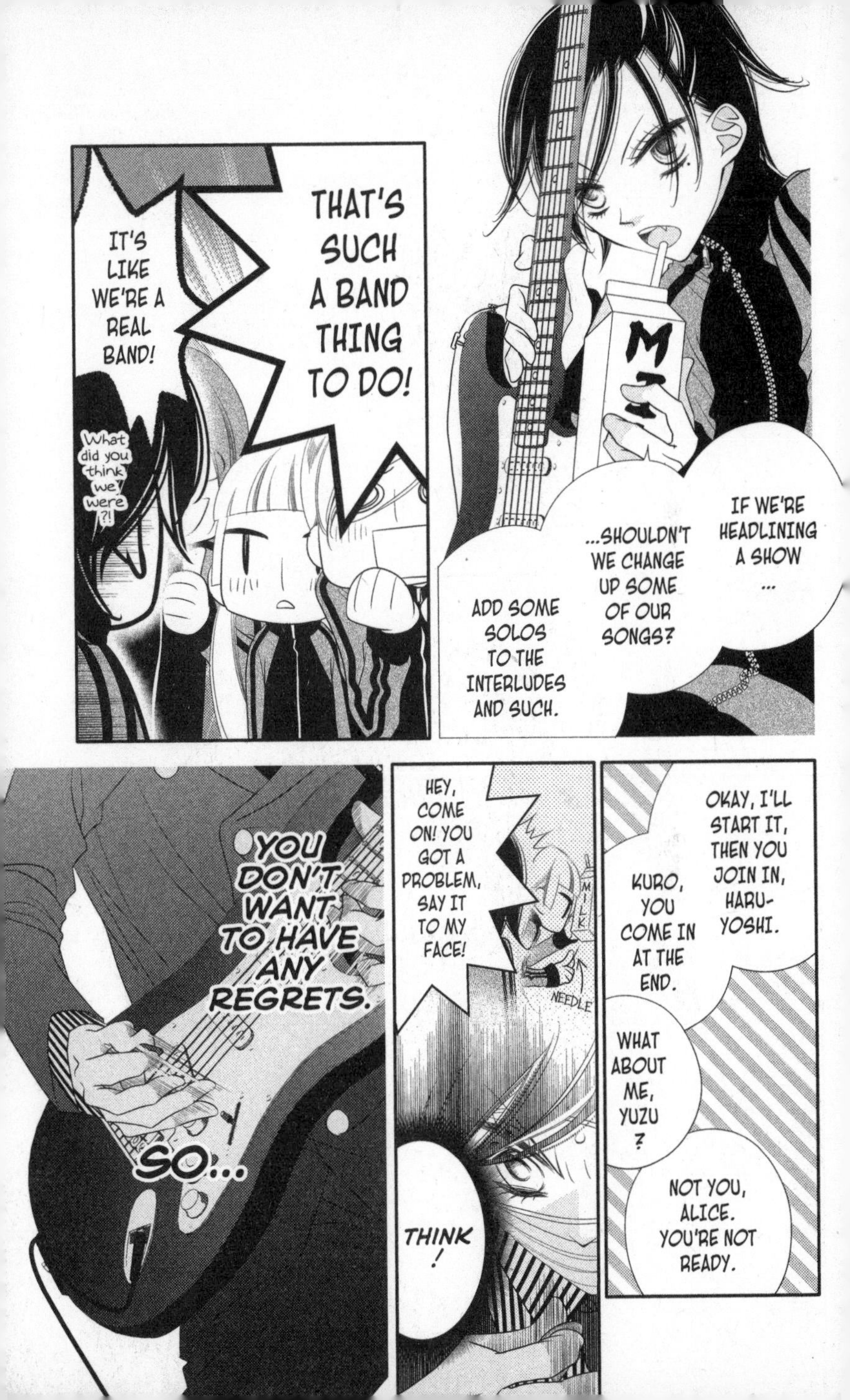
IF WE'RE HEADLINING A SHOW ...
...SHOULDN'T WE CHANGE UP SOME OF OUR SONGS?
ADD SOME SOLOS TO THE INTERLUDES AND SUCH.
THAT'S SUCH A BAND THING TO DO!
IT'S LIKE WE'RE A REAL BAND!
What did you think we were?!
OKAY, I'LL START IT, THEN YOU JOIN IN, HARU-YOSHI.
KURO, YOU COME IN AT THE END.
WHAT ABOUT ME, YUZU?
NOT YOU, ALICE. YOU'RE NOT READY.
HEY, COME ON! YOU GOT A PROBLEM, SAY IT TO MY FACE!
MILK
NEEDLE
THINK!
YOU DON'T WANT TO HAVE ANY REGRETS.
SO...

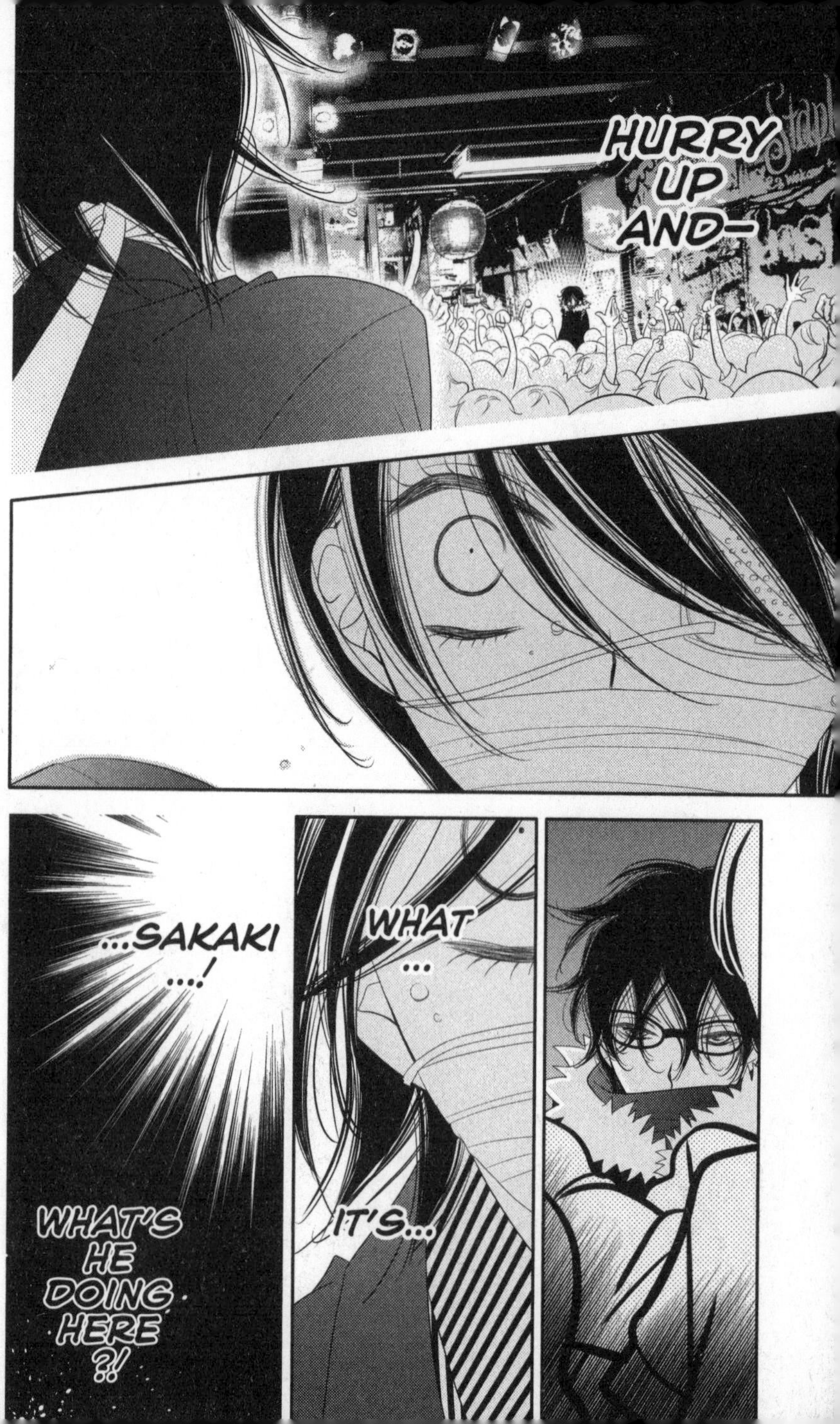

HURRY UP AND-
WHAT...
IT'S...
...SAKAKI...!
WHAT'S HE DOING HERE?!

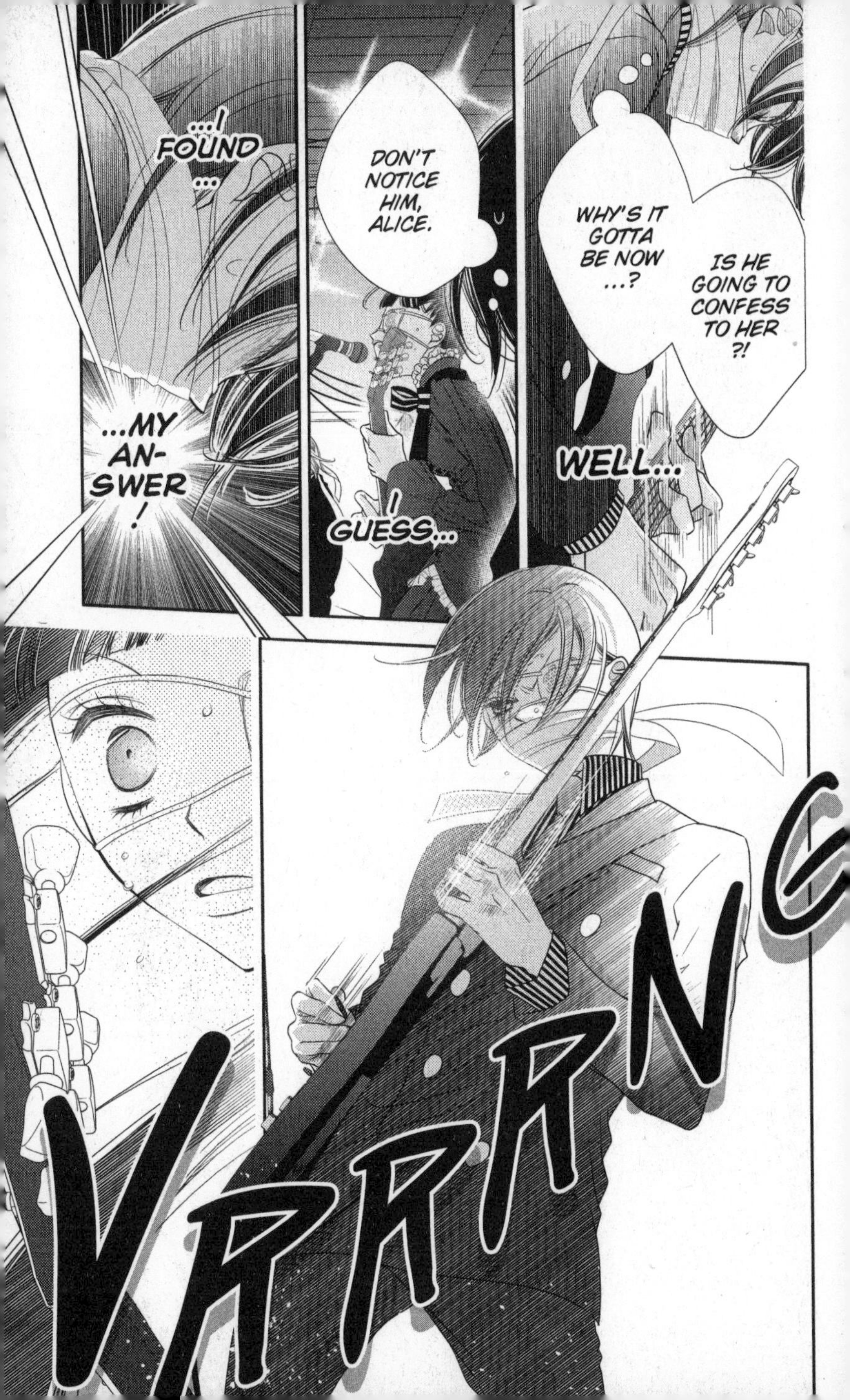
IS HE GOING TO CONFESS TO HER?!
WHY'S IT GOTTA BE NOW ...?
WELL...
DON'T NOTICE HIM, ALICE.
I GUESS...
...I FOUND ...
...MY AN-SWER!
VRRANG

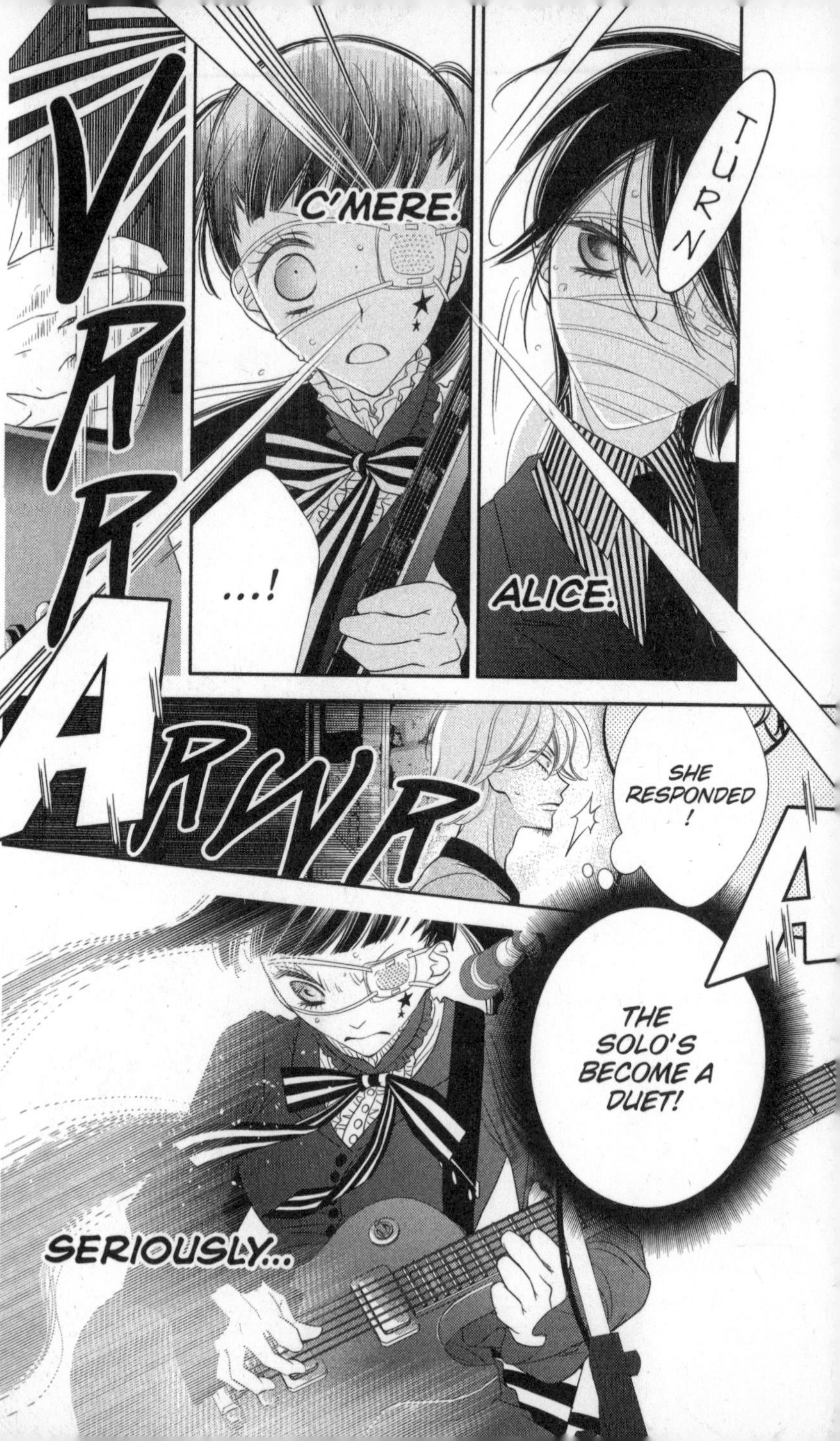
TURN
ALICE.
C'MERE.
...!
SHE RESPONDED!
THE SOLO'S BECOME A DUET!
SERIOUSLY...

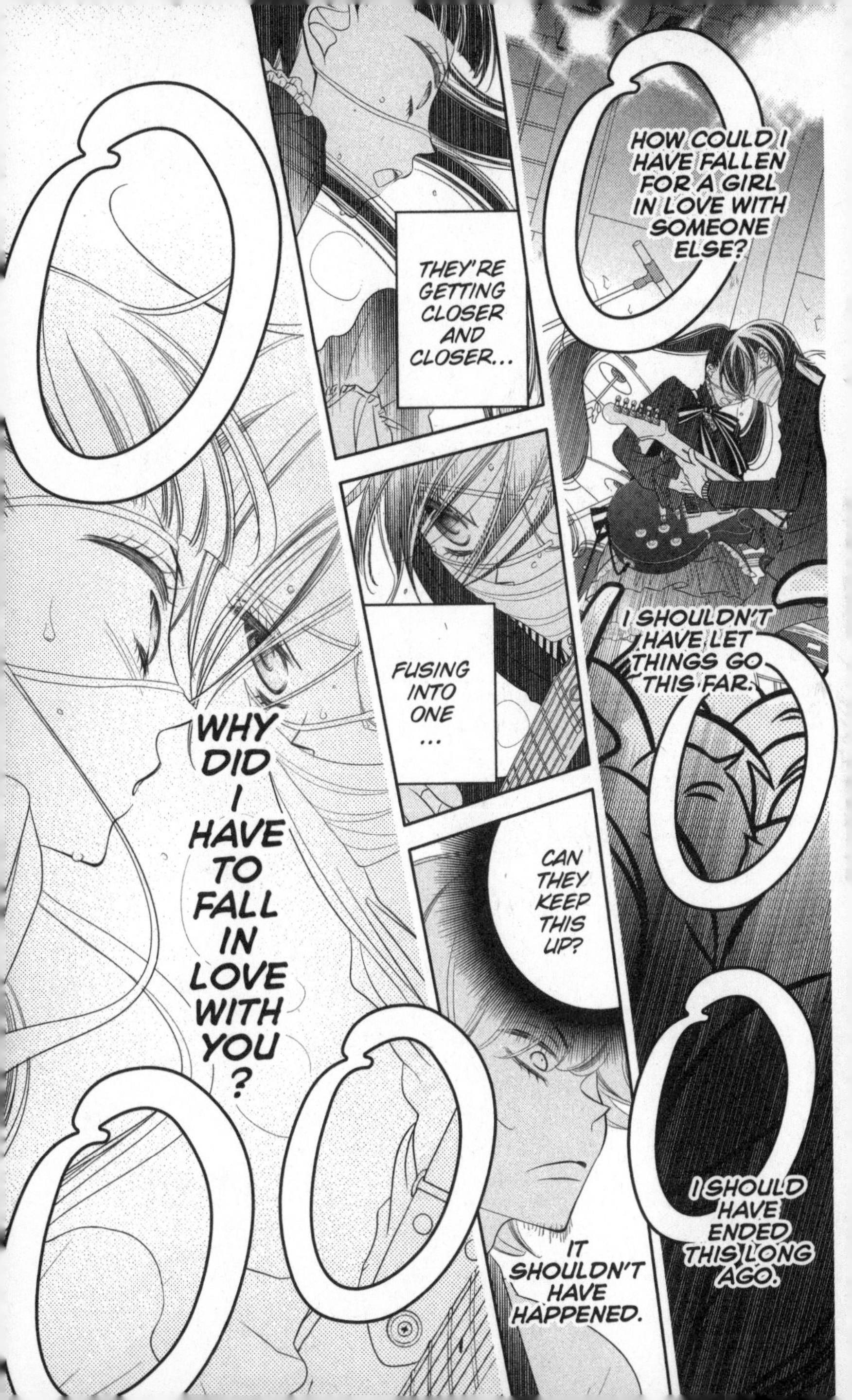
HOW COULD I HAVE FALLEN FOR A GIRL IN LOVE WITH SOMEONE ELSE?
I SHOULDN'T HAVE LET THINGS GO THIS FAR.
I SHOULD HAVE ENDED THIS LONG AGO.
THEY'RE GETTING CLOSER AND CLOSER...
FUSING INTO ONE...
CAN THEY KEEP THIS UP?
IT SHOULDN'T HAVE HAPPENED.
WHY DID I HAVE TO FALL IN LOVE WITH YOU?

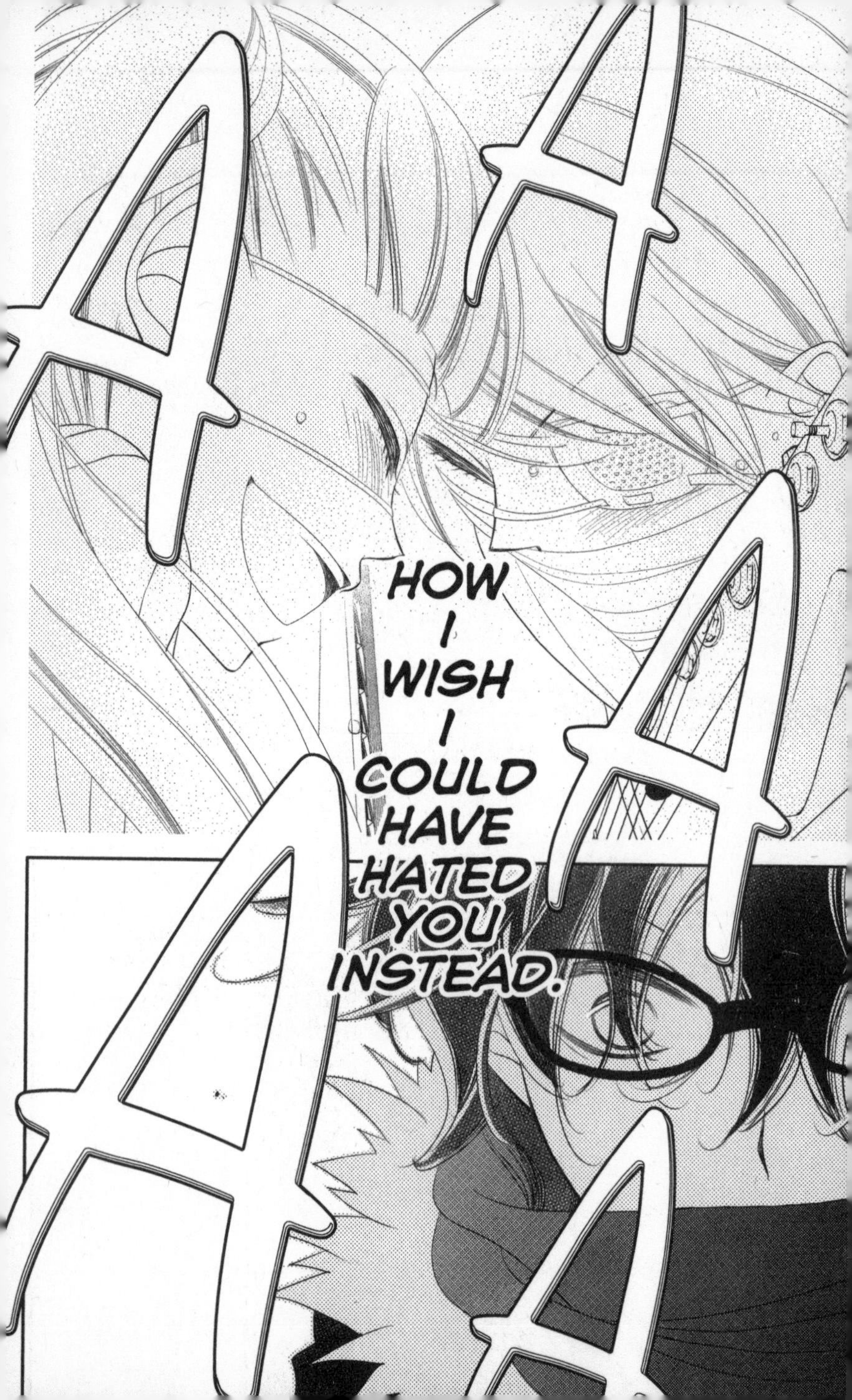
AAAAAA
HOW I WISH I COULD HAVE HATED YOU INSTEAD.

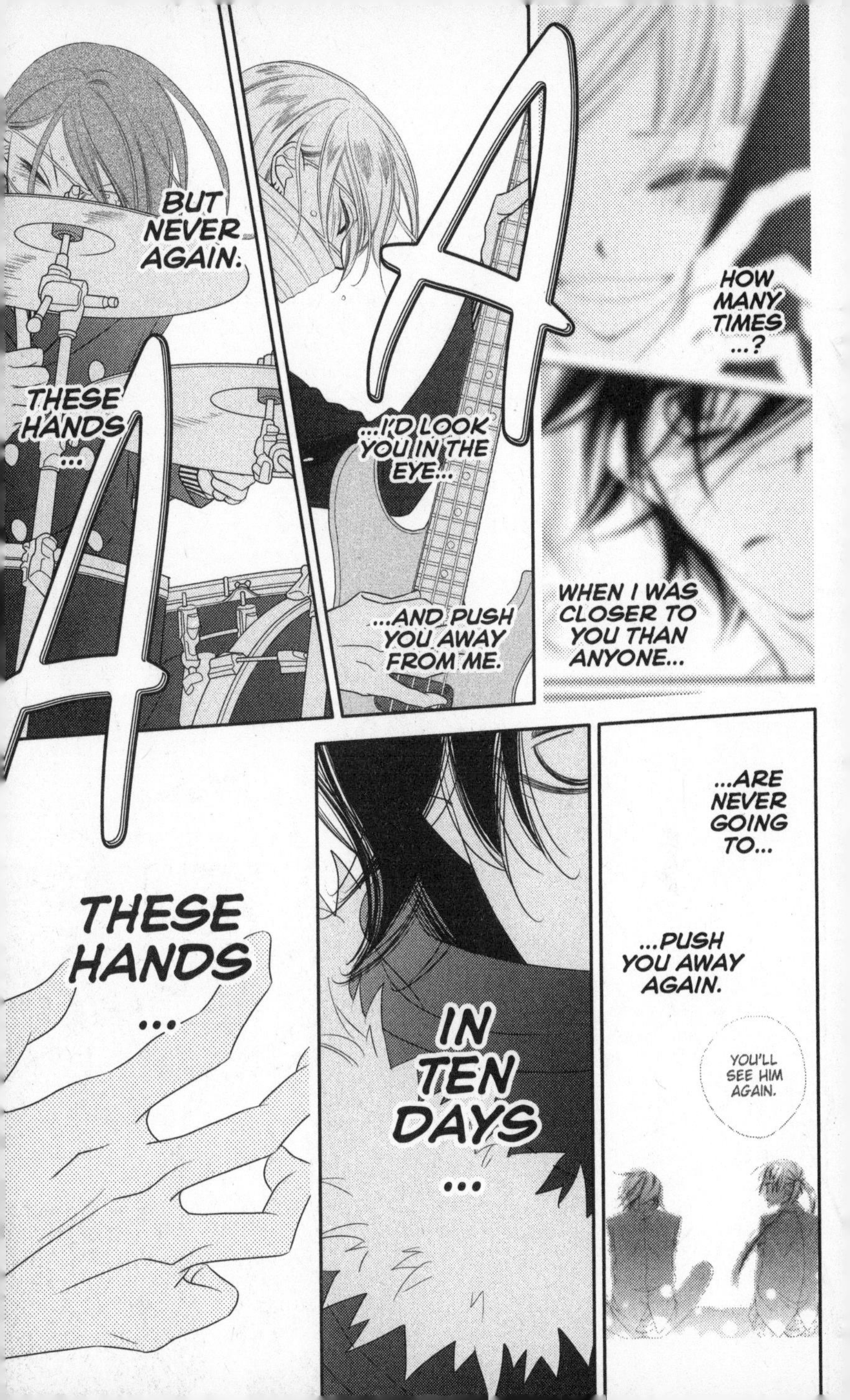
HOW MANY TIMES ...?
WHEN I WAS CLOSER TO YOU THAN ANYONE...
...I'D LOOK YOU IN THE EYE...
...AND PUSH YOU AWAY FROM ME.
BUT NEVER AGAIN.
THESE HANDS ...
...ARE NEVER GOING TO...
...PUSH YOU AWAY AGAIN.
YOU'LL SEE HIM AGAIN.
IN TEN DAYS ...
THESE HANDS ...

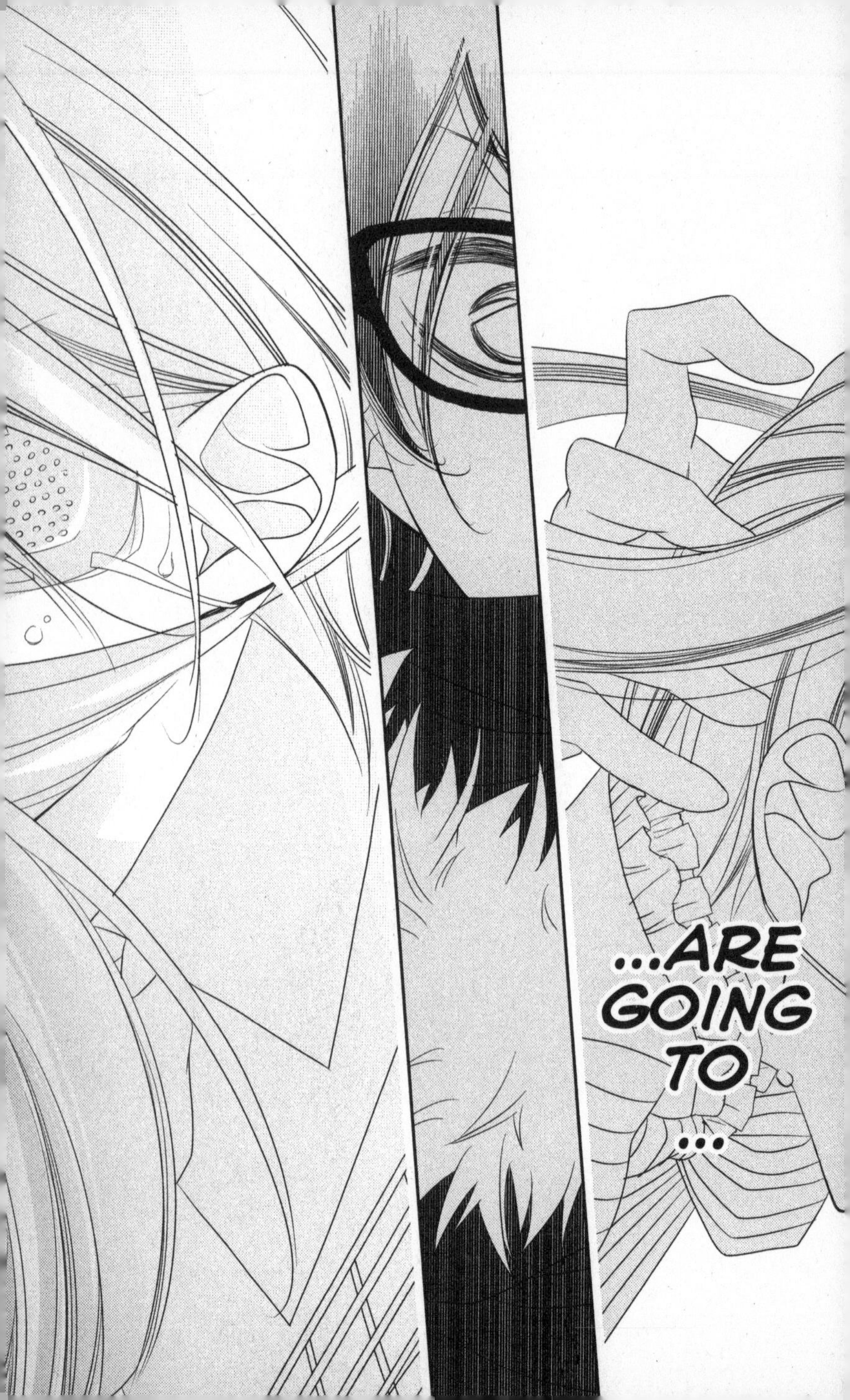
...ARE GOING TO ...

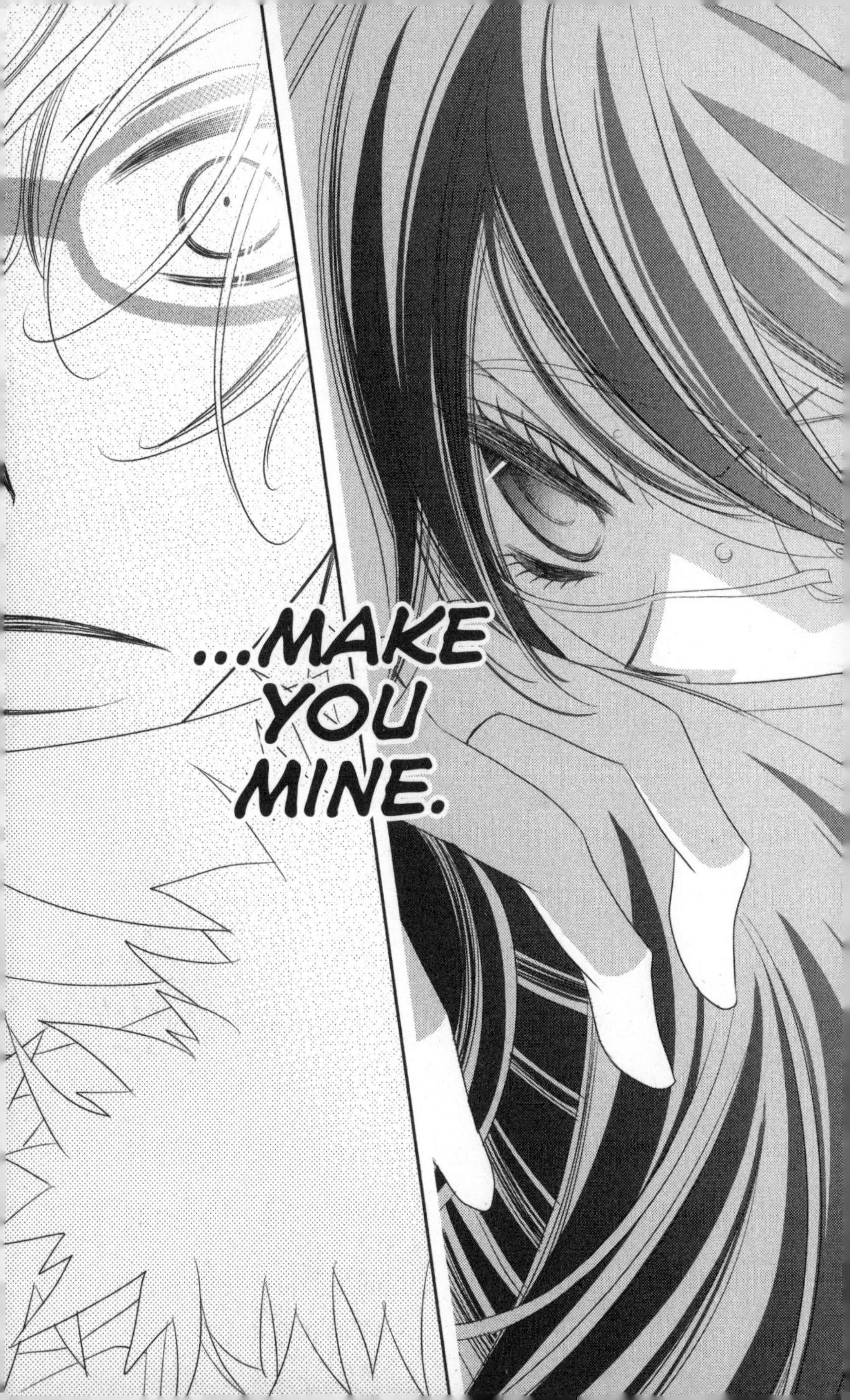
...MAKE YOU MINE.

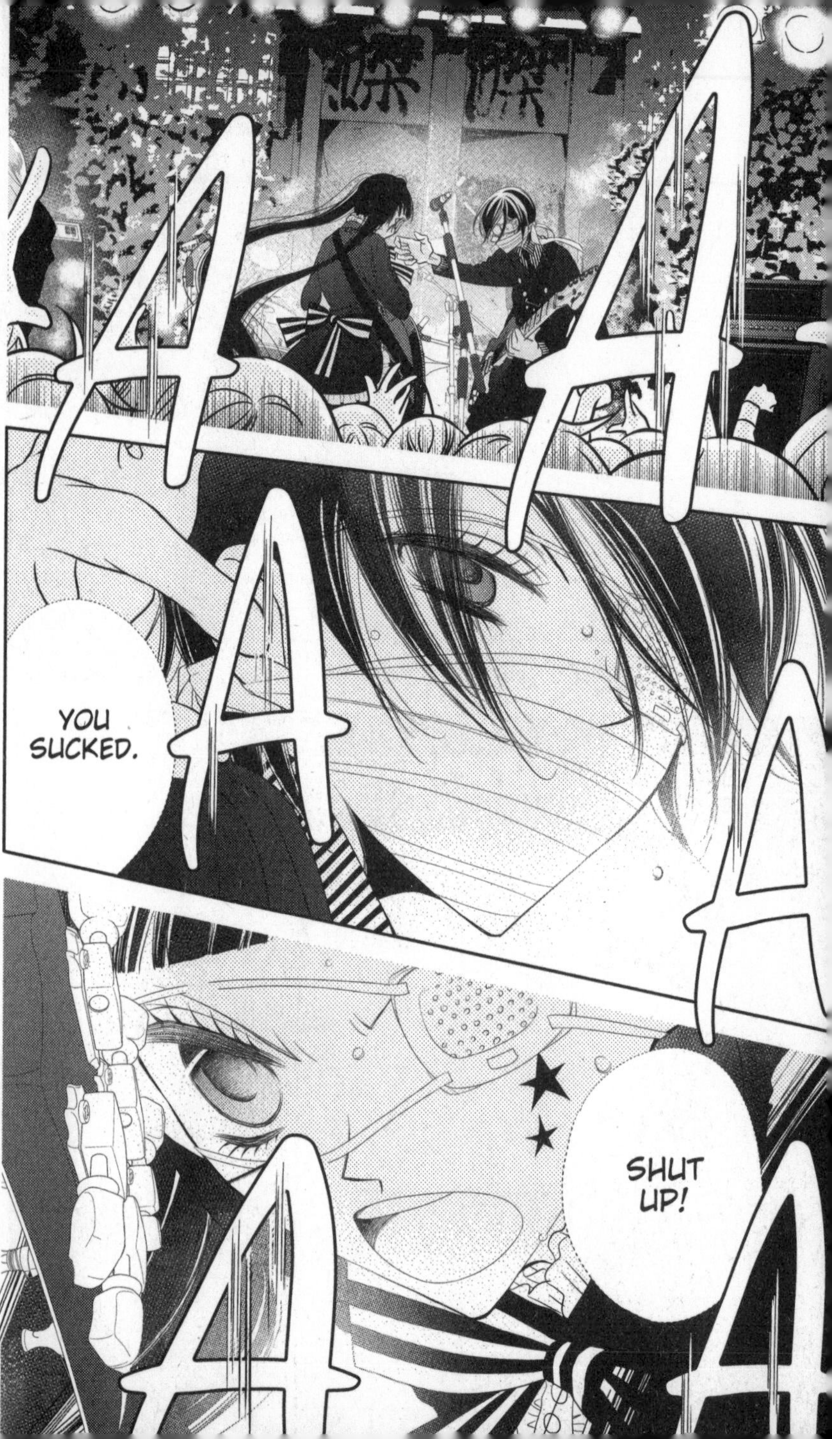
YOU SUCKED.
SHUT UP!

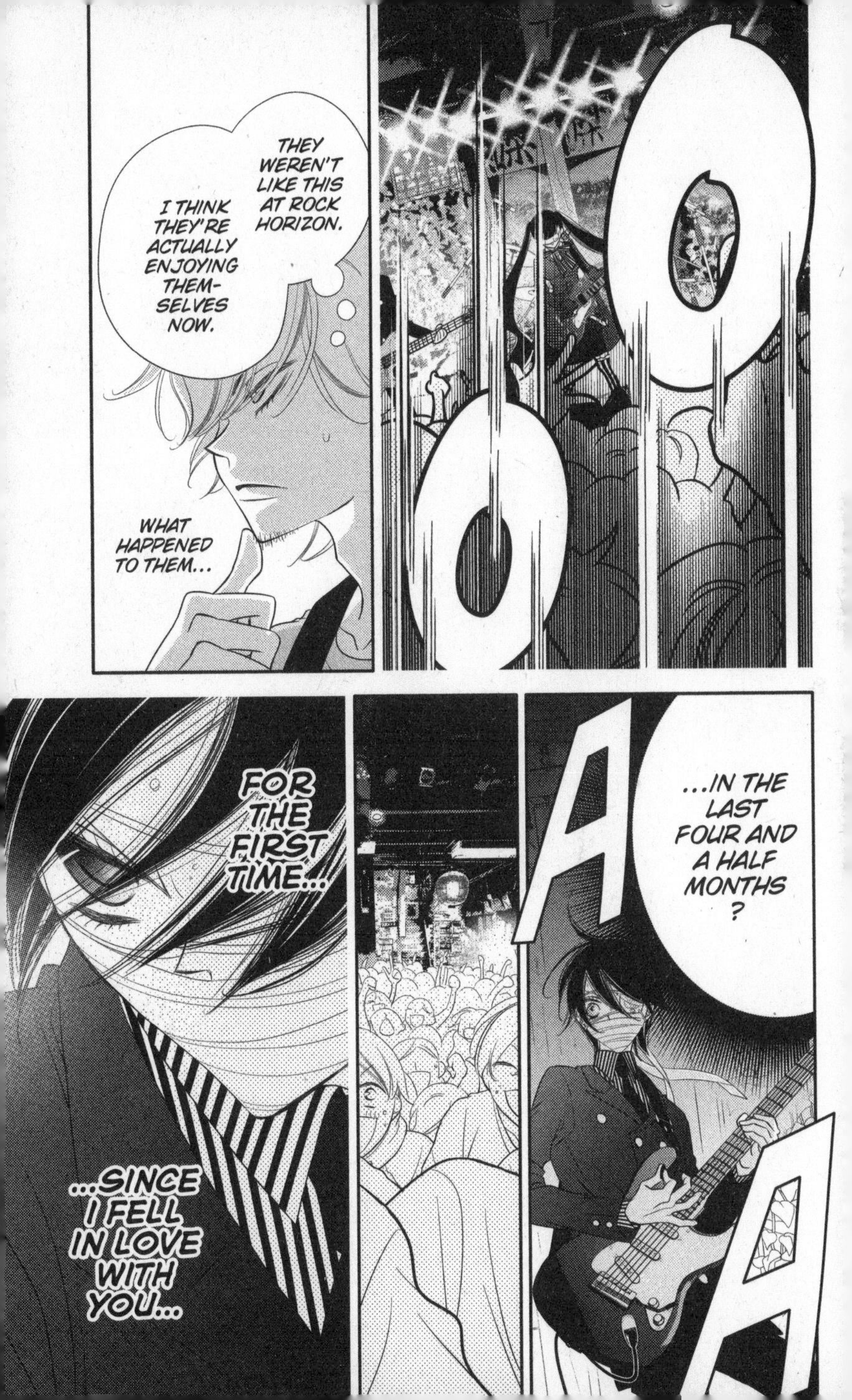
OO
THEY WEREN'T LIKE THIS AT ROCK HORIZON.
I THINK THEY'RE ACTUALLY ENJOYING THEM-SELVES NOW.
WHAT HAPPENED TO THEM...
AO
...IN THE LAST FOUR AND A HALF MONTHS?
A
FOR THE FIRST TIME...
...SINCE I FELL IN LOVE WITH YOU...

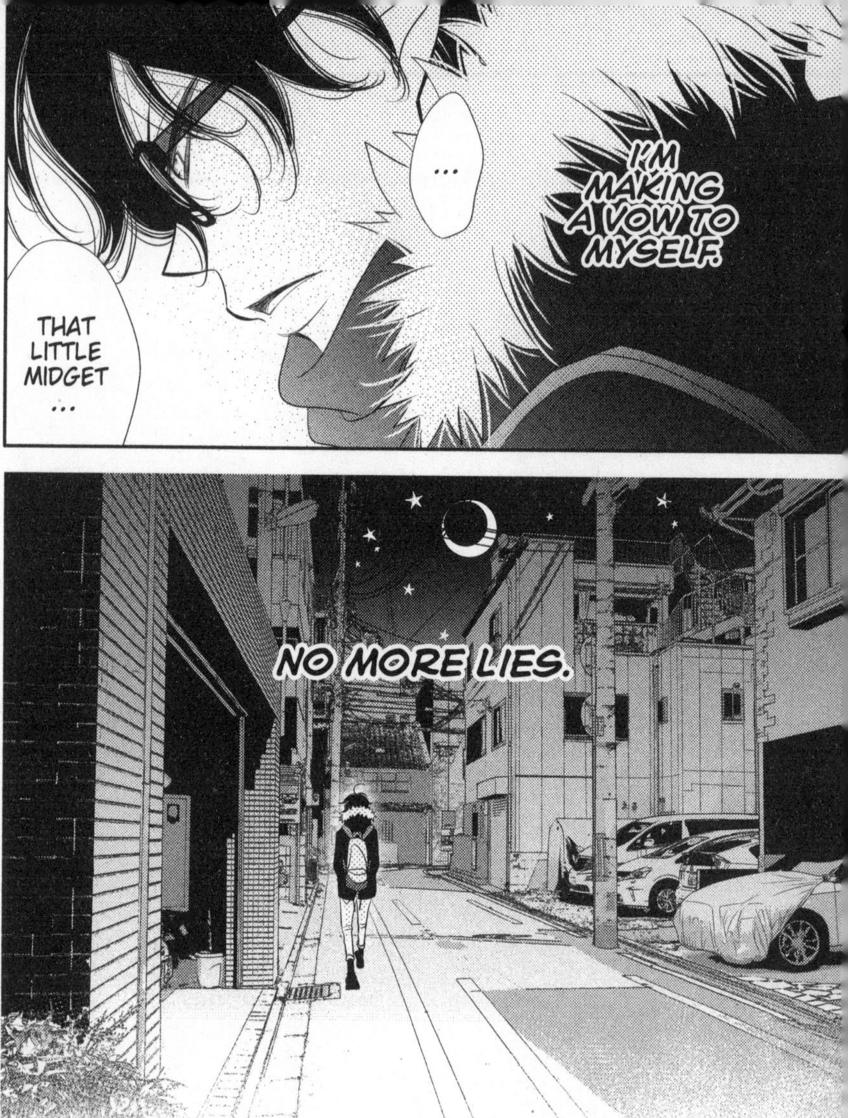
I'M MAKING A VOW TO MYSELF.
...
THAT LITTLE MIDGET ...
NO MORE LIES.

I'M GOING TO TELL YOU THE TRUTH.

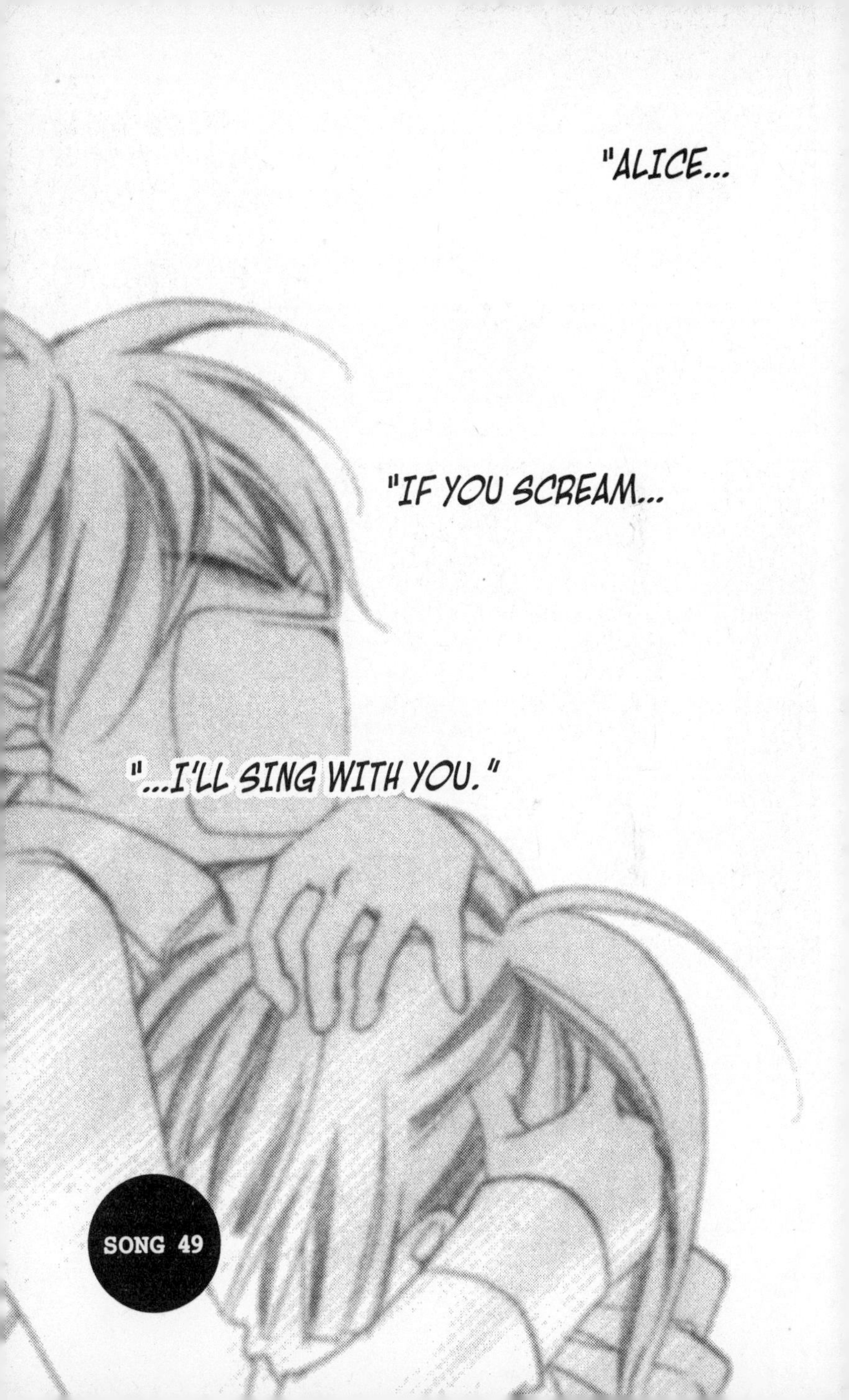
"ALICE...
"IF YOU SCREAM...
"...I'LL SING WITH YOU."
SONG 49

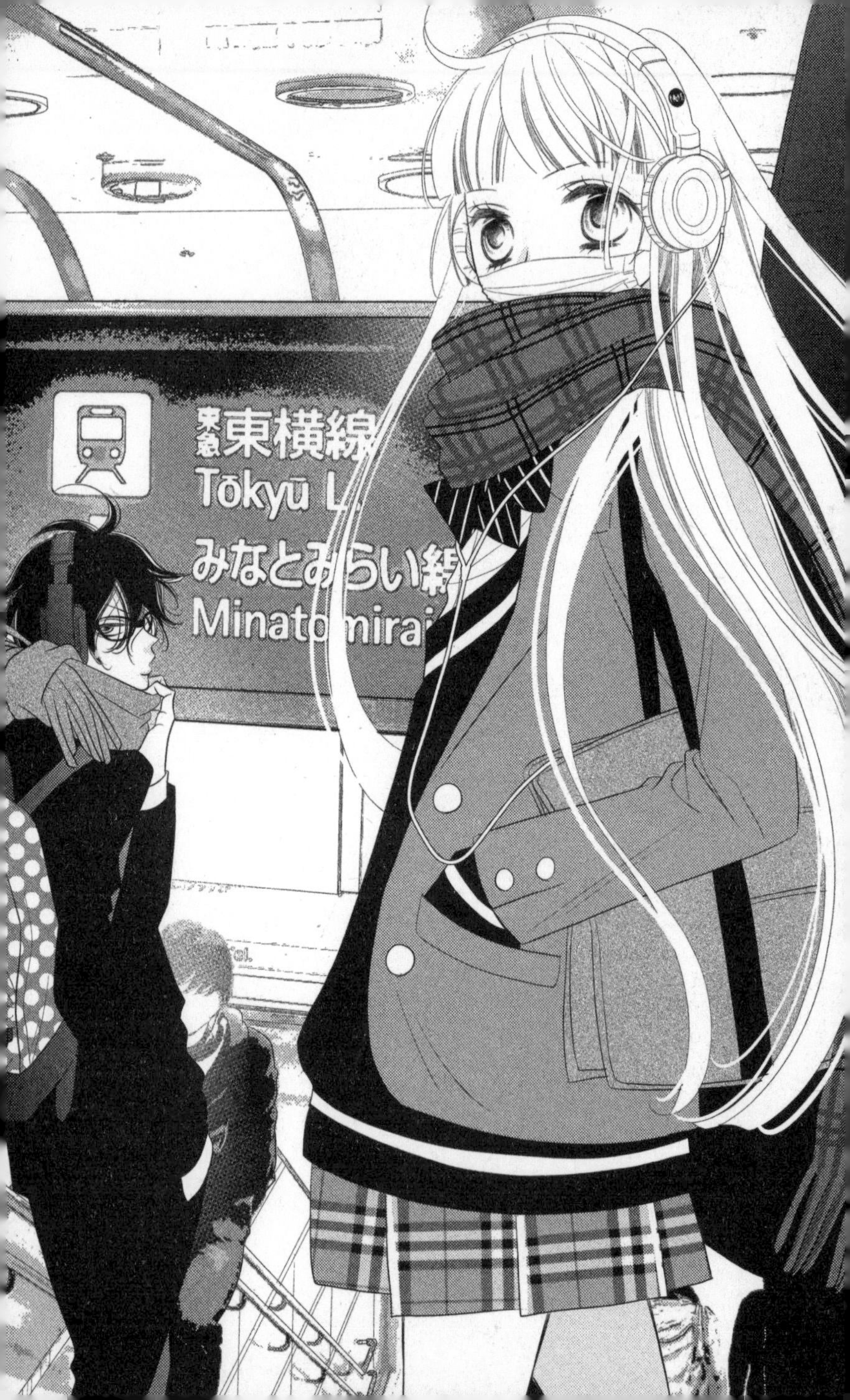
東急東横線
Tōkyū L
みなとみらい
Minatomirai

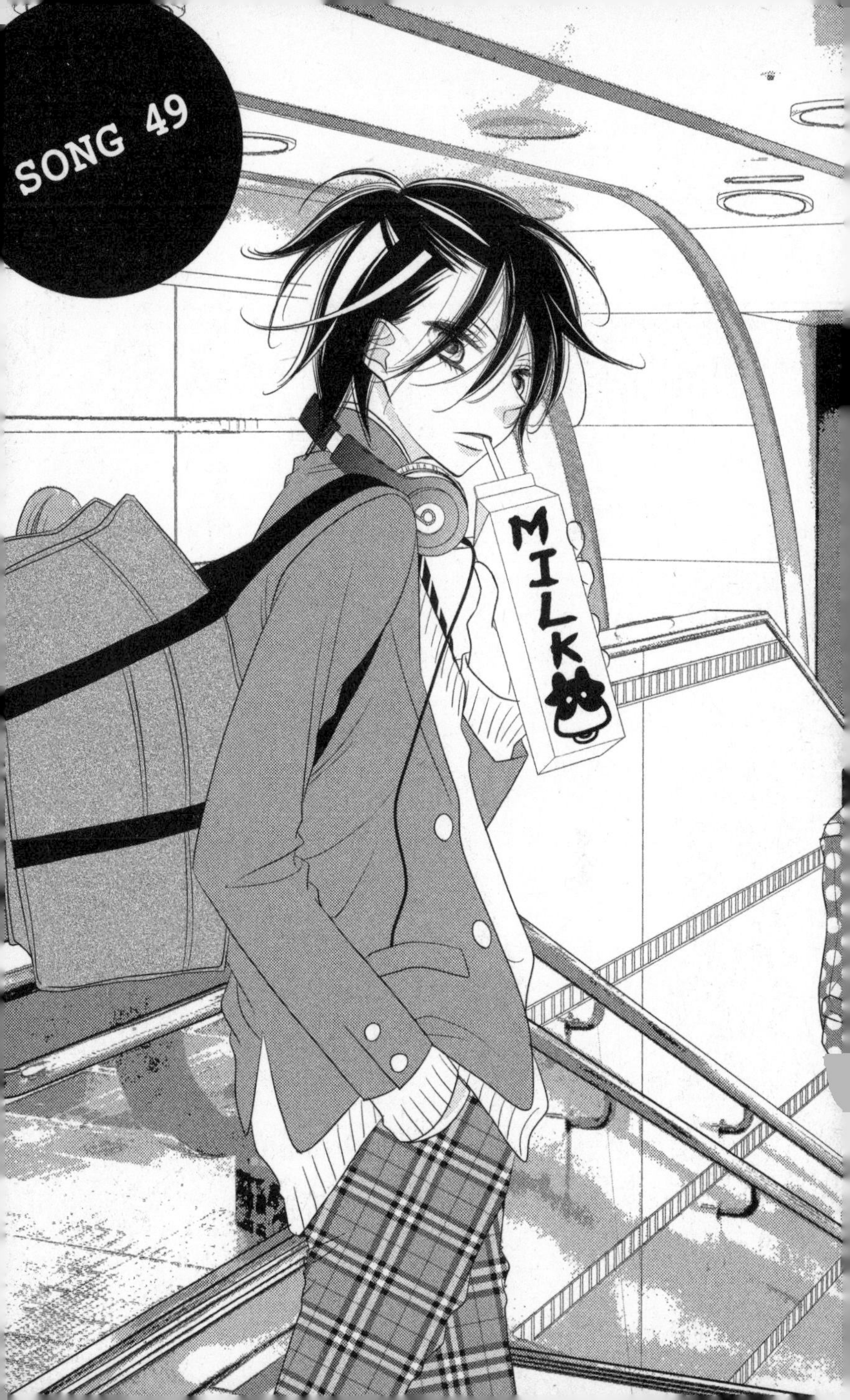
SONG 49
MILK

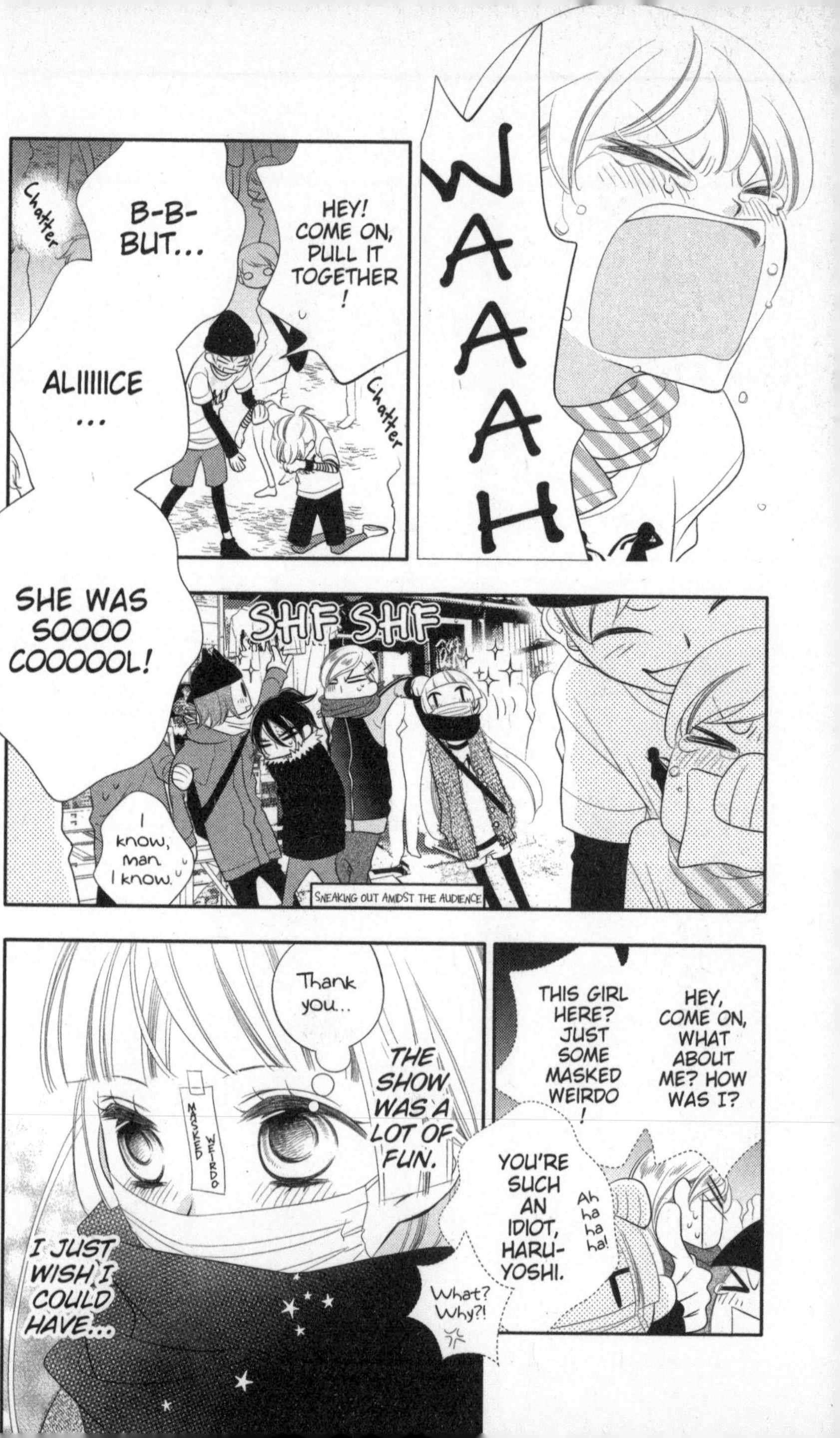
WAAAH
HEY! COME ON, PULL IT TOGETHER!
B-B-BUT...
Chatter
ALIIIIICE...
Chatter
SHE WAS SOOOO COOOOOL!
SHF SHF
I know, man. I know.
SNEAKING OUT AMIDST THE AUDIENCE
HEY, COME ON, WHAT ABOUT ME? HOW WAS I?
THIS GIRL HERE? JUST SOME MASKED WEIRDO!
YOU'RE SUCH AN IDIOT, HARUYOSHI.
Ah ha ha ha!
What? Why?!
Thank you...
THE SHOW WAS A LOT OF FUN.
MASKED WEIRDO
I JUST WISH I COULD HAVE...

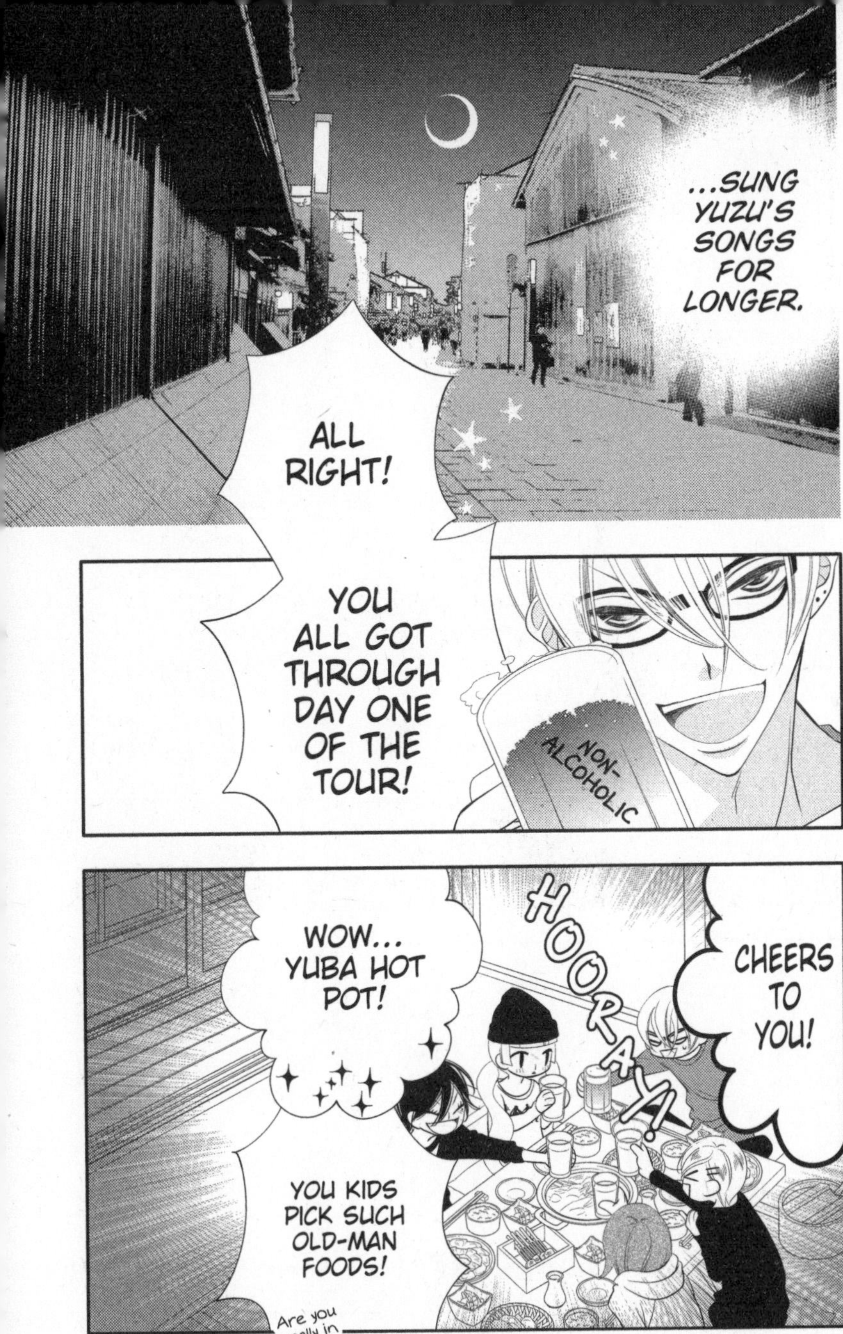
...SUNG YUZU'S SONGS FOR LONGER.
ALL RIGHT!
YOU ALL GOT THROUGH DAY ONE OF THE TOUR!
NON-ALCOHOLIC
CHEERS TO YOU!
HOORAY!
WOW... YUBA HOT POT!
YOU KIDS PICK SUCH OLD-MAN FOODS!
Are you really in high school?!

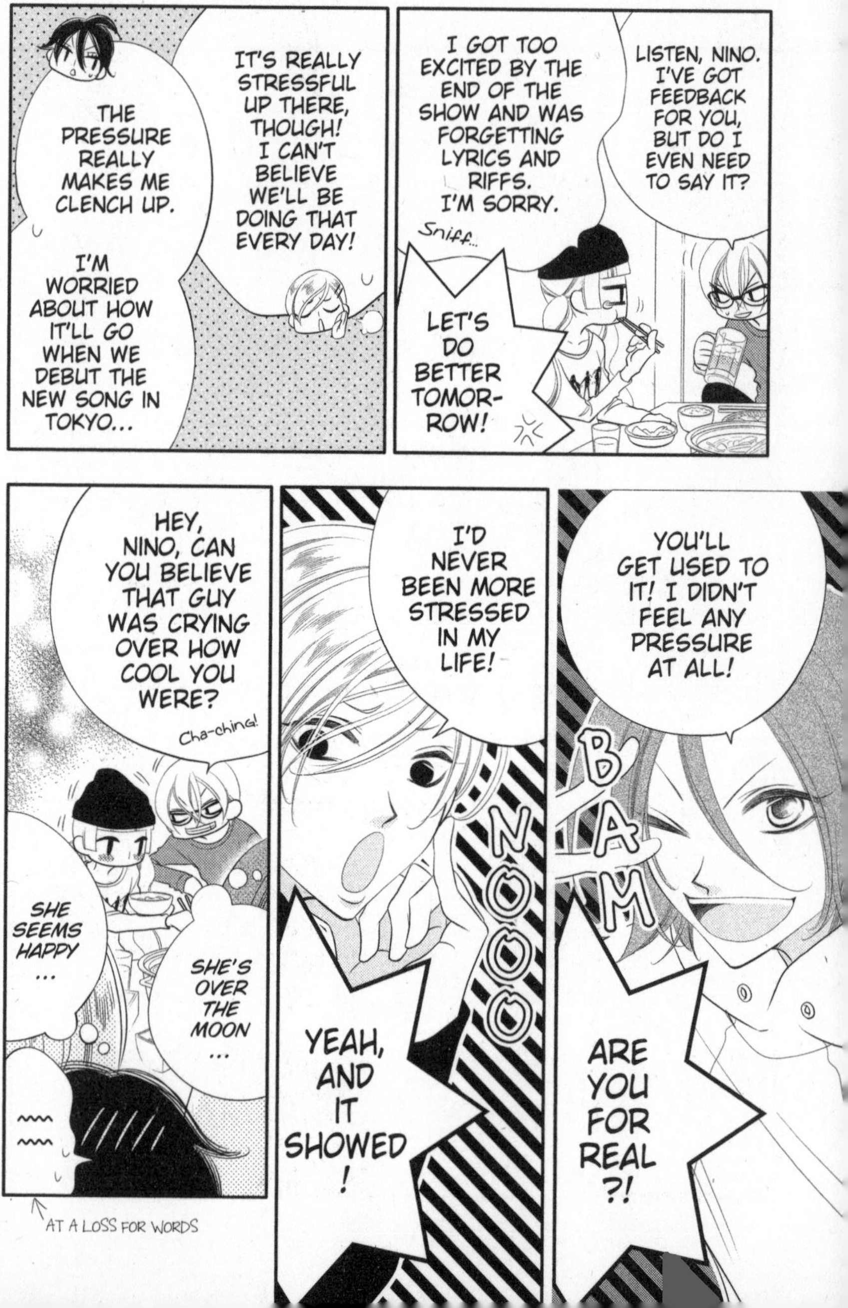
LISTEN, NINO. I'VE GOT FEEDBACK FOR YOU, BUT DO I EVEN NEED TO SAY IT?
I GOT TOO EXCITED BY THE END OF THE SHOW AND WAS FORGETTING LYRICS AND RIFFS. I'M SORRY.
Sniff...
LET'S DO BETTER TOMORROW!
IT'S REALLY STRESSFUL UP THERE, THOUGH! I CAN'T BELIEVE WE'LL BE DOING THAT EVERY DAY!
THE PRESSURE REALLY MAKES ME CLENCH UP.
I'M WORRIED ABOUT HOW IT'LL GO WHEN WE DEBUT THE NEW SONG IN TOKYO...
YOU'LL GET USED TO IT! I DIDN'T FEEL ANY PRESSURE AT ALL!
BAM
ARE YOU FOR REAL?!
I'D NEVER BEEN MORE STRESSED IN MY LIFE!
NOOOO
YEAH, AND IT SHOWED!
HEY, NINO, CAN YOU BELIEVE THAT GUY WAS CRYING OVER HOW COOL YOU WERE?
Cha-ching!
SHE'S OVER THE MOON...
SHE SEEMS HAPPY...
AT A LOSS FOR WORDS

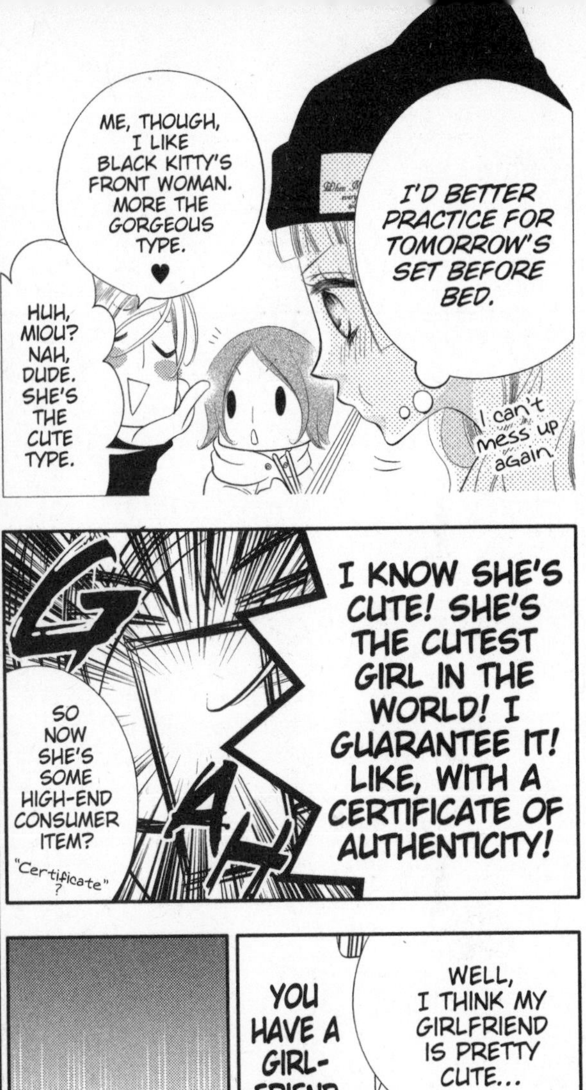
I'D BETTER PRACTICE FOR TOMORROW'S SET BEFORE BED.
I can't mess up again.
ME, THOUGH, I LIKE BLACK KITTY'S FRONT WOMAN. MORE THE GORGEOUS TYPE. ♥
HUH, MIOU? NAH, DUDE. SHE'S THE CUTE TYPE.
I KNOW SHE'S CUTE! SHE'S THE CUTEST GIRL IN THE WORLD! I GUARANTEE IT! LIKE, WITH A CERTIFICATE OF AUTHENTICITY!
GAH
SO NOW SHE'S SOME HIGH-END CONSUMER ITEM?
"Certificate"?
WELL, I THINK MY GIRLFRIEND IS PRETTY CUTE...
YOU HAVE A GIRL-FRIEND?!

3

I've been involved with the preparations for this for a really long time, and it feels like I've had to wait forever before I could make it public! I'm so happy that I can finally share the news. I'm still in the thick of preparing for it, and I promise to keep working hard!

Making an anime has long been a dream of mine. Maybe that's why this still doesn't feel real to me yet? I have this weird feeling like I'm just drifting around the whole time. Needless to say, I'm going to give this anime my all, but I won't let that stop me from working even harder than before on the manga. I hope you'll continue to support Anonymous Noise!

MORE INFO TO COME!

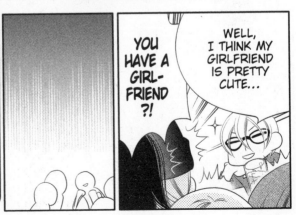

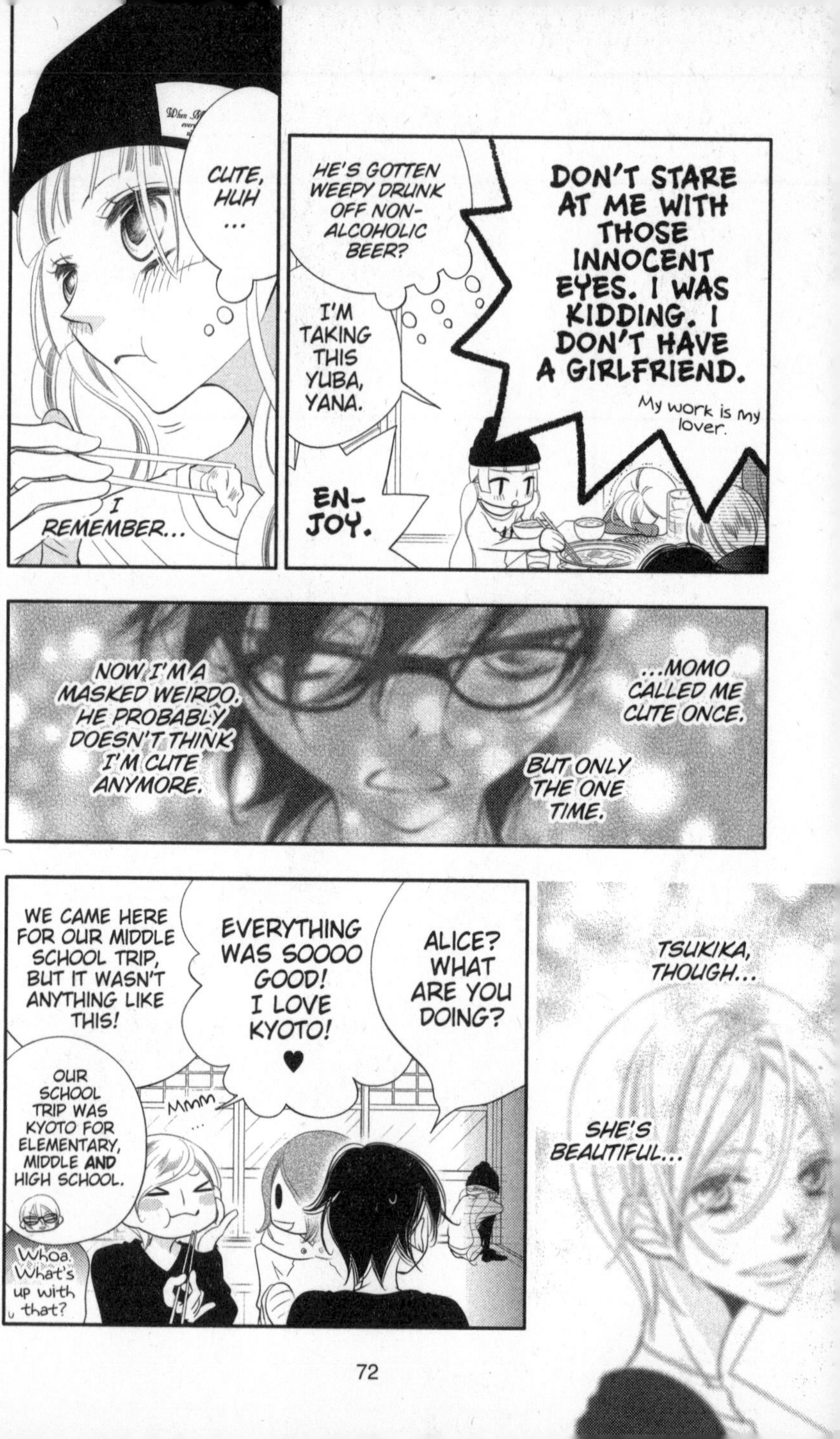
DON'T STARE AT ME WITH THOSE INNOCENT EYES. I WAS KIDDING. I DON'T HAVE A GIRLFRIEND.
My work is my lover.
HE'S GOTTEN WEEPY DRUNK OFF NON-ALCOHOLIC BEER?
I'M TAKING THIS YUBA, YANA.
EN-JOY.
CUTE, HUH...
I REMEMBER...
...MOMO CALLED ME CUTE ONCE.
BUT ONLY THE ONE TIME.
NOW I'M A MASKED WEIRDO. HE PROBABLY DOESN'T THINK I'M CUTE ANYMORE.
TSUKIKA, THOUGH...
SHE'S BEAUTIFUL...
ALICE? WHAT ARE YOU DOING?
EVERYTHING WAS SOOOO GOOD! I LOVE KYOTO! ♥
WE CAME HERE FOR OUR MIDDLE SCHOOL TRIP, BUT IT WASN'T ANYTHING LIKE THIS!
Mmm...
OUR SCHOOL TRIP WAS KYOTO FOR ELEMENTARY, MIDDLE AND HIGH SCHOOL.
Whoa. What's up with that?

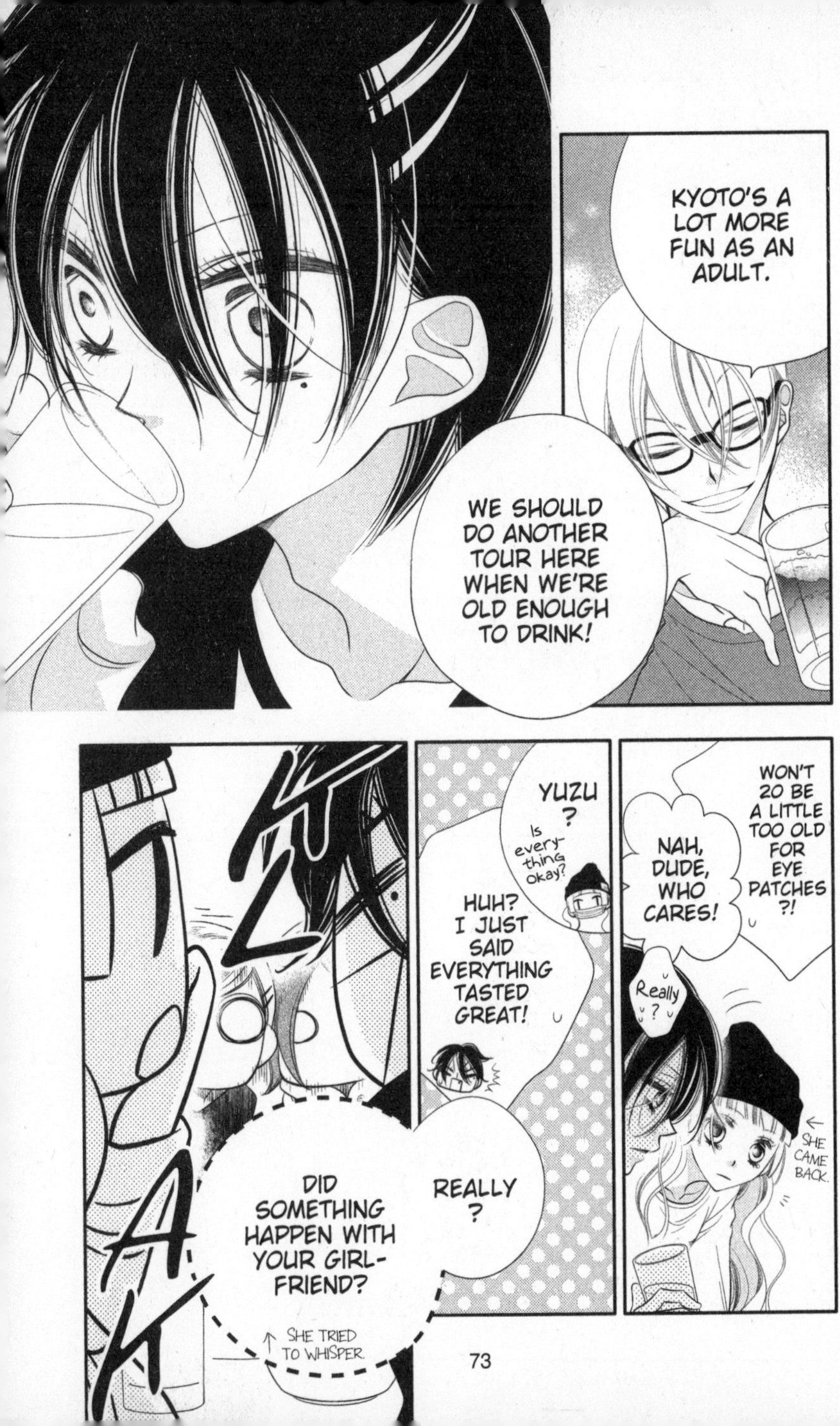
KYOTO'S A LOT MORE FUN AS AN ADULT.
WE SHOULD DO ANOTHER TOUR HERE WHEN WE'RE OLD ENOUGH TO DRINK!
WON'T 20 BE A LITTLE TOO OLD FOR EYE PATCHES ?!
NAH, DUDE, WHO CARES!
Really ?
SHE CAME BACK.
YUZU ?
Is everything okay?
HUH? I JUST SAID EVERYTHING TASTED GREAT!
REALLY ?
DID SOMETHING HAPPEN WITH YOUR GIRLFRIEND?
SHE TRIED TO WHISPER.

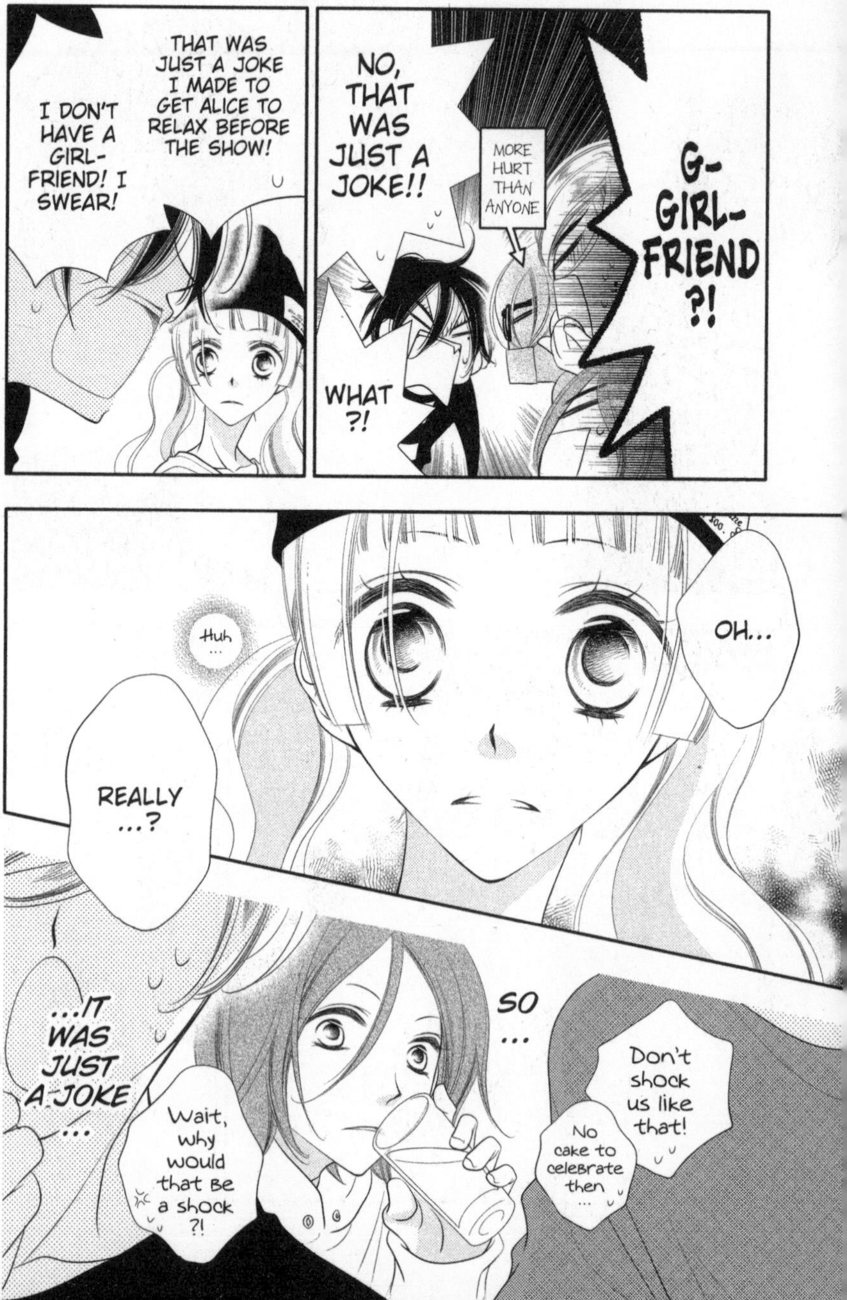
G-GIRL-FRIEND?!
MORE HURT THAN ANYONE
NO, THAT WAS JUST A JOKE!!
WHAT?!
THAT WAS JUST A JOKE I MADE TO GET ALICE TO RELAX BEFORE THE SHOW!
I DON'T HAVE A GIRL-FRIEND! I SWEAR!
OH...
Huh...
REALLY...?
Don't shock us like that!
SO...
No cake to celebrate then...
Wait, why would that be a shock?!
...IT WAS JUST A JOKE...

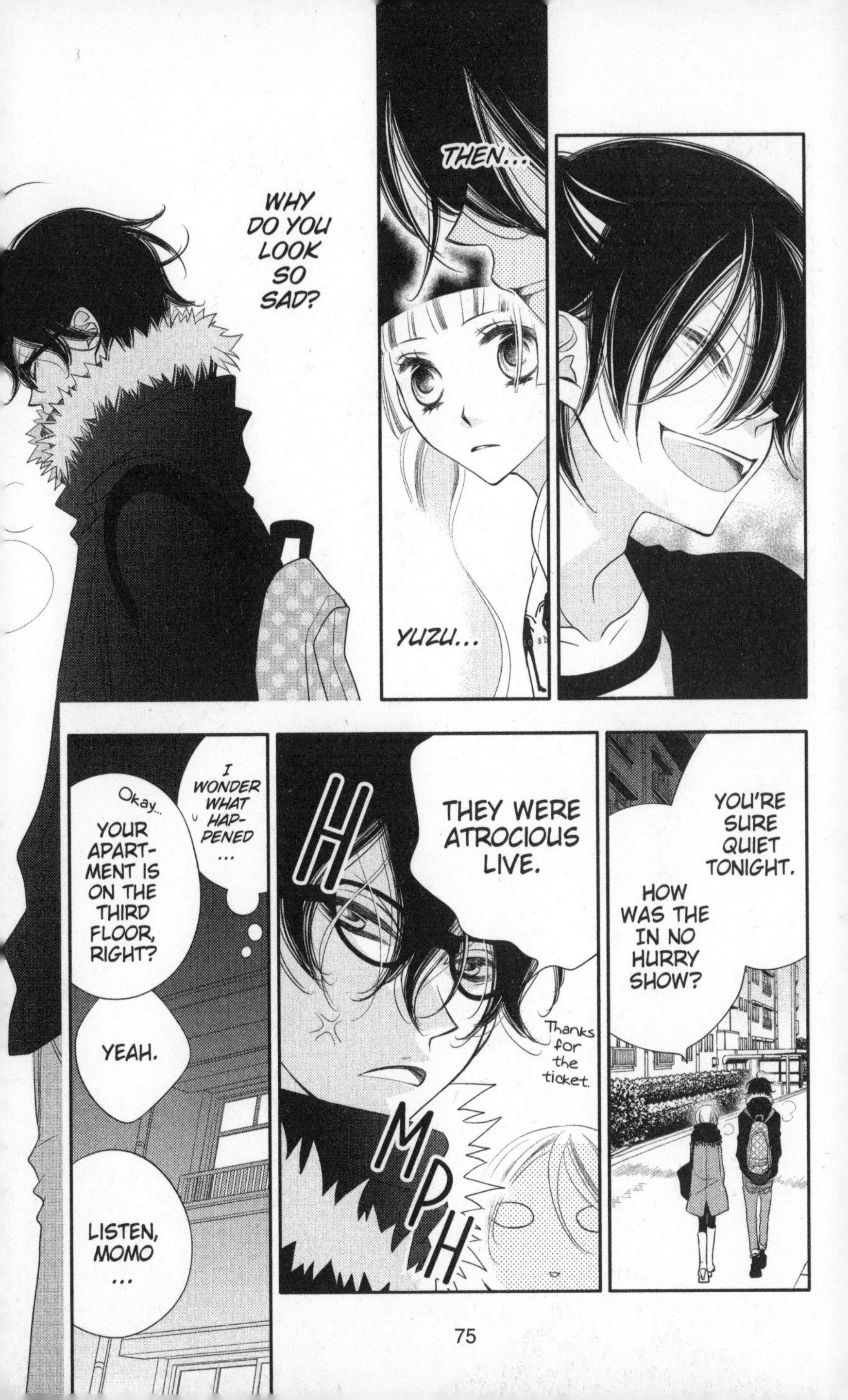
THEN...
YUZU...
WHY DO YOU LOOK SO SAD?
YOU'RE SURE QUIET TONIGHT.
HOW WAS THE IN NO HURRY SHOW?
THEY WERE ATROCIOUS LIVE.
HMPH
Thanks for the ticket.
I WONDER WHAT HAP-PENED...
Okay...
YOUR APART-MENT IS ON THE THIRD FLOOR, RIGHT?
YEAH.
LISTEN, MOMO...

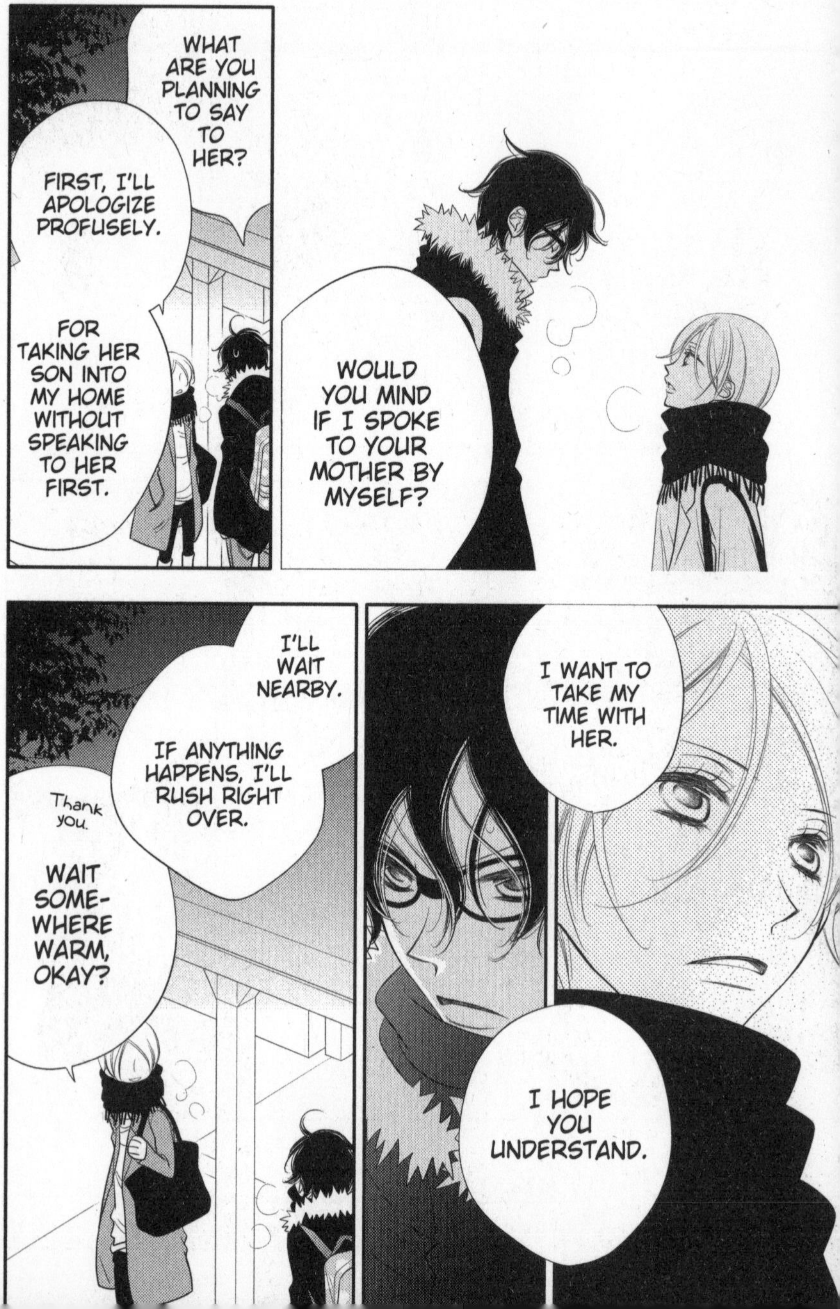
WOULD YOU MIND IF I SPOKE TO YOUR MOTHER BY MYSELF?
WHAT ARE YOU PLANNING TO SAY TO HER?
FIRST, I'LL APOLOGIZE PROFUSELY.
FOR TAKING HER SON INTO MY HOME WITHOUT SPEAKING TO HER FIRST.
I WANT TO TAKE MY TIME WITH HER.
I HOPE YOU UNDERSTAND.
I'LL WAIT NEARBY.
IF ANYTHING HAPPENS, I'LL RUSH RIGHT OVER.
Thank you.
WAIT SOME-WHERE WARM, OKAY?

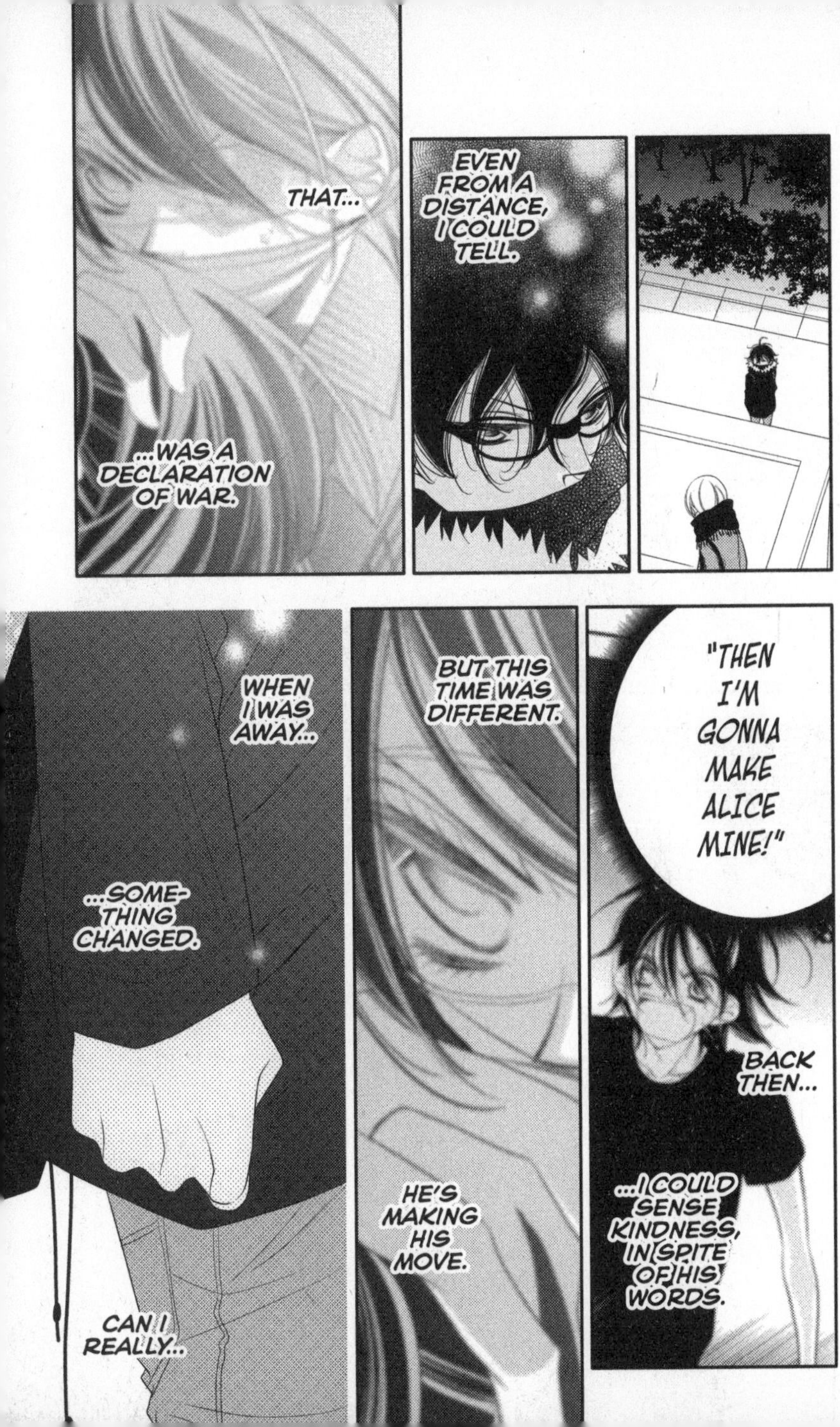
EVEN FROM A DISTANCE, I COULD TELL.
THAT...
...WAS A DECLARATION OF WAR.
"THEN I'M GONNA MAKE ALICE MINE!"
BACK THEN...
...I COULD SENSE KINDNESS, IN SPITE OF HIS WORDS.
BUT THIS TIME WAS DIFFERENT.
HE'S MAKING HIS MOVE.
WHEN I WAS AWAY...
...SOME-THING CHANGED.
CAN I REALLY...

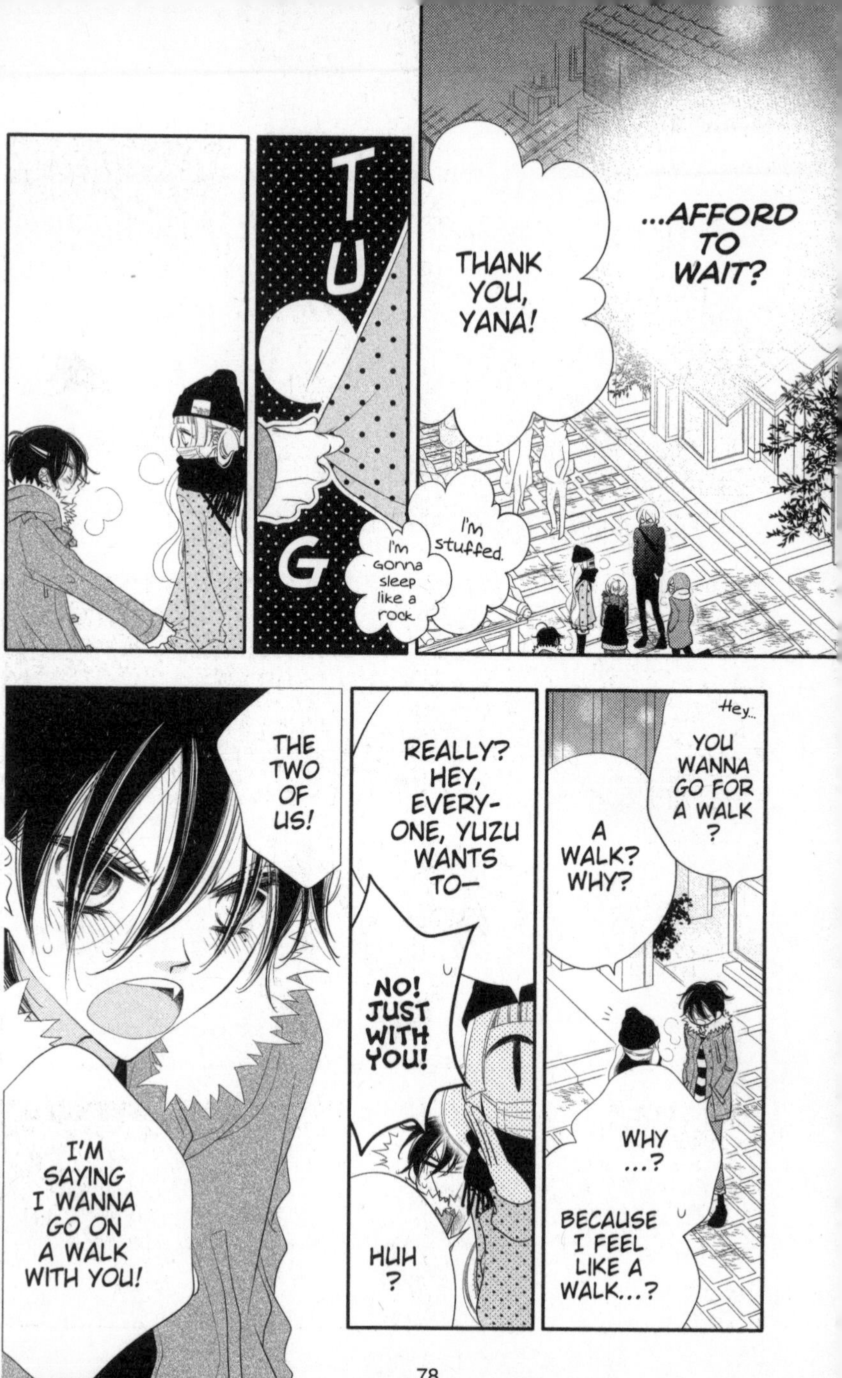
...AFFORD TO WAIT?
THANK YOU, YANA!
I'm stuffed.
I'm gonna sleep like a rock.
TUG
Hey...
YOU WANNA GO FOR A WALK?
A WALK? WHY?
WHY...?
BECAUSE I FEEL LIKE A WALK...?
REALLY? HEY, EVERYONE, YUZU WANTS TO—
NO! JUST WITH YOU!
HUH?
THE TWO OF US!
I'M SAYING I WANNA GO ON A WALK WITH YOU!

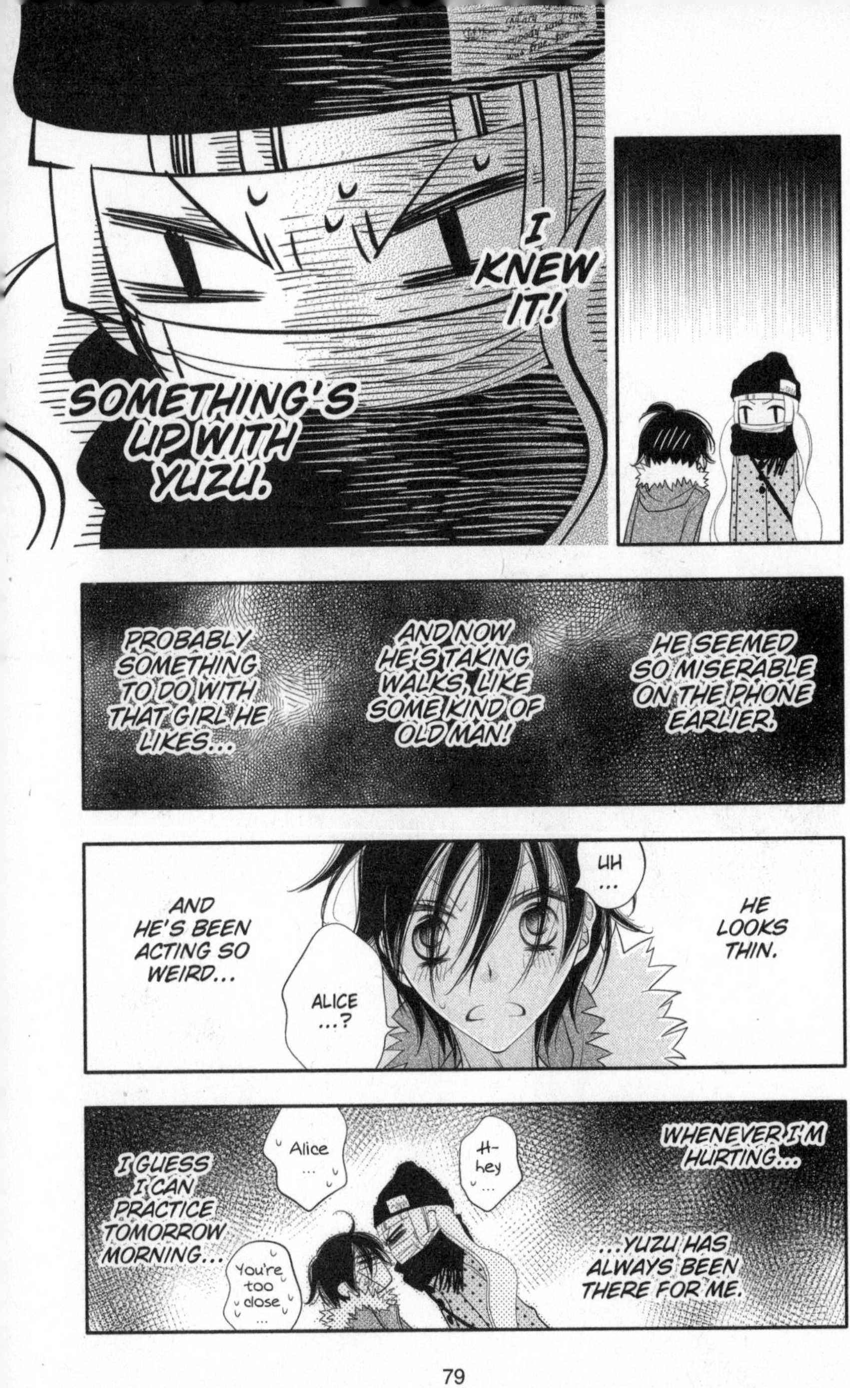
I KNEW IT!
SOMETHING'S UP WITH YUZU.
HE SEEMED SO MISERABLE ON THE PHONE EARLIER.
AND NOW HE'S TAKING WALKS, LIKE SOME KIND OF OLD MAN!
PROBABLY SOMETHING TO DO WITH THAT GIRL HE LIKES...
HE LOOKS THIN.
UH...
ALICE...?
AND HE'S BEEN ACTING SO WEIRD...
WHENEVER I'M HURTING...
H-hey...
Alice...
...YUZU HAS ALWAYS BEEN THERE FOR ME.
You're too close...
I GUESS I CAN PRACTICE TOMORROW MORNING...

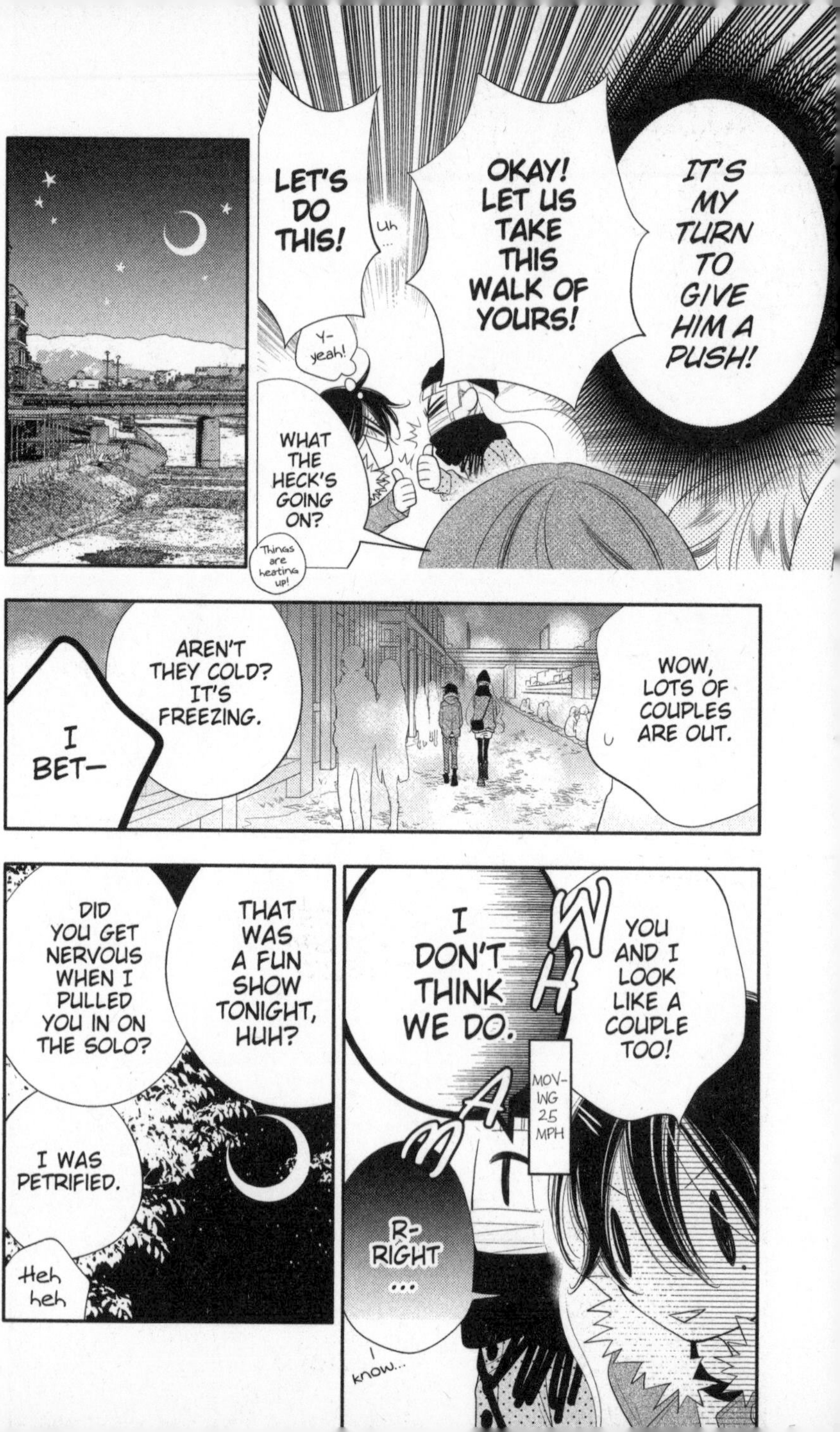
IT'S MY TURN TO GIVE HIM A PUSH!
OKAY! LET US TAKE THIS WALK OF YOURS!
Uh ...
LET'S DO THIS!
Y-yeah!
WHAT THE HECK'S GOING ON?
Things are heating up!
WOW, LOTS OF COUPLES ARE OUT.
AREN'T THEY COLD? IT'S FREEZING.
I BET—
YOU AND I LOOK LIKE A COUPLE TOO!
WHAM
I DON'T THINK WE DO.
MOVING 25 MPH
R-RIGHT...
I know...
THAT WAS A FUN SHOW TONIGHT, HUH?
DID YOU GET NERVOUS WHEN I PULLED YOU IN ON THE SOLO?
I WAS PETRIFIED.
Heh heh

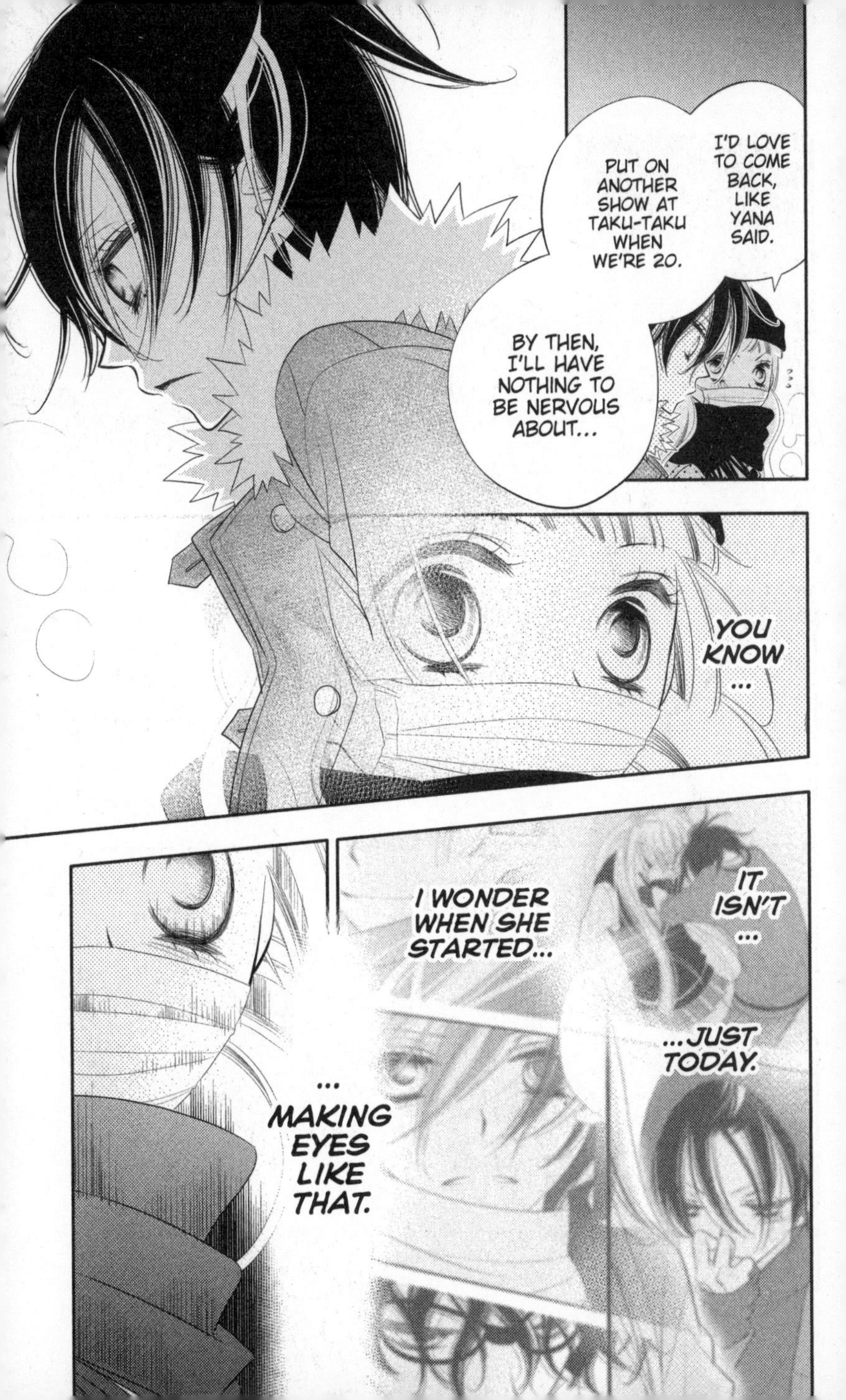
I'D LOVE TO COME BACK, LIKE YANA SAID.
PUT ON ANOTHER SHOW AT TAKU-TAKU WHEN WE'RE 20.
BY THEN, I'LL HAVE NOTHING TO BE NERVOUS ABOUT...
YOU KNOW...
IT ISN'T...
...JUST TODAY.
I WONDER WHEN SHE STARTED...
...MAKING EYES LIKE THAT.

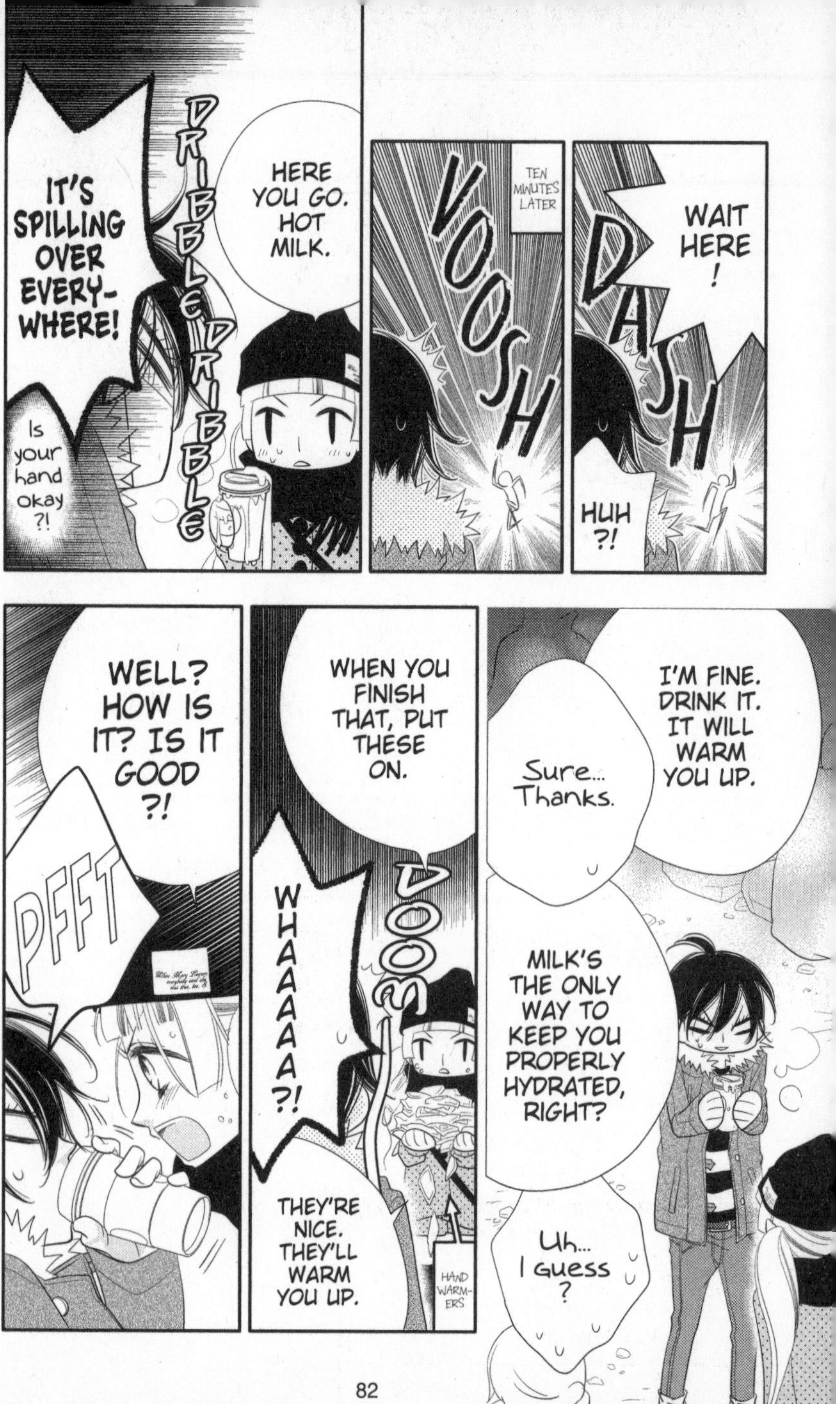
WAIT HERE!
DASH
HUH?!
TEN MINUTES LATER
VOOSH
HERE YOU GO. HOT MILK.
DRIBBLE DRIBBLE
IT'S SPILLING OVER EVERY-WHERE!
Is your hand okay?!
I'M FINE. DRINK IT. IT WILL WARM YOU UP.
Sure... Thanks.
MILK'S THE ONLY WAY TO KEEP YOU PROPERLY HYDRATED, RIGHT?
Uh... I guess?
WHEN YOU FINISH THAT, PUT THESE ON.
DOOM
WHAAAAAA?!
THEY'RE NICE. THEY'LL WARM YOU UP.
HAND WARMERS
WELL? HOW IS IT? IS IT GOOD?!
PFFT

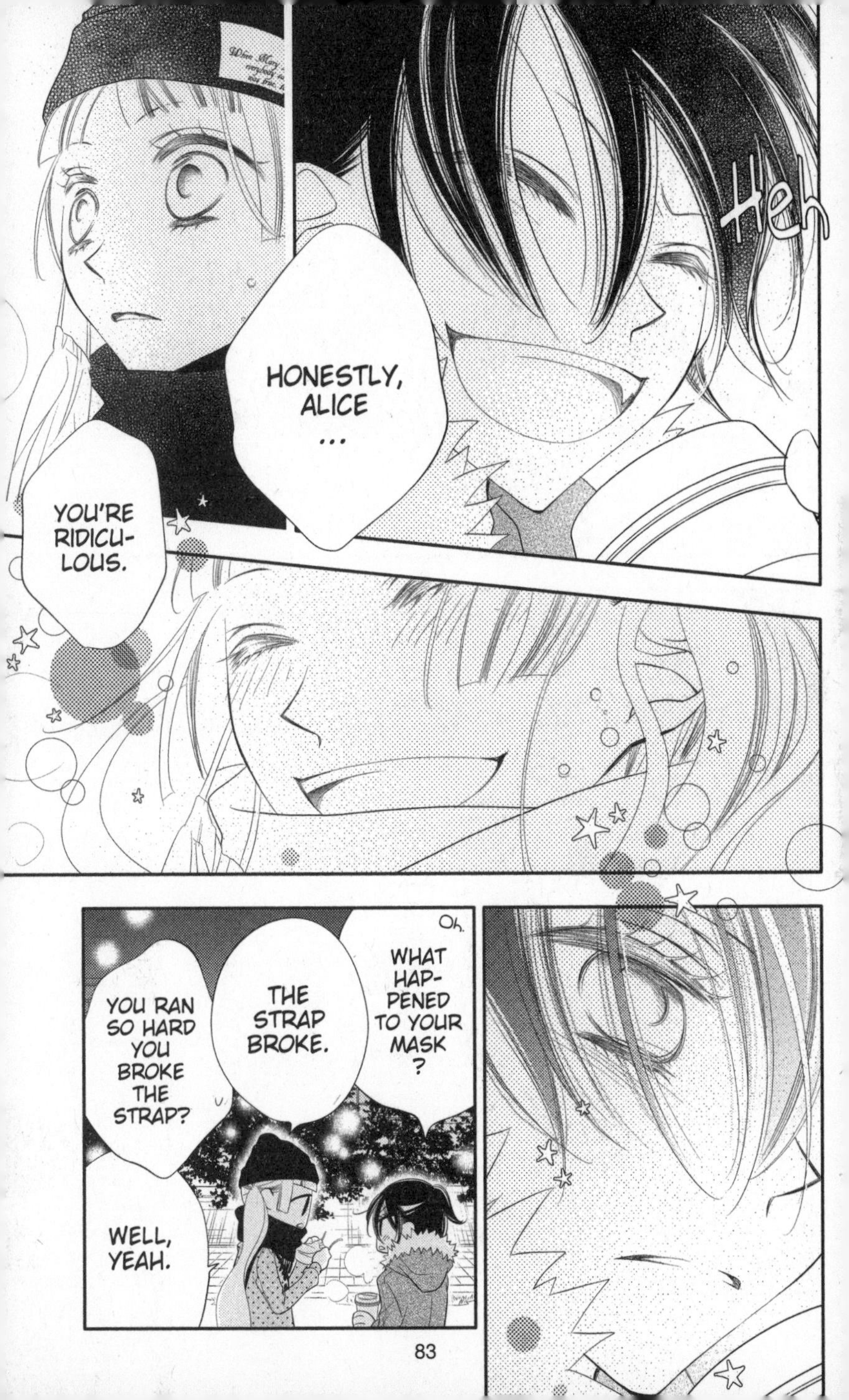
Heh
HONESTLY, ALICE ...
YOU'RE RIDICULOUS.
Oh.
WHAT HAPPENED TO YOUR MASK?
THE STRAP BROKE.
YOU RAN SO HARD YOU BROKE THE STRAP?
WELL, YEAH.

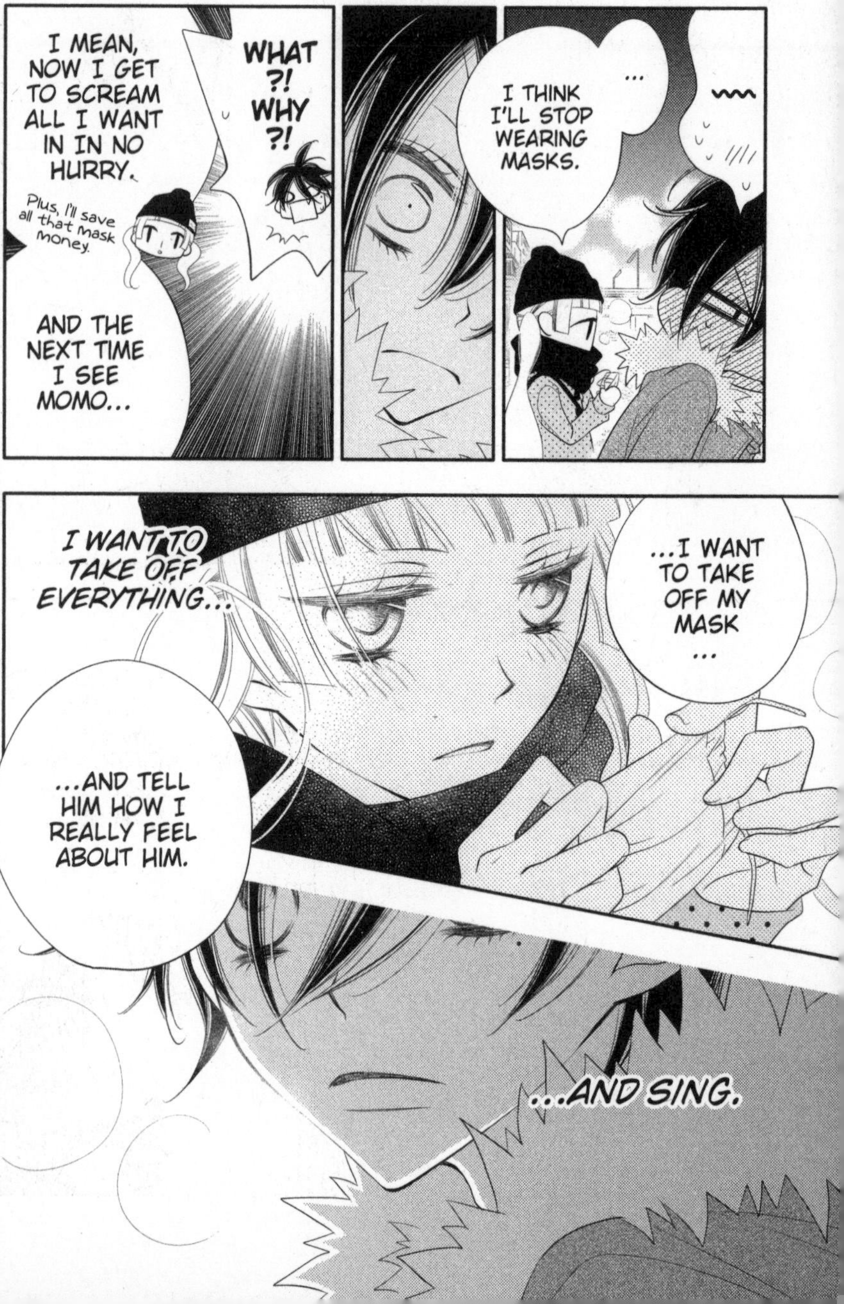
...
I THINK I'LL STOP WEARING MASKS.
WHAT?! WHY?!
I MEAN, NOW I GET TO SCREAM ALL I WANT IN IN NO HURRY.
Plus, I'll save all that mask money.
AND THE NEXT TIME I SEE MOMO...
...I WANT TO TAKE OFF MY MASK...
I WANT TO TAKE OFF EVERYTHING...
...AND TELL HIM HOW I REALLY FEEL ABOUT HIM.
...AND SING.

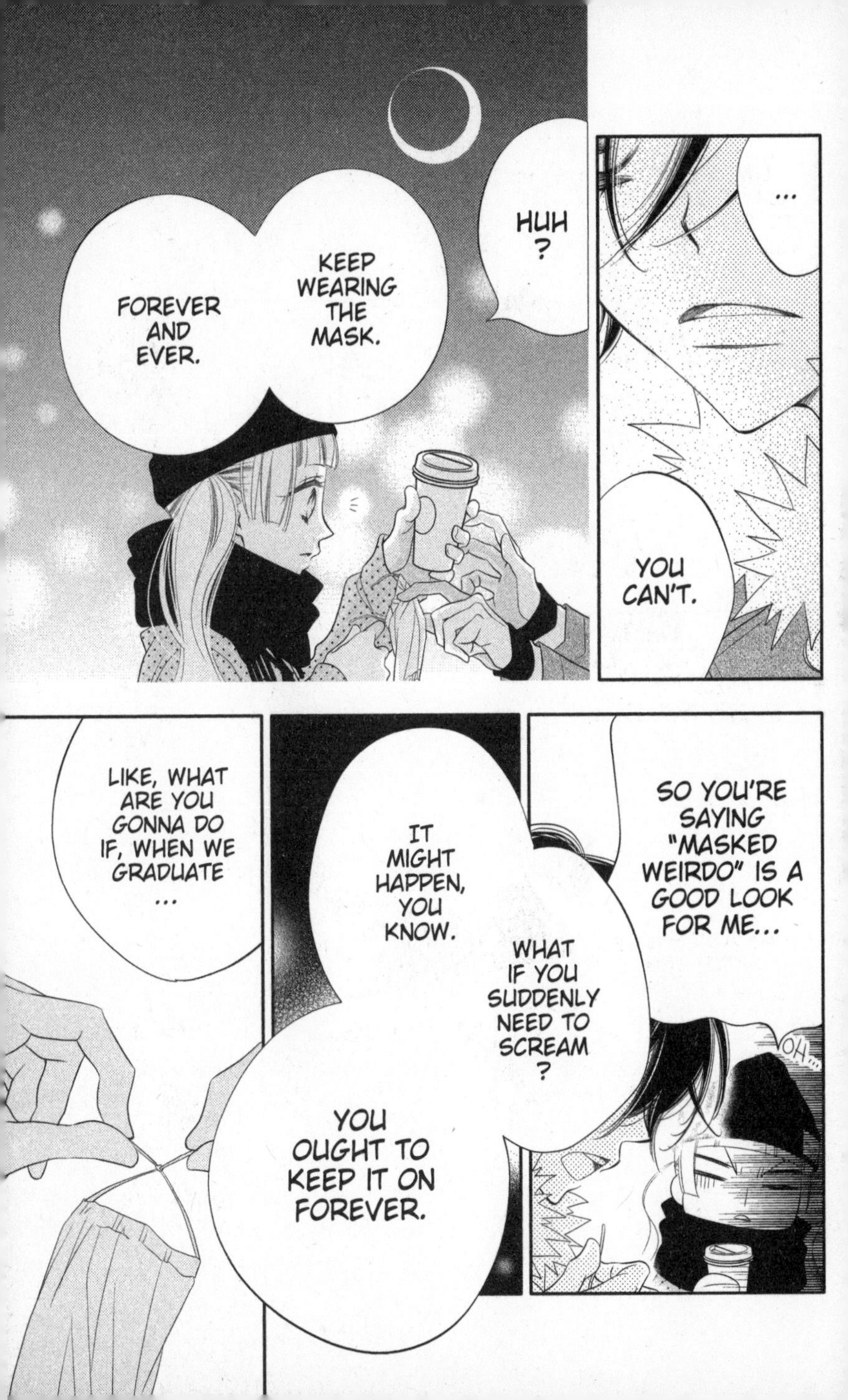
...
YOU CAN'T.
HUH?
KEEP WEARING THE MASK.
FOREVER AND EVER.
SO YOU'RE SAYING "MASKED WEIRDO" IS A GOOD LOOK FOR ME...
OH...
LIKE, WHAT ARE YOU GONNA DO IF, WHEN WE GRADUATE...
WHAT IF YOU SUDDENLY NEED TO SCREAM?
IT MIGHT HAPPEN, YOU KNOW.
YOU OUGHT TO KEEP IT ON FOREVER.

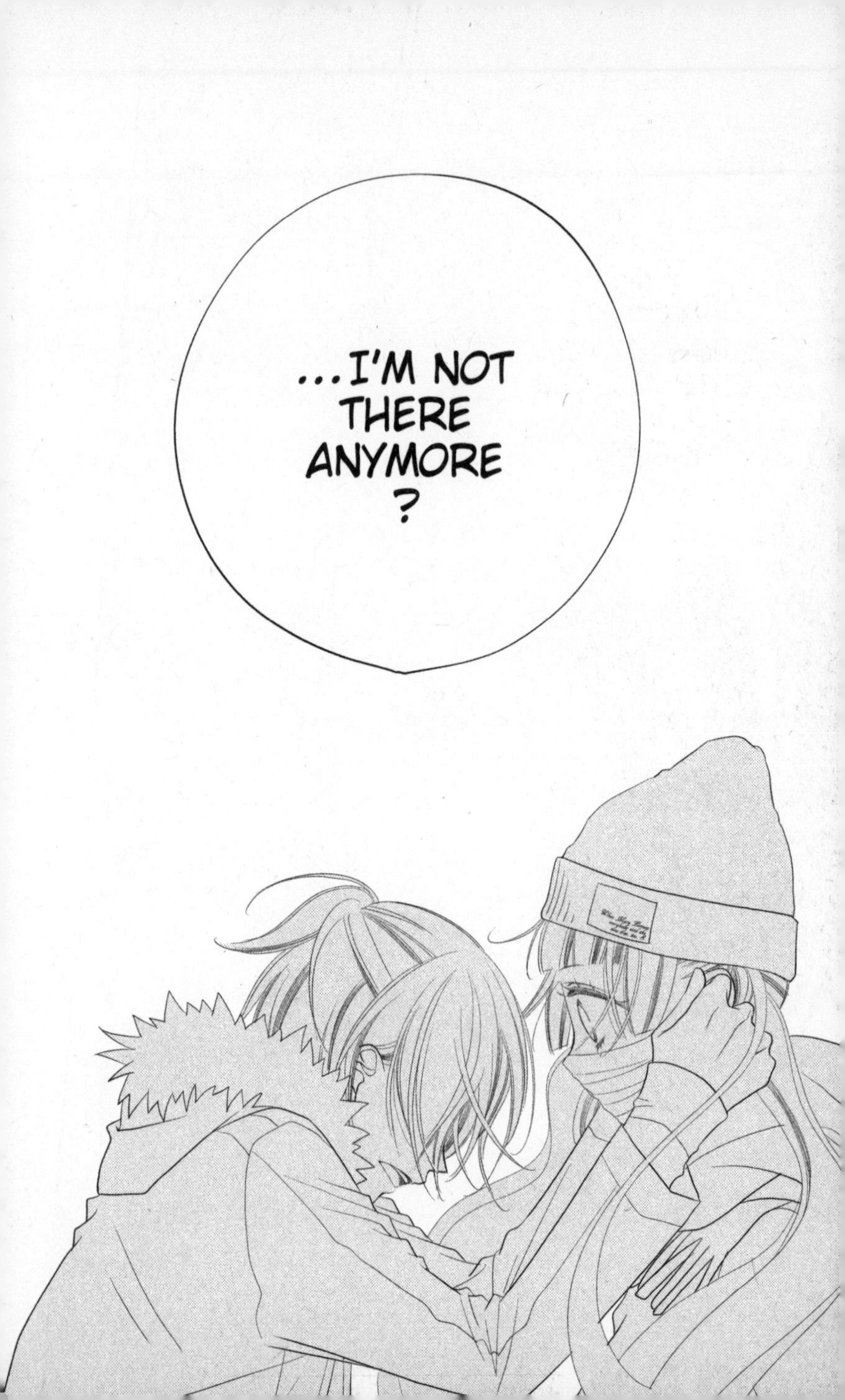
...I'M NOT THERE ANYMORE ?

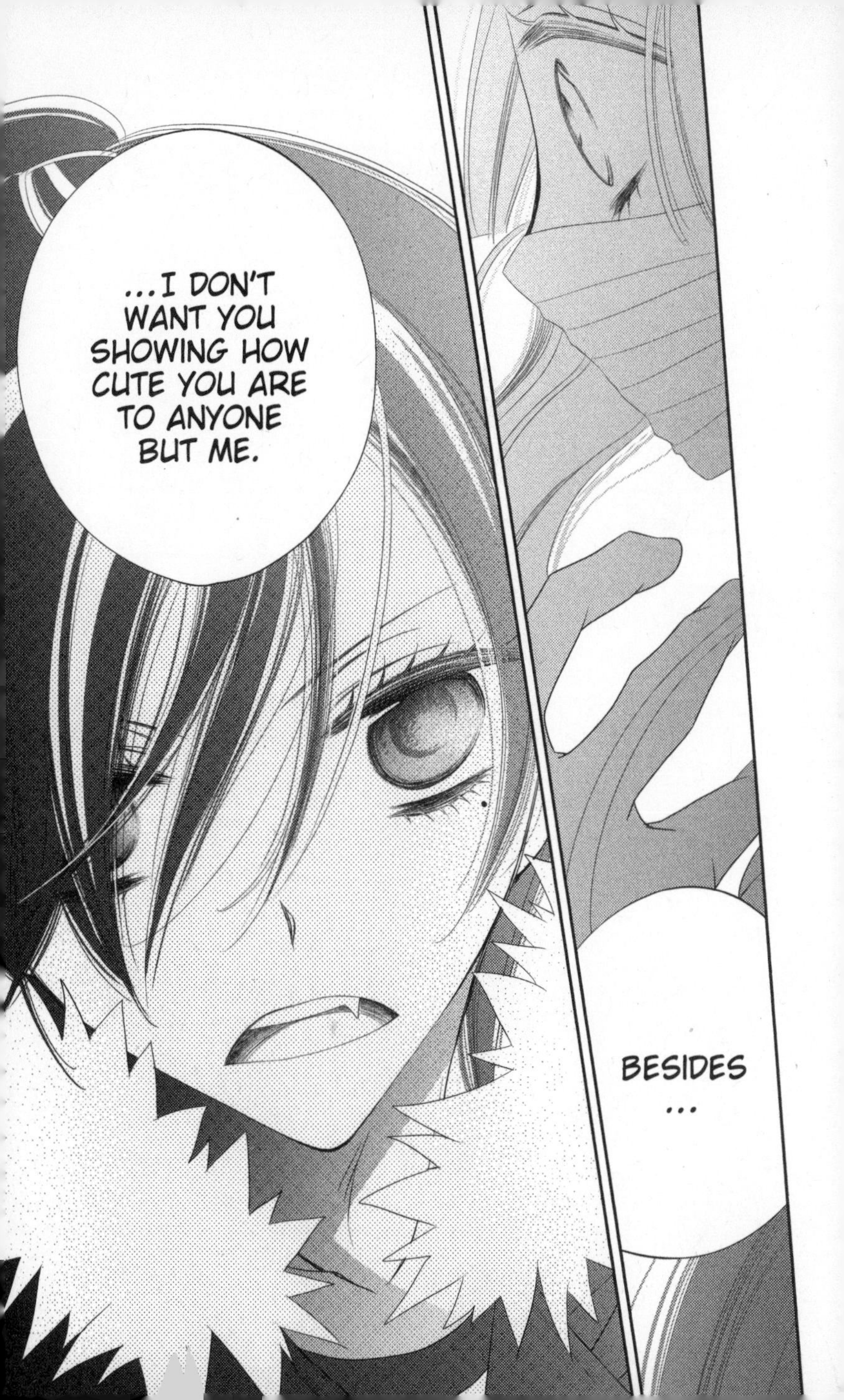
...I DON'T WANT YOU SHOWING HOW CUTE YOU ARE TO ANYONE BUT ME.
BESIDES ...

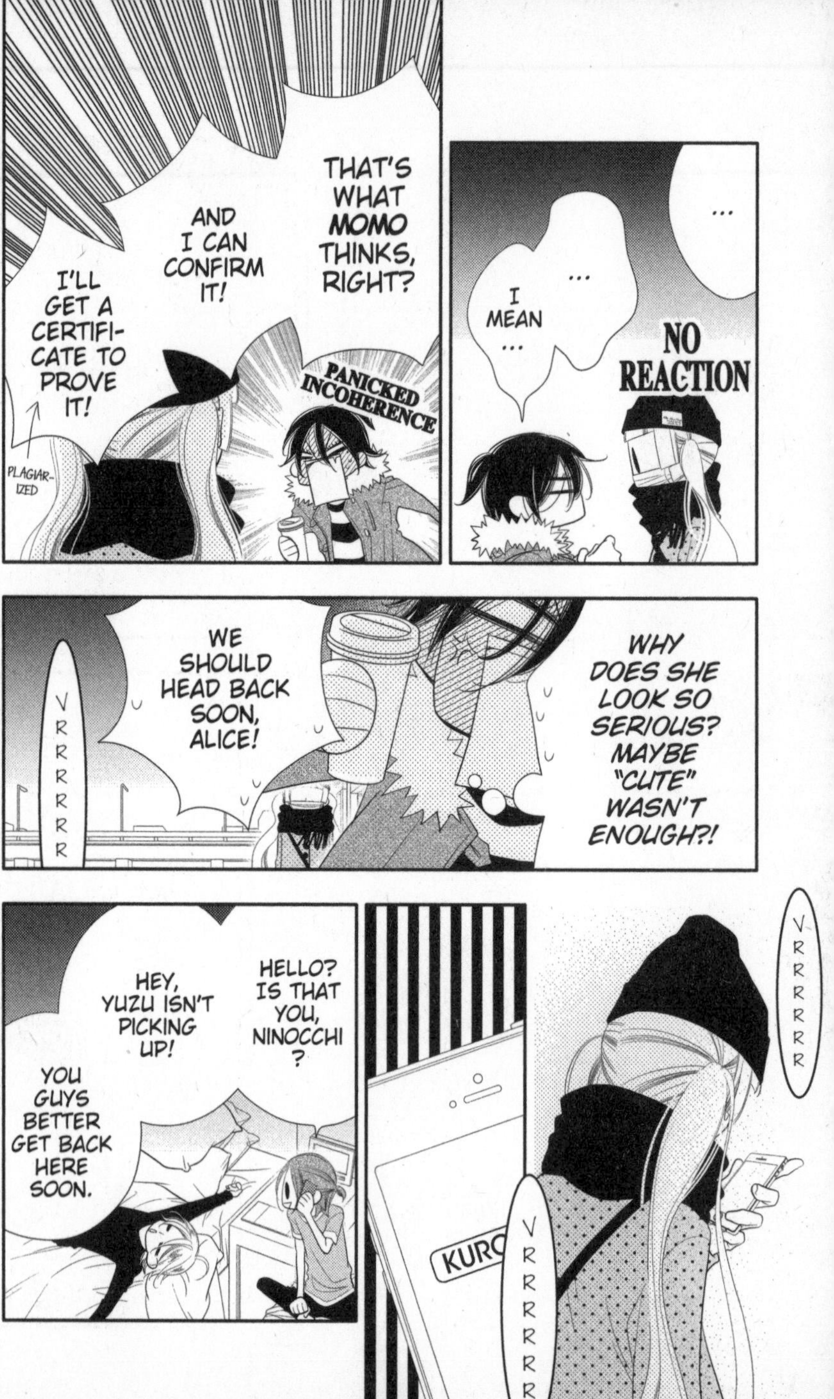
...
... I MEAN ...
NO REACTION
THAT'S WHAT MOMO THINKS, RIGHT?
PANICKED INCOHERENCE
AND I CAN CONFIRM IT!
I'LL GET A CERTIFI-CATE TO PROVE IT!
PLAGIAR-IZED
WHY DOES SHE LOOK SO SERIOUS? MAYBE "CUTE" WASN'T ENOUGH?!
WE SHOULD HEAD BACK SOON, ALICE!
VRRRRRR
VRRRRRR
KURO
VRRRRRR
HELLO? IS THAT YOU, NINOCCHI?
HEY, YUZU ISN'T PICKING UP!
YOU GUYS BETTER GET BACK HERE SOON.

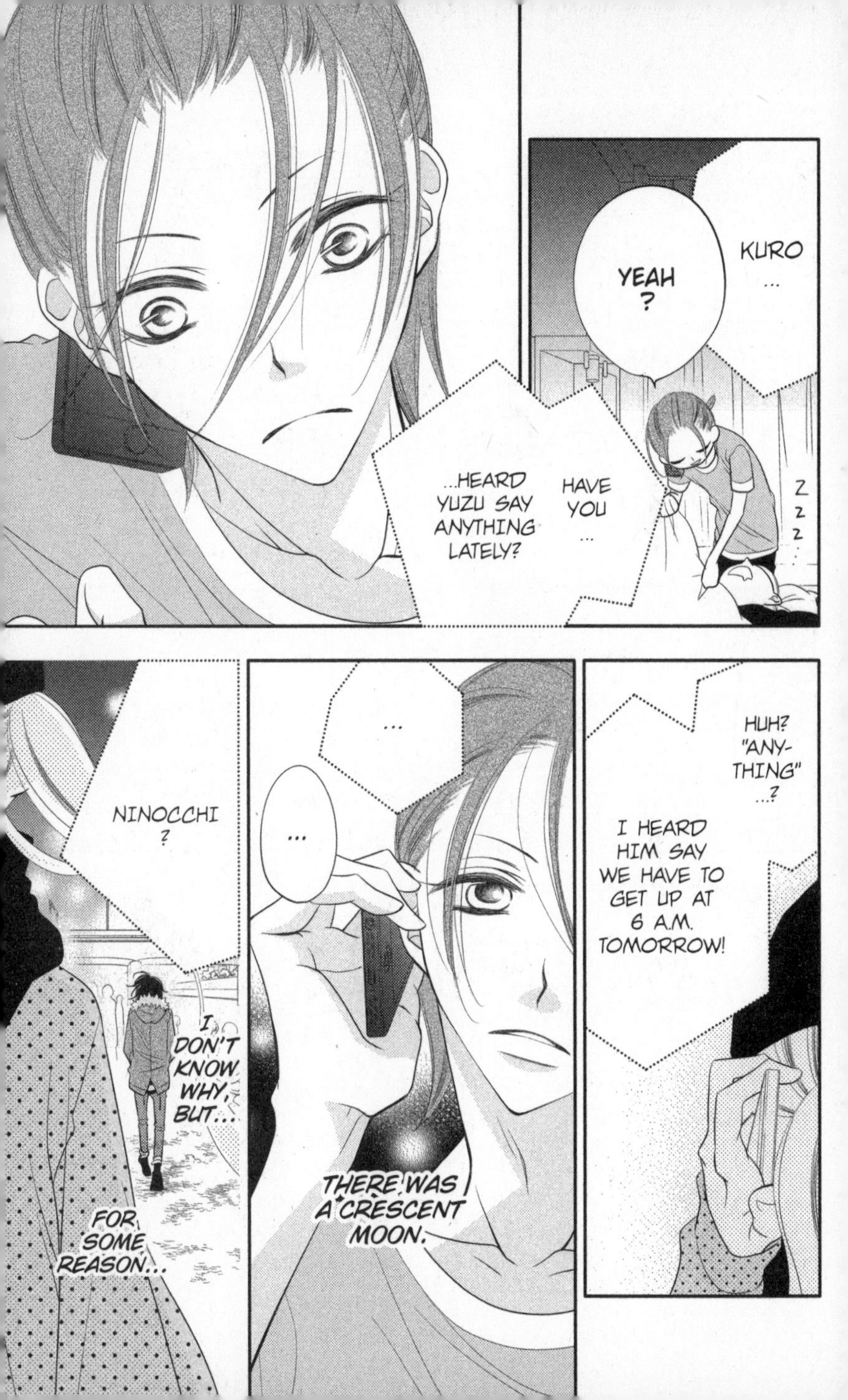
KURO ...
YEAH ?
Z Z Z
HAVE YOU ...
...HEARD YUZU SAY ANYTHING LATELY?
HUH? "ANY-THING" ...?
I HEARD HIM SAY WE HAVE TO GET UP AT 6 A.M. TOMORROW!
...
...
THERE WAS A CRESCENT MOON.
NINOCCHI ?
I DON'T KNOW WHY, BUT...
FOR SOME REASON...

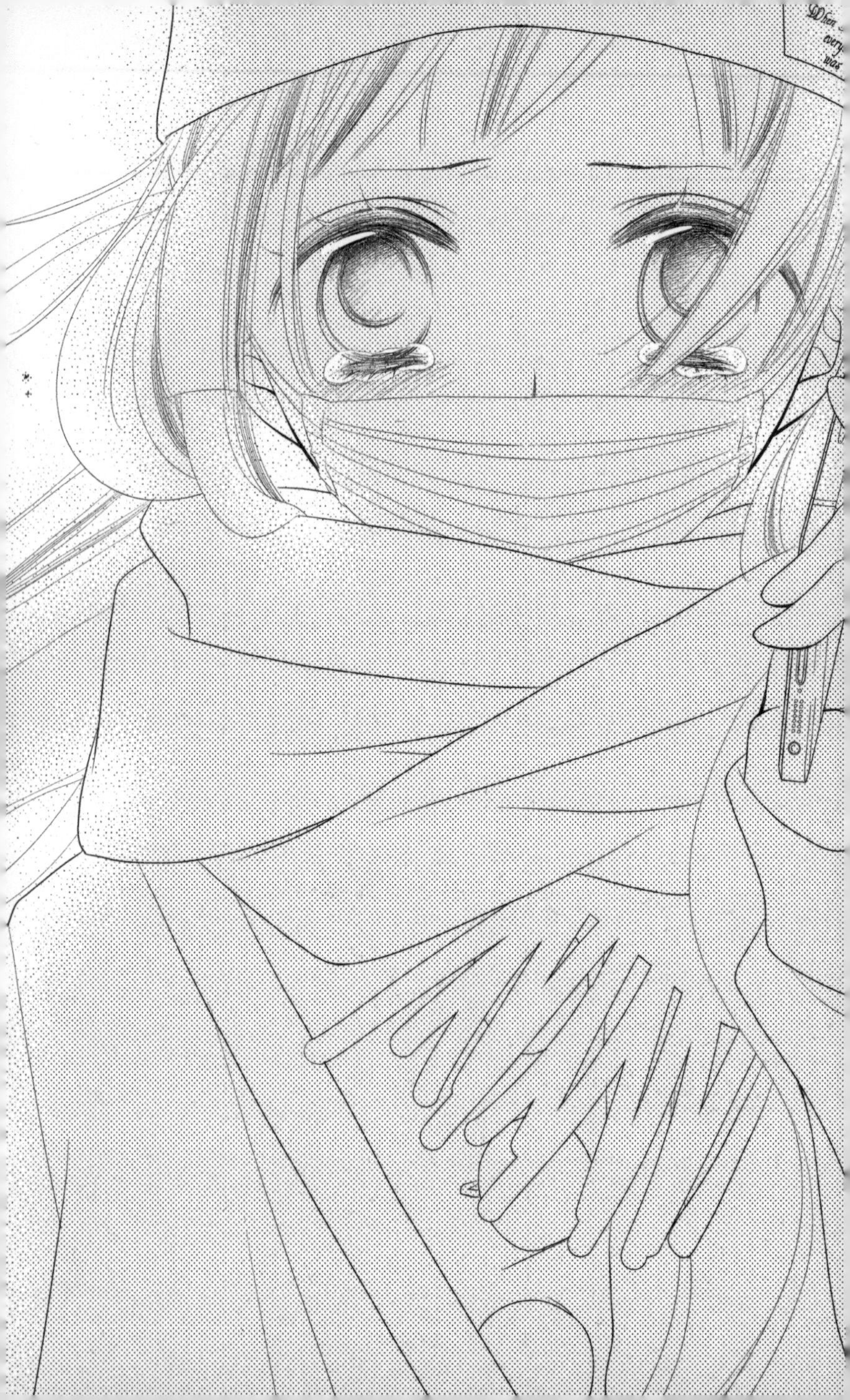
When
every
was

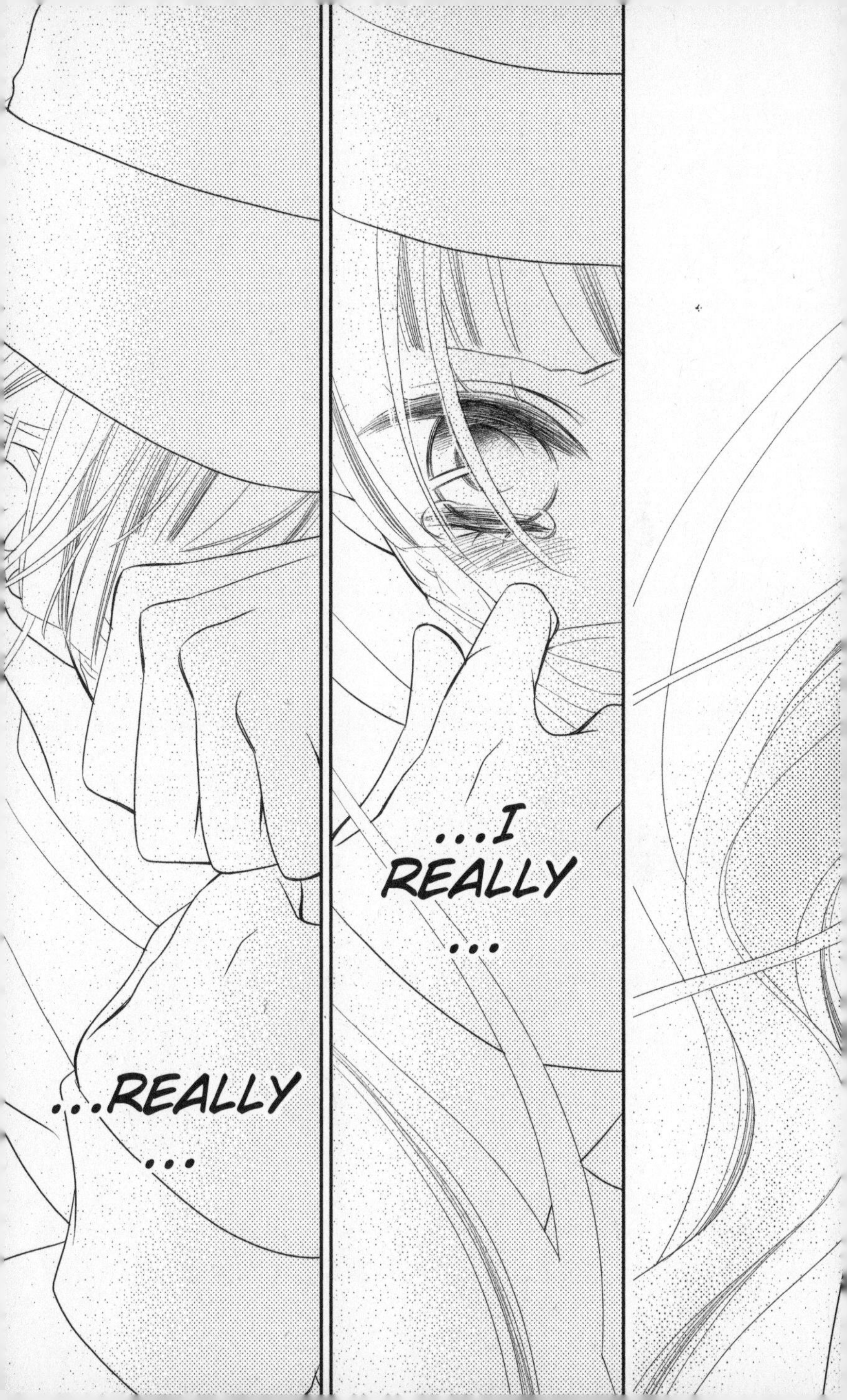
...I REALLY ...
...REALLY ...

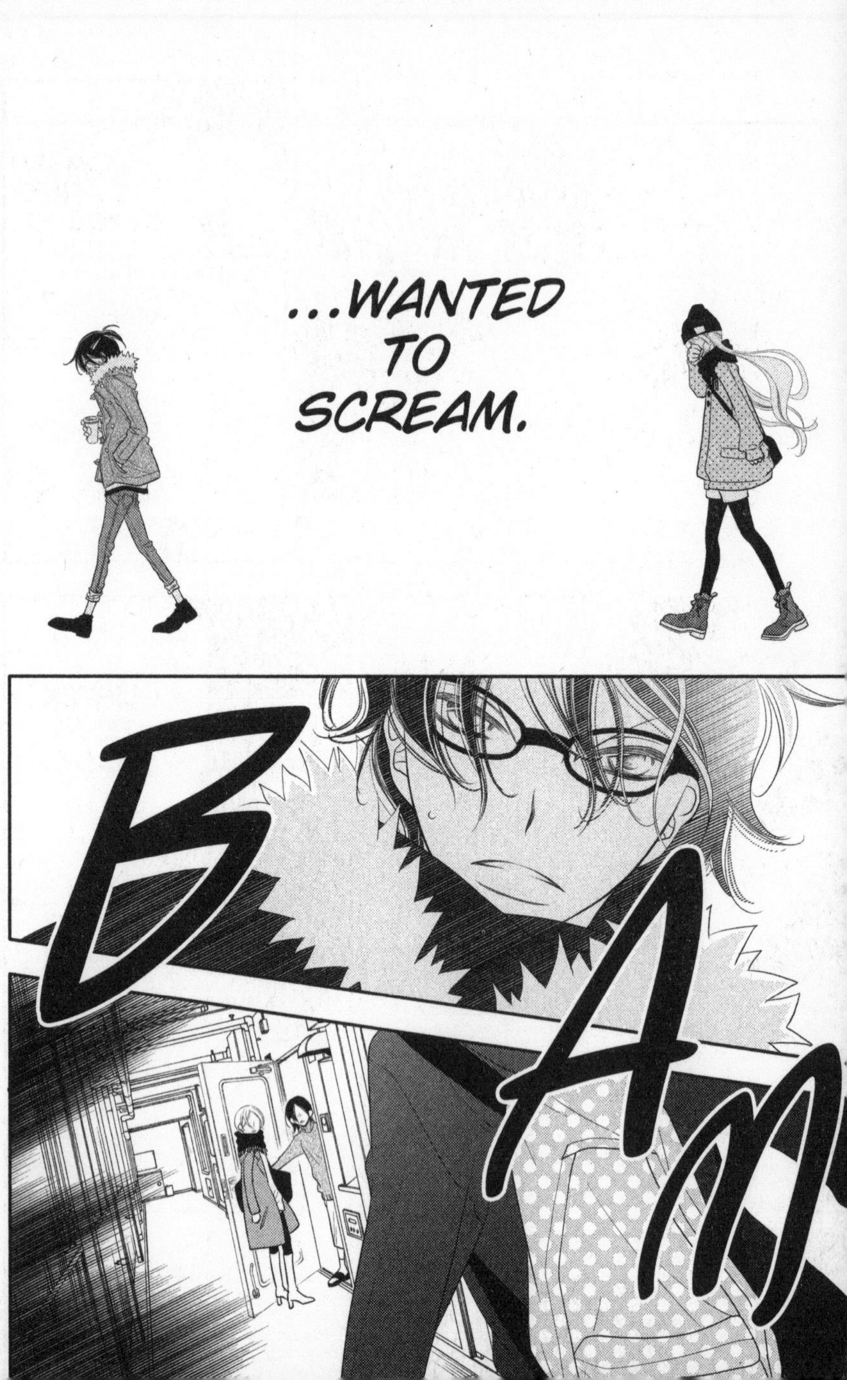
...WANTED TO SCREAM.
BAM

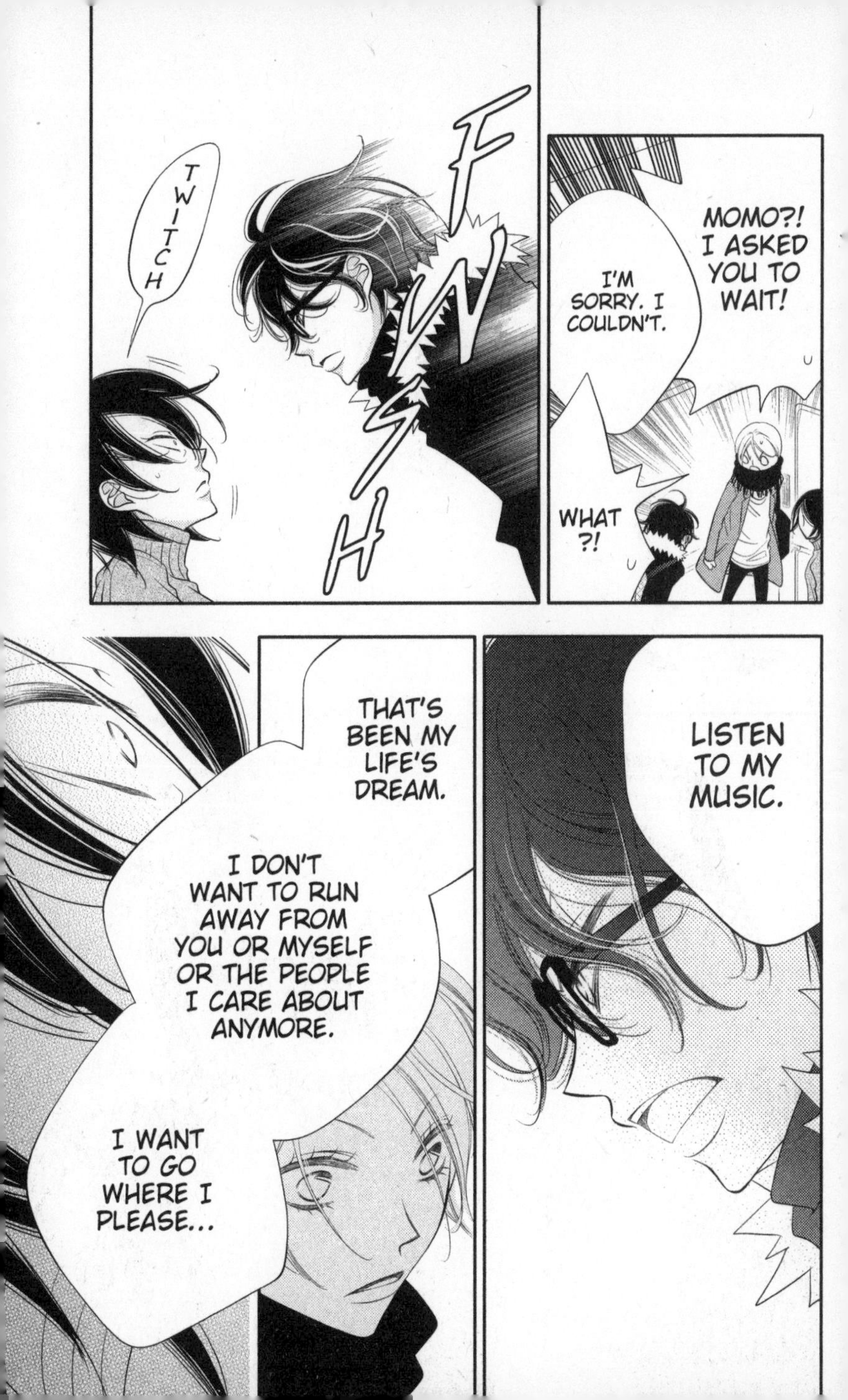

MOMO?! I ASKED YOU TO WAIT!
I'M SORRY. I COULDN'T.
WHAT?!
FWSH
TWITCH
LISTEN TO MY MUSIC.
THAT'S BEEN MY LIFE'S DREAM.
I DON'T WANT TO RUN AWAY FROM YOU OR MYSELF OR THE PEOPLE I CARE ABOUT ANYMORE.
I WANT TO GO WHERE I PLEASE...

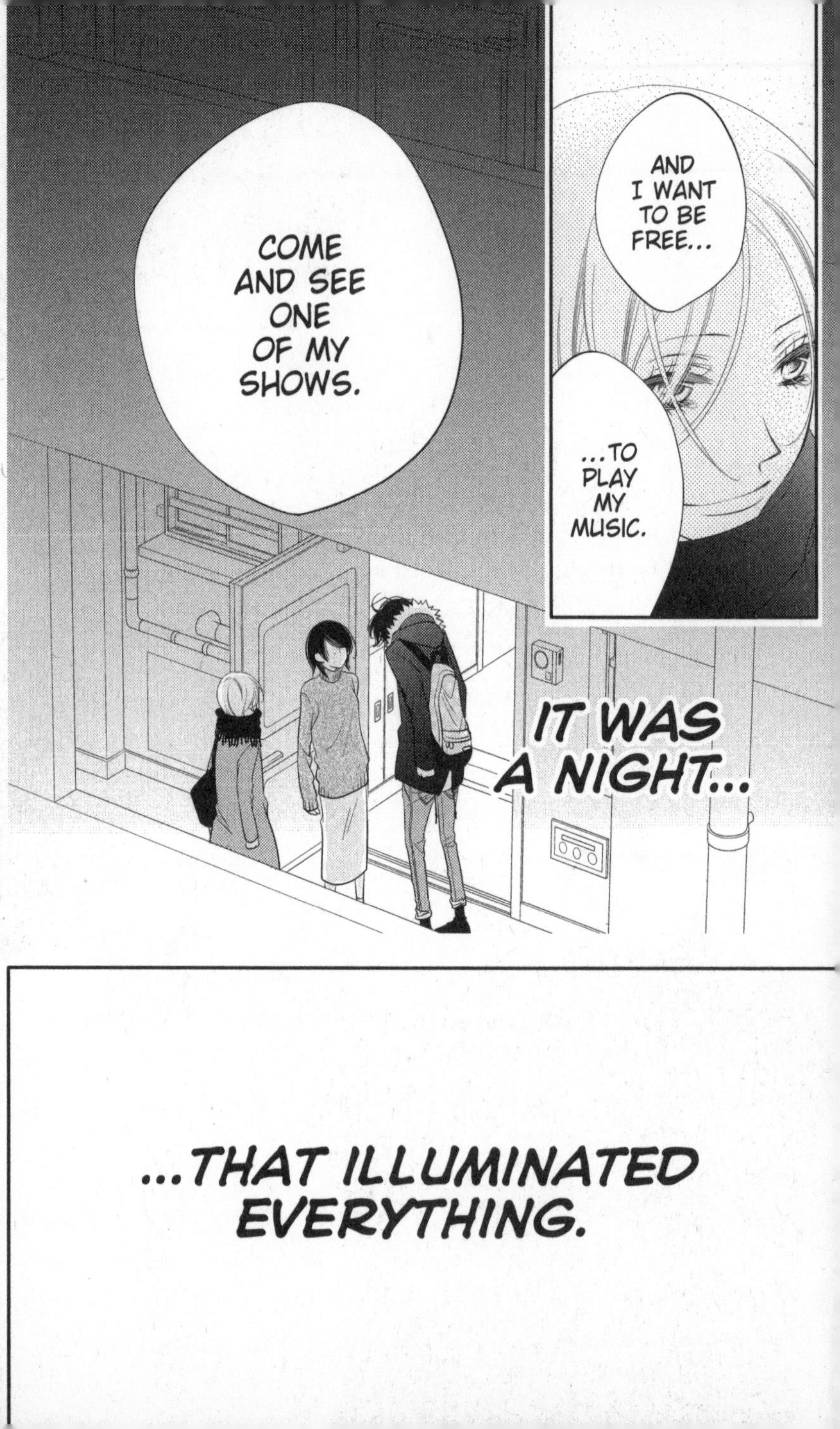
AND I WANT TO BE FREE...
...TO PLAY MY MUSIC.
COME AND SEE ONE OF MY SHOWS.
IT WAS A NIGHT...
...THAT ILLUMINATED EVERYTHING.

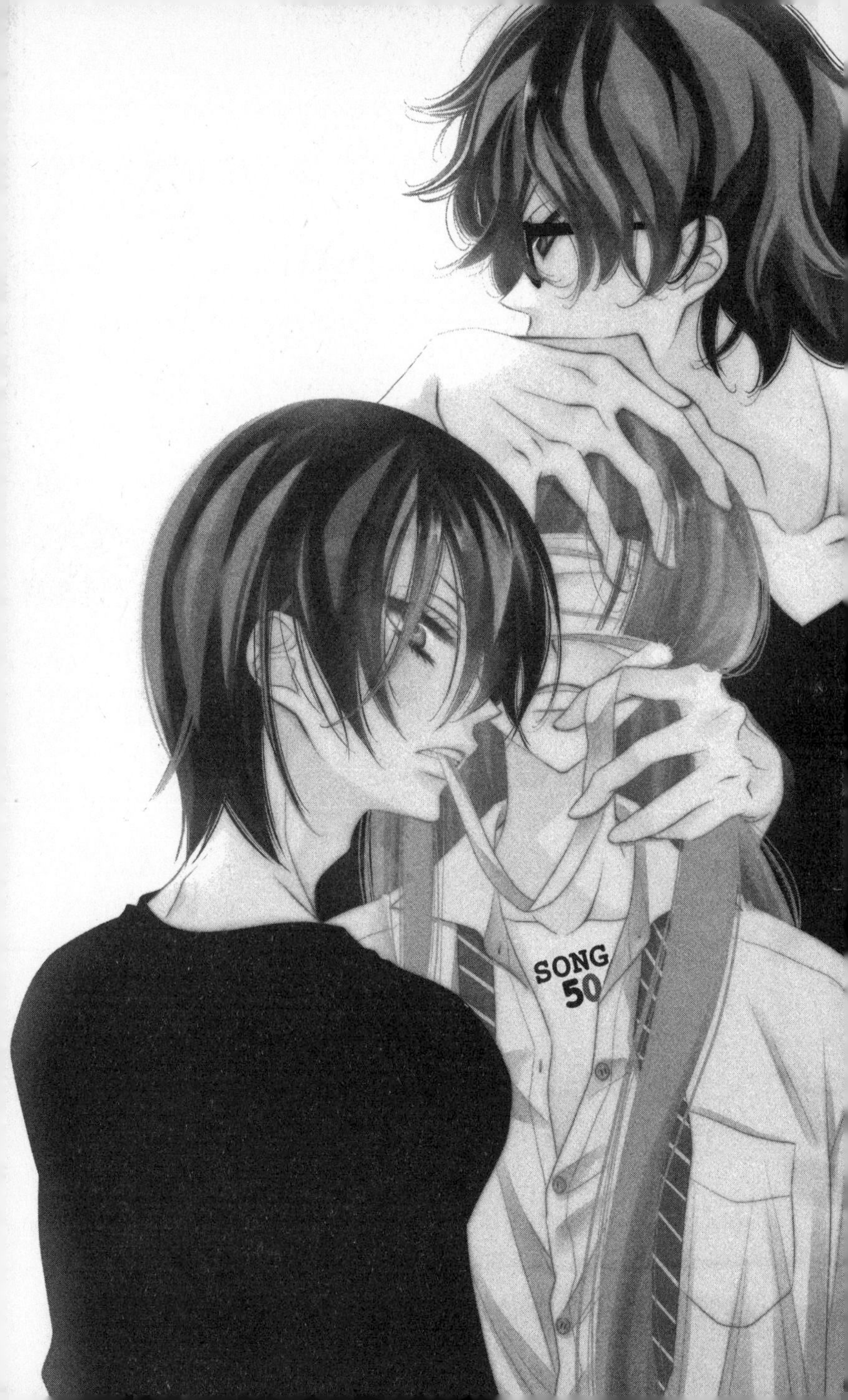
SONG
50

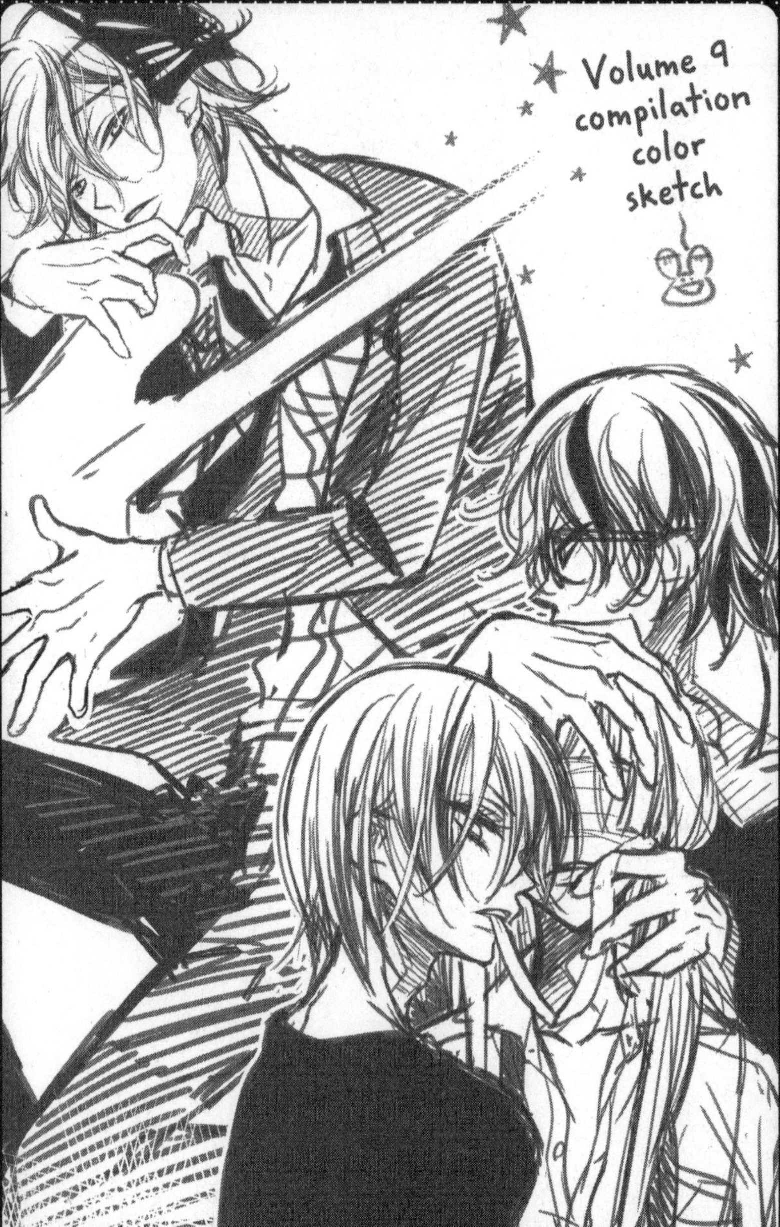
Volume 9
compilation
color
sketch

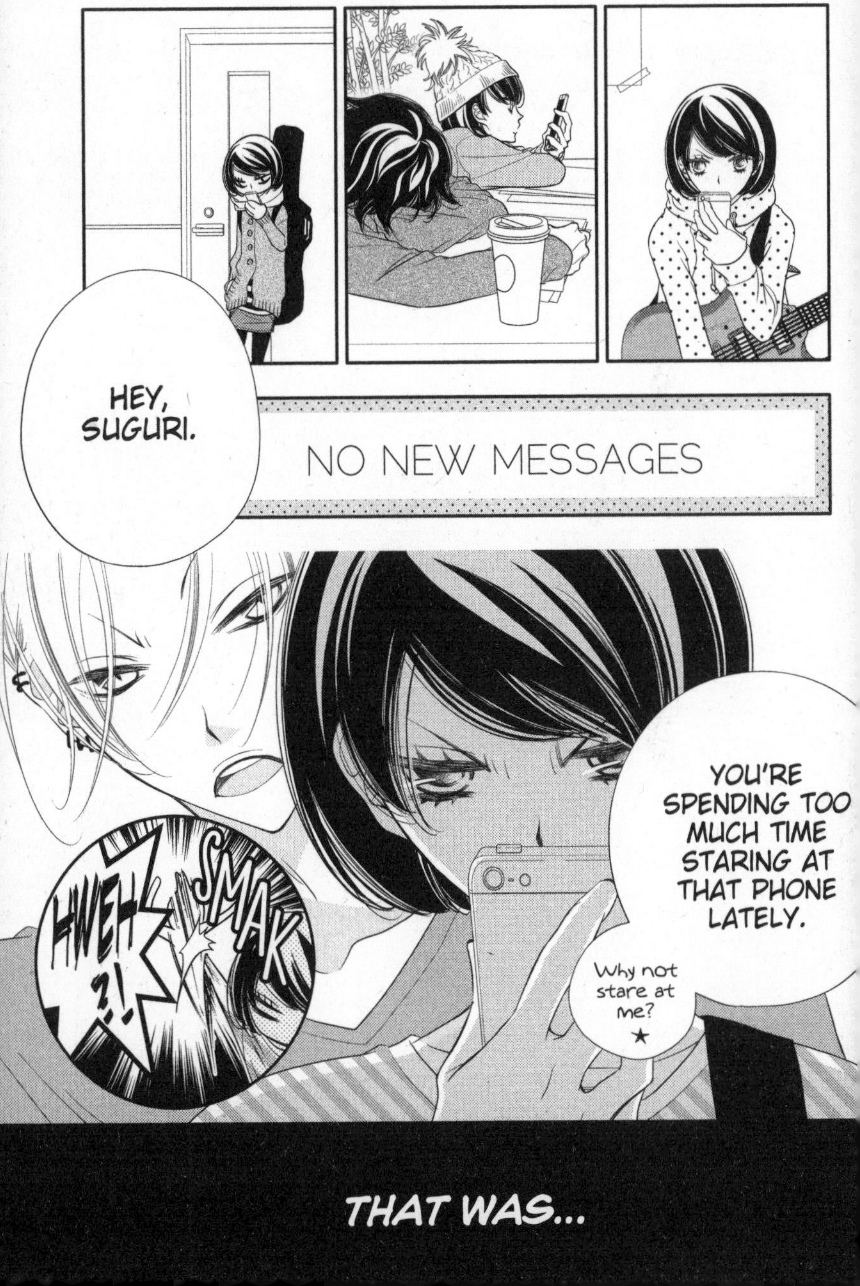
NO NEW MESSAGES
HEY, SUGURI.
YOU'RE SPENDING TOO MUCH TIME STARING AT THAT PHONE LATELY.
Why not stare at me? ★
SMAK
HWEH ?!
THAT WAS...

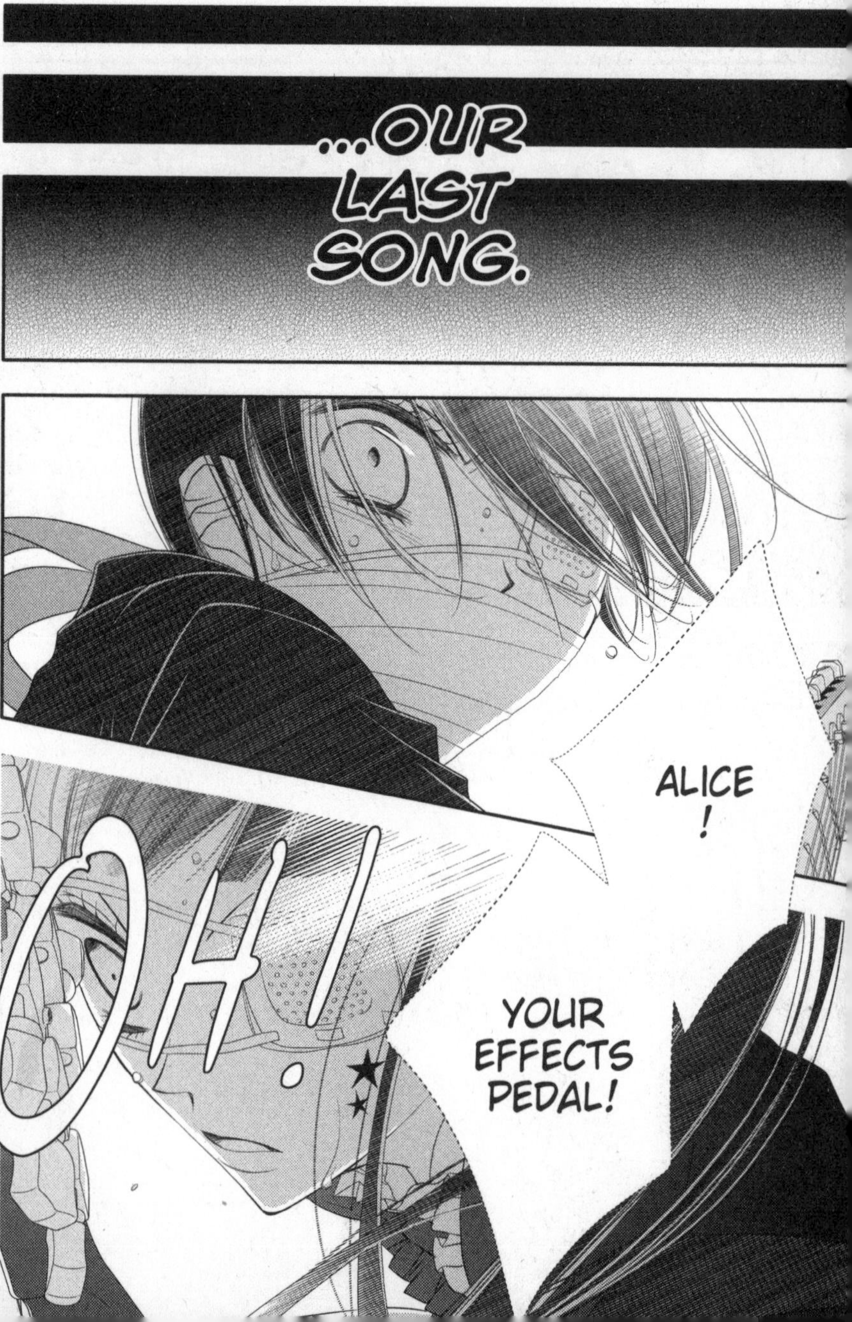
...OUR LAST SONG.
ALICE!
YOUR EFFECTS PEDAL!
OH!

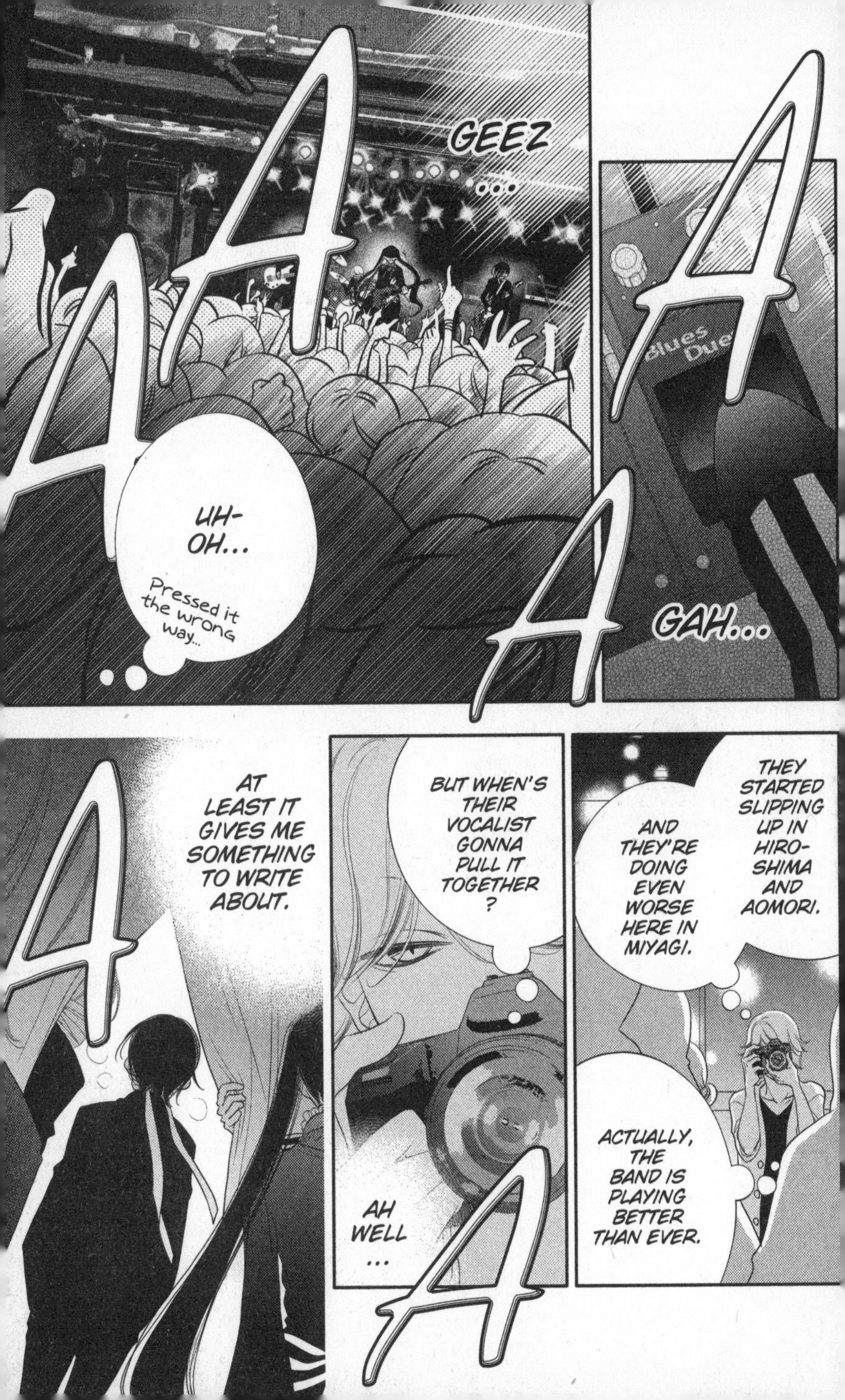
AAAAAA
Blues Due
GAH...
GEEZ...
UH-OH...
Pressed it the wrong way...
THEY STARTED SLIPPING UP IN HIRO-SHIMA AND AOMORI.
AND THEY'RE DOING EVEN WORSE HERE IN MIYAGI.
ACTUALLY, THE BAND IS PLAYING BETTER THAN EVER.
BUT WHEN'S THEIR VOCALIST GONNA PULL IT TOGETHER?
AH WELL...
AT LEAST IT GIVES ME SOMETHING TO WRITE ABOUT.

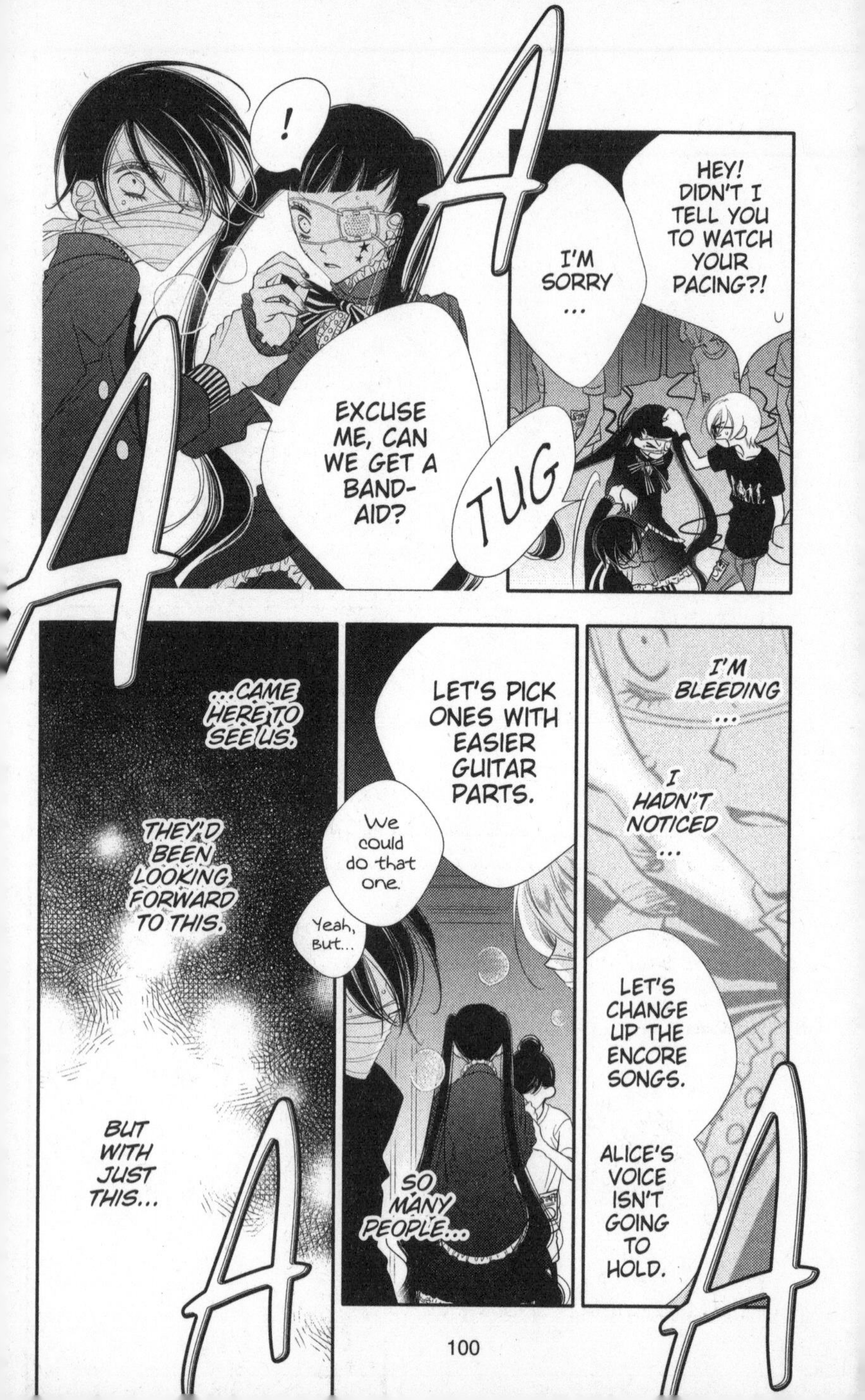
HEY! DIDN'T I TELL YOU TO WATCH YOUR PACING?!
I'M SORRY...
!
TUG
EXCUSE ME, CAN WE GET A BAND-AID?
I'M BLEEDING...
I HADN'T NOTICED...
LET'S CHANGE UP THE ENCORE SONGS.
ALICE'S VOICE ISN'T GOING TO HOLD.
LET'S PICK ONES WITH EASIER GUITAR PARTS.
We could do that one.
Yeah, but...
SO MANY PEOPLE...
...CAME HERE TO SEE US.
THEY'D BEEN LOOKING FORWARD TO THIS.
BUT WITH JUST THIS...

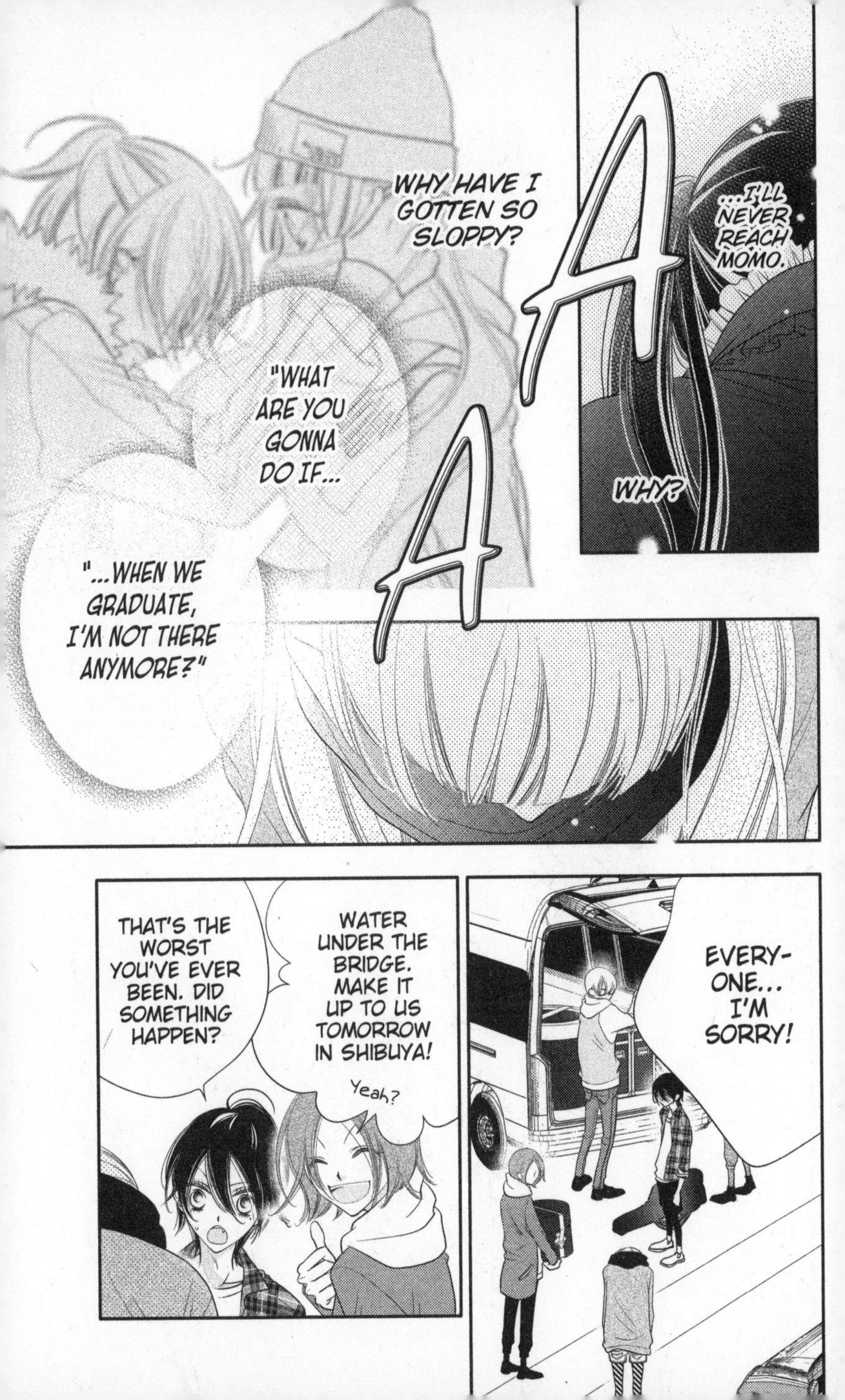
...I'LL NEVER REACH MOMO.
WHY?
WHY HAVE I GOTTEN SO SLOPPY?
AA
"WHAT ARE YOU GONNA DO IF...
"...WHEN WE GRADUATE, I'M NOT THERE ANYMORE?"
EVERY-ONE... I'M SORRY!
WATER UNDER THE BRIDGE. MAKE IT UP TO US TOMORROW IN SHIBUYA!
Yeah?
THAT'S THE WORST YOU'VE EVER BEEN. DID SOMETHING HAPPEN?

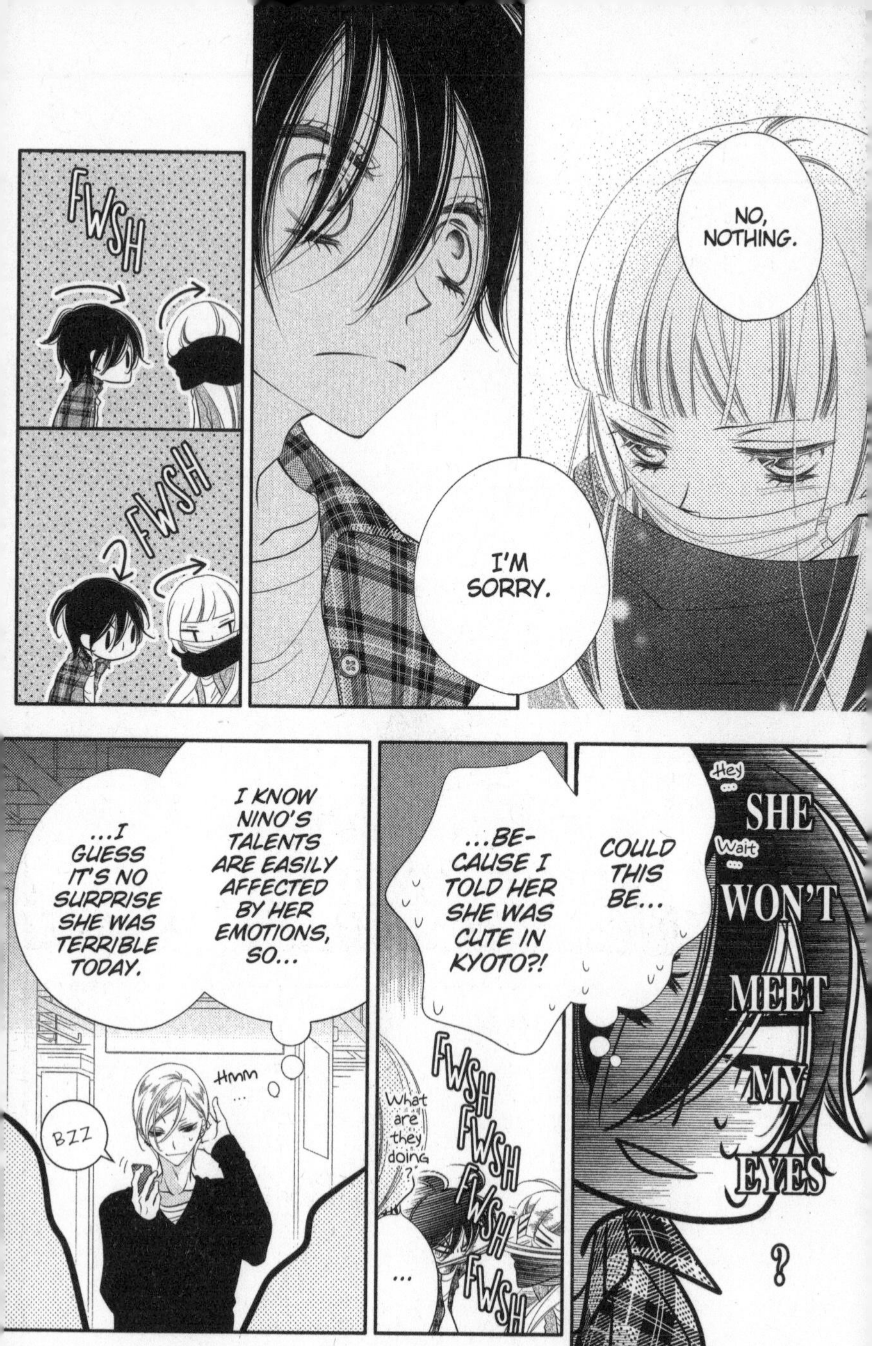
NO, NOTHING.
I'M SORRY.
FWSH
FWSH
Hey...
SHE WON'T MEET MY EYES?
Wait...
COULD THIS BE...
...BE-CAUSE I TOLD HER SHE WAS CUTE IN KYOTO?!
What are they doing?
FWSH FWSH FWSH FWSH
...
I KNOW NINO'S TALENTS ARE EASILY AFFECTED BY HER EMOTIONS, SO...
...I GUESS IT'S NO SURPRISE SHE WAS TERRIBLE TODAY.
Hmm...
BZZ

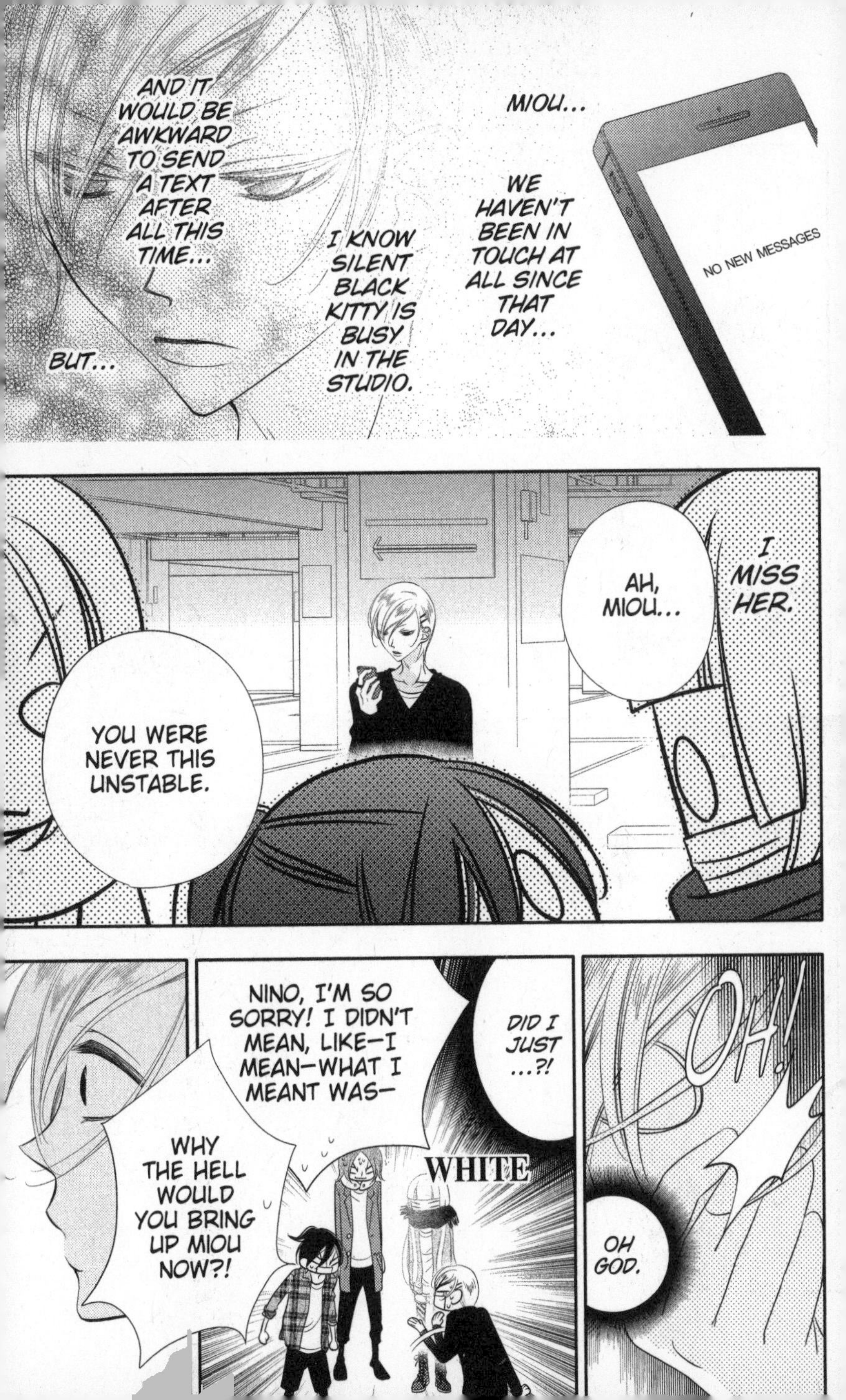
NO NEW MESSAGES
MIOU...
WE HAVEN'T BEEN IN TOUCH AT ALL SINCE THAT DAY...
I KNOW SILENT BLACK KITTY IS BUSY IN THE STUDIO.
AND IT WOULD BE AWKWARD TO SEND A TEXT AFTER ALL THIS TIME...
BUT...
I MISS HER.
AH, MIOU...
YOU WERE NEVER THIS UNSTABLE.
OH!
OH GOD.
DID I JUST ...?!
NINO, I'M SO SORRY! I DIDN'T MEAN, LIKE—I MEAN—WHAT I MEANT WAS—
WHITE
WHY THE HELL WOULD YOU BRING UP MIOU NOW?!

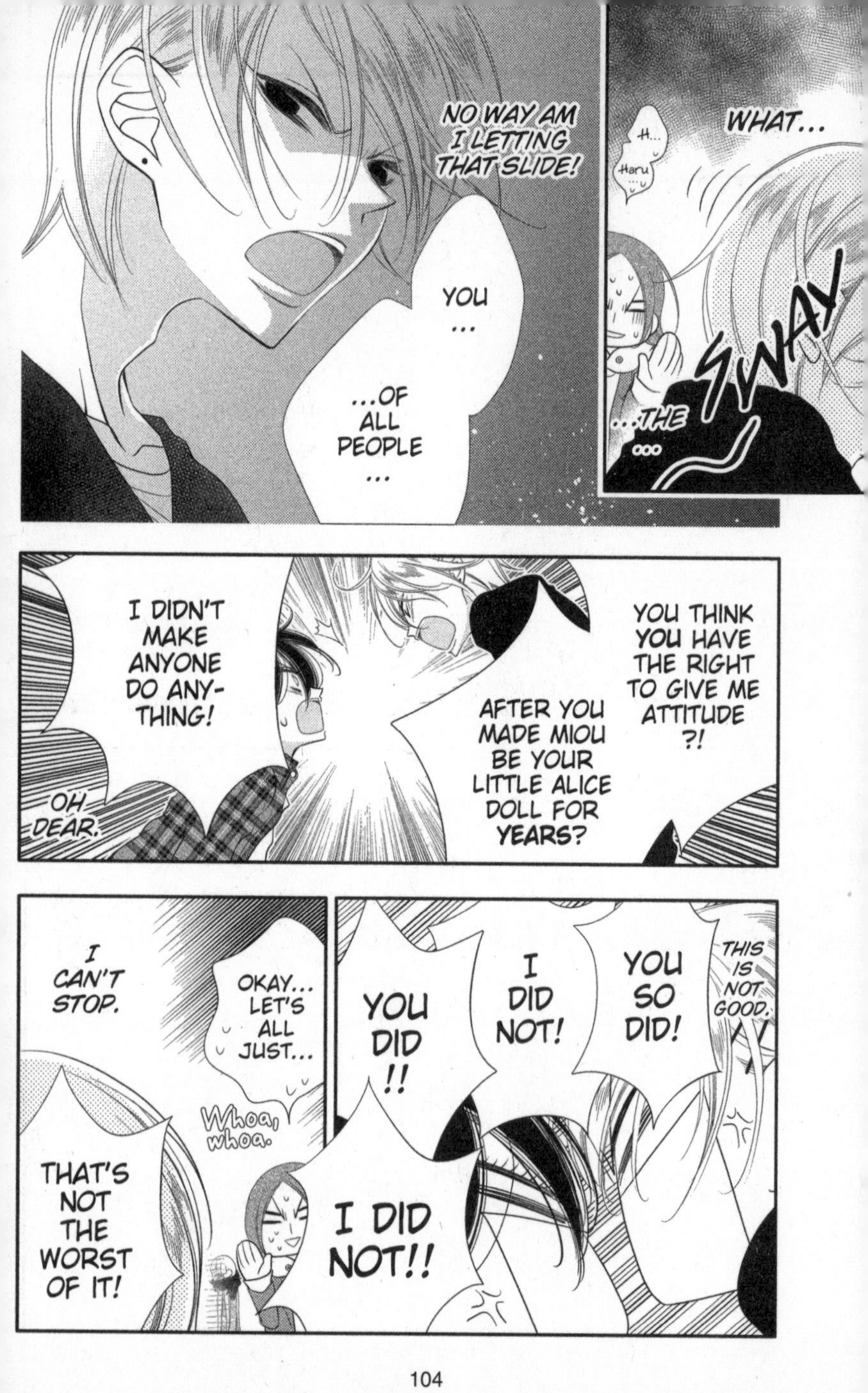
WHAT...
H... Haru...
...THE...
SWAY
NO WAY AM I LETTING THAT SLIDE!
YOU...
...OF ALL PEOPLE...
YOU THINK YOU HAVE THE RIGHT TO GIVE ME ATTITUDE?!
AFTER YOU MADE MIOU BE YOUR LITTLE ALICE DOLL FOR YEARS?
I DIDN'T MAKE ANYONE DO ANY-THING!
OH DEAR.
THIS IS NOT GOOD.
YOU SO DID!
I DID NOT!
YOU DID!!
I DID NOT!!
I CAN'T STOP.
OKAY... LET'S ALL JUST...
Whoa, whoa.
THAT'S NOT THE WORST OF IT!

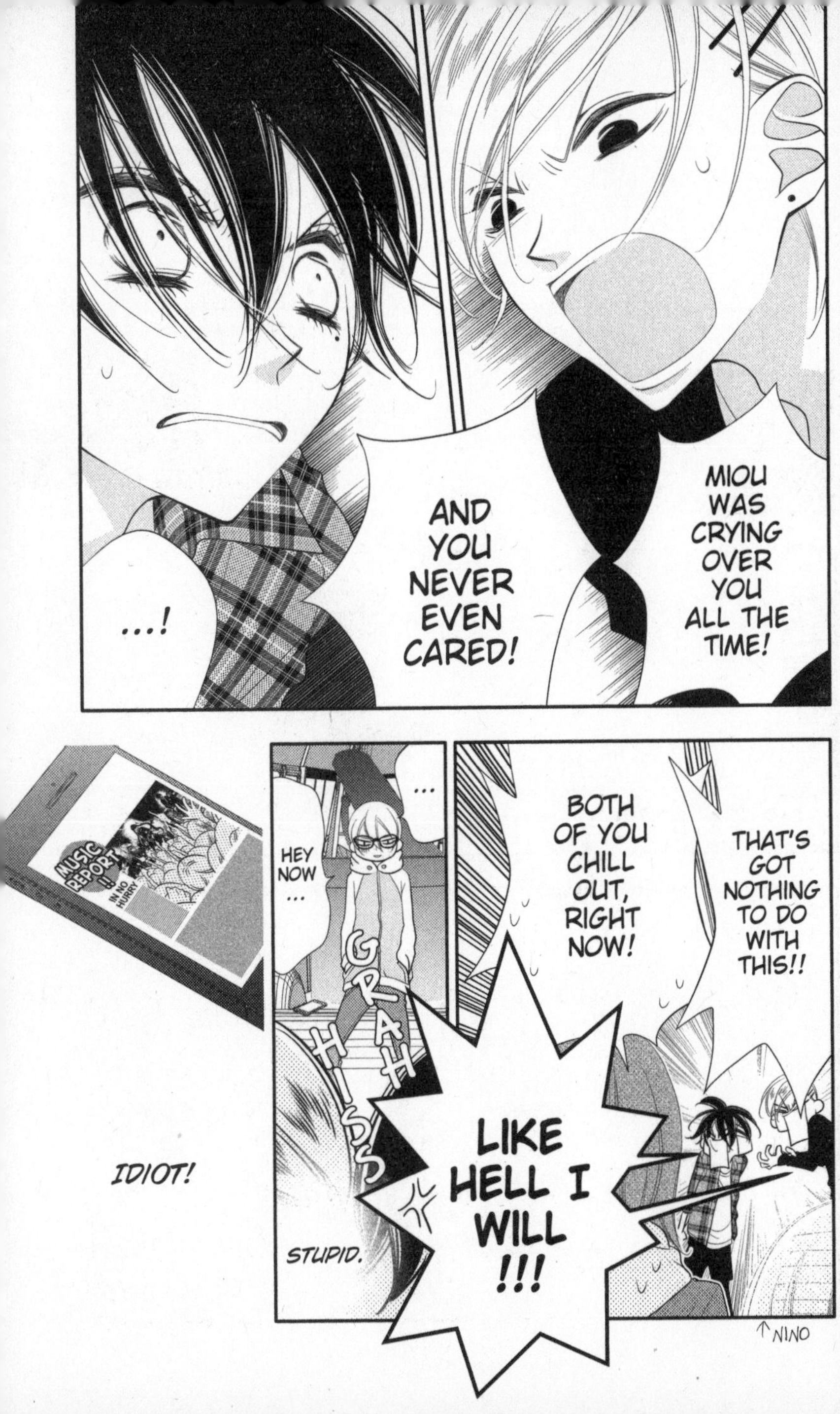
MIOU WAS CRYING OVER YOU ALL THE TIME!
AND YOU NEVER EVEN CARED!
...!
THAT'S GOT NOTHING TO DO WITH THIS!!
BOTH OF YOU CHILL OUT, RIGHT NOW!
LIKE HELL I WILL!!!
STUPID.
↑NINO
...
HEY NOW ...
GRAH
HISS
MUSIC REPORT!!
IN NO HURRY
IDIOT!

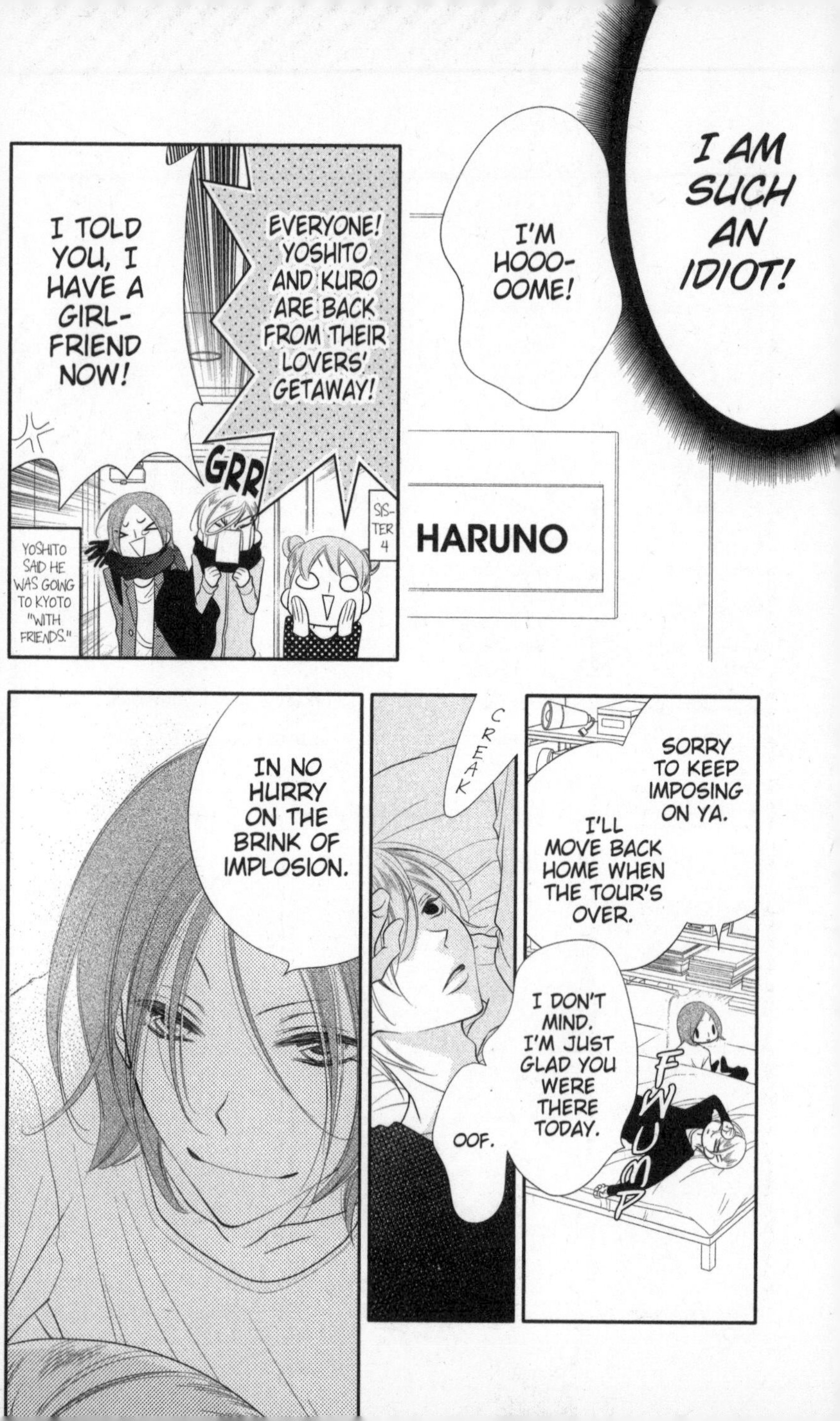
I AM SUCH AN IDIOT!
I'M HOOOO-OOME!
HARUNO
EVERYONE! YOSHITO AND KURO ARE BACK FROM THEIR LOVERS' GETAWAY!
SIS-TER 4
GRR
I TOLD YOU, I HAVE A GIRL-FRIEND NOW!
YOSHITO SAID HE WAS GOING TO KYOTO "WITH FRIENDS."
SORRY TO KEEP IMPOSING ON YA.
I'LL MOVE BACK HOME WHEN THE TOUR'S OVER.
FWUMP
I DON'T MIND. I'M JUST GLAD YOU WERE THERE TODAY.
OOF.
CREAK
IN NO HURRY ON THE BRINK OF IMPLOSION.

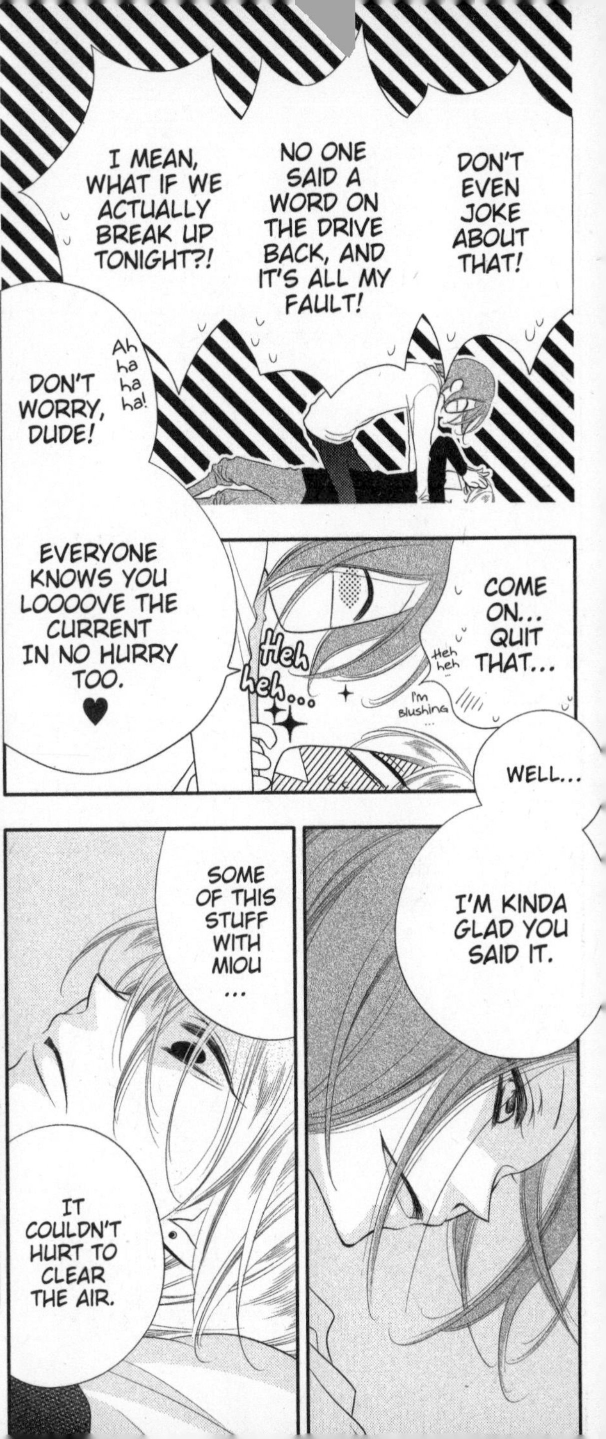
DON'T EVEN JOKE ABOUT THAT!
NO ONE SAID A WORD ON THE DRIVE BACK, AND IT'S ALL MY FAULT!
I MEAN, WHAT IF WE ACTUALLY BREAK UP TONIGHT?!
Ah ha ha ha!
DON'T WORRY, DUDE!
COME ON... QUIT THAT...
Heh heh...
I'm blushing...
Heh heh...
EVERYONE KNOWS YOU LOOOOVE THE CURRENT IN NO HURRY TOO. ♥
WELL...
I'M KINDA GLAD YOU SAID IT.
SOME OF THIS STUFF WITH MIOU...
IT COULDN'T HURT TO CLEAR THE AIR.

4

Chara-ani is making licensed Anonymous Noise merchandise!

This isn't related to the anime or anything—we've actually been talking about this for a long time. Now they're finally for sale at:

http://www.chara-ani.com

At the time I'm writing this (March 2016), there's a banner you can click on their home page, but if that isn't there anymore, please use the search function!

I can't believe how much stuff they've made. It's so exciting!

It's been a long time since I've been involved with merchandising like this, and it makes me really happy! I hope you enjoy it!

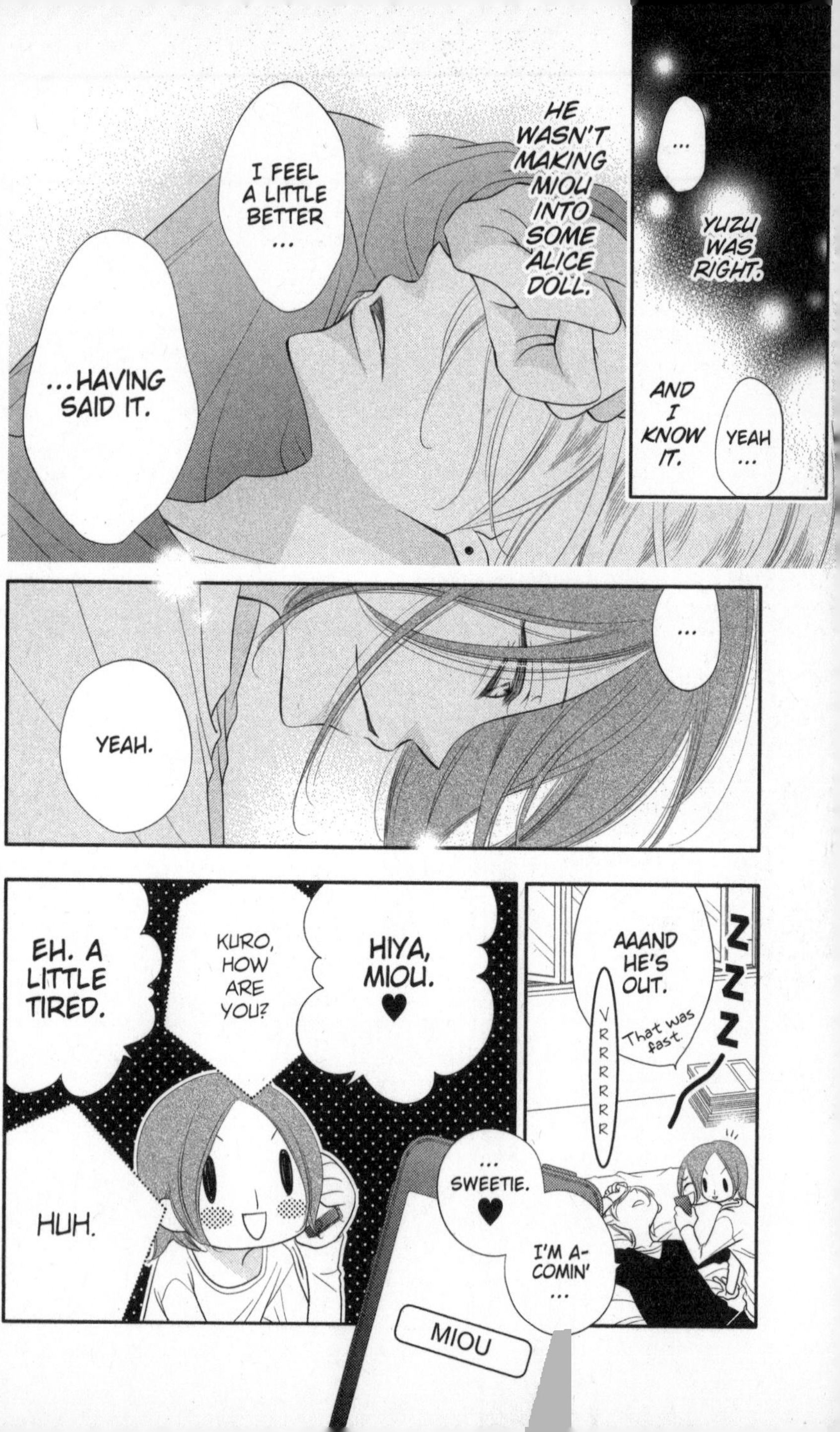
...
YUZU WAS RIGHT.
YEAH...
AND I KNOW IT.
HE WASN'T MAKING MIOU INTO SOME ALICE DOLL.
I FEEL A LITTLE BETTER...
...HAVING SAID IT.
...
YEAH.
AAAND HE'S OUT.
That was fast.
ZZZ
VRRRRRR
...SWEETIE.
I'M A-COMIN'...
MIOU
HIYA, MIOU.
KURO, HOW ARE YOU?
EH. A LITTLE TIRED.
HUH.

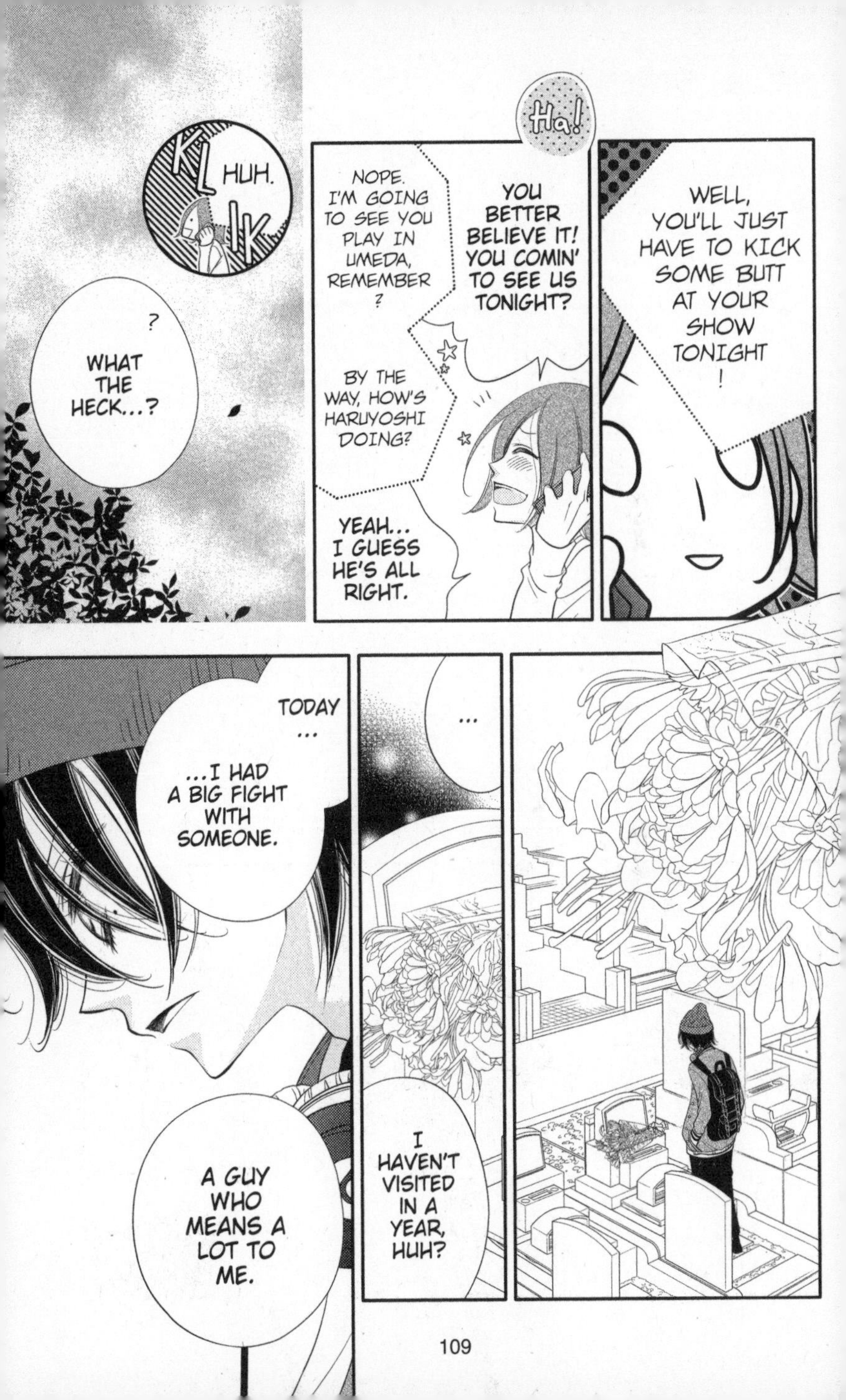
WELL, YOU'LL JUST HAVE TO KICK SOME BUTT AT YOUR SHOW TONIGHT!
Ha!
YOU BETTER BELIEVE IT! YOU COMIN' TO SEE US TONIGHT?
NOPE. I'M GOING TO SEE YOU PLAY IN UMEDA, REMEMBER?
BY THE WAY, HOW'S HARUYOSHI DOING?
YEAH... I GUESS HE'S ALL RIGHT.
KLIK
HUH.
WHAT THE HECK...?
...
I HAVEN'T VISITED IN A YEAR, HUH?
TODAY...
...I HAD A BIG FIGHT WITH SOMEONE.
A GUY WHO MEANS A LOT TO ME.

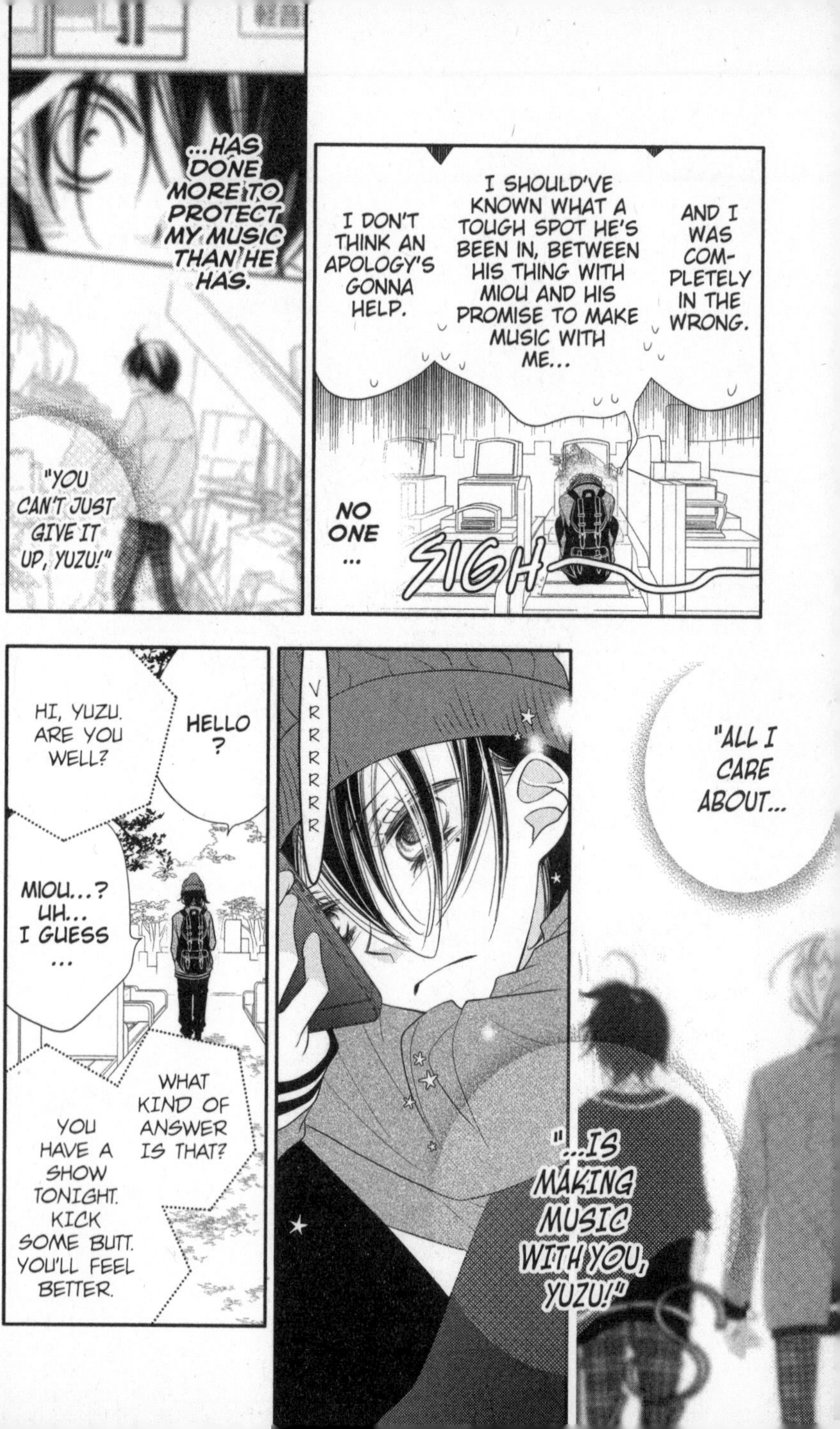
AND I WAS COMPLETELY IN THE WRONG.
I SHOULD'VE KNOWN WHAT A TOUGH SPOT HE'S BEEN IN, BETWEEN HIS THING WITH MIOU AND HIS PROMISE TO MAKE MUSIC WITH ME...
I DON'T THINK AN APOLOGY'S GONNA HELP.
SIGH
NO ONE...
...HAS DONE MORE TO PROTECT MY MUSIC THAN HE HAS.
"YOU CAN'T JUST GIVE IT UP, YUZU!"
"ALL I CARE ABOUT...
"...IS MAKING MUSIC WITH YOU, YUZU!"
VRRRRRR
HELLO?
HI, YUZU. ARE YOU WELL?
MIOU...? UH... I GUESS...
WHAT KIND OF ANSWER IS THAT?
YOU HAVE A SHOW TONIGHT. KICK SOME BUTT. YOU'LL FEEL BETTER.

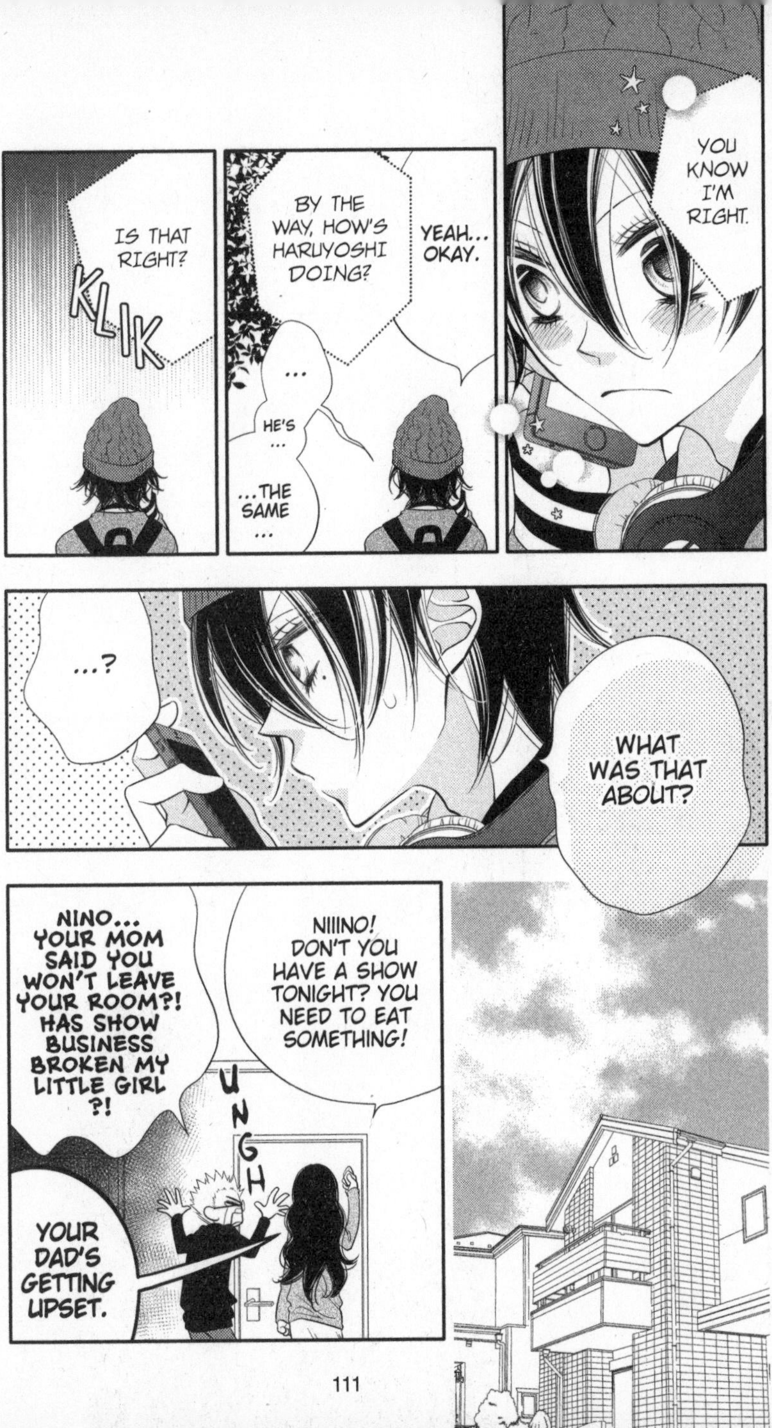
YOU KNOW I'M RIGHT.
YEAH... OKAY.
BY THE WAY, HOW'S HARUYOSHI DOING?
...
HE'S ...
...THE SAME ...
IS THAT RIGHT?
KLIK
WHAT WAS THAT ABOUT?
...?
NIIINO! DON'T YOU HAVE A SHOW TONIGHT? YOU NEED TO EAT SOMETHING!
NINO... YOUR MOM SAID YOU WON'T LEAVE YOUR ROOM?! HAS SHOW BUSINESS BROKEN MY LITTLE GIRL ?!
UNGH
YOUR DAD'S GETTING UPSET.

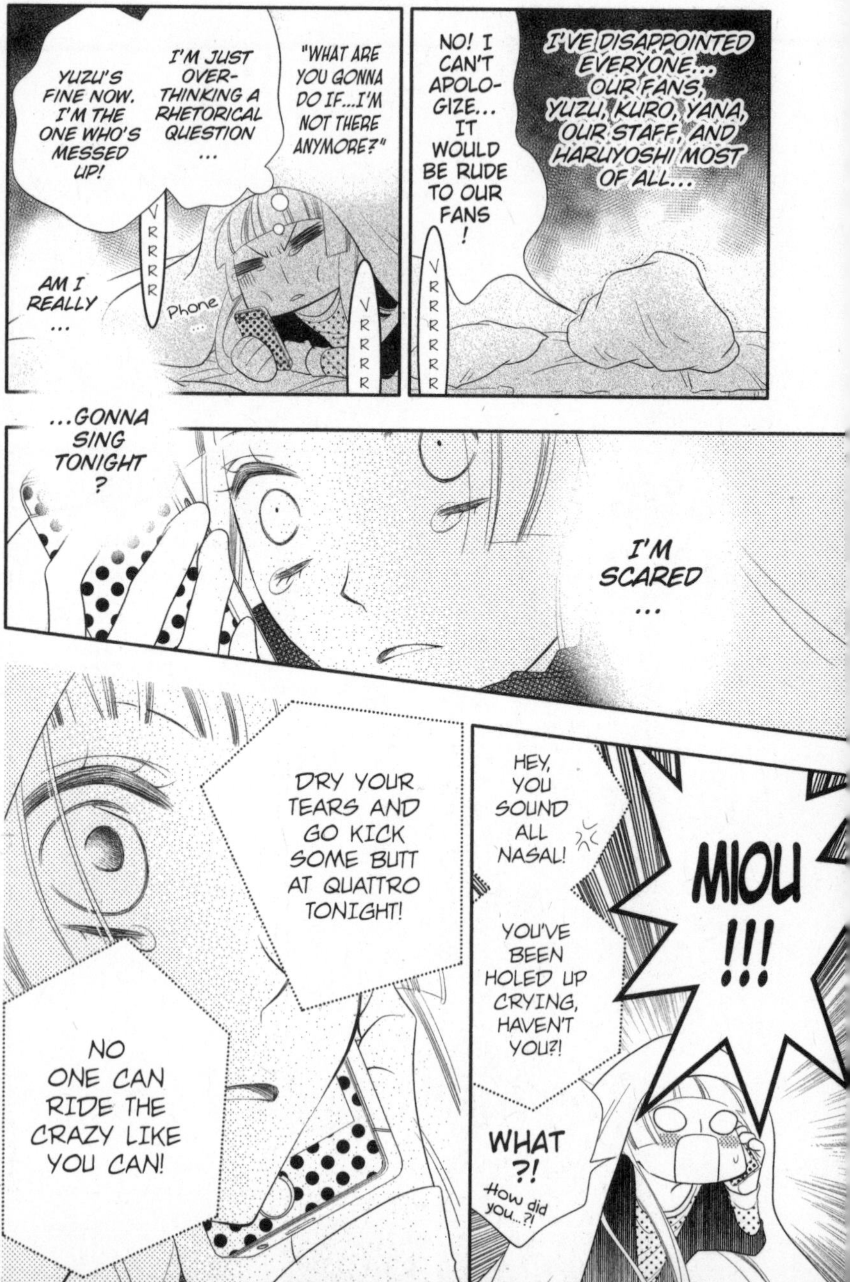
I'VE DISAPPOINTED EVERYONE... OUR FANS, YUZU, KURO, YANA, OUR STAFF, AND HARUYOSHI MOST OF ALL...
NO! I CAN'T APOLOGIZE... IT WOULD BE RUDE TO OUR FANS!
VRRRRR
"WHAT ARE YOU GONNA DO IF...I'M NOT THERE ANYMORE?"
I'M JUST OVER-THINKING A RHETORICAL QUESTION...
YUZU'S FINE NOW. I'M THE ONE WHO'S MESSED UP!
VRRRR
VRRRR
Phone...
AM I REALLY...
...GONNA SING TONIGHT?
I'M SCARED...
MIOU!!!
HEY, YOU SOUND ALL NASAL!
YOU'VE BEEN HOLED UP CRYING, HAVEN'T YOU?!
WHAT?!
How did you...?!
DRY YOUR TEARS AND GO KICK SOME BUTT AT QUATTRO TONIGHT!
NO ONE CAN RIDE THE CRAZY LIKE YOU CAN!

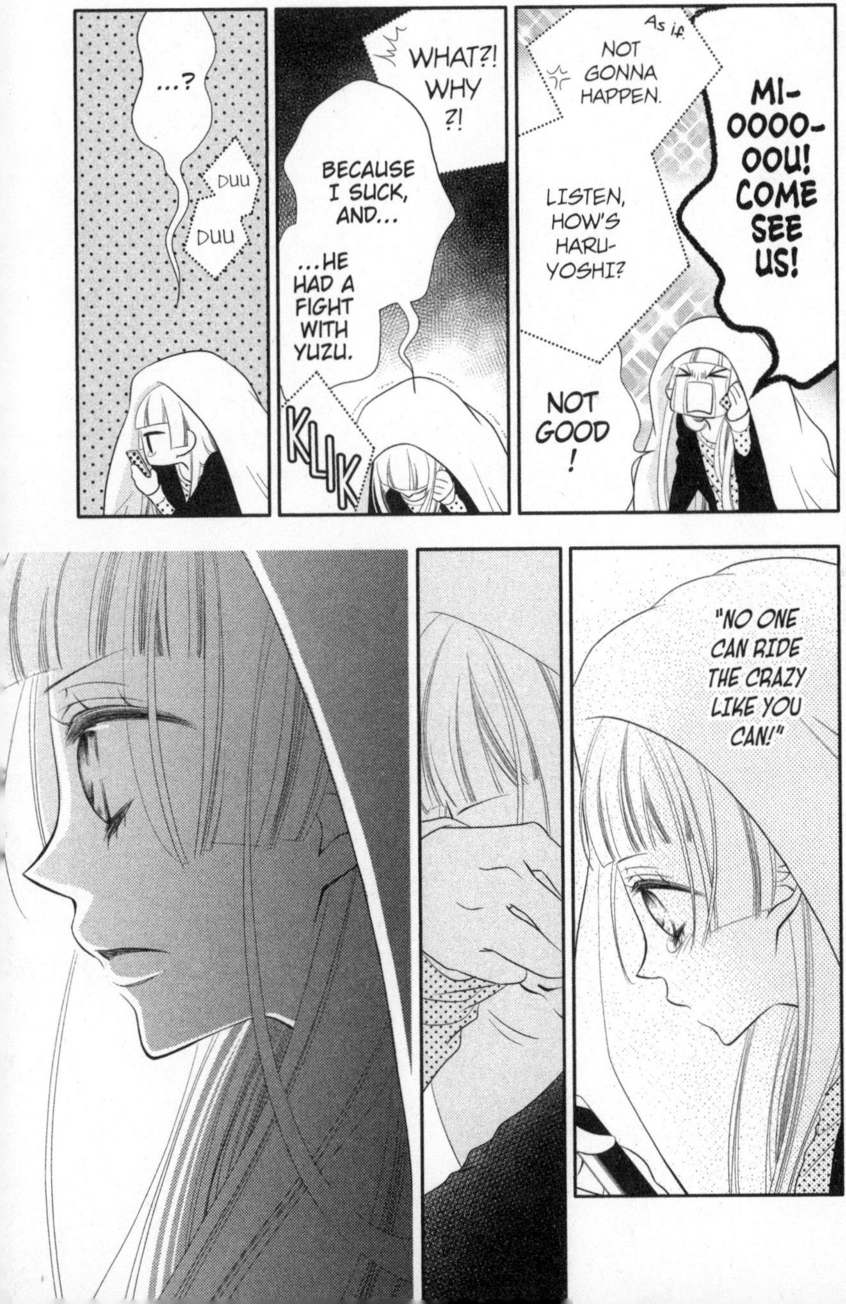
MI-OOOO-OOU! COME SEE US!
As if.
NOT GONNA HAPPEN.
LISTEN, HOW'S HARU-YOSHI?
NOT GOOD!
WHAT?! WHY?!
BECAUSE I SUCK, AND...
...HE HAD A FIGHT WITH YUZU.
KLIK
...?
DUU
DUU
"NO ONE CAN RIDE THE CRAZY LIKE YOU CAN!"

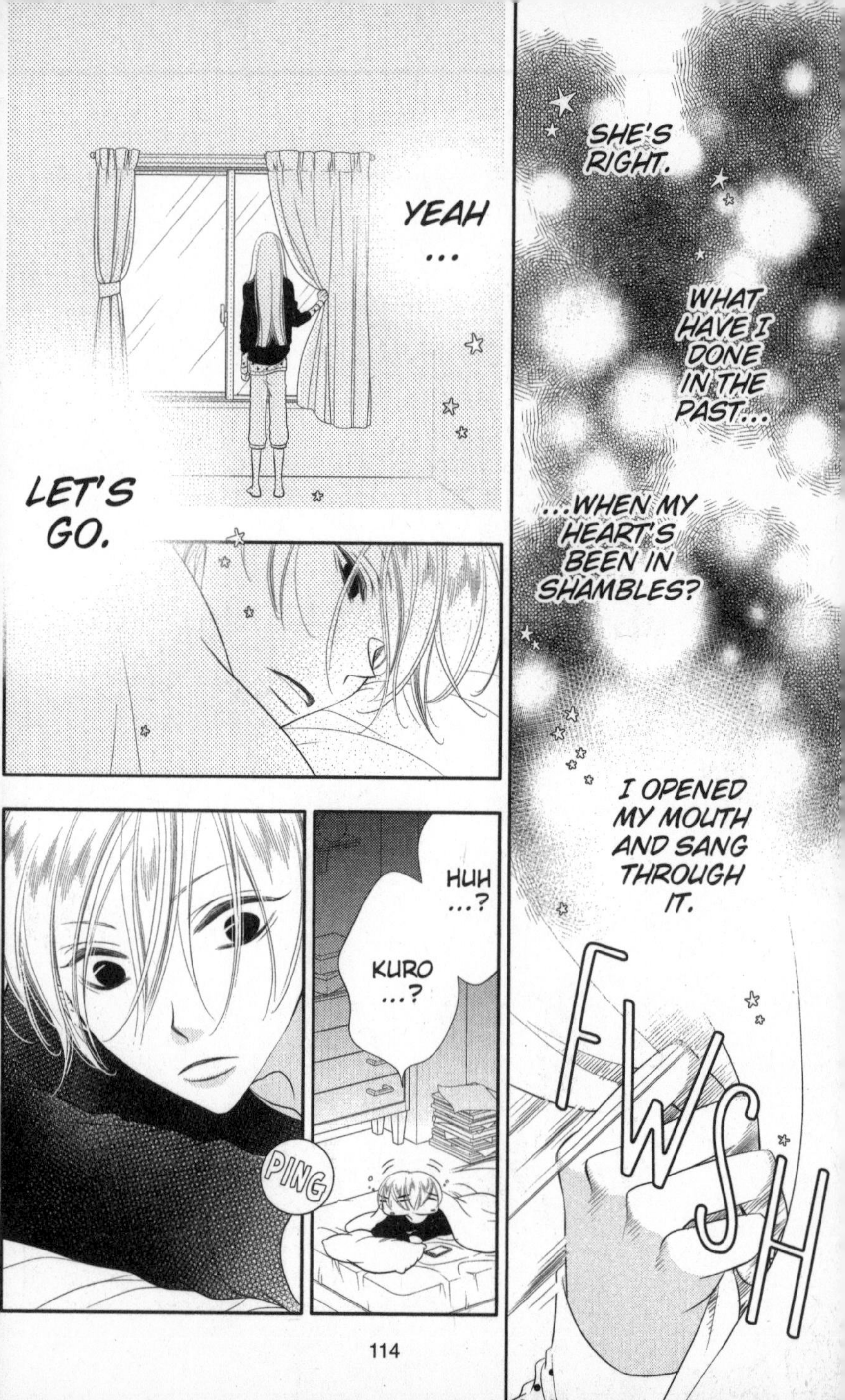

SHE'S RIGHT.
WHAT HAVE I DONE IN THE PAST...
...WHEN MY HEART'S BEEN IN SHAMBLES?
I OPENED MY MOUTH AND SANG THROUGH IT.
FWSH
YEAH ...
LET'S GO.
HUH ...?
KURO ...?
PING

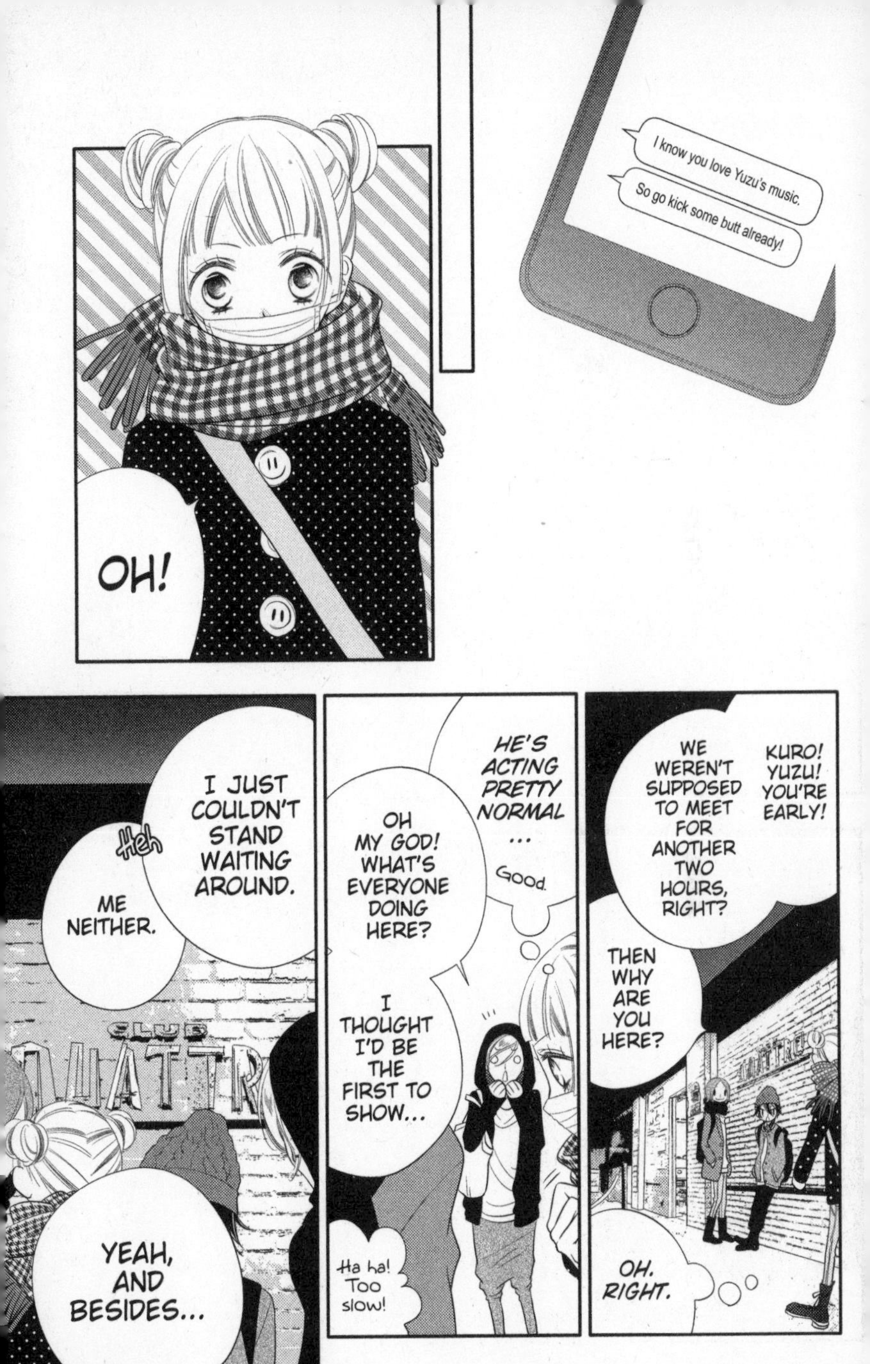
I know you love Yuzu's music.
So go kick some butt already!
OH!
KURO! YUZU! YOU'RE EARLY!
WE WEREN'T SUPPOSED TO MEET FOR ANOTHER TWO HOURS, RIGHT?
THEN WHY ARE YOU HERE?
OH. RIGHT.
HE'S ACTING PRETTY NORMAL ...
Good.
OH MY GOD! WHAT'S EVERYONE DOING HERE?
I THOUGHT I'D BE THE FIRST TO SHOW...
Ha ha! Too slow!
I JUST COULDN'T STAND WAITING AROUND.
Heh
ME NEITHER.
CLUB
YEAH, AND BESIDES...

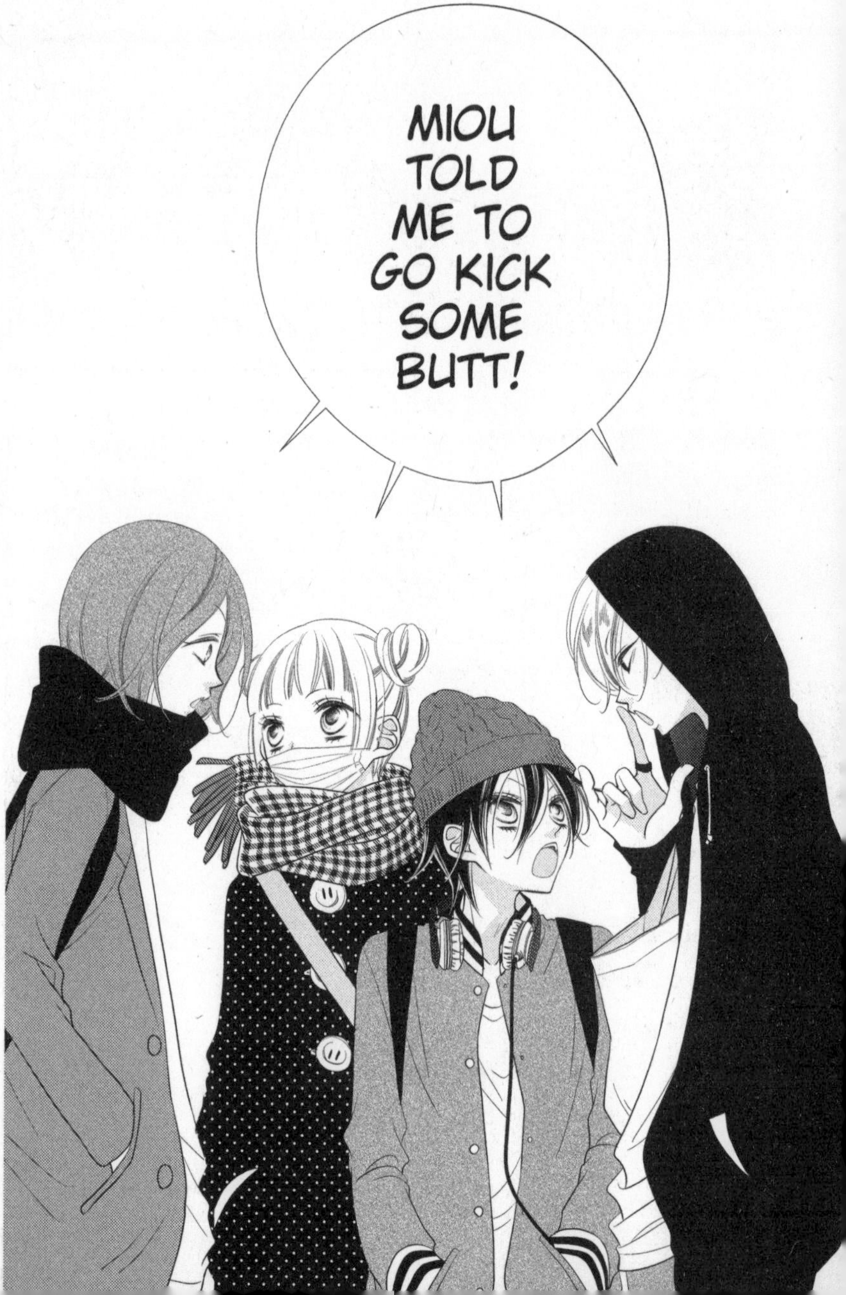
MIOU TOLD ME TO GO KICK SOME BUTT!

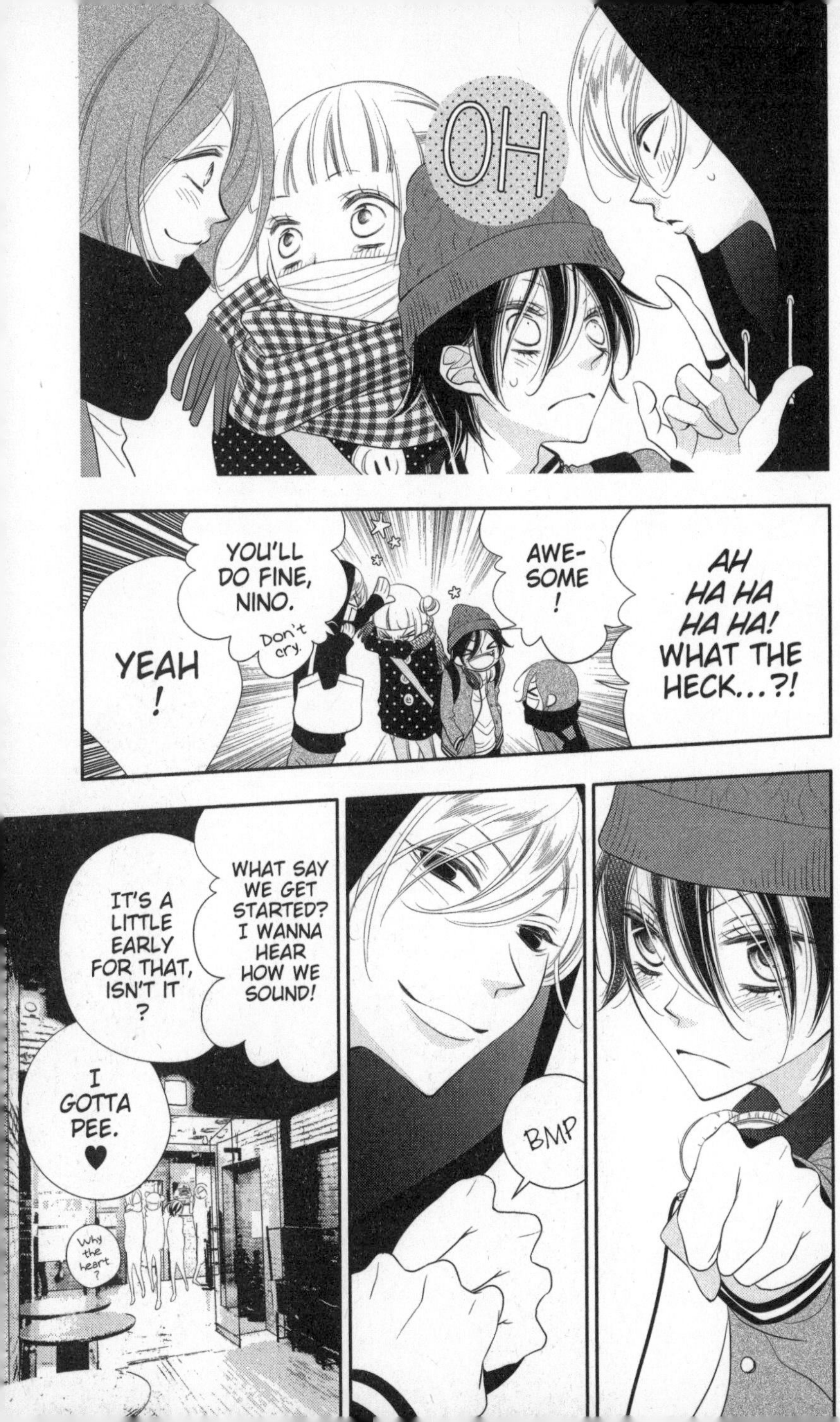
OH
AH HA HA HA HA! WHAT THE HECK...?!
AWE-SOME!
YOU'LL DO FINE, NINO.
Don't cry.
YEAH!
BMP
WHAT SAY WE GET STARTED? I WANNA HEAR HOW WE SOUND!
IT'S A LITTLE EARLY FOR THAT, ISN'T IT?
I GOTTA PEE. ♥
Why the heart?

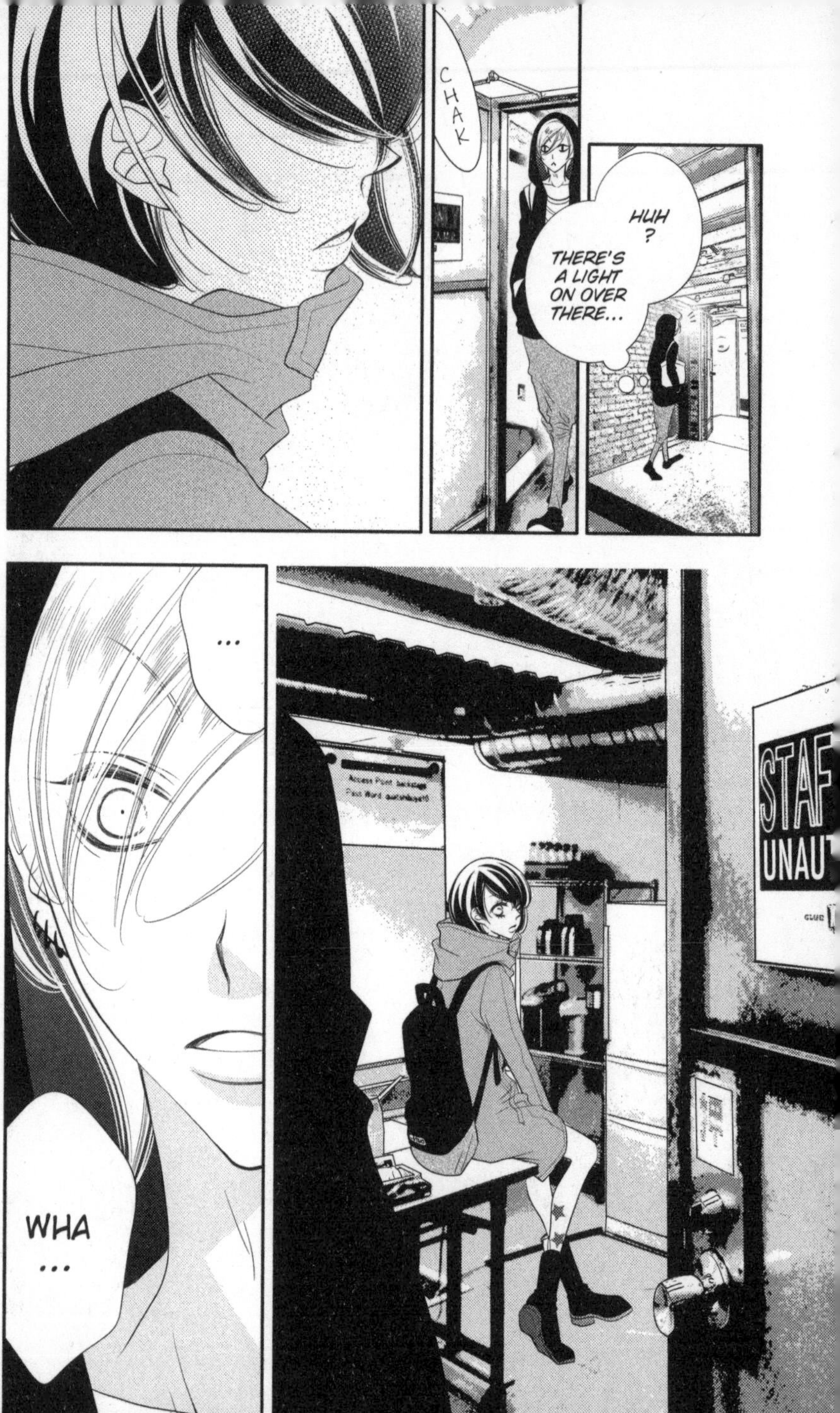

HUH?
THERE'S A LIGHT ON OVER THERE...
CHAK
STAF
UNAU
...
WHA...

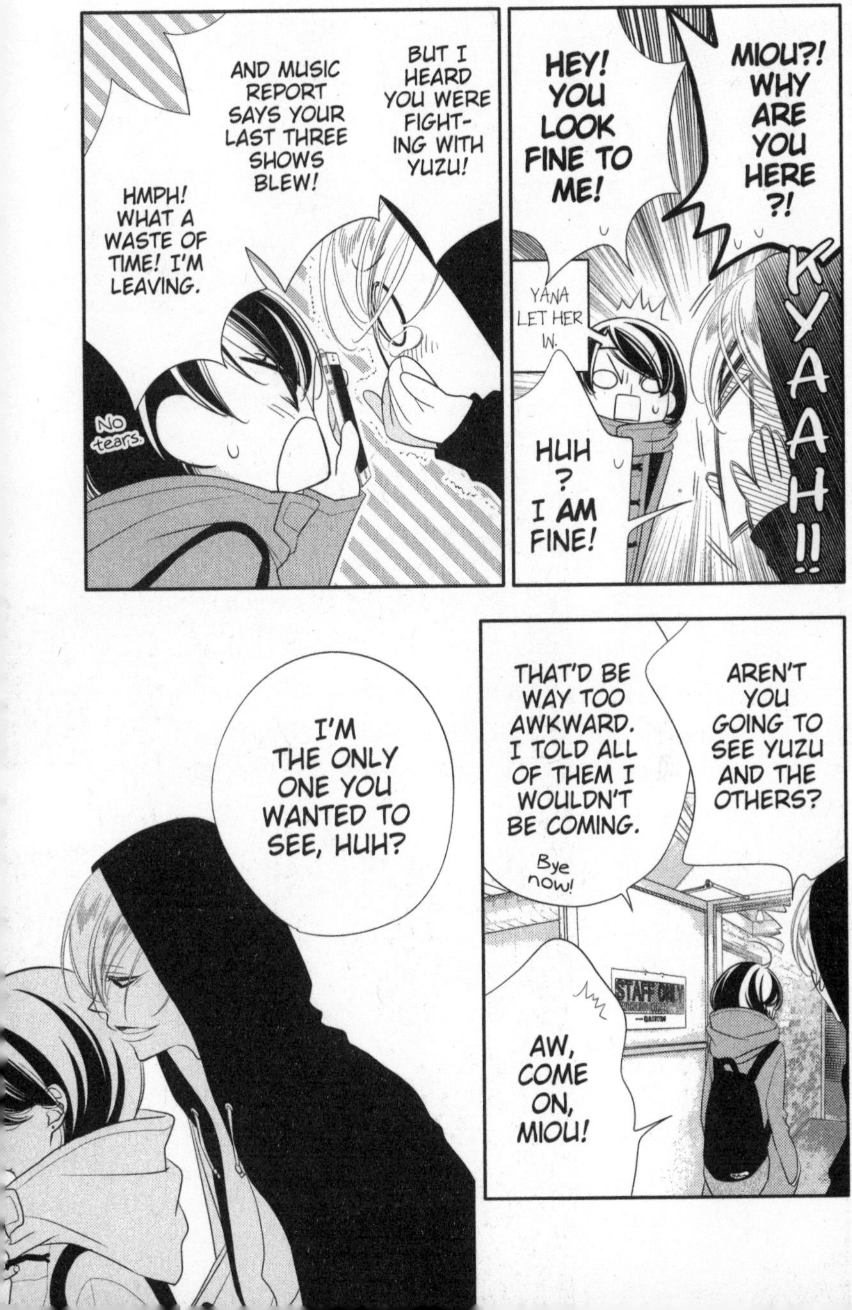
MIOU?! WHY ARE YOU HERE?!
KYAAAH!!
HEY! YOU LOOK FINE TO ME!
YANA LET HER IN.
HUH? I AM FINE!
BUT I HEARD YOU WERE FIGHT-ING WITH YUZU!
AND MUSIC REPORT SAYS YOUR LAST THREE SHOWS BLEW!
HMPH! WHAT A WASTE OF TIME! I'M LEAVING.
No tears.
AREN'T YOU GOING TO SEE YUZU AND THE OTHERS?
THAT'D BE WAY TOO AWKWARD. I TOLD ALL OF THEM I WOULDN'T BE COMING.
Bye now!
AW, COME ON, MIOU!
I'M THE ONLY ONE YOU WANTED TO SEE, HUH?

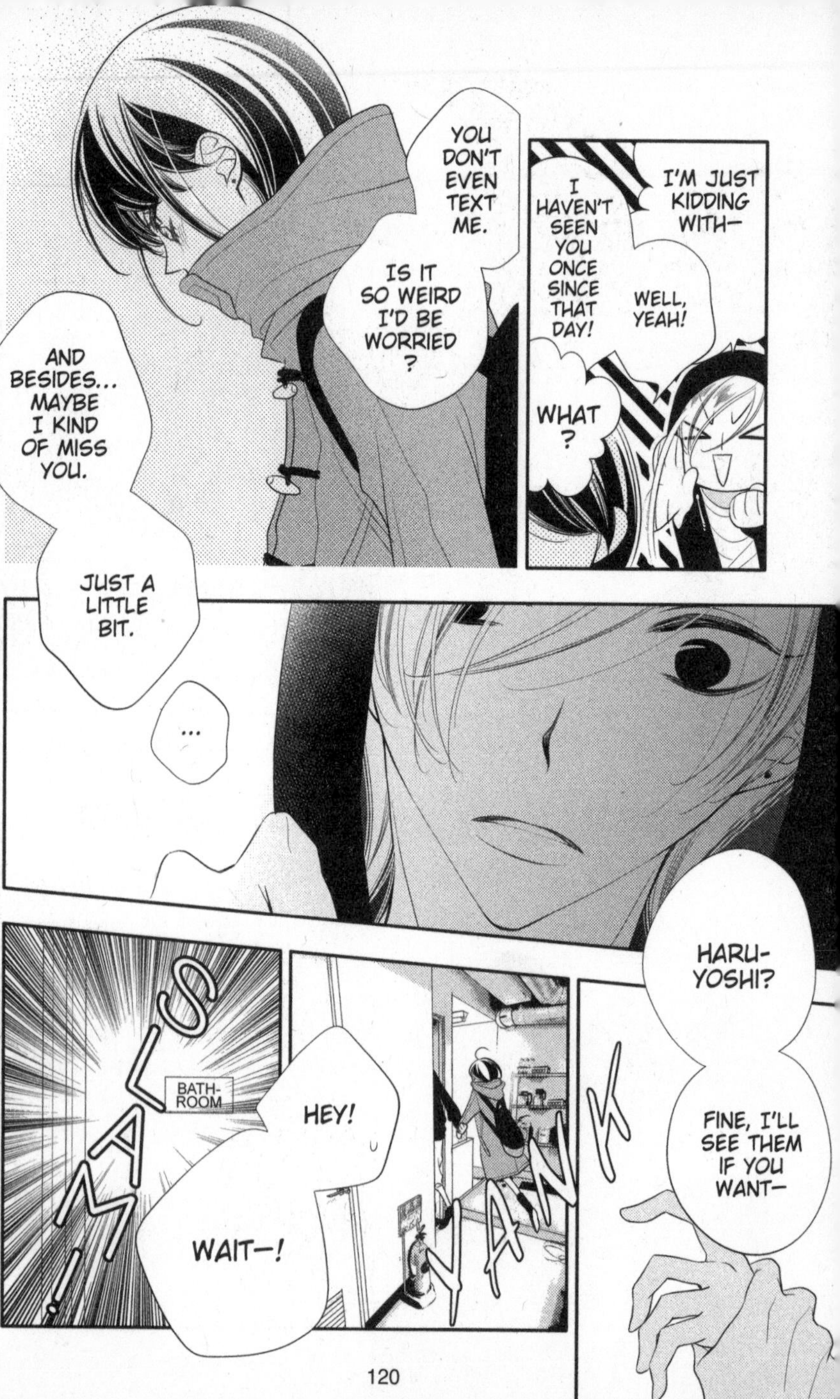
I'M JUST KIDDING WITH—
I HAVEN'T SEEN YOU ONCE SINCE THAT DAY!
WELL, YEAH!
WHAT?
YOU DON'T EVEN TEXT ME.
IS IT SO WEIRD I'D BE WORRIED?
AND BESIDES... MAYBE I KIND OF MISS YOU.
JUST A LITTLE BIT.
...
HARU-YOSHI?
FINE, I'LL SEE THEM IF YOU WANT—
YANK
HEY!
WAIT—!
SLAM
BATH-ROOM

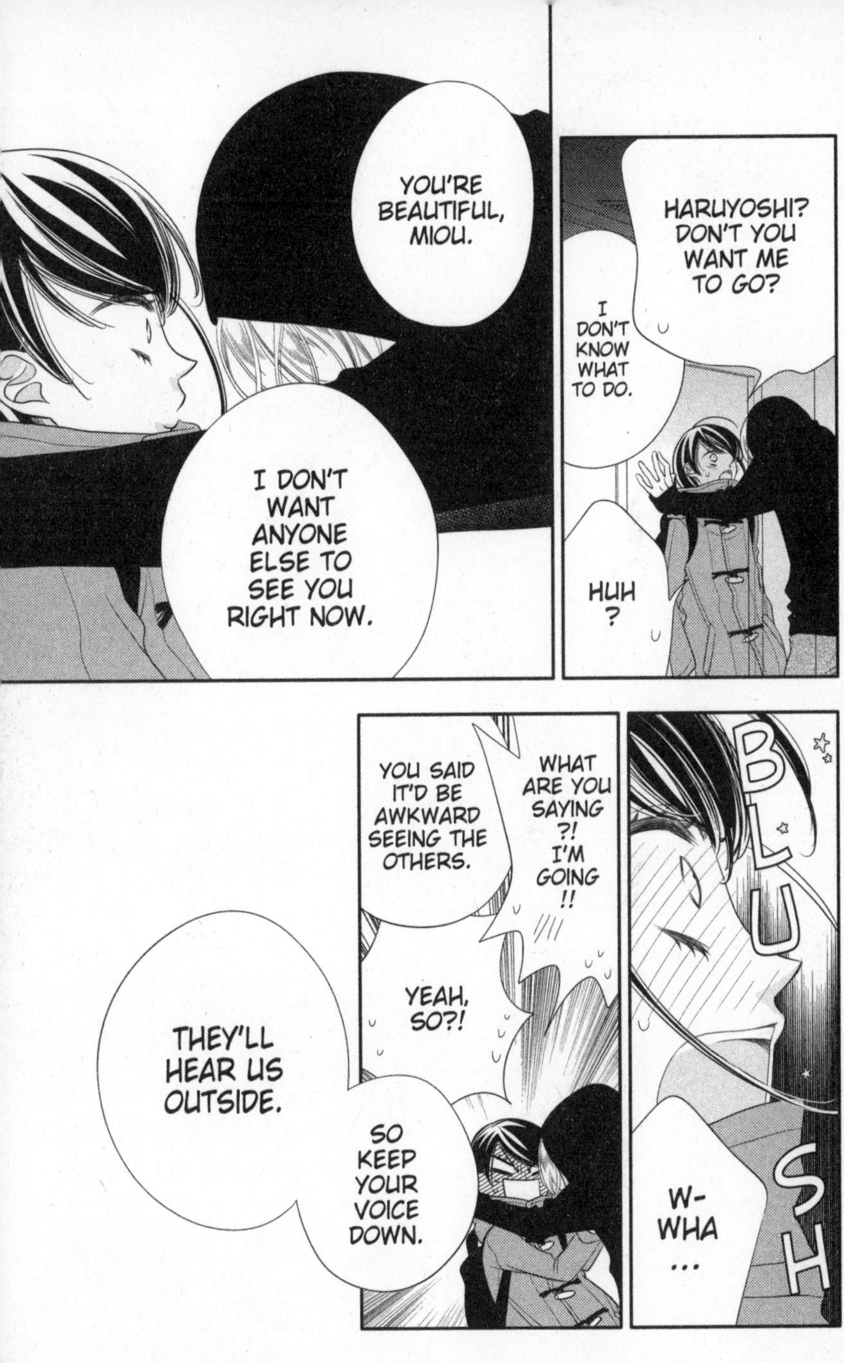
HARUYOSHI? DON'T YOU WANT ME TO GO?
I DON'T KNOW WHAT TO DO.
HUH?
YOU'RE BEAUTIFUL, MIOU.
I DON'T WANT ANYONE ELSE TO SEE YOU RIGHT NOW.
BLUSH
W-WHA...
WHAT ARE YOU SAYING?! I'M GOING!!
YOU SAID IT'D BE AWKWARD SEEING THE OTHERS.
YEAH, SO?!
THEY'LL HEAR US OUTSIDE.
SO KEEP YOUR VOICE DOWN.

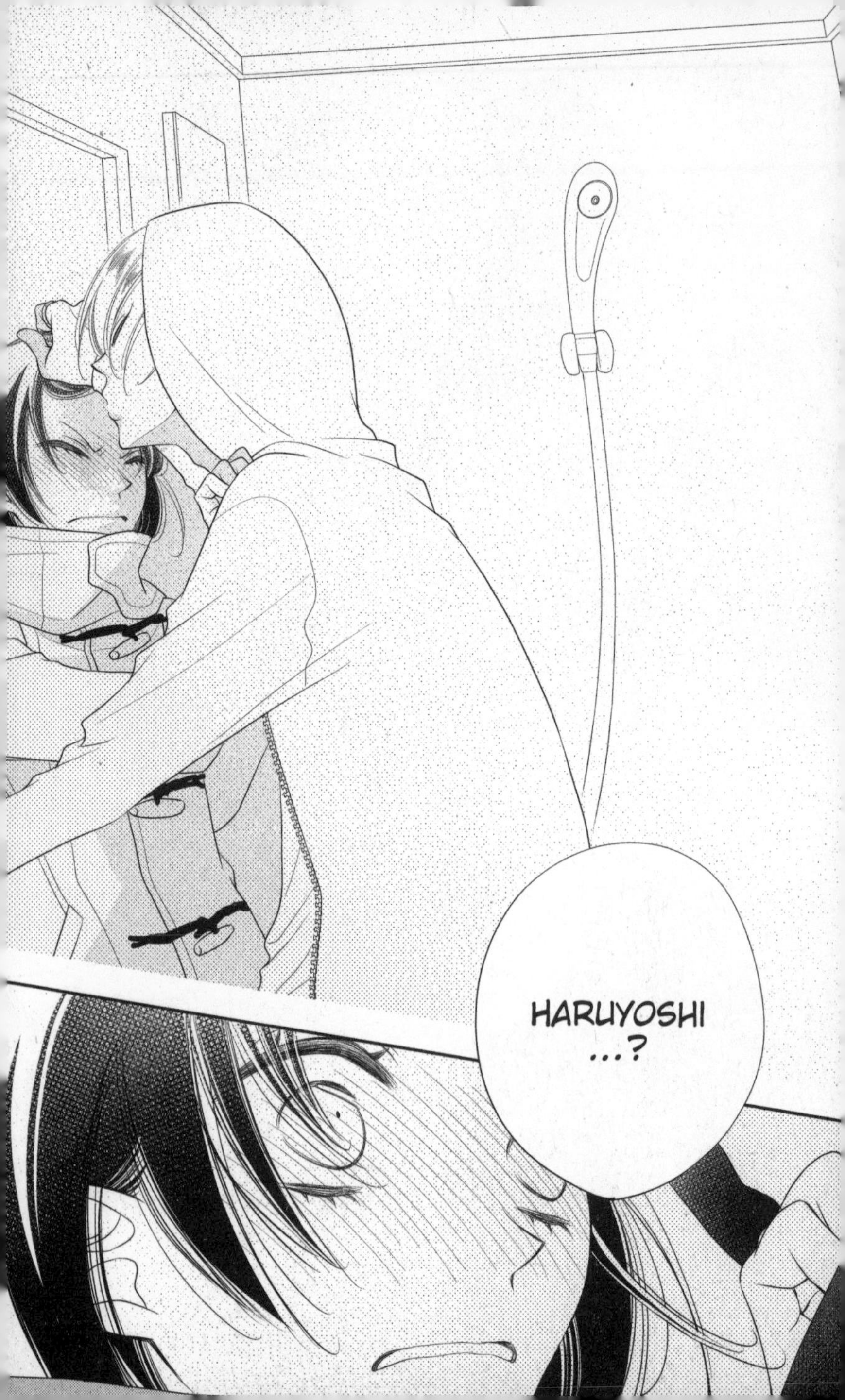
HARUYOSHI ...?

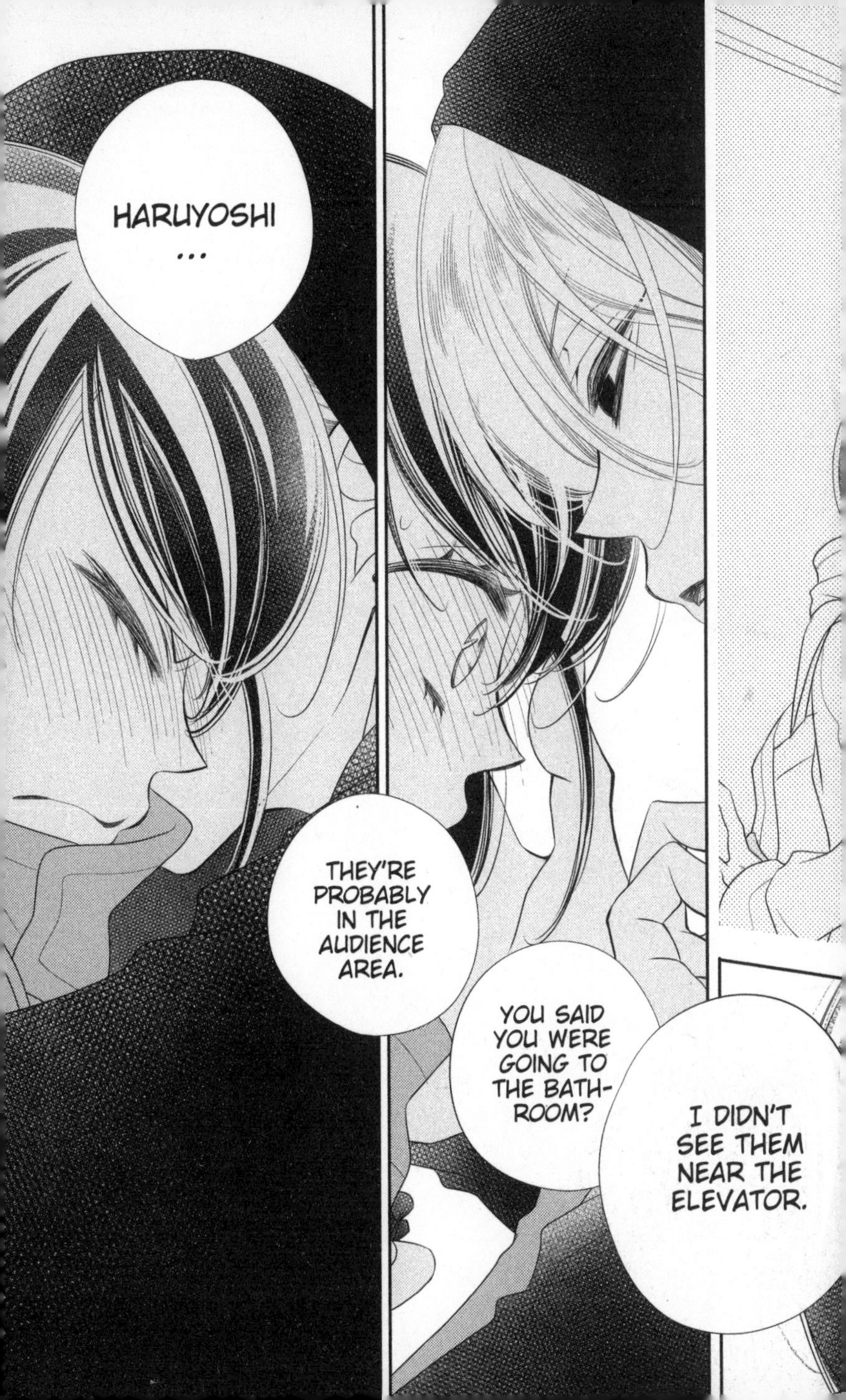
I DIDN'T SEE THEM NEAR THE ELEVATOR.
YOU SAID YOU WERE GOING TO THE BATH-ROOM?
THEY'RE PROBABLY IN THE AUDIENCE AREA.
HARUYOSHI ...

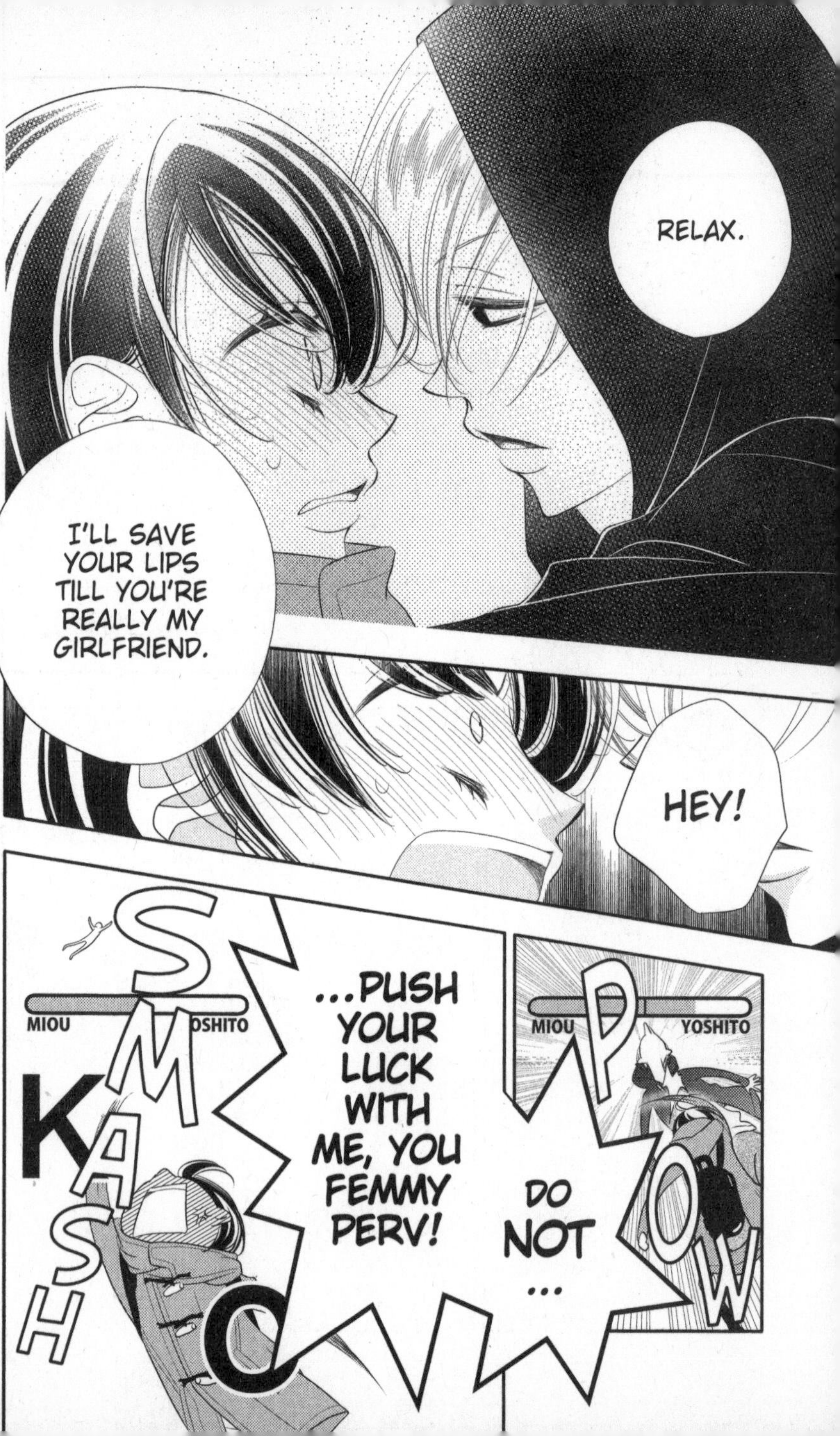
RELAX.
I'LL SAVE YOUR LIPS TILL YOU'RE REALLY MY GIRLFRIEND.
HEY!
MIOU
YOSHITO
POW
DO NOT ...
...PUSH YOUR LUCK WITH ME, YOU FEMMY PERV!
MIOU
YOSHITO
SMASH

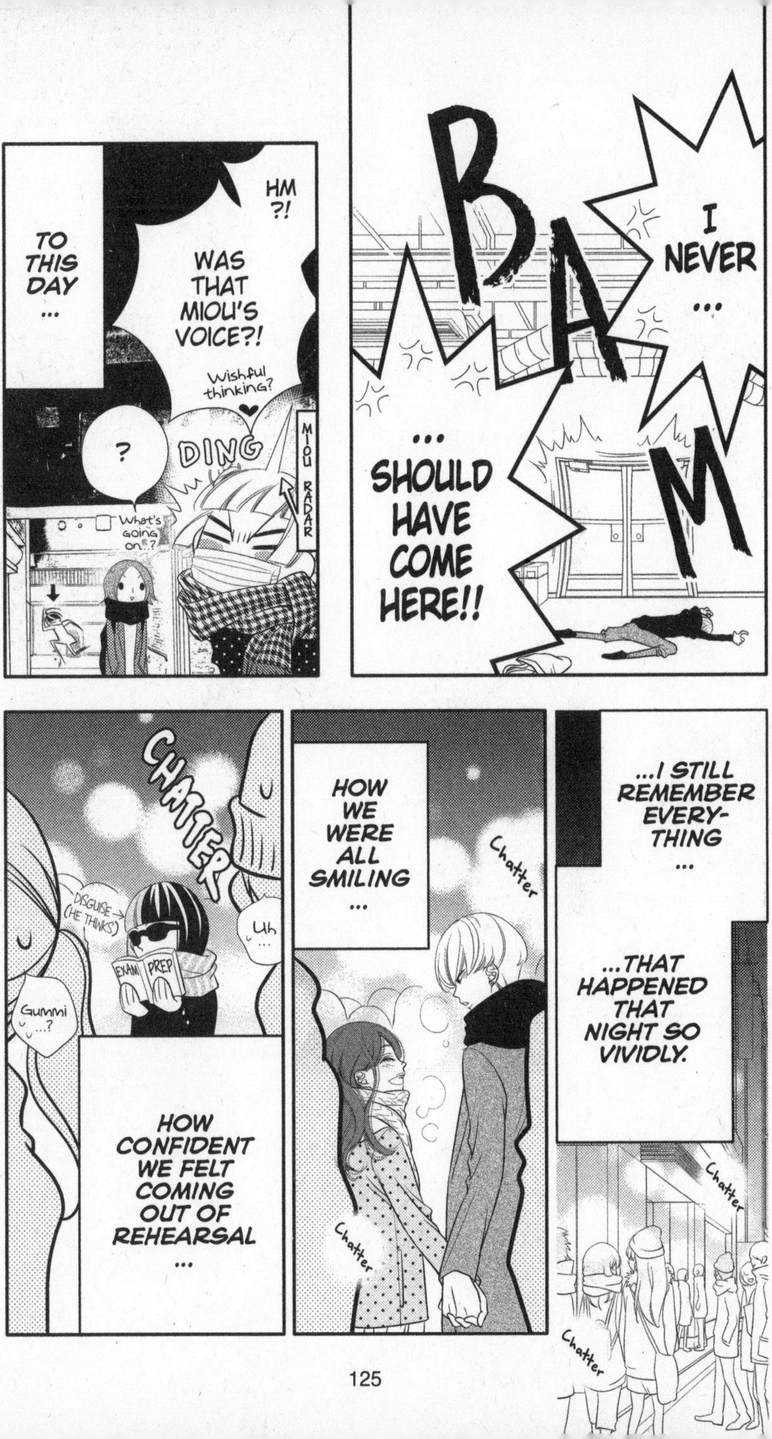
BAM
I NEVER ...
... SHOULD HAVE COME HERE!!
HM ?!
WAS THAT MIOU'S VOICE?!
TO THIS DAY ...
Wishful thinking?
MIOU RADAR
DING
?
What's going on..?
...I STILL REMEMBER EVERY-THING ...
...THAT HAPPENED THAT NIGHT SO VIVIDLY.
Chatter
Chatter
HOW WE WERE ALL SMILING ...
Chatter
Chatter
CHATTER
Uh ...
DISGUISE (HE THINKS)
EXAM PREP
Gummi ...?
HOW CONFIDENT WE FELT COMING OUT OF REHEARSAL ...

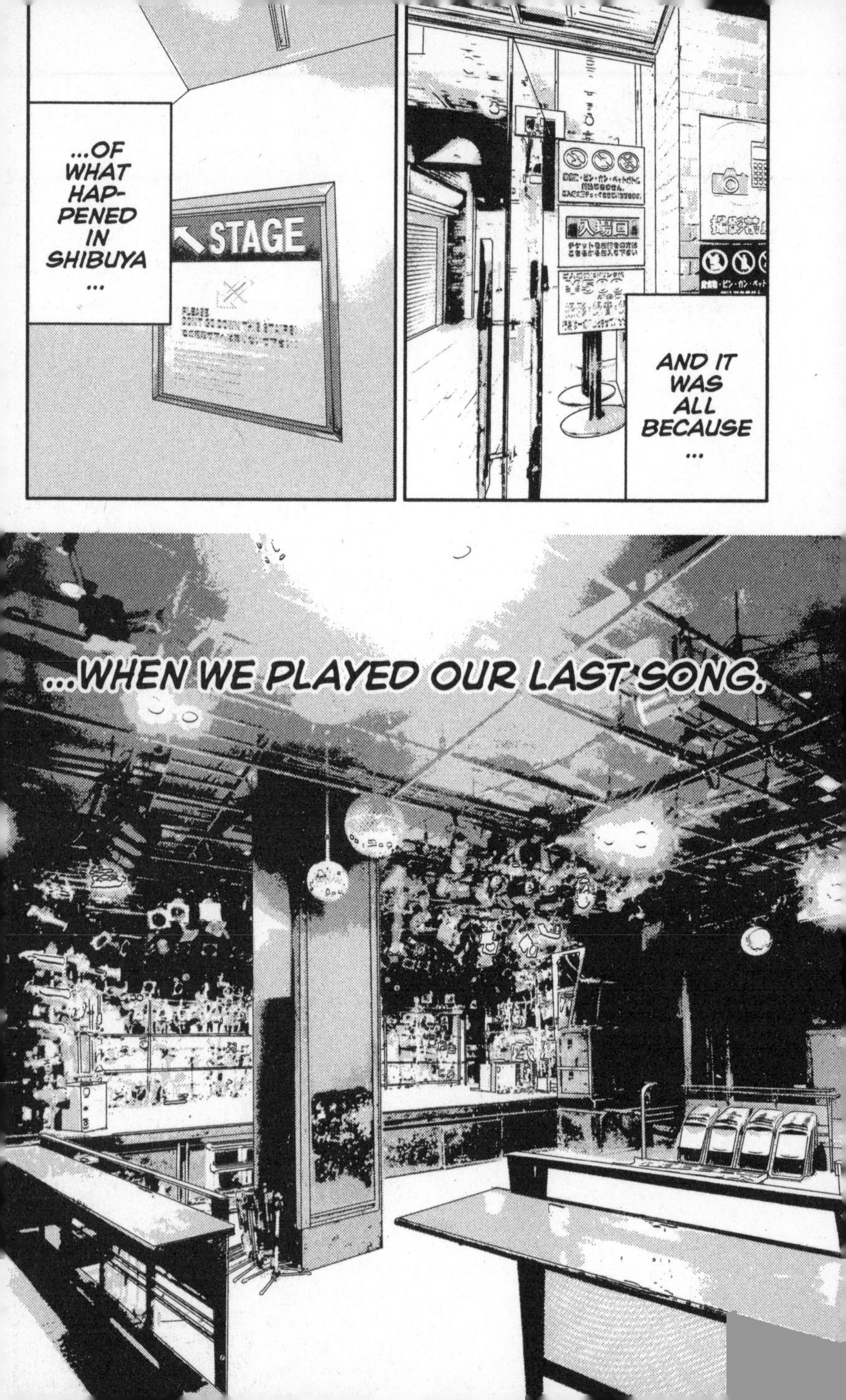
入場口
AND IT WAS ALL BECAUSE ...
...OF WHAT HAP-PENED IN SHIBUYA ...
STAGE
...WHEN WE PLAYED OUR LAST SONG.

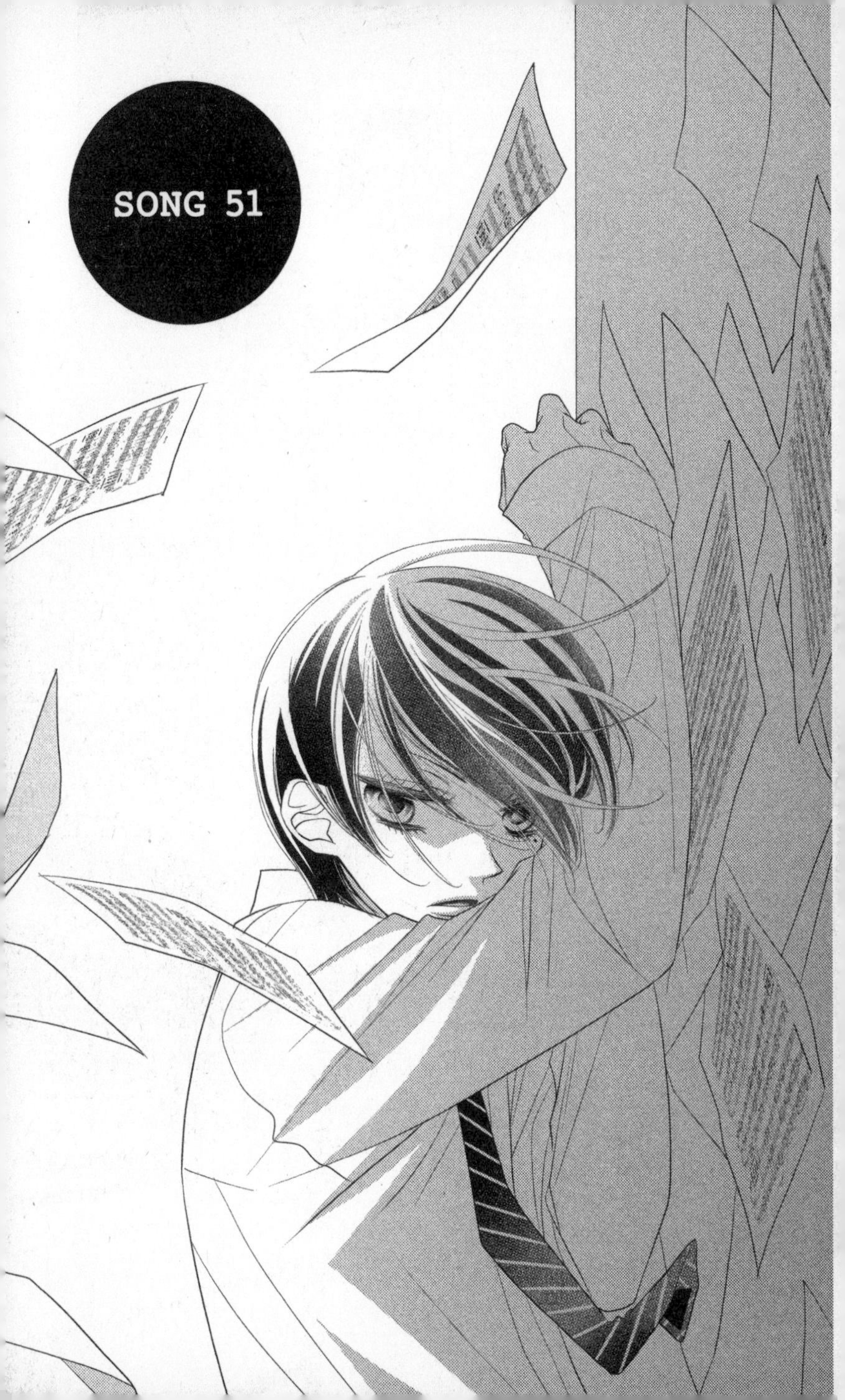
SONG 51

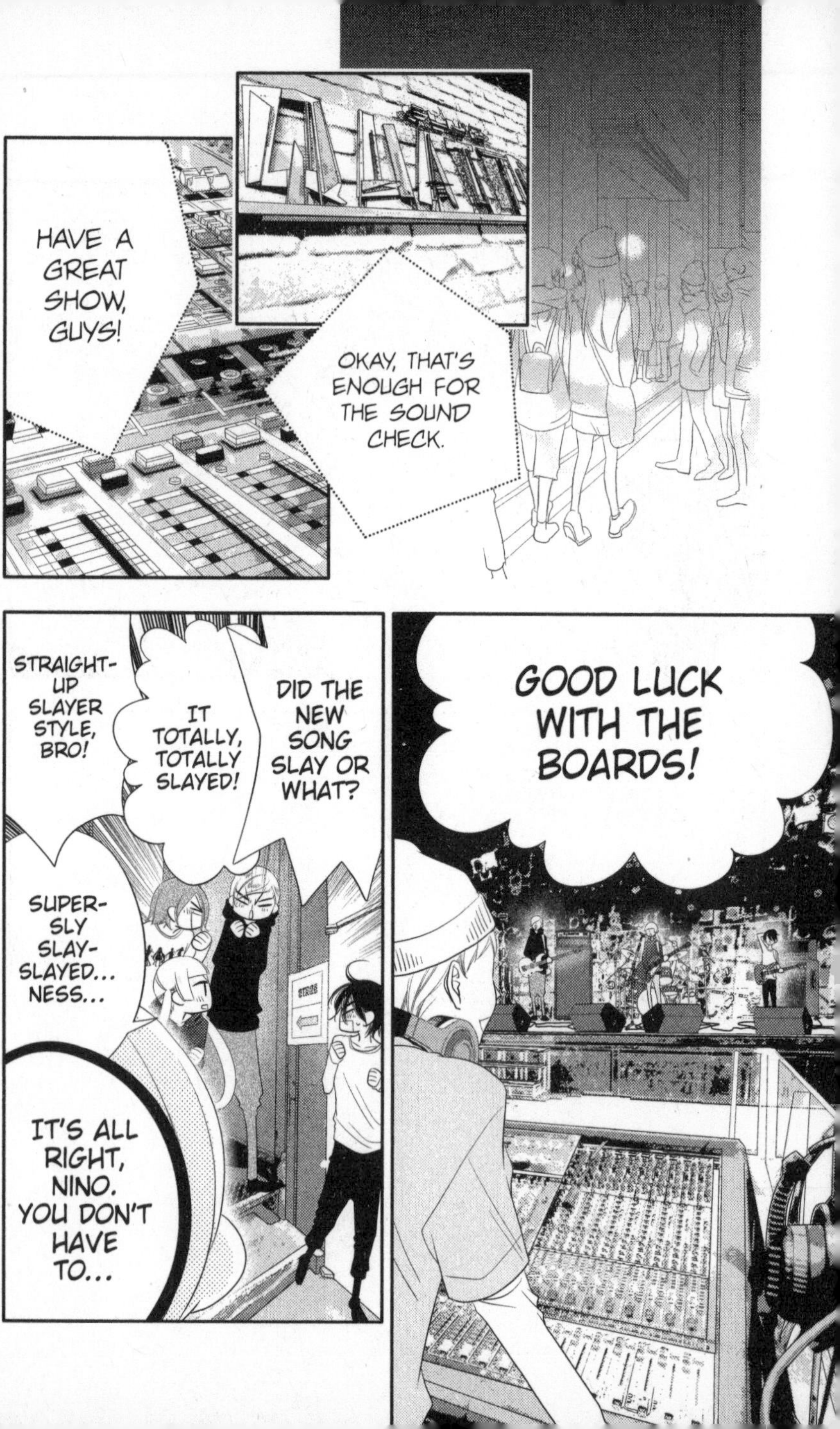
OKAY, THAT'S ENOUGH FOR THE SOUND CHECK.
HAVE A GREAT SHOW, GUYS!
GOOD LUCK WITH THE BOARDS!
DID THE NEW SONG SLAY OR WHAT?
IT TOTALLY, TOTALLY SLAYED!
STRAIGHT-UP SLAYER STYLE, BRO!
SUPER-SLY SLAY-SLAYED... NESS...
IT'S ALL RIGHT, NINO. YOU DON'T HAVE TO...

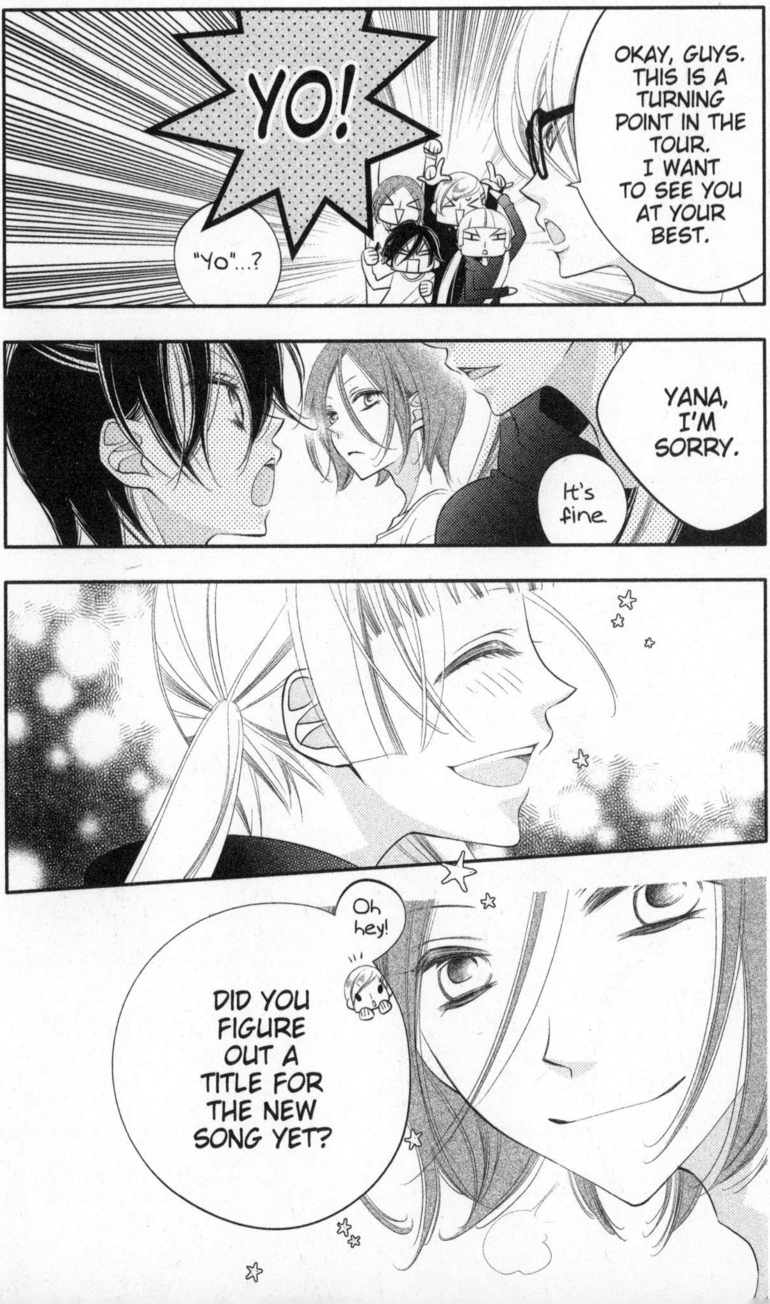
OKAY, GUYS. THIS IS A TURNING POINT IN THE TOUR. I WANT TO SEE YOU AT YOUR BEST.
YO!
"Yo"...?
YANA, I'M SORRY.
It's fine.
Oh hey!
DID YOU FIGURE OUT A TITLE FOR THE NEW SONG YET?

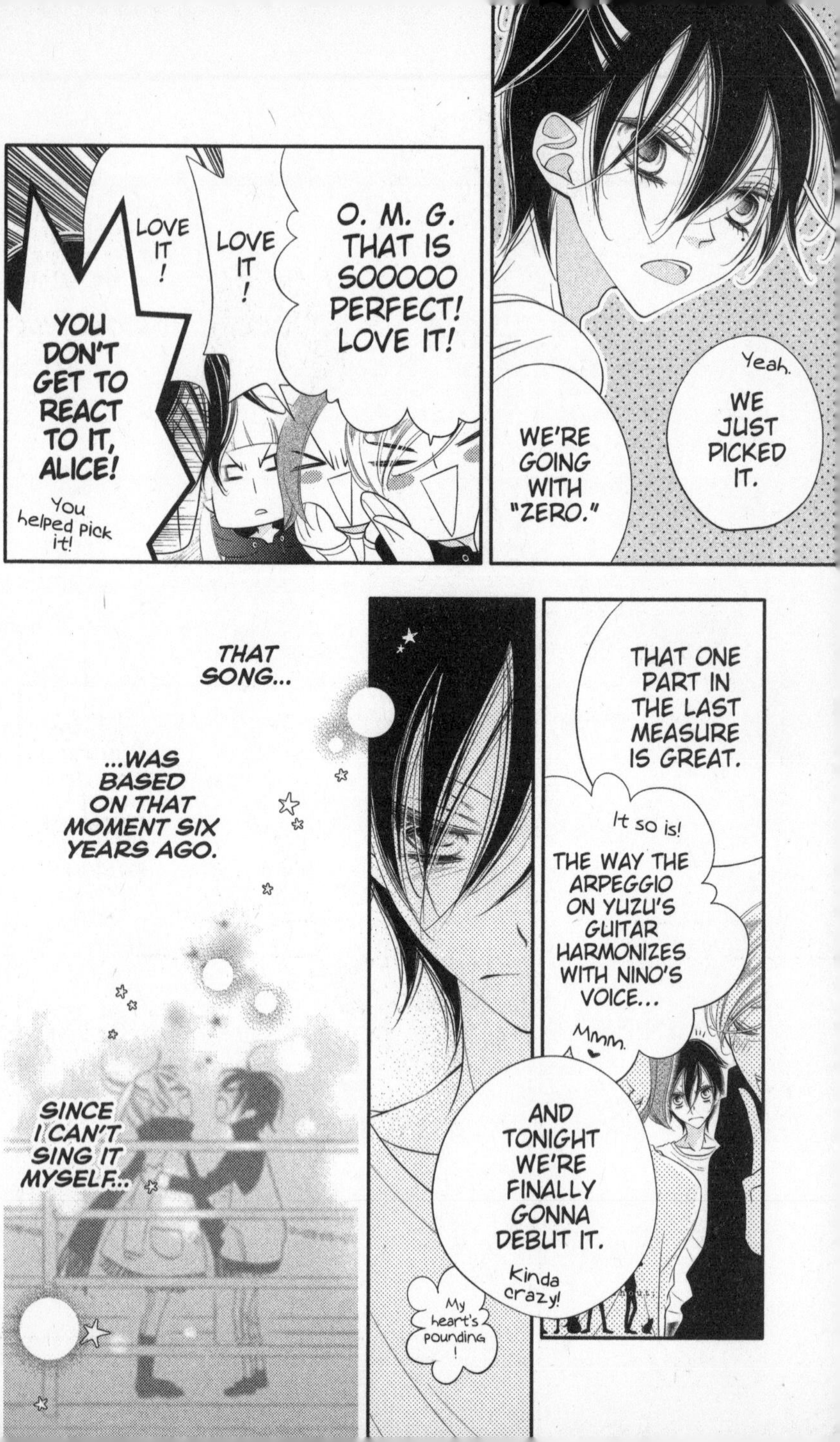
Yeah.
WE JUST PICKED IT.
WE'RE GOING WITH "ZERO."
O. M. G. THAT IS SOOOOO PERFECT! LOVE IT!
LOVE IT!
LOVE IT!
YOU DON'T GET TO REACT TO IT, ALICE!
You helped pick it!
THAT ONE PART IN THE LAST MEASURE IS GREAT.
It so is!
THE WAY THE ARPEGGIO ON YUZU'S GUITAR HARMONIZES WITH NINO'S VOICE...
Mmm.
AND TONIGHT WE'RE FINALLY GONNA DEBUT IT.
Kinda crazy!
My heart's pounding!
THAT SONG...
...WAS BASED ON THAT MOMENT SIX YEARS AGO.
SINCE I CAN'T SING IT MYSELF...

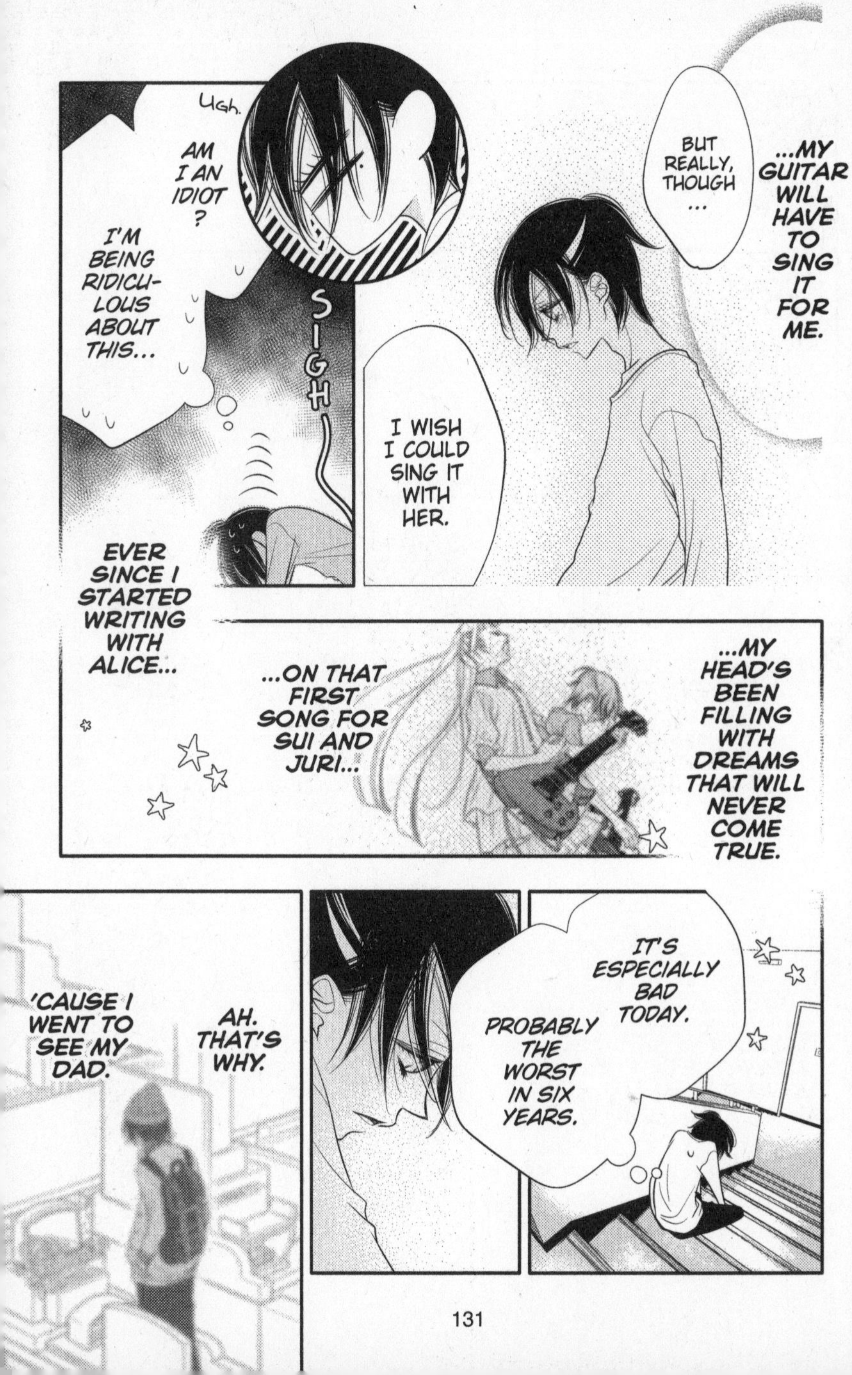
...MY GUITAR WILL HAVE TO SING IT FOR ME.
BUT REALLY, THOUGH...
I WISH I COULD SING IT WITH HER.
Ugh.
AM I AN IDIOT?
I'M BEING RIDICU-LOUS ABOUT THIS...
SIGH
EVER SINCE I STARTED WRITING WITH ALICE...
...MY HEAD'S BEEN FILLING WITH DREAMS THAT WILL NEVER COME TRUE.
...ON THAT FIRST SONG FOR SUI AND JURI...
IT'S ESPECIALLY BAD TODAY.
PROBABLY THE WORST IN SIX YEARS.
AH. THAT'S WHY.
'CAUSE I WENT TO SEE MY DAD.

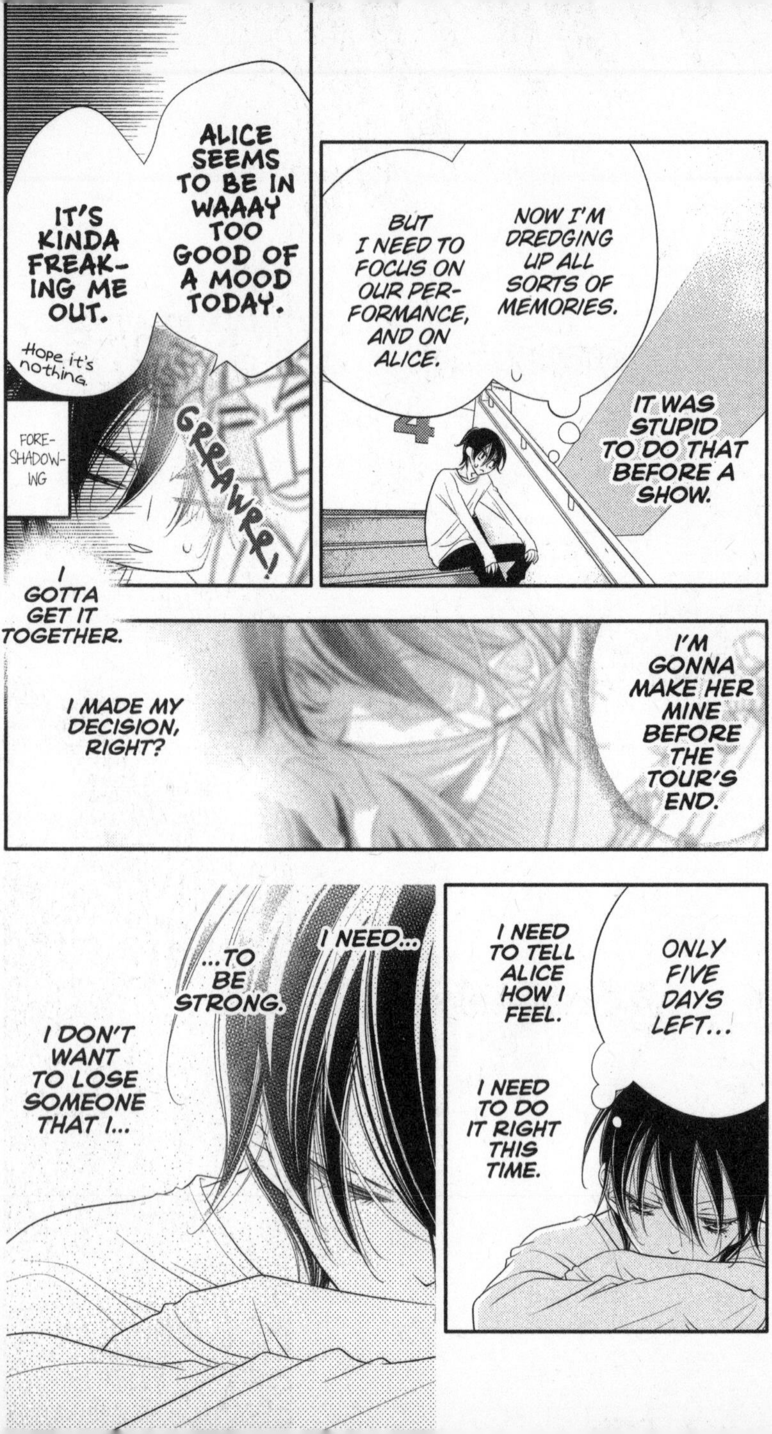
NOW I'M DREDGING UP ALL SORTS OF MEMORIES.
BUT I NEED TO FOCUS ON OUR PER-FORMANCE, AND ON ALICE.
IT WAS STUPID TO DO THAT BEFORE A SHOW.
ALICE SEEMS TO BE IN WAAAY TOO GOOD OF A MOOD TODAY.
IT'S KINDA FREAK-ING ME OUT.
Hope it's nothing.
GRRAWRR!
FORE-SHADOW-ING
I'M GONNA MAKE HER MINE BEFORE THE TOUR'S END.
I MADE MY DECISION, RIGHT?
I GOTTA GET IT TOGETHER.
ONLY FIVE DAYS LEFT...
I NEED TO TELL ALICE HOW I FEEL.
I NEED TO DO IT RIGHT THIS TIME.
I NEED...
...TO BE STRONG.
I DON'T WANT TO LOSE SOMEONE THAT I...

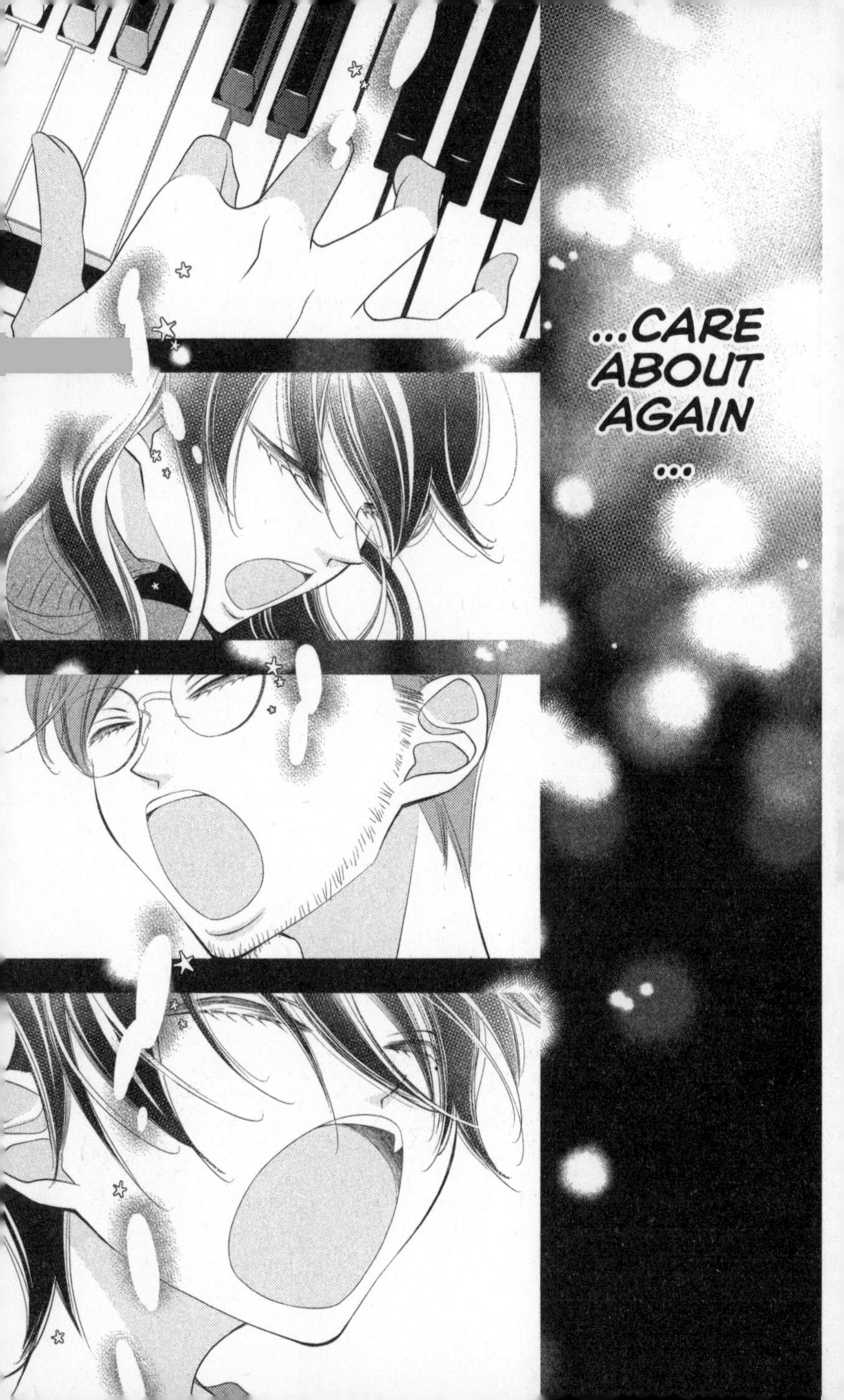
...CARE ABOUT AGAIN ...

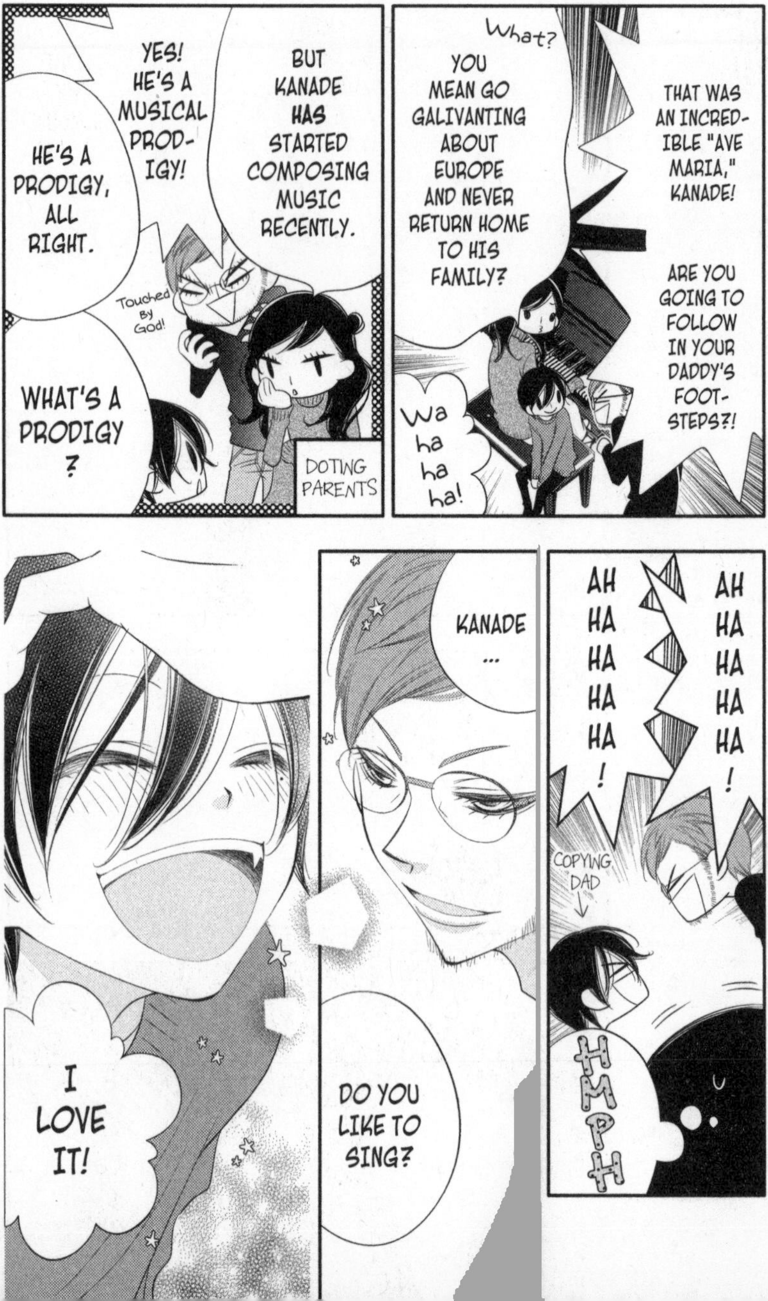
THAT WAS AN INCREDIBLE "AVE MARIA," KANADE!
ARE YOU GOING TO FOLLOW IN YOUR DADDY'S FOOTSTEPS?!
What?
YOU MEAN GO GALIVANTING ABOUT EUROPE AND NEVER RETURN HOME TO HIS FAMILY?
Wa ha ha ha!
BUT KANADE HAS STARTED COMPOSING MUSIC RECENTLY.
YES! HE'S A MUSICAL PRODIGY!
HE'S A PRODIGY, ALL RIGHT.
Touched By God!
DOTING PARENTS
WHAT'S A PRODIGY?
AH HA HA HA HA!
AH HA HA HA HA!
COPYING DAD
HMPH
KANADE...
DO YOU LIKE TO SING?
I LOVE IT!

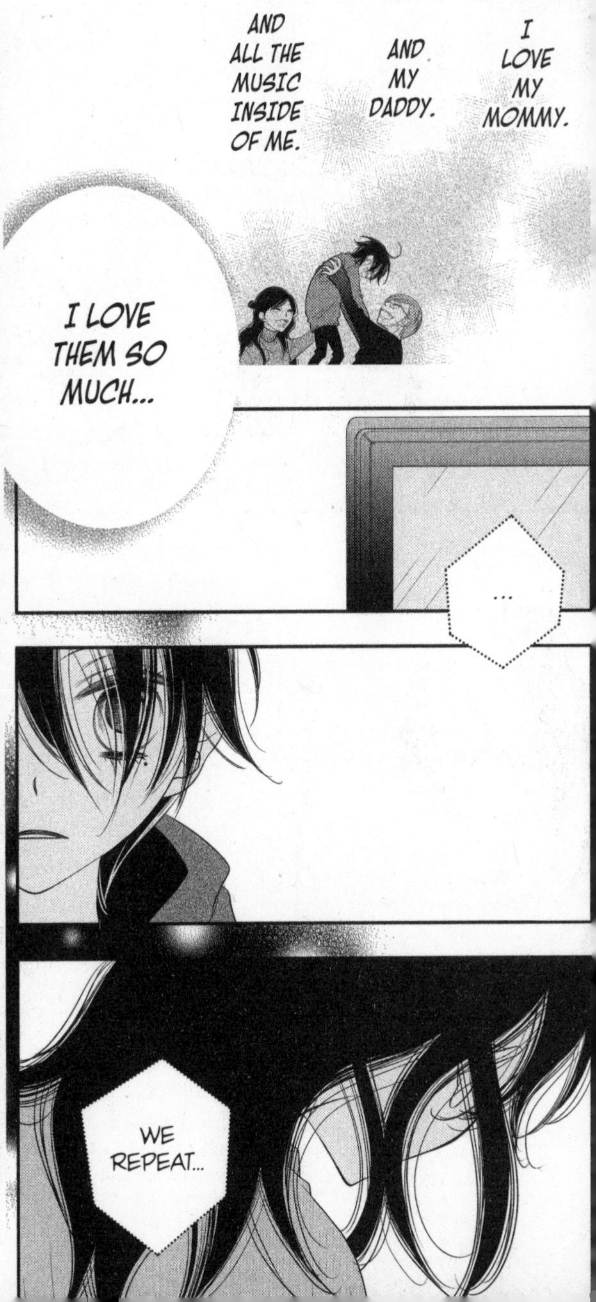
I LOVE MY MOMMY.
AND MY DADDY.
AND ALL THE MUSIC INSIDE OF ME.
I LOVE THEM SO MUCH...
...
WE REPEAT...

5

It's the tour arc! I mentioned it in the last volume, but three clubs let me inside to gather materials for this story:

Kyoto's Taku-Taku, Umeya's Club Quattro and Shibuya's Club Quattro.

I could not be more grateful for their help!

WAAH!

Everyone at all three clubs was incredibly nice. They turned on the houselights for me, let me stand on the club floor and even set up their fencing for me. I really can't thank them enough for that.

Personally, I used to go to Club Quattro in Shibuya all the time, so that visit was especially moving for me.

SO INCREDIBLE!

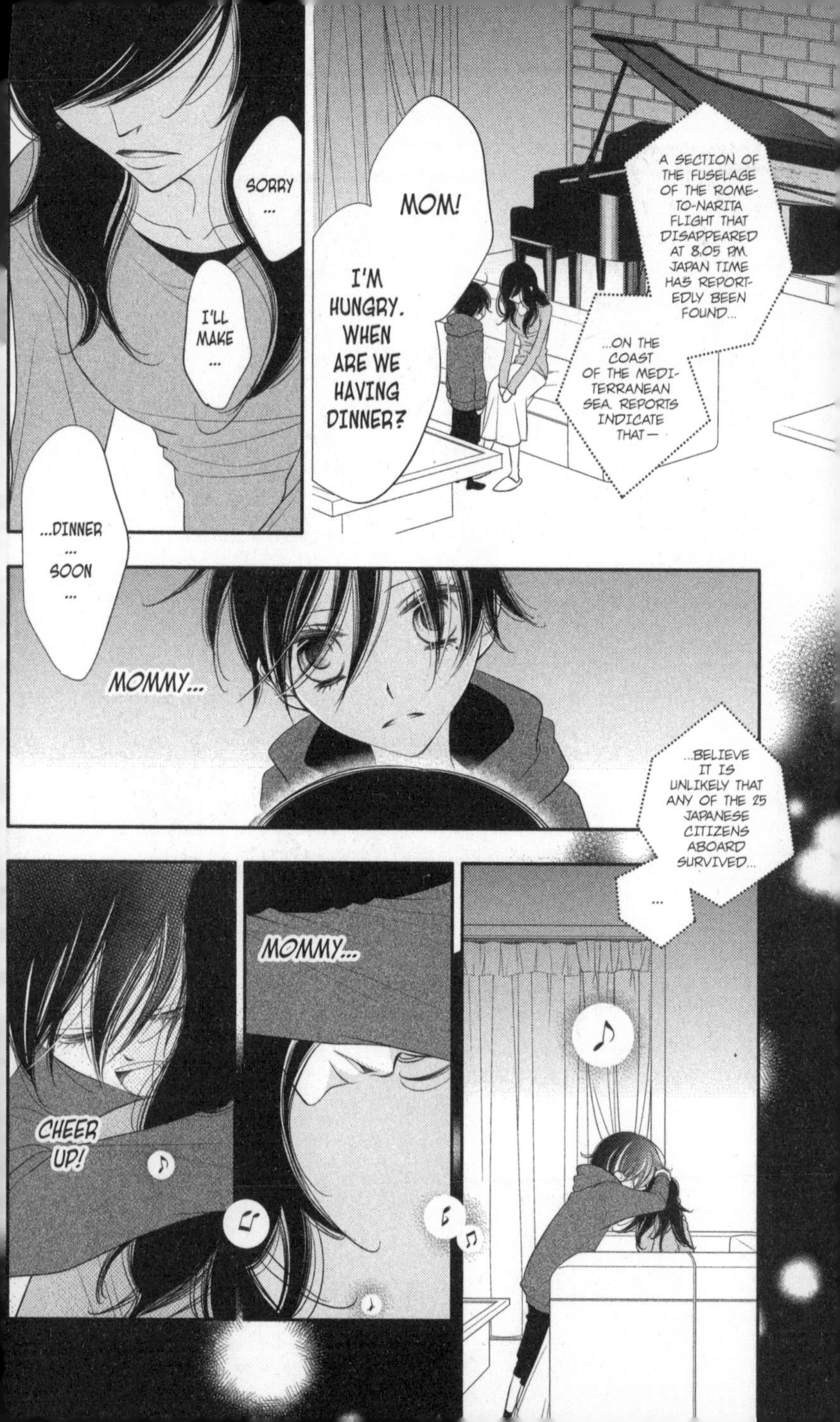

A SECTION OF THE FUSELAGE OF THE ROME-TO-NARITA FLIGHT THAT DISAPPEARED AT 8:05 P.M. JAPAN TIME HAS REPORTEDLY BEEN FOUND...
...ON THE COAST OF THE MEDITERRANEAN SEA. REPORTS INDICATE THAT—
MOM!
I'M HUNGRY. WHEN ARE WE HAVING DINNER?
SORRY...
I'LL MAKE...
...DINNER... SOON...
MOMMY...
...BELIEVE IT IS UNLIKELY THAT ANY OF THE 25 JAPANESE CITIZENS ABOARD SURVIVED...
...
MOMMY...
CHEER UP!

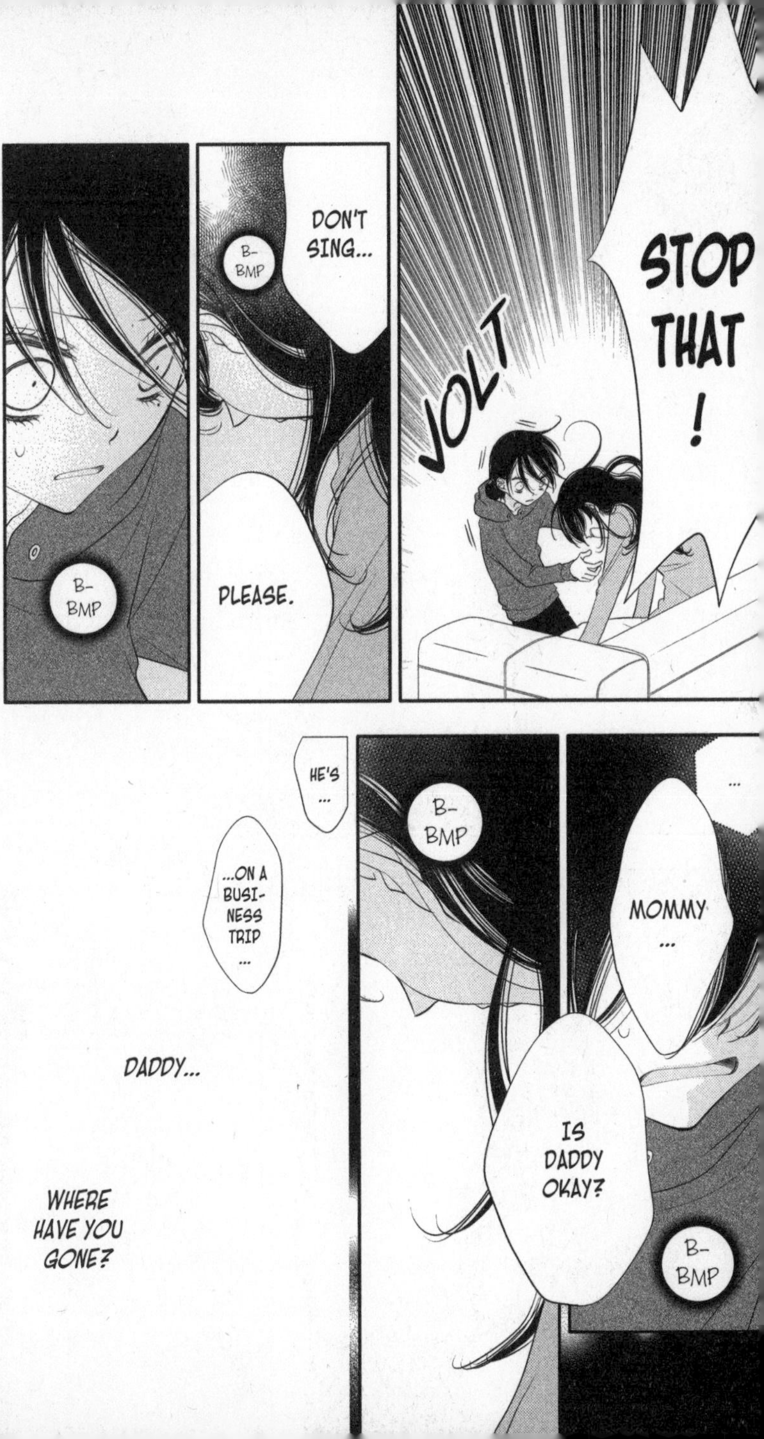
STOP THAT !
JOLT
B-BMP
DON'T SING...
PLEASE.
B-BMP
...
MOMMY ...
IS DADDY OKAY?
B-BMP
B-BMP
HE'S ...
...ON A BUSINESS TRIP ...
DADDY...
WHERE HAVE YOU GONE?

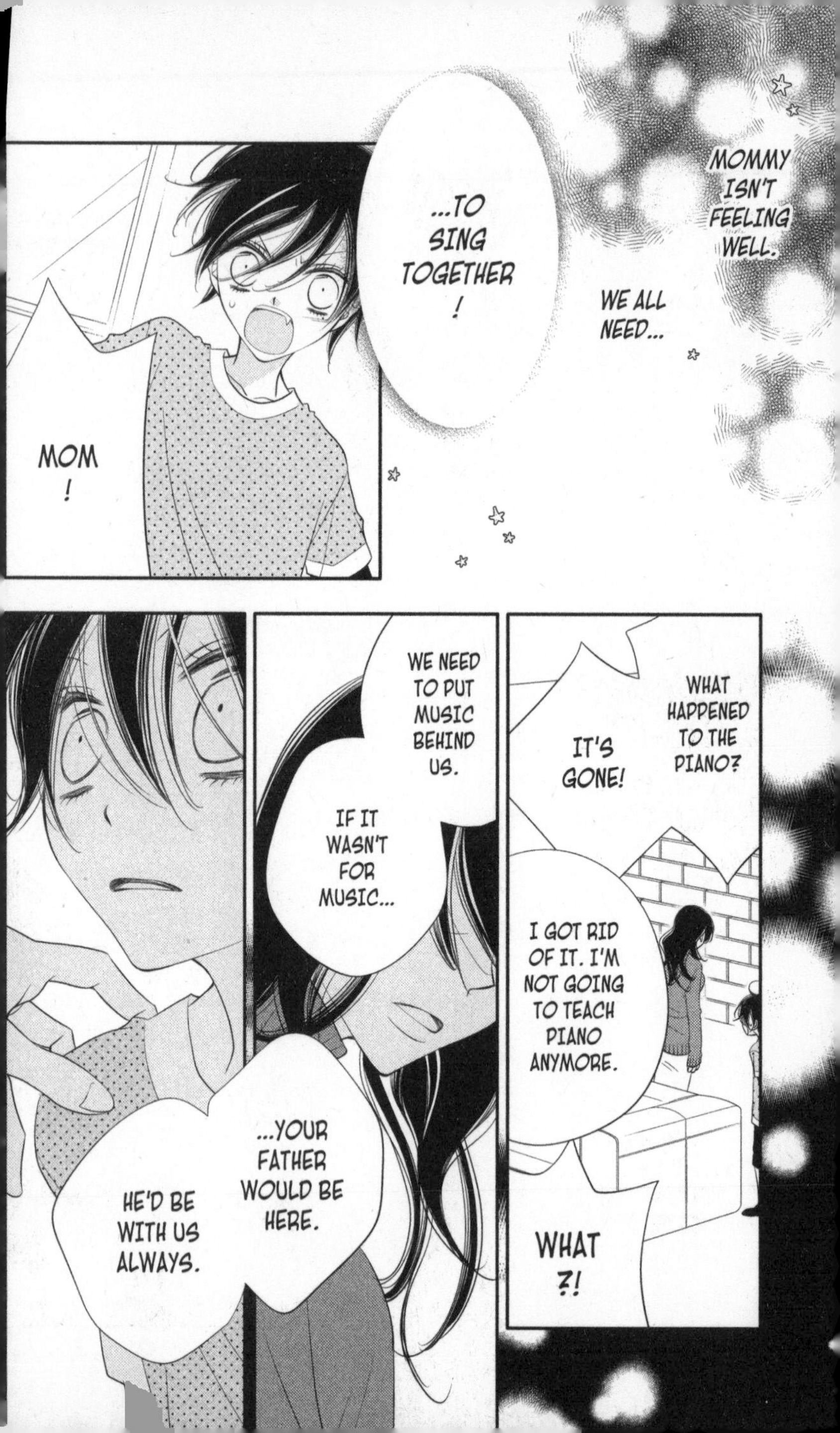
MOMMY ISN'T FEELING WELL.
WE ALL NEED...
...TO SING TOGETHER!
MOM!
WHAT HAPPENED TO THE PIANO?
IT'S GONE!
I GOT RID OF IT. I'M NOT GOING TO TEACH PIANO ANYMORE.
WHAT?!
WE NEED TO PUT MUSIC BEHIND US.
IF IT WASN'T FOR MUSIC...
...YOUR FATHER WOULD BE HERE.
HE'D BE WITH US ALWAYS.

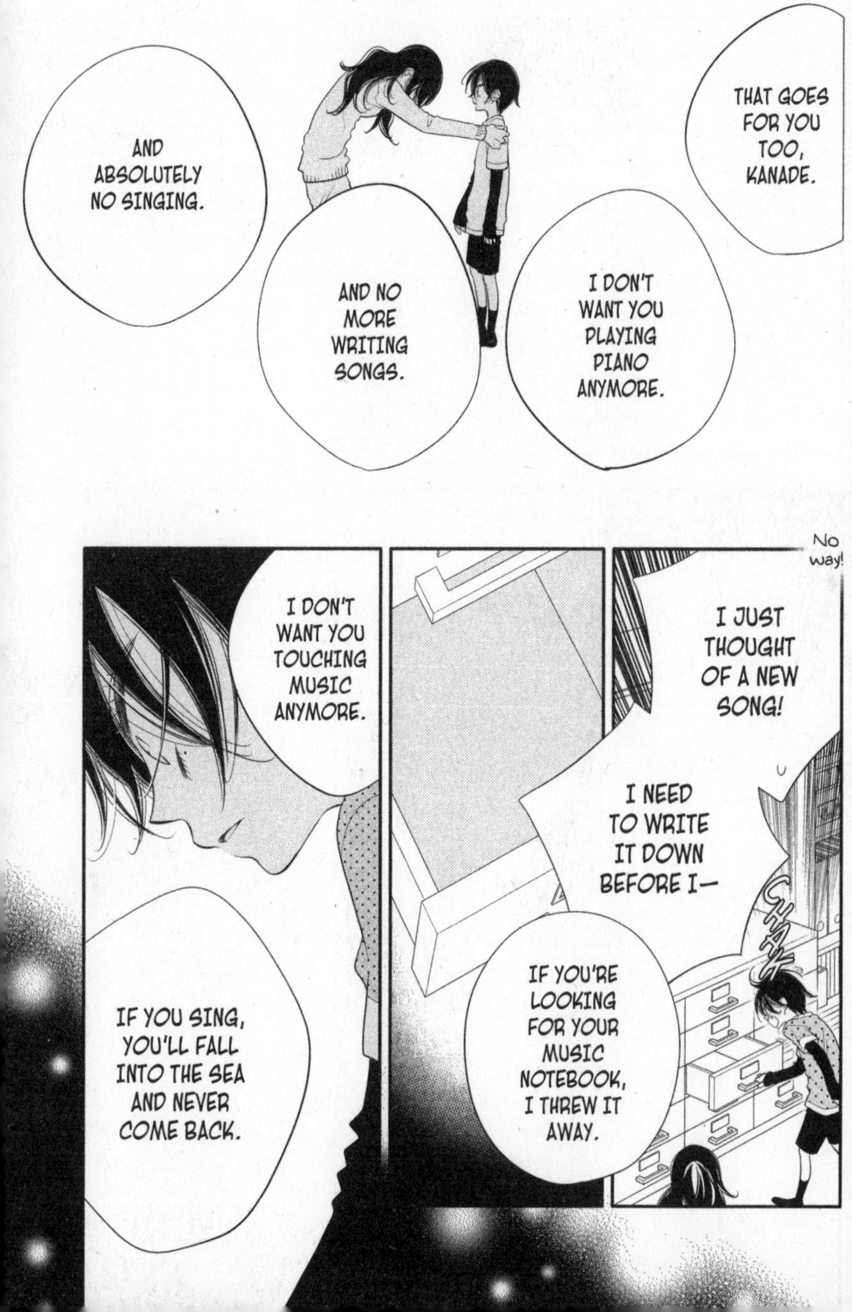
THAT GOES FOR YOU TOO, KANADE.
I DON'T WANT YOU PLAYING PIANO ANYMORE.
AND NO MORE WRITING SONGS.
AND ABSOLUTELY NO SINGING.
No way!
I JUST THOUGHT OF A NEW SONG!
I NEED TO WRITE IT DOWN BEFORE I—
CHAK
IF YOU'RE LOOKING FOR YOUR MUSIC NOTEBOOK, I THREW IT AWAY.
I DON'T WANT YOU TOUCHING MUSIC ANYMORE.
IF YOU SING, YOU'LL FALL INTO THE SEA AND NEVER COME BACK.

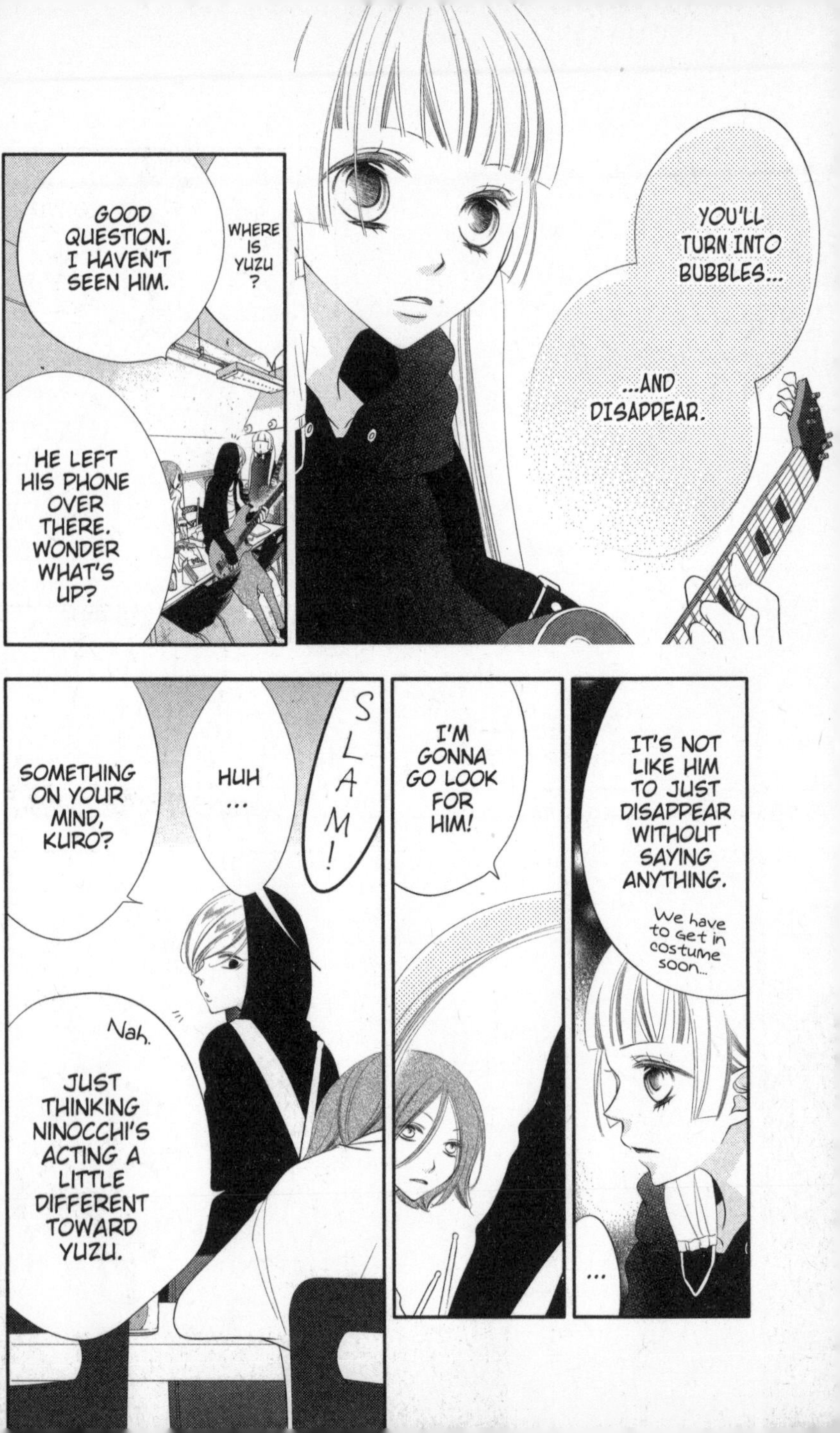
YOU'LL TURN INTO BUBBLES...
...AND DISAPPEAR.
WHERE IS YUZU ?
GOOD QUESTION. I HAVEN'T SEEN HIM.
HE LEFT HIS PHONE OVER THERE. WONDER WHAT'S UP?
IT'S NOT LIKE HIM TO JUST DISAPPEAR WITHOUT SAYING ANYTHING.
We have to get in costume soon...
...
I'M GONNA GO LOOK FOR HIM!
SLAM!
HUH ...
SOMETHING ON YOUR MIND, KURO?
Nah.
JUST THINKING NINOCCHI'S ACTING A LITTLE DIFFERENT TOWARD YUZU.

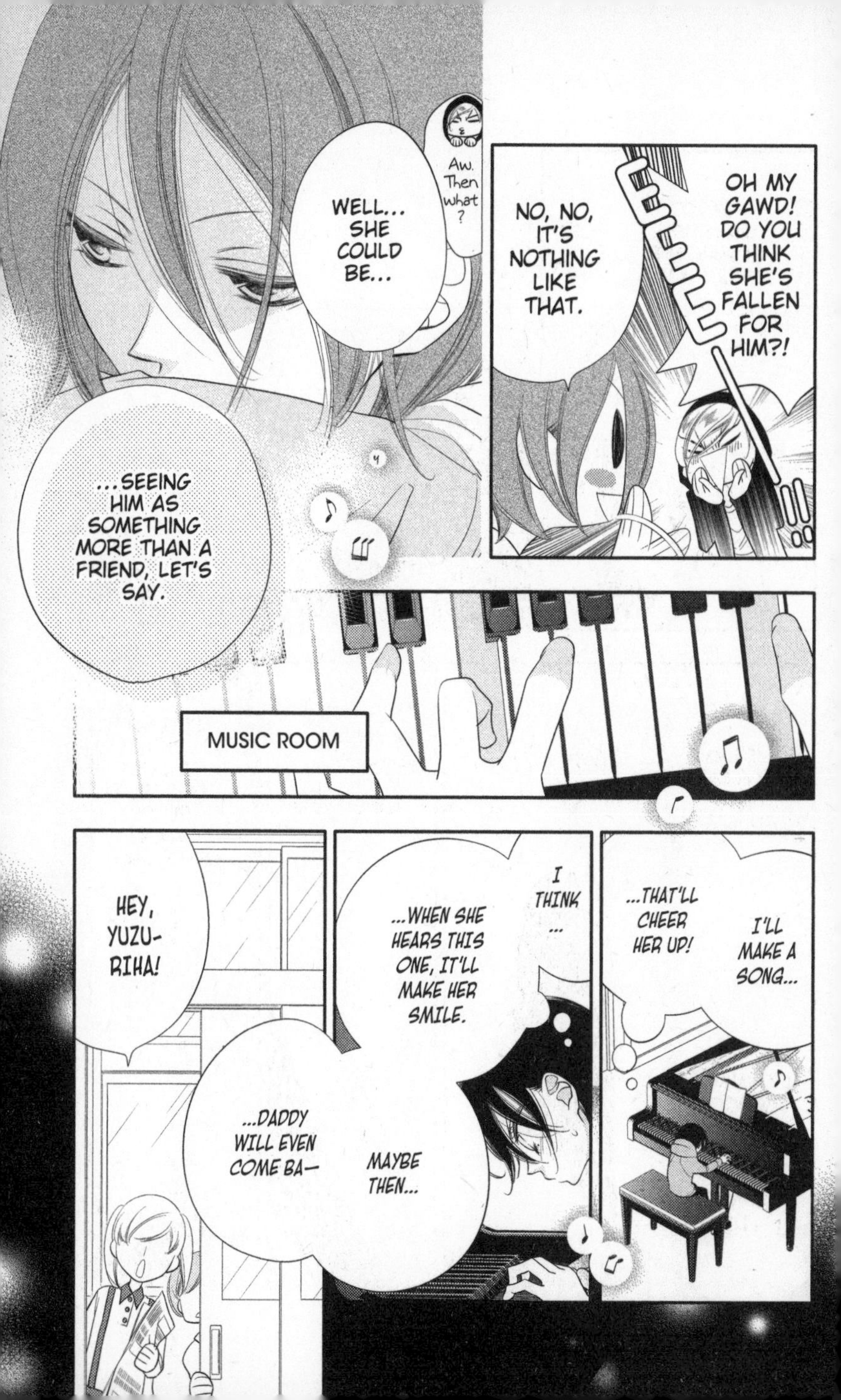

OH MY GAWD! DO YOU THINK SHE'S FALLEN FOR HIM?!
NO, NO, IT'S NOTHING LIKE THAT.
WELL... SHE COULD BE...
Aw. Then what?
...SEEING HIM AS SOMETHING MORE THAN A FRIEND, LET'S SAY.
MUSIC ROOM
I'LL MAKE A SONG...
...THAT'LL CHEER HER UP!
I THINK...
...WHEN SHE HEARS THIS ONE, IT'LL MAKE HER SMILE.
MAYBE THEN...
...DADDY WILL EVEN COME BA—
HEY, YUZURIHA!

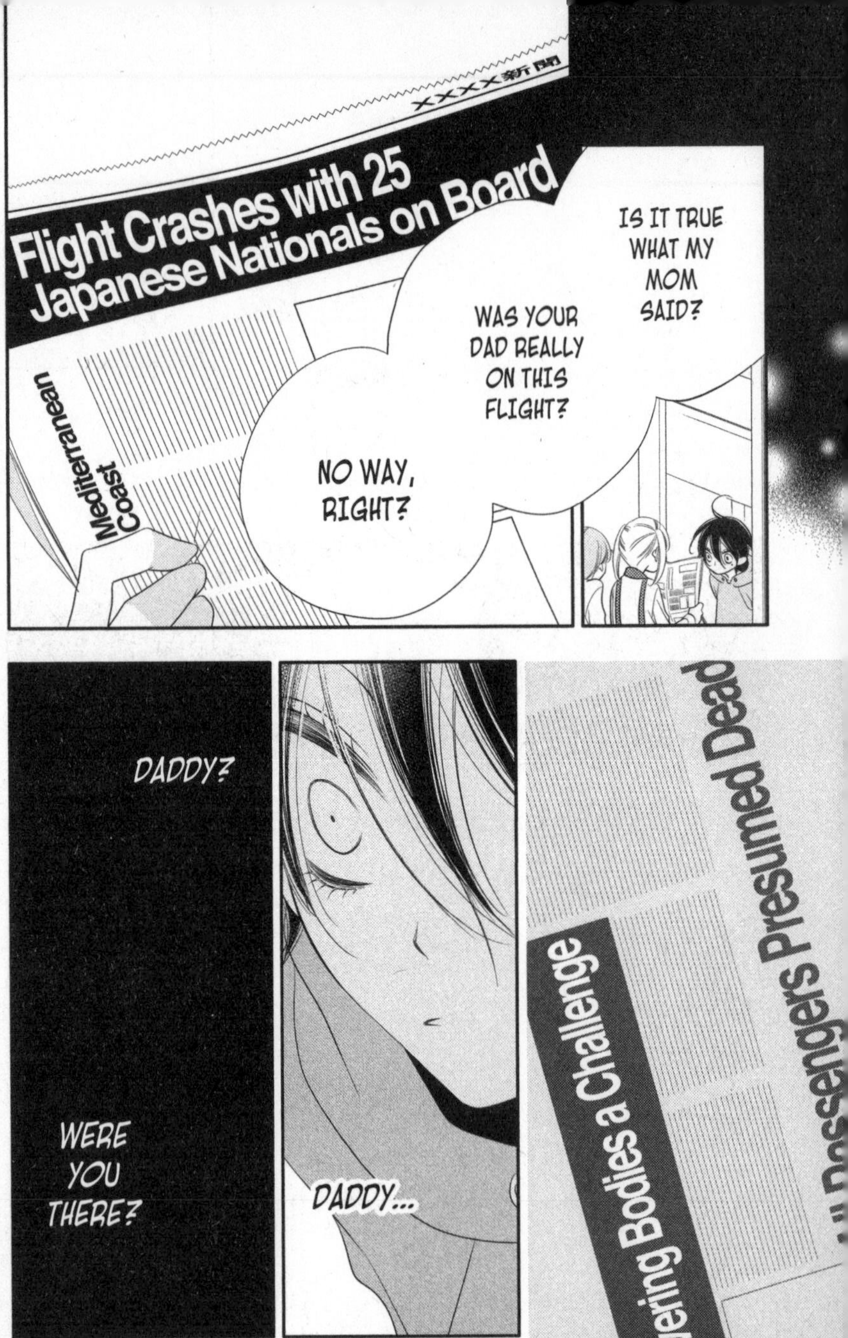
XXXX新聞
IS IT TRUE WHAT MY MOM SAID?
WAS YOUR DAD REALLY ON THIS FLIGHT?
Flight Crashes with 25 Japanese Nationals on Board
NO WAY, RIGHT?
Mediterranean Coast
Passengers Presumed Dead
Recovering Bodies a Challenge
DADDY...
DADDY?
WERE YOU THERE?

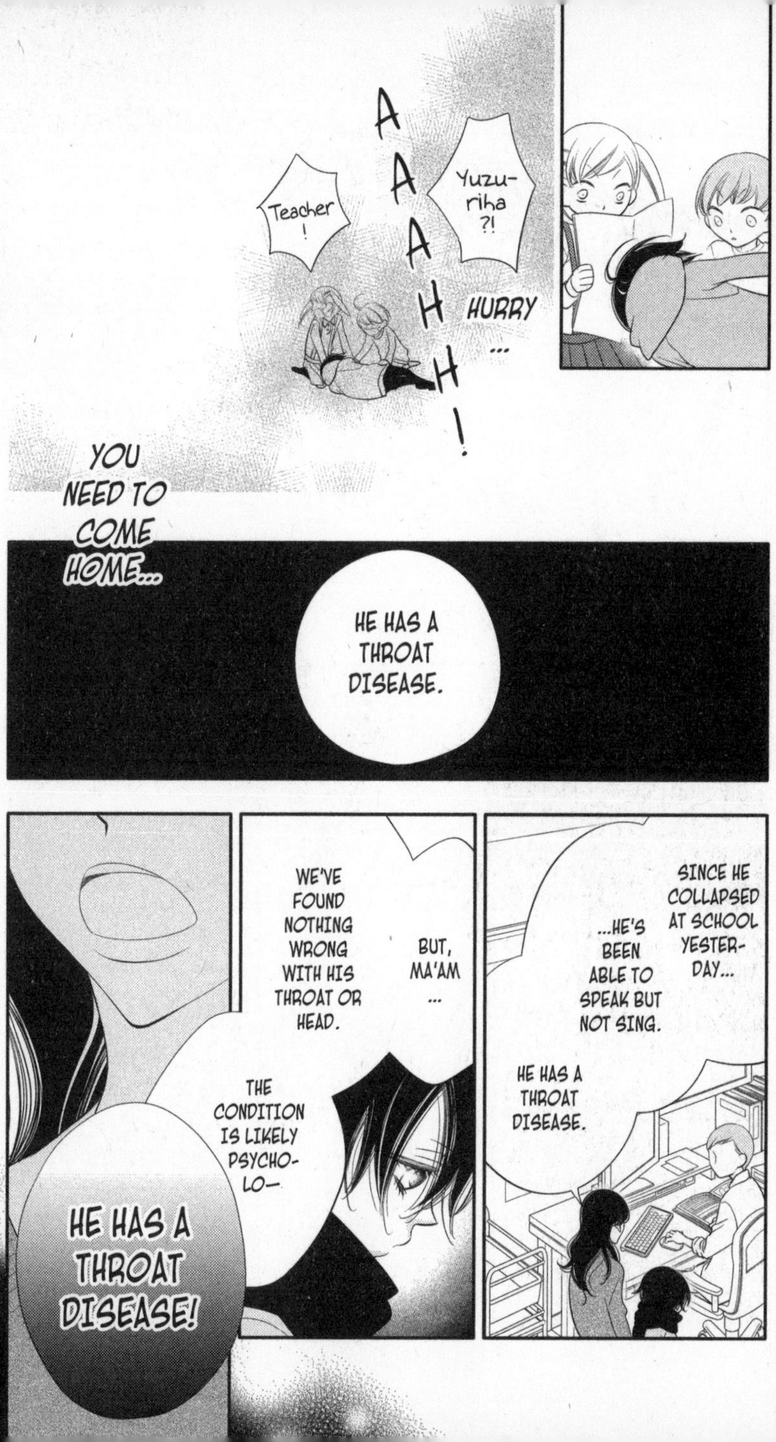
Yuzu-riha ?!
AAAAHH!
Teacher!
HURRY...
YOU NEED TO COME HOME...
HE HAS A THROAT DISEASE.
SINCE HE COLLAPSED AT SCHOOL YESTER-DAY...
...HE'S BEEN ABLE TO SPEAK BUT NOT SING.
HE HAS A THROAT DISEASE.
BUT, MA'AM...
WE'VE FOUND NOTHING WRONG WITH HIS THROAT OR HEAD.
THE CONDITION IS LIKELY PSYCHO-LO—
HE HAS A THROAT DISEASE!

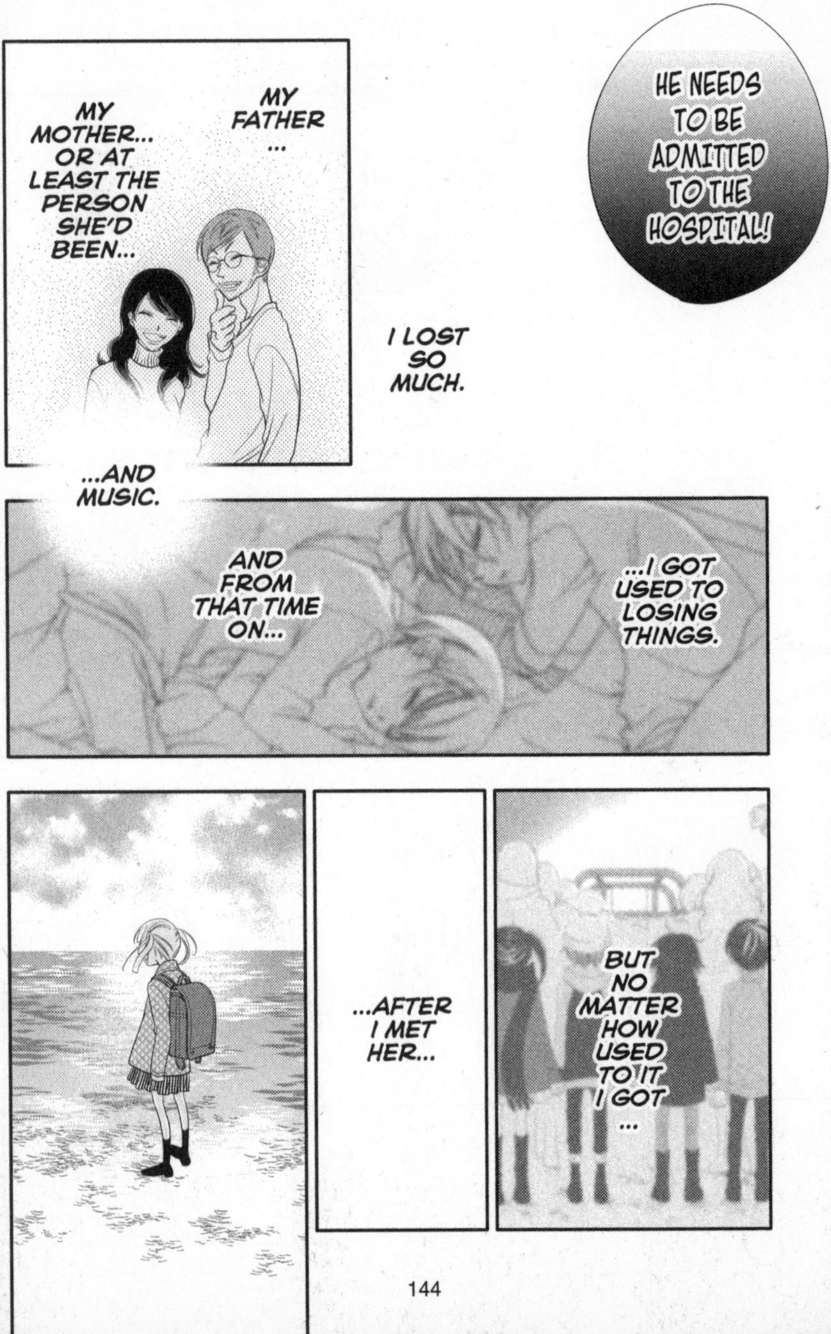
HE NEEDS TO BE ADMITTED TO THE HOSPITAL!
I LOST SO MUCH.
MY FATHER ...
MY MOTHER... OR AT LEAST THE PERSON SHE'D BEEN...
...AND MUSIC.
...I GOT USED TO LOSING THINGS.
AND FROM THAT TIME ON...
BUT NO MATTER HOW USED TO IT I GOT ...
...AFTER I MET HER...

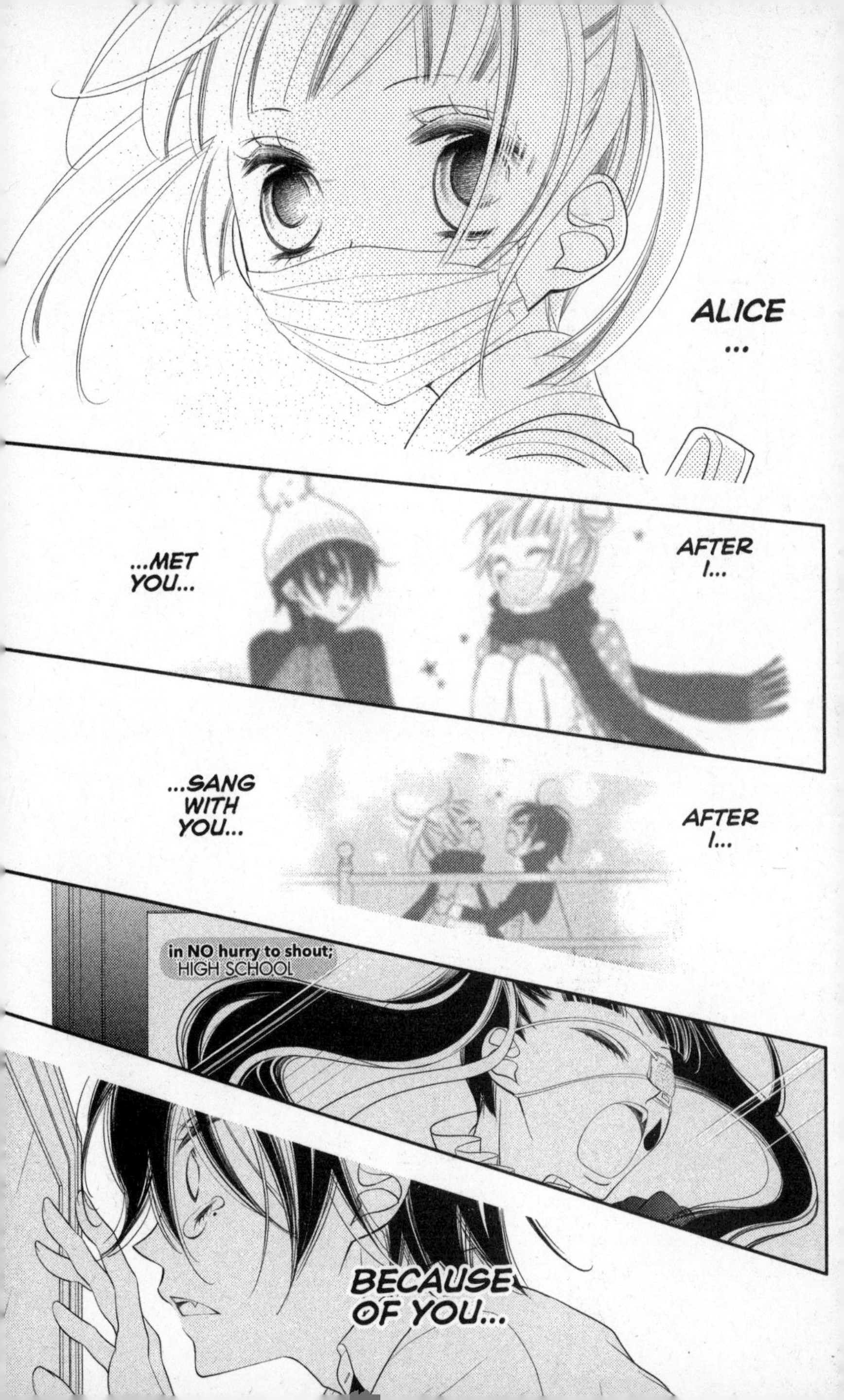
ALICE
...
AFTER I...
...MET YOU...
AFTER I...
...SANG WITH YOU...
in NO hurry to shout;
HIGH SCHOOL
BECAUSE OF YOU...

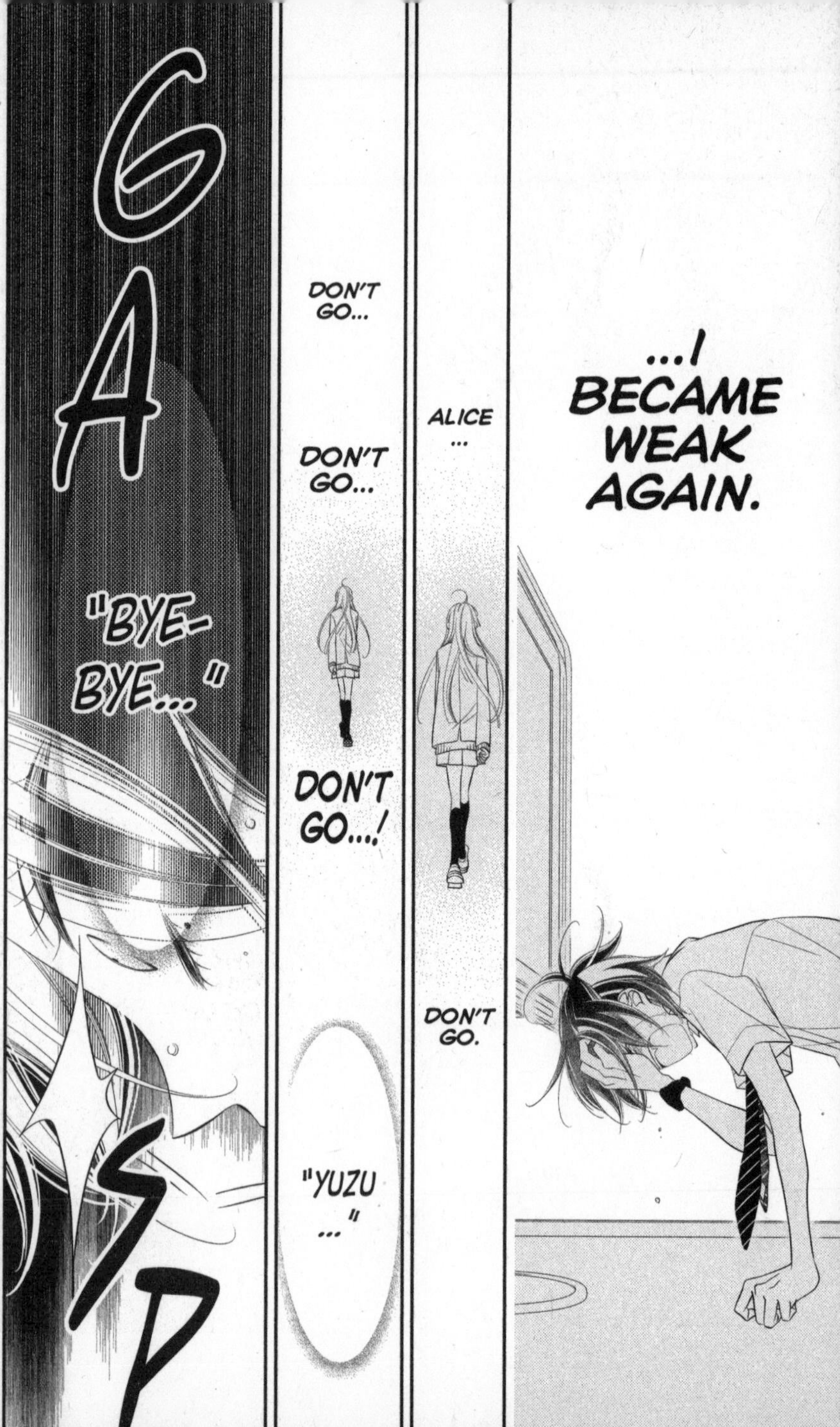
...I BECAME WEAK AGAIN.
ALICE ...
DON'T GO.
DON'T GO...
DON'T GO...
DON'T GO...!
"YUZU ..." ...
GA
"BYE-BYE..."
SP

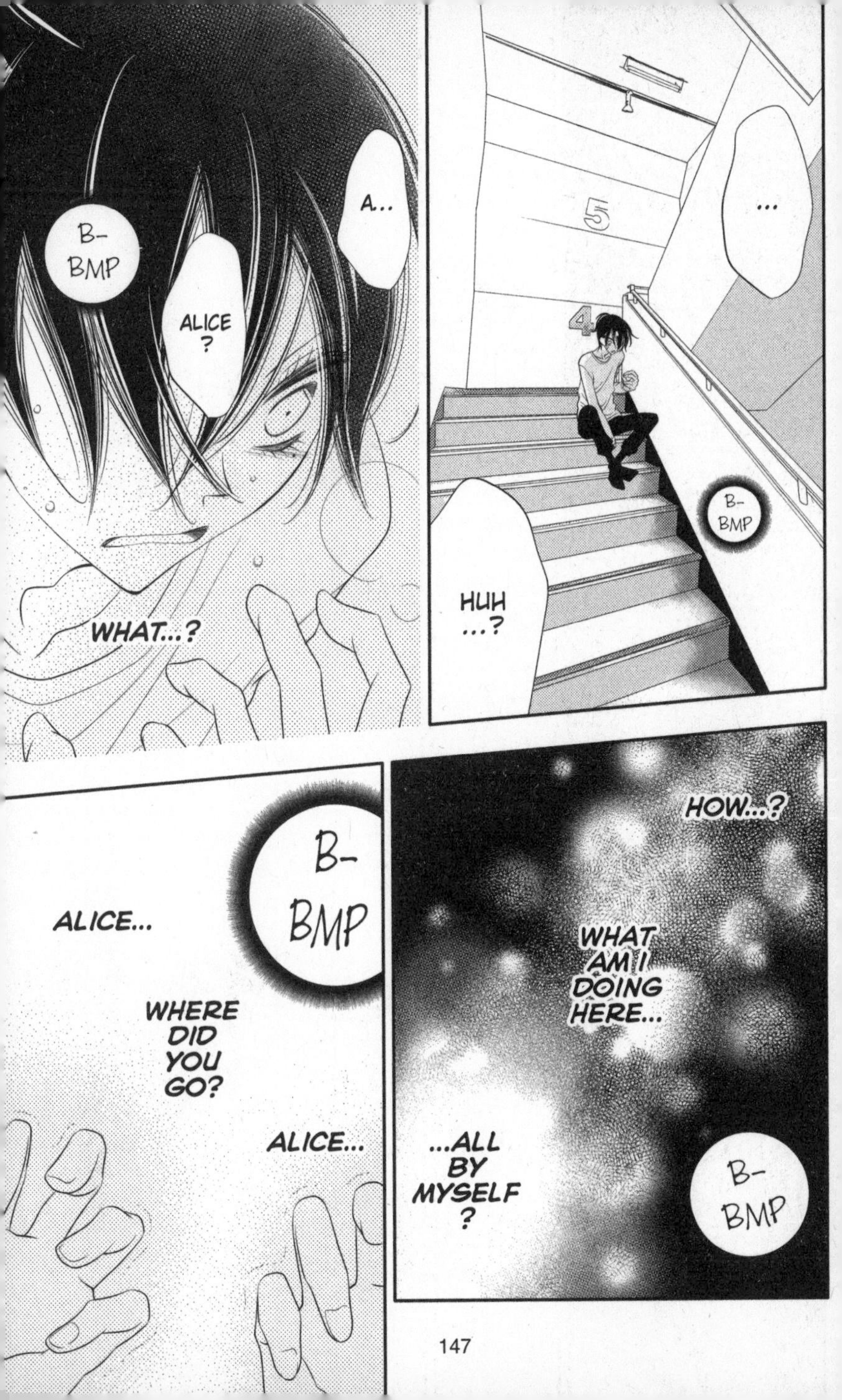
...
B-BMP
HUH ...?
A...
ALICE ?
B-BMP
WHAT...?
HOW...?
WHAT AM I DOING HERE...
...ALL BY MYSELF ?
B-BMP
B-BMP
ALICE...
WHERE DID YOU GO?
ALICE...

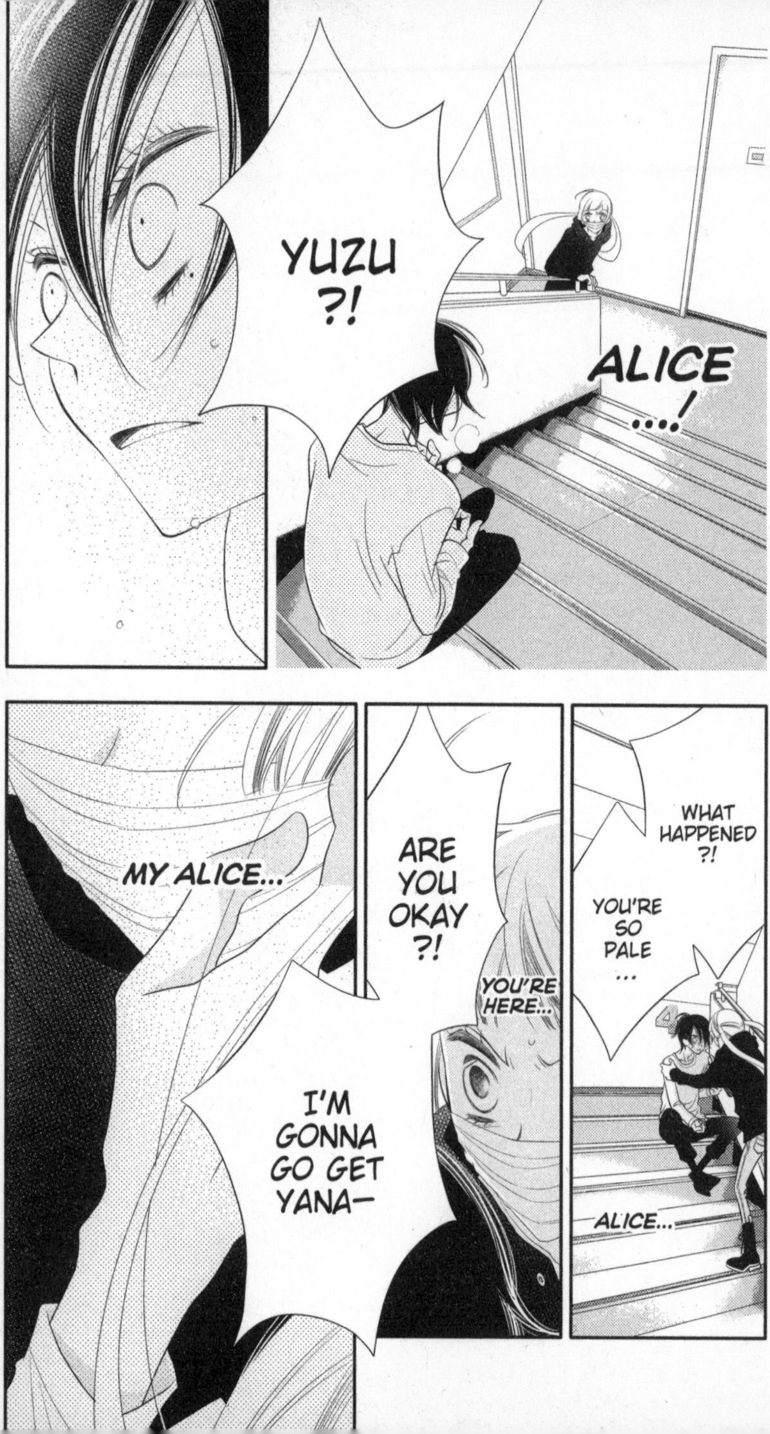
YUZU ?!
ALICE ...!
WHAT HAPPENED ?!
YOU'RE SO PALE ...
ALICE...
ARE YOU OKAY ?!
YOU'RE HERE...
MY ALICE...
I'M GONNA GO GET YANA—

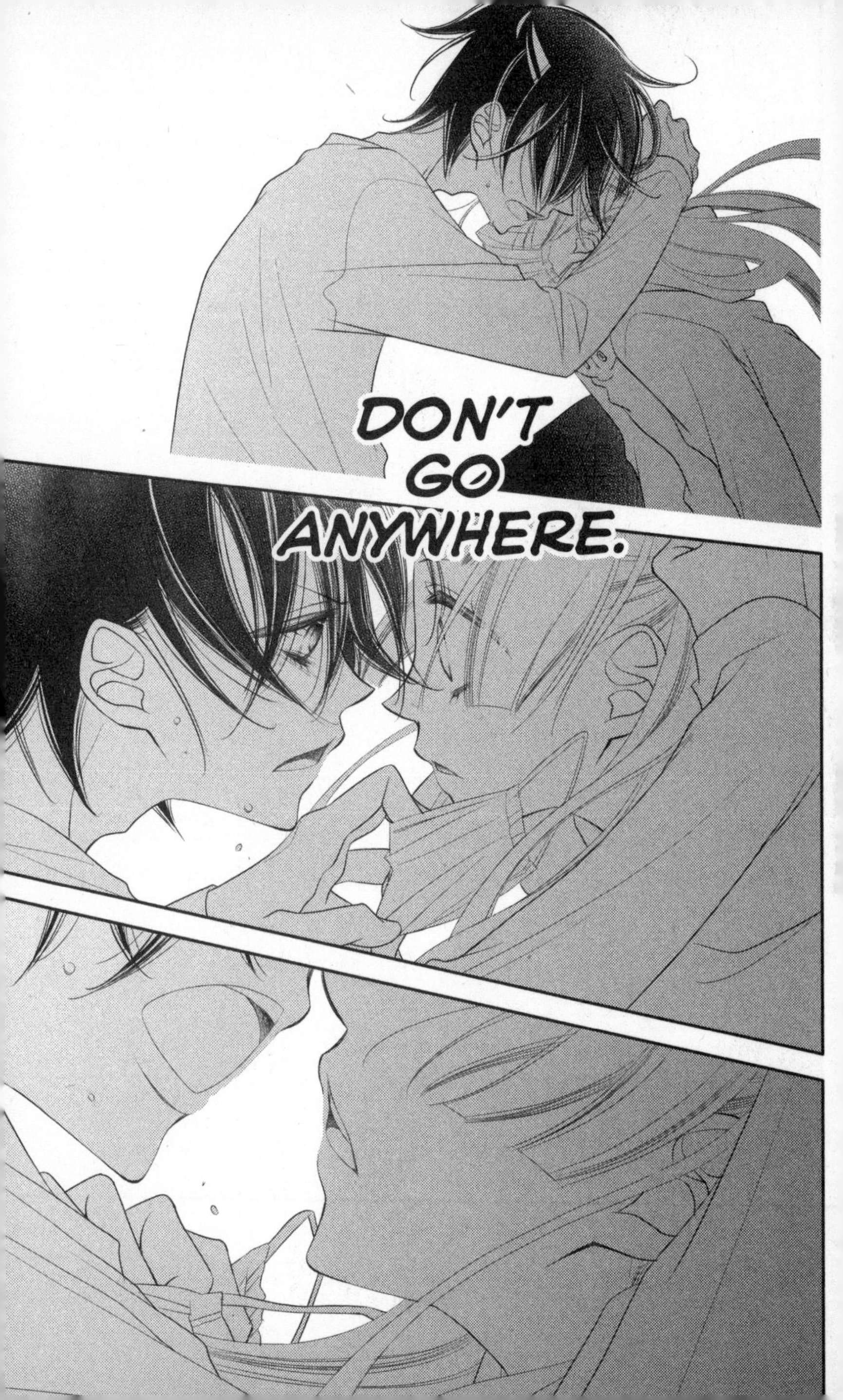
DON'T GO ANYWHERE.

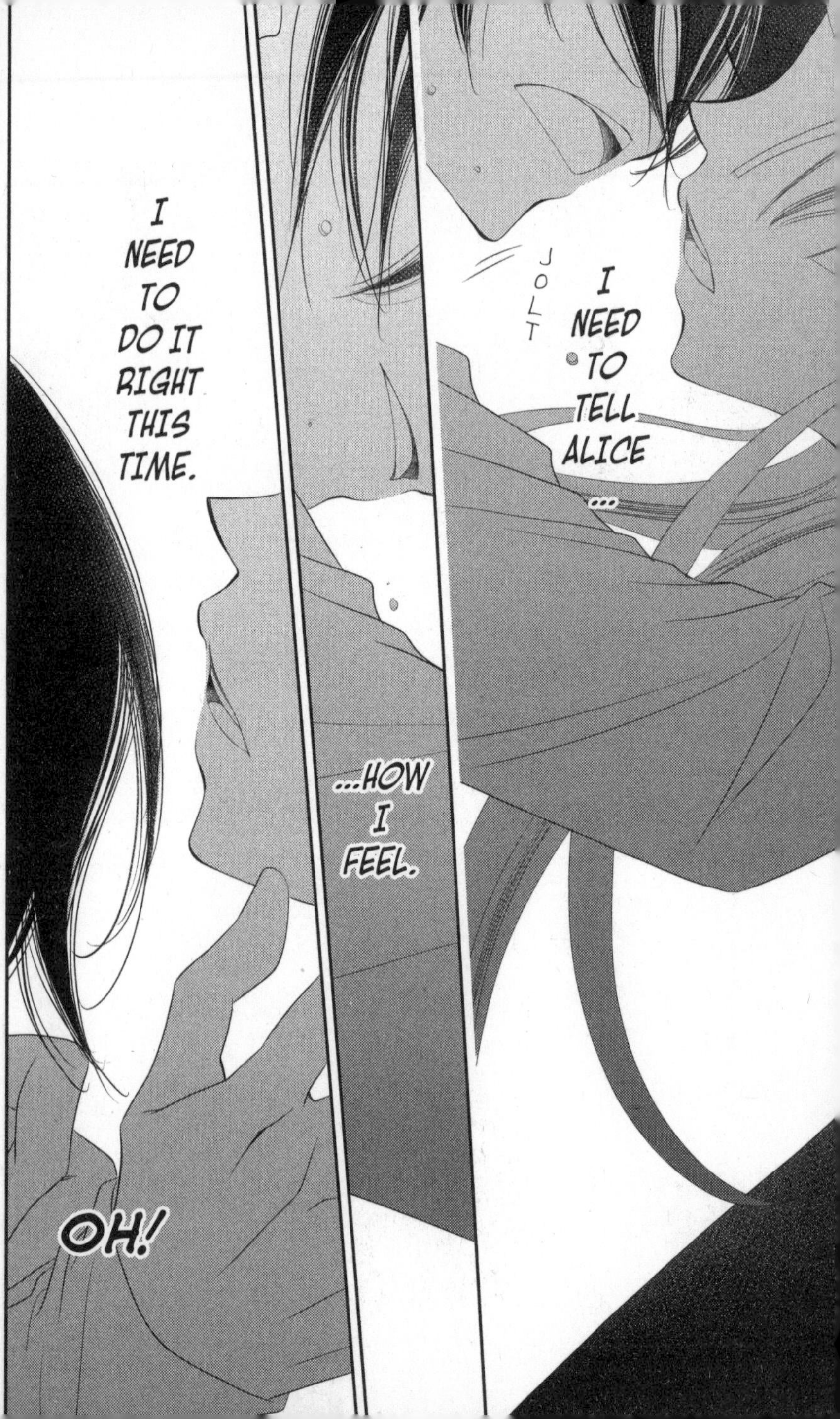
JOLT
I NEED TO TELL ALICE ...
...HOW I FEEL.
I NEED TO DO IT RIGHT THIS TIME.
OH!

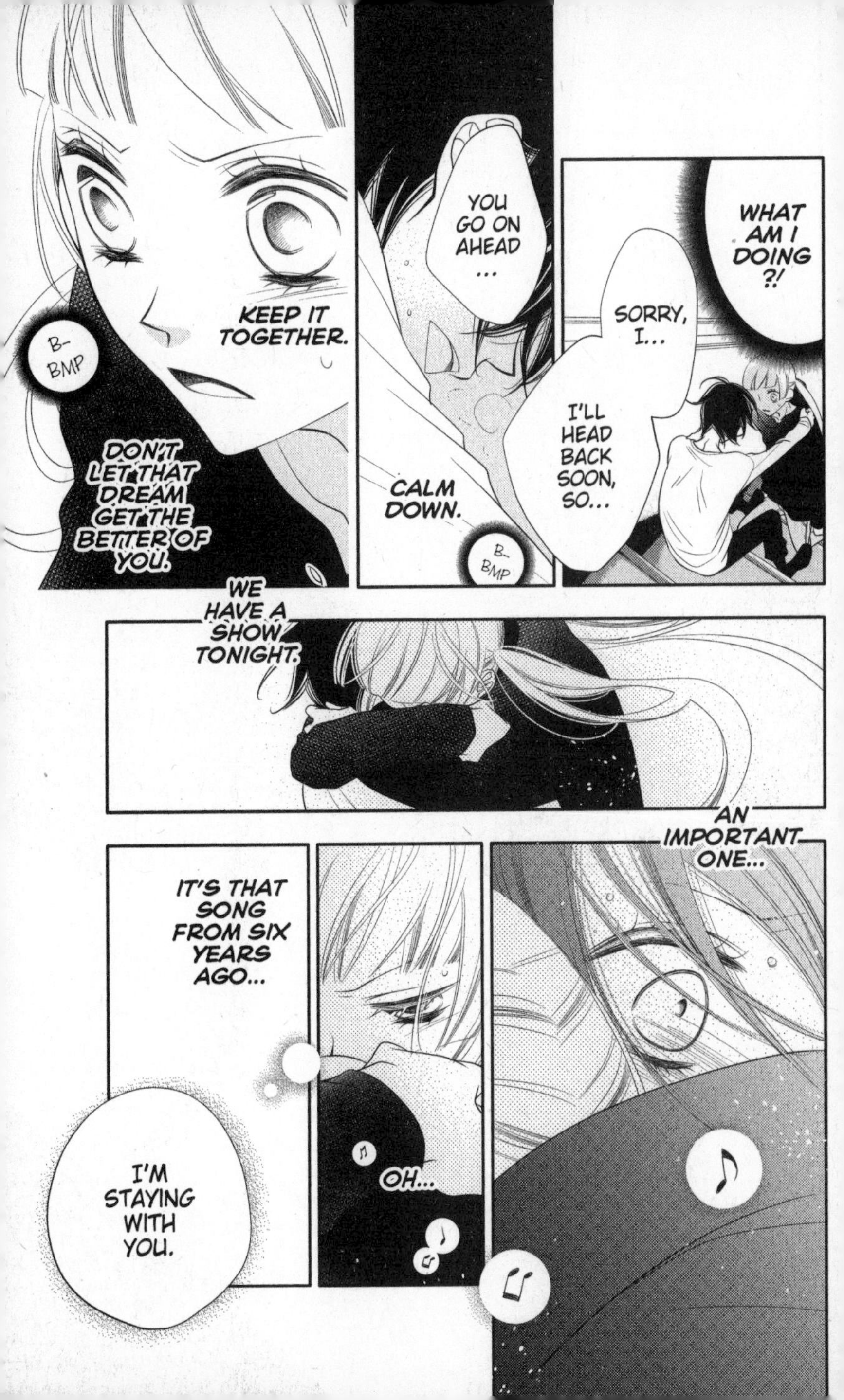
WHAT AM I DOING ?!
SORRY, I...
I'LL HEAD BACK SOON, SO...
YOU GO ON AHEAD ...
CALM DOWN.
B-BMP
KEEP IT TOGETHER.
B-BMP
DON'T LET THAT DREAM GET THE BETTER OF YOU.
WE HAVE A SHOW TONIGHT.
AN IMPORTANT ONE...
OH...
IT'S THAT SONG FROM SIX YEARS AGO...
I'M STAYING WITH YOU.

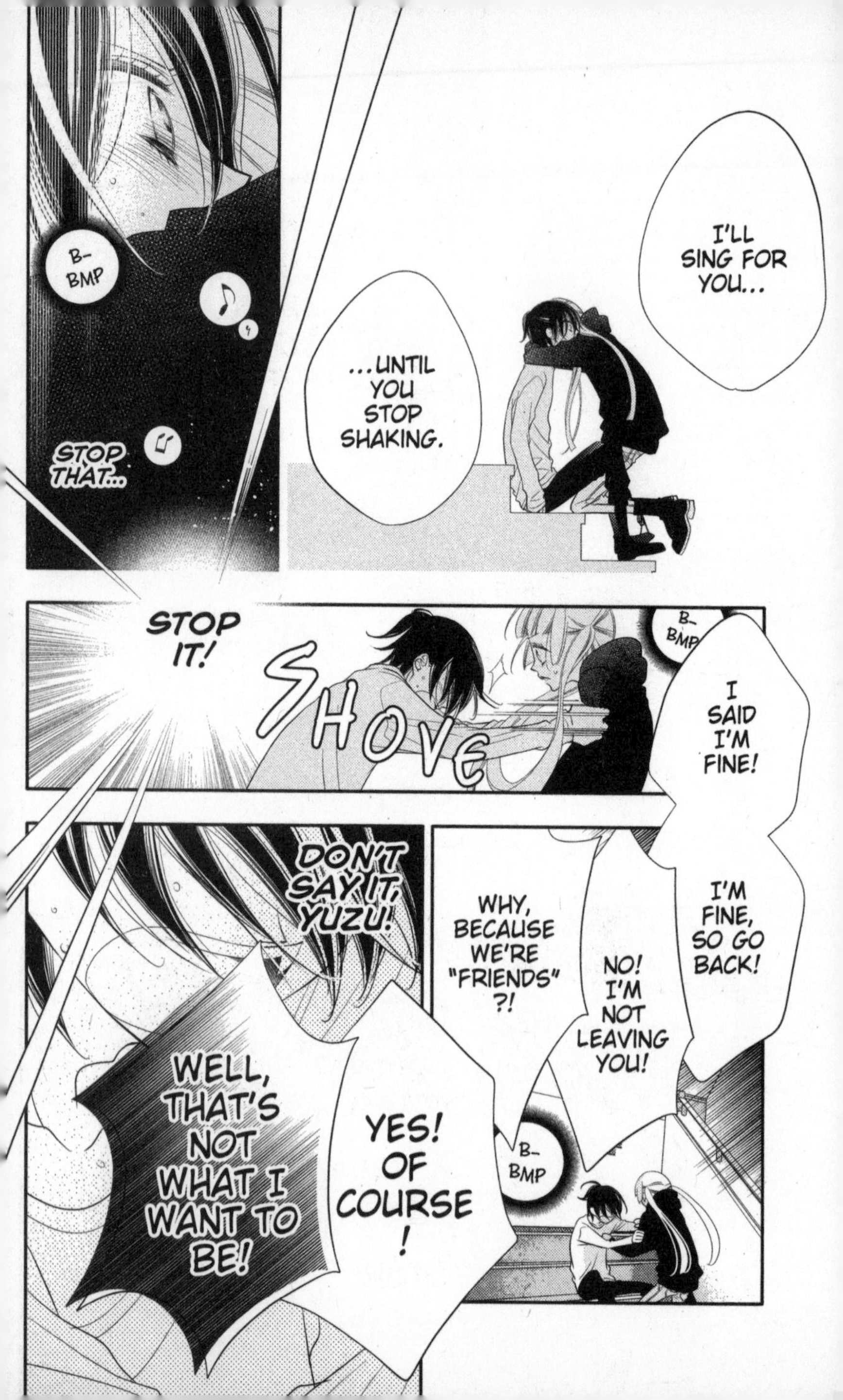
I'LL SING FOR YOU...
...UNTIL YOU STOP SHAKING.
B-BMP
STOP THAT...
B-BMP
I SAID I'M FINE!
SHOVE
STOP IT!
I'M FINE, SO GO BACK!
NO! I'M NOT LEAVING YOU!
WHY, BECAUSE WE'RE "FRIENDS"?!
B-BMP
YES! OF COURSE!
DON'T SAY IT, YUZU!
WELL, THAT'S NOT WHAT I WANT TO BE!

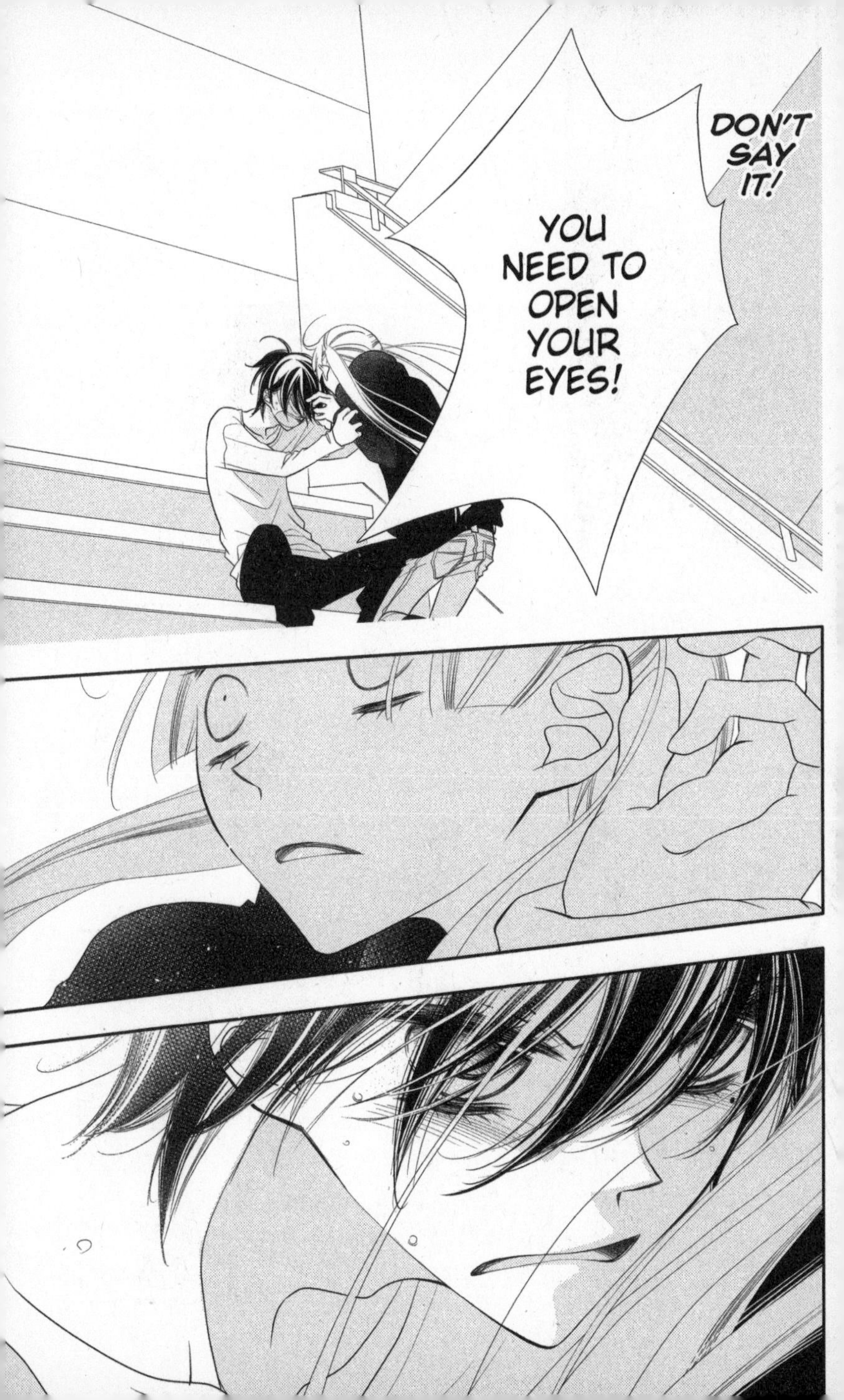
DON'T SAY IT!
YOU NEED TO OPEN YOUR EYES!

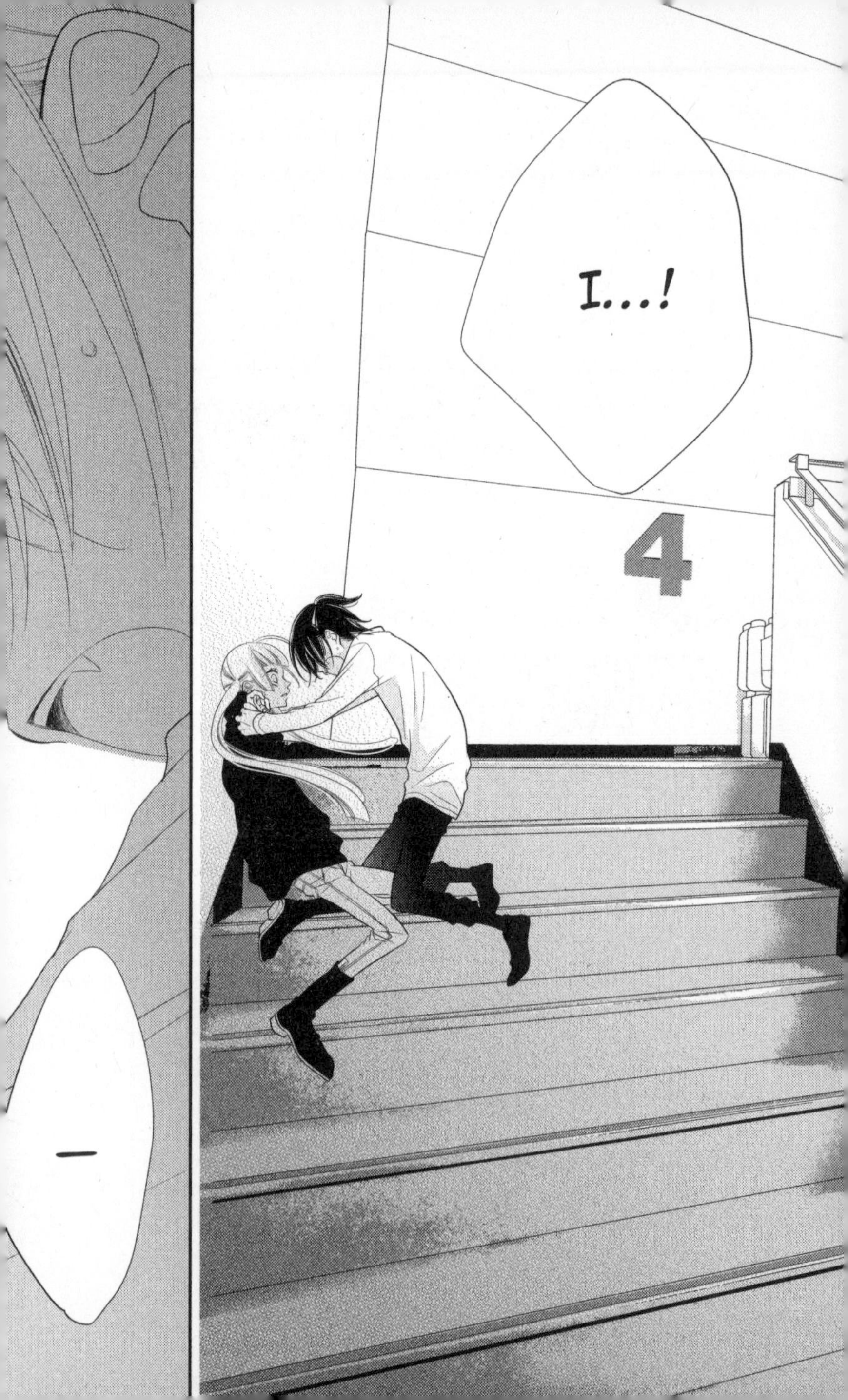
I...!
—

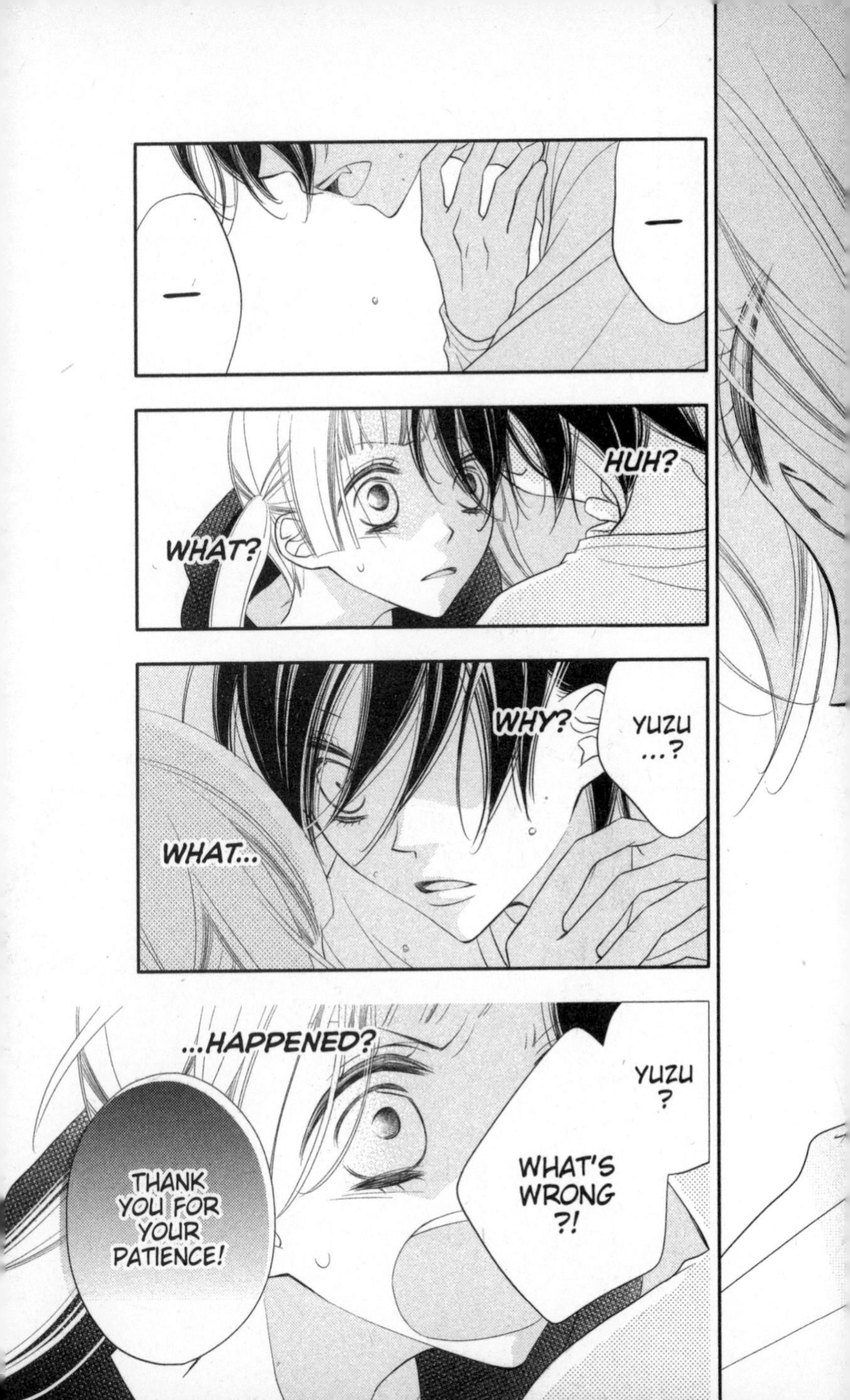
HUH?
WHAT?
YUZU ...?
WHY?
WHAT...
YUZU ?
WHAT'S WRONG ?!
...HAPPENED?
THANK YOU FOR YOUR PATIENCE!

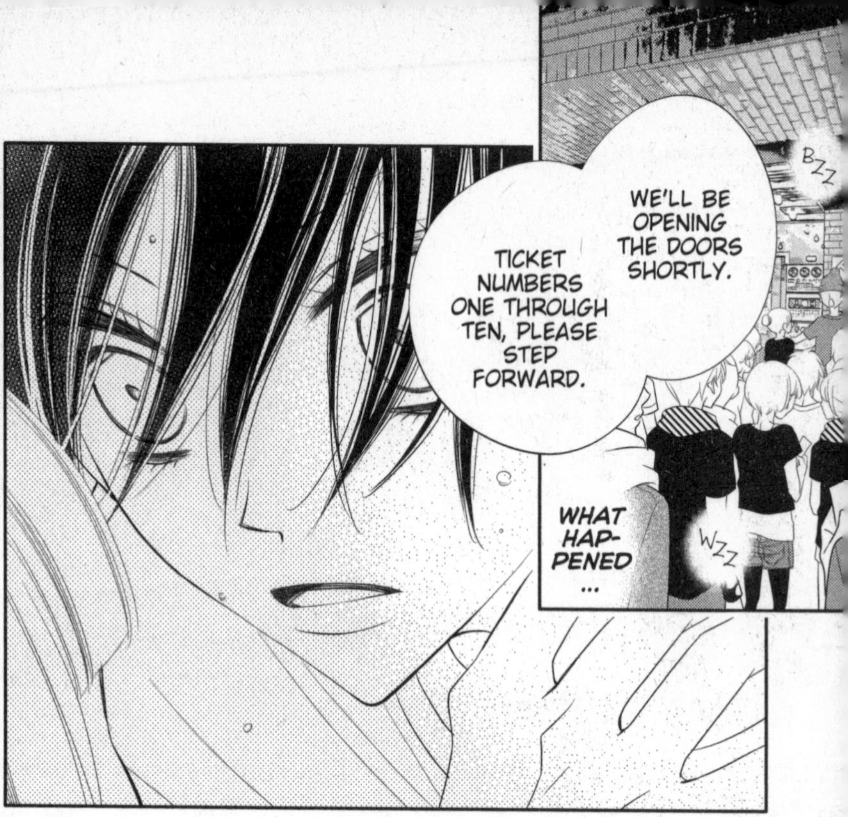
BZZ
WE'LL BE OPENING THE DOORS SHORTLY.
TICKET NUMBERS ONE THROUGH TEN, PLEASE STEP FORWARD.
WHAT HAP-PENED ...
WZZ

...TO MY VOICE?

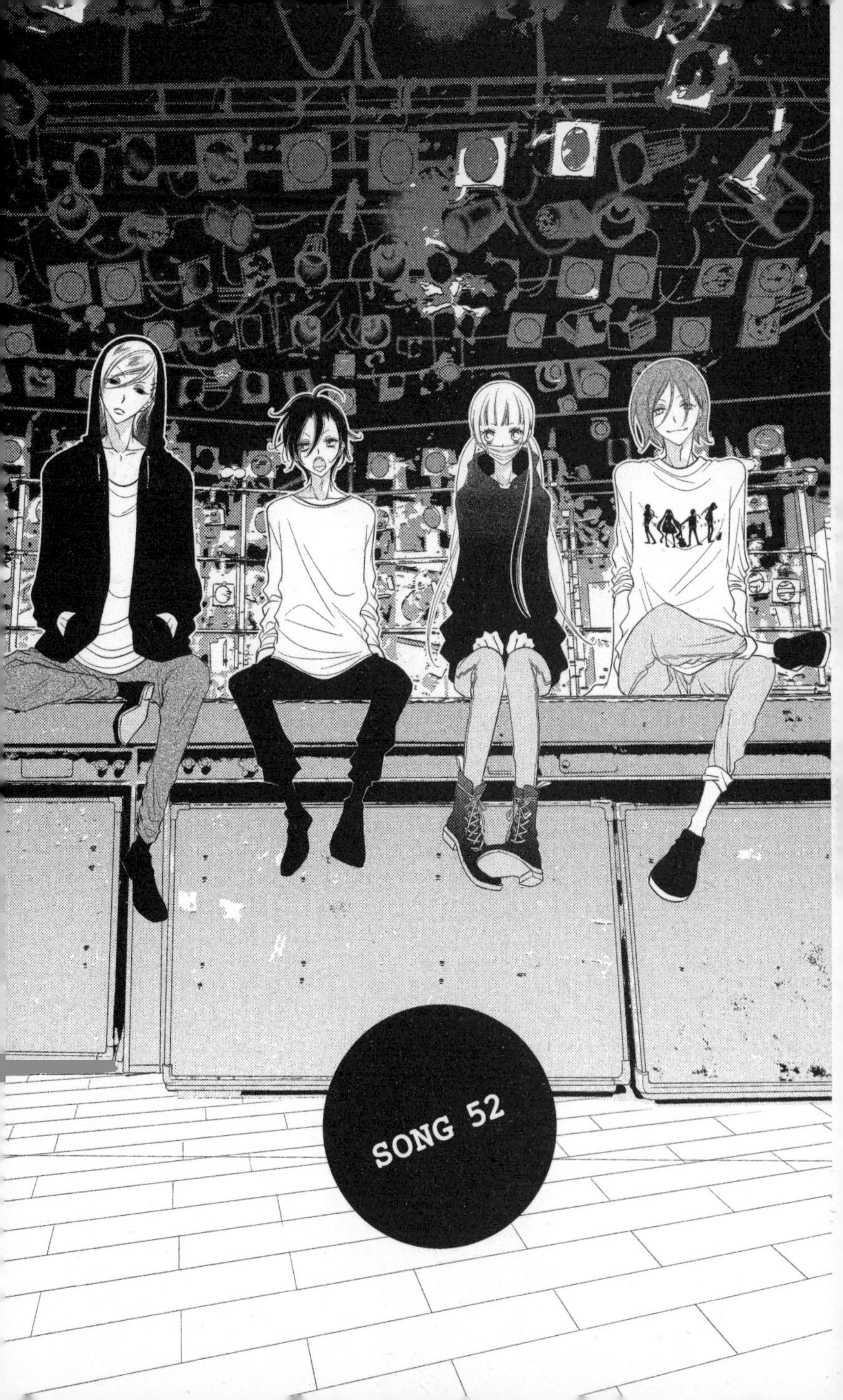
SONG 52

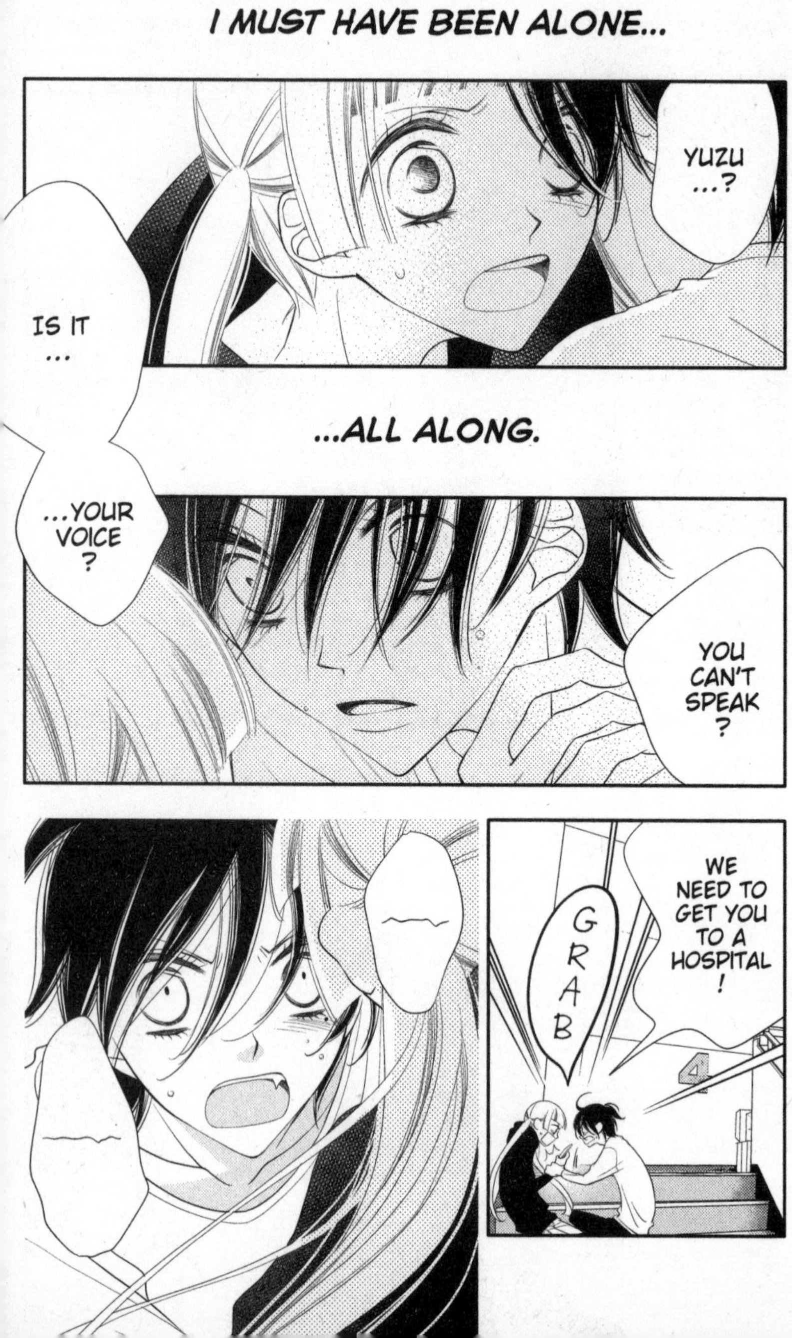
I MUST HAVE BEEN ALONE...
YUZU ...?
IS IT ...
...ALL ALONG.
...YOUR VOICE?
YOU CAN'T SPEAK?
WE NEED TO GET YOU TO A HOSPITAL!
GRAB

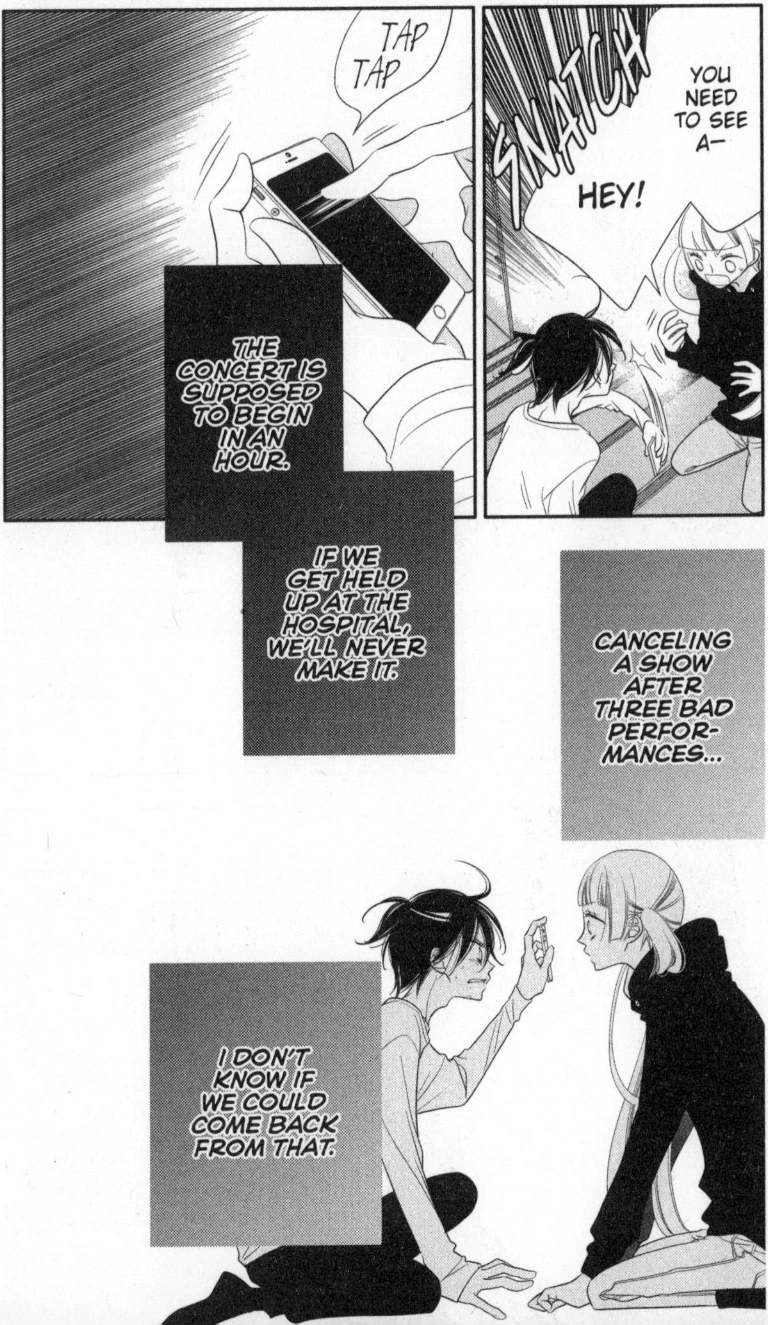
YOU NEED TO SEE A—
SNATCH
HEY!
TAP TAP
THE CONCERT IS SUPPOSED TO BEGIN IN AN HOUR.
IF WE GET HELD UP AT THE HOSPITAL, WE'LL NEVER MAKE IT.
CANCELING A SHOW AFTER THREE BAD PERFORMANCES...
I DON'T KNOW IF WE COULD COME BACK FROM THAT.

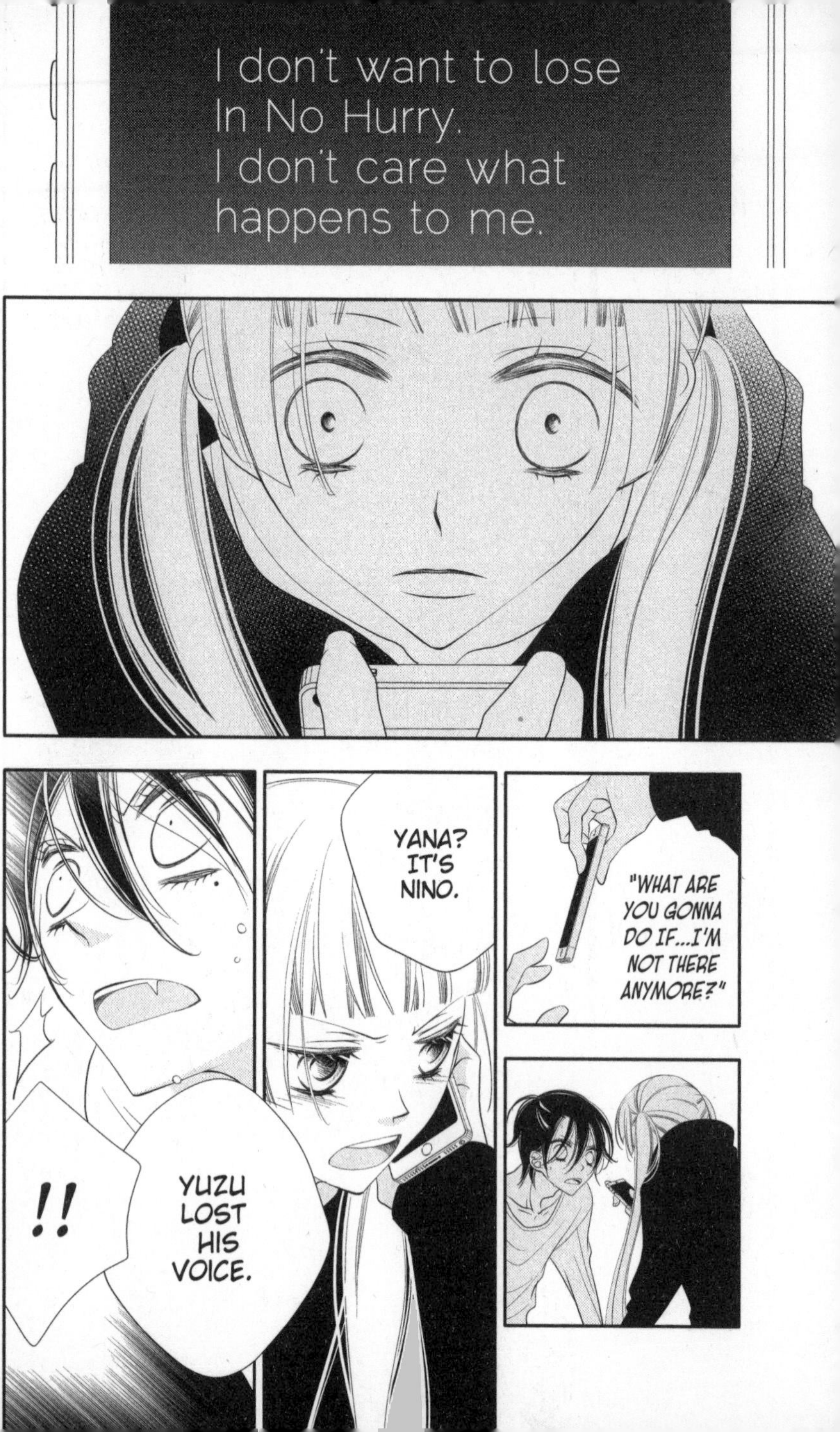
I don't want to lose
In No Hurry.
I don't care what
happens to me.
"WHAT ARE YOU GONNA DO IF...I'M NOT THERE ANYMORE?"
YANA? IT'S NINO.
YUZU LOST HIS VOICE.
!!

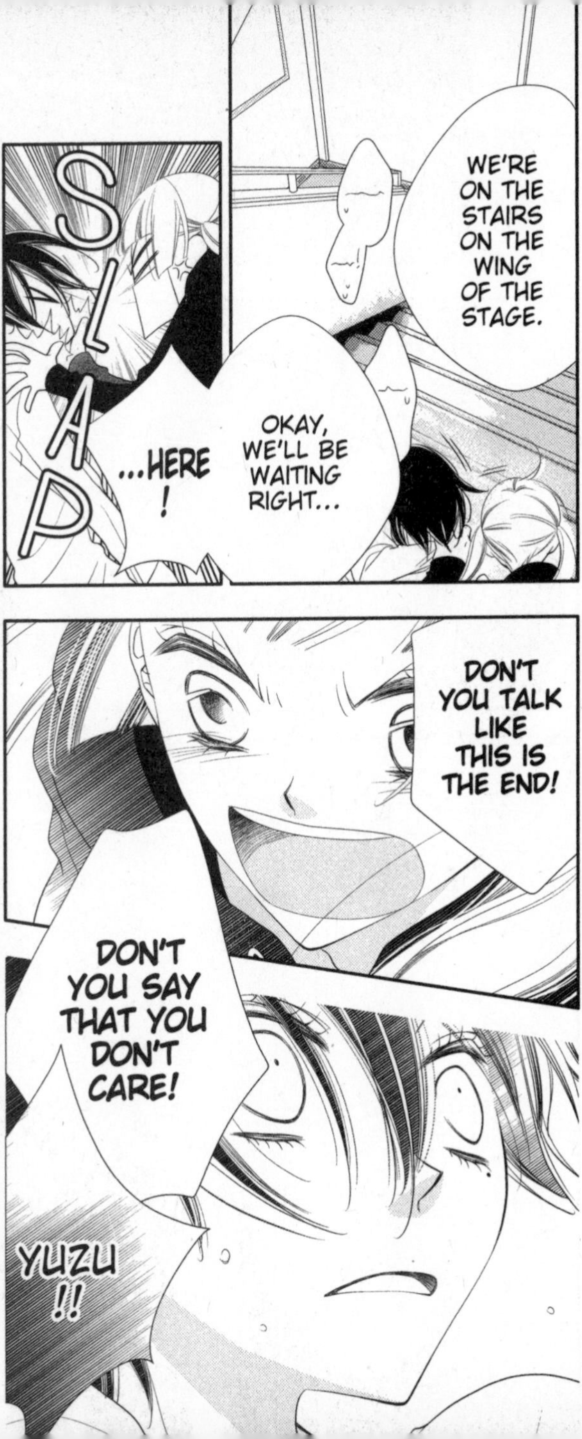
WE'RE ON THE STAIRS ON THE WING OF THE STAGE.
OKAY, WE'LL BE WAITING RIGHT...
...HERE!
SLAP
DON'T YOU TALK LIKE THIS IS THE END!
DON'T YOU SAY THAT YOU DON'T CARE!
YUZU!!

6

So, when all is said and done, what did you think of Anonymous Noise 9?

We ended up spending more time at the Shibuya Quattro than I'd expected, but I hope you'll look forward to the continuation of the tour arc! I hope to see you again in volume 10.

Thank you for reading!

[SPECIAL THANKS]
MOSAGE
TAKAYUKI NAGASHIMA
KENJU NORO
MY FAMILY
MY FRIENDS
AND YOU!!

Ryoko Fukuyama
c/o Anonymous Noise Editor
VIZ Media
P.O. Box 77010
San Francisco, CA 94107

HP http://ryoconet/
@ryocoryocoryoco
http://facebook.com/ryocoryocoryoco/

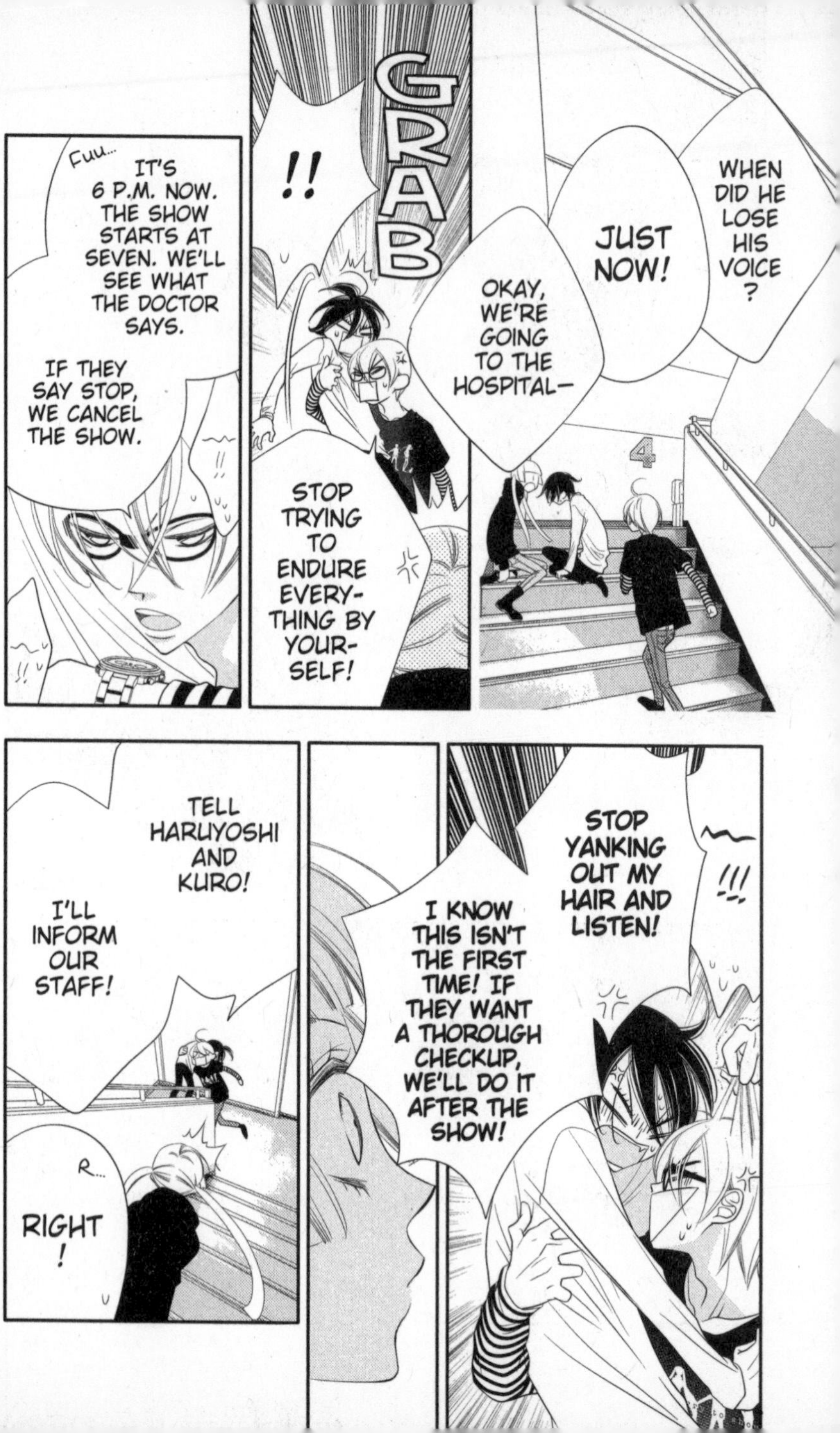
WHEN DID HE LOSE HIS VOICE?
JUST NOW!
OKAY, WE'RE GOING TO THE HOSPITAL—
GRAB
!!
STOP TRYING TO ENDURE EVERY-THING BY YOUR-SELF!
Fuu...
IT'S 6 P.M. NOW. THE SHOW STARTS AT SEVEN. WE'LL SEE WHAT THE DOCTOR SAYS.
IF THEY SAY STOP, WE CANCEL THE SHOW.
!!!
STOP YANKING OUT MY HAIR AND LISTEN!
I KNOW THIS ISN'T THE FIRST TIME! IF THEY WANT A THOROUGH CHECKUP, WE'LL DO IT AFTER THE SHOW!
TELL HARUYOSHI AND KURO!
I'LL INFORM OUR STAFF!
R...
RIGHT!

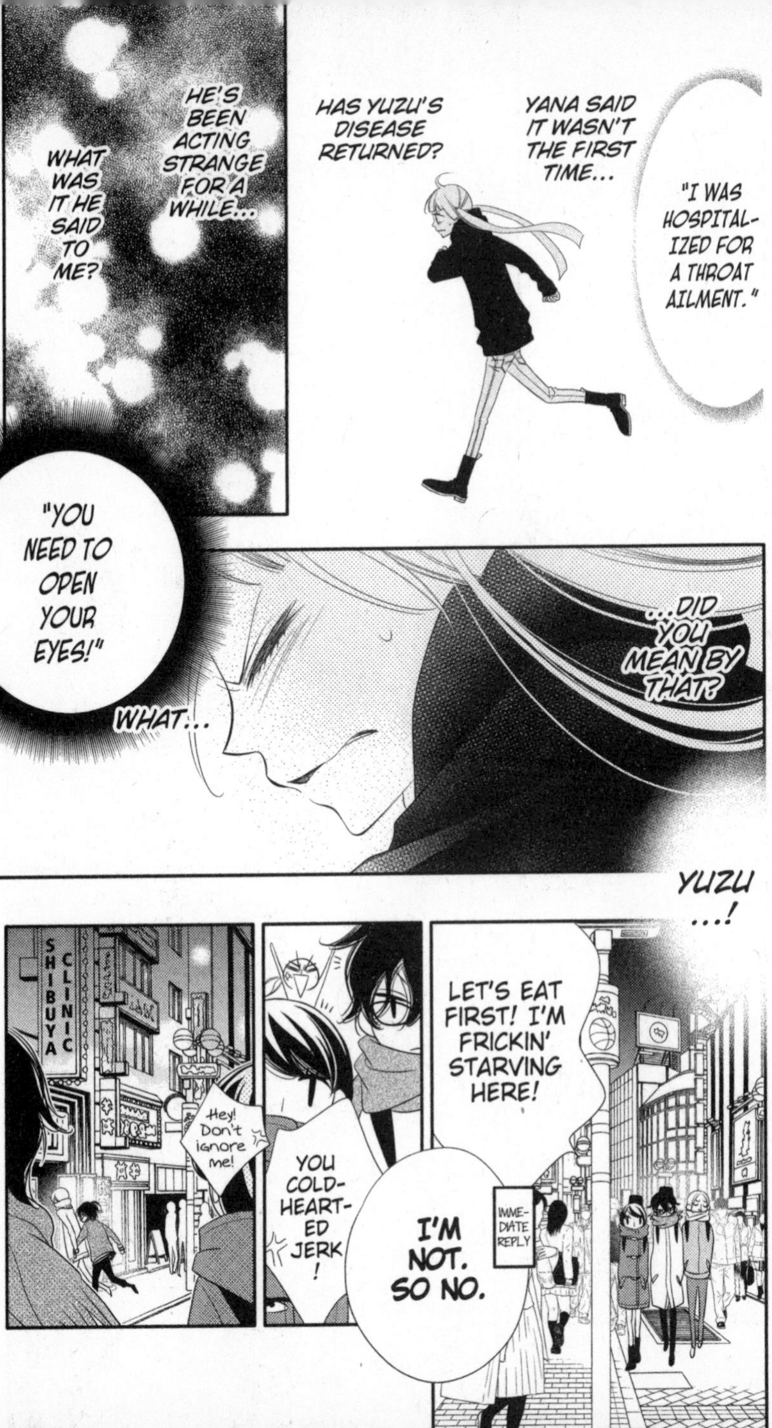
"I WAS HOSPITALIZED FOR A THROAT AILMENT."
YANA SAID IT WASN'T THE FIRST TIME...
HAS YUZU'S DISEASE RETURNED?
HE'S BEEN ACTING STRANGE FOR A WHILE...
WHAT WAS IT HE SAID TO ME?
"YOU NEED TO OPEN YOUR EYES!"
WHAT...
...DID YOU MEAN BY THAT?
YUZU...!
LET'S EAT FIRST! I'M FRICKIN' STARVING HERE!
IMMEDIATE REPLY
I'M NOT. SO NO.
YOU COLD-HEARTED JERK!
Hey! Don't ignore me!
SHIBUYA CLINIC

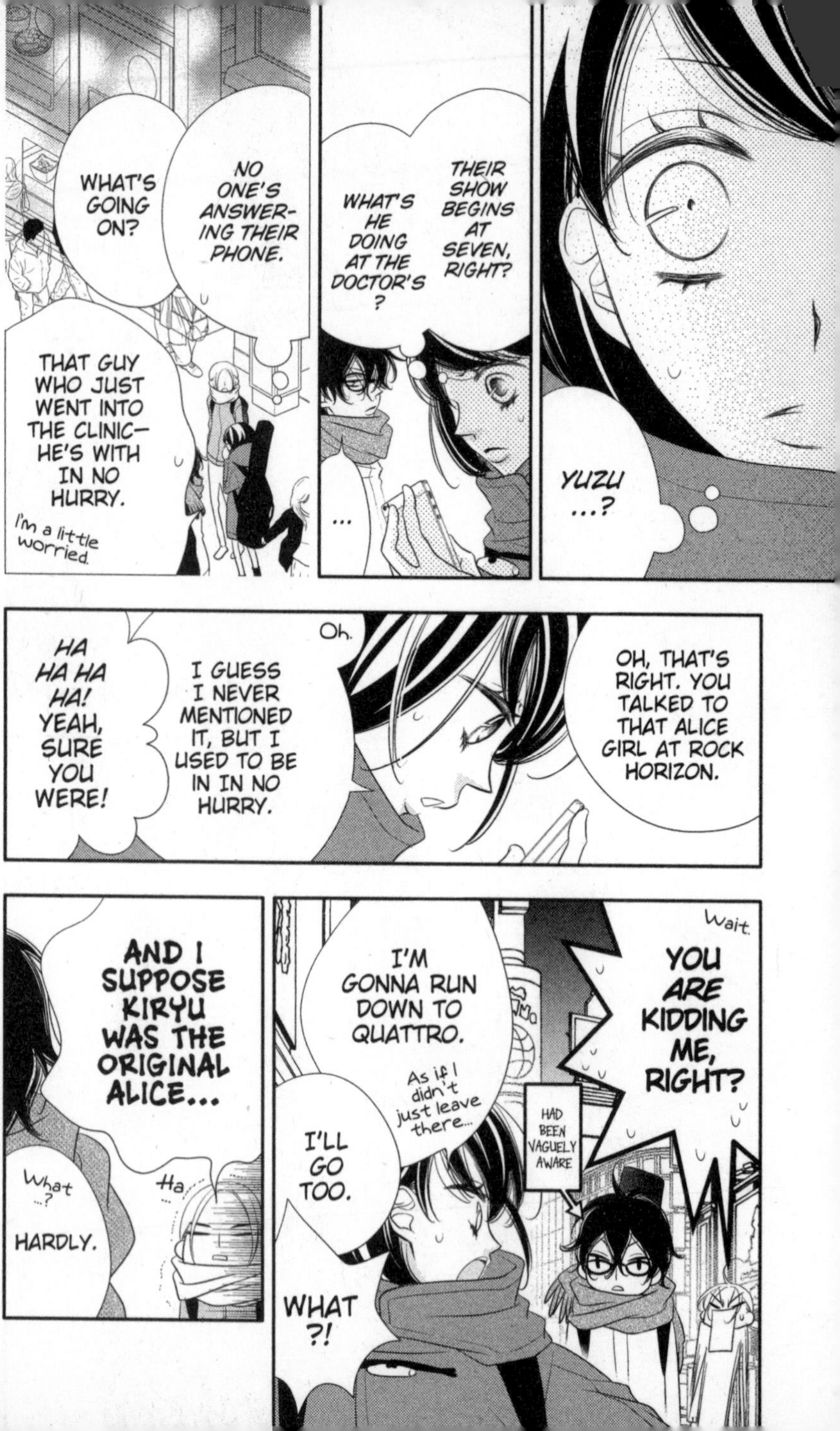
YUZU ...?
THEIR SHOW BEGINS AT SEVEN, RIGHT?
WHAT'S HE DOING AT THE DOCTOR'S?
...
NO ONE'S ANSWERING THEIR PHONE.
WHAT'S GOING ON?
THAT GUY WHO JUST WENT INTO THE CLINIC— HE'S WITH IN NO HURRY.
I'm a little worried.
Oh.
OH, THAT'S RIGHT. YOU TALKED TO THAT ALICE GIRL AT ROCK HORIZON.
I GUESS I NEVER MENTIONED IT, BUT I USED TO BE IN IN NO HURRY.
HA HA HA HA! YEAH, SURE YOU WERE!
Wait.
YOU ARE KIDDING ME, RIGHT?
I'M GONNA RUN DOWN TO QUATTRO.
As if I didn't just leave there...
HAD BEEN VAGUELY AWARE
I'LL GO TOO.
WHAT?!
AND I SUPPOSE KIRYU WAS THE ORIGINAL ALICE...
Ha...
What...?
HARDLY.

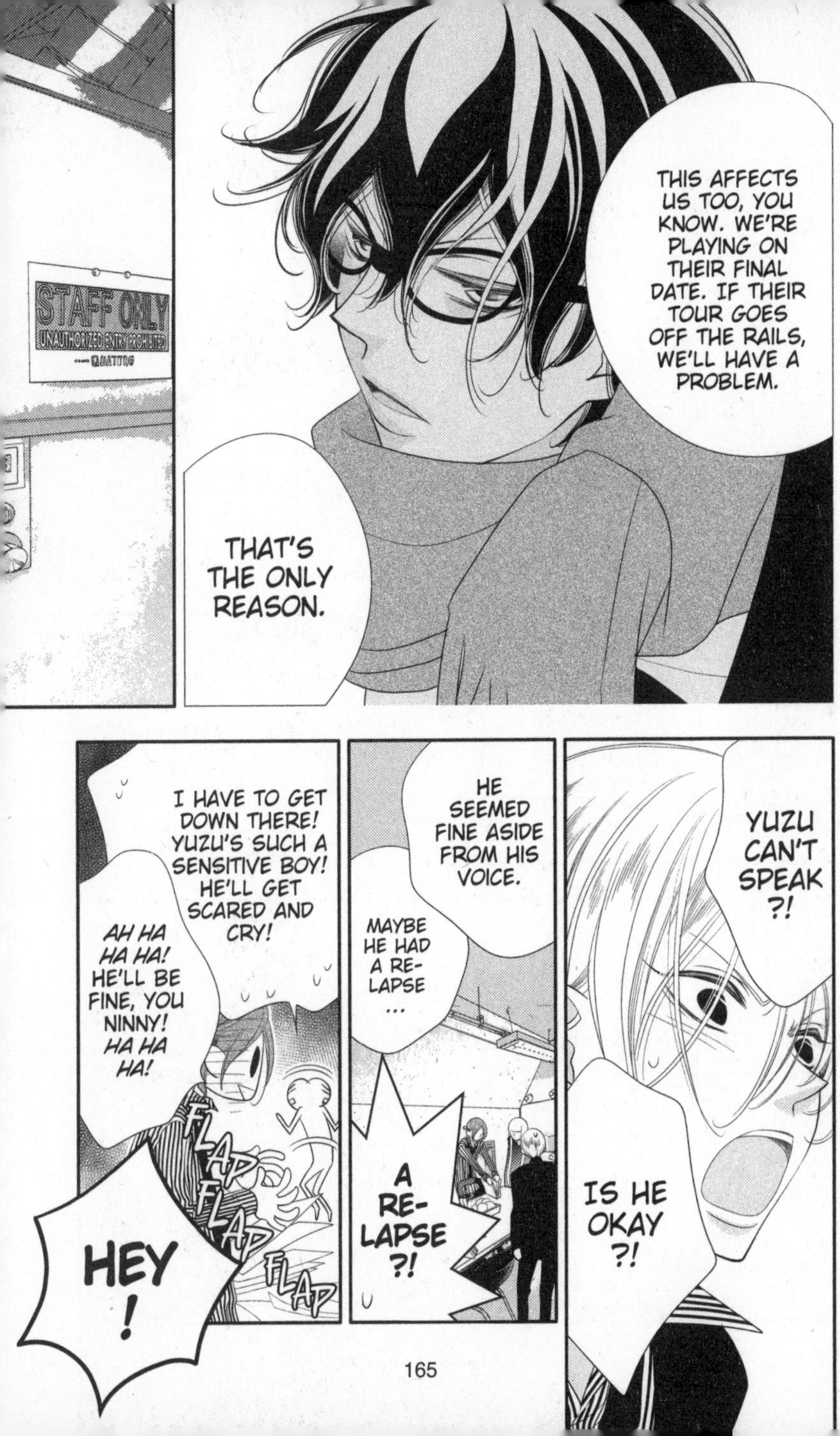

THIS AFFECTS US TOO, YOU KNOW. WE'RE PLAYING ON THEIR FINAL DATE. IF THEIR TOUR GOES OFF THE RAILS, WE'LL HAVE A PROBLEM.
THAT'S THE ONLY REASON.
STAFF ONLY
UNAUTHORIZED ENTRY PROHIBITED
YUZU CAN'T SPEAK ?!
IS HE OKAY ?!
HE SEEMED FINE ASIDE FROM HIS VOICE.
MAYBE HE HAD A RE-LAPSE ...
A RE-LAPSE ?!
I HAVE TO GET DOWN THERE! YUZU'S SUCH A SENSITIVE BOY! HE'LL GET SCARED AND CRY!
AH HA HA HA! HE'LL BE FINE, YOU NINNY! HA HA HA!
FLAP FLAP FLAP FLAP
HEY !

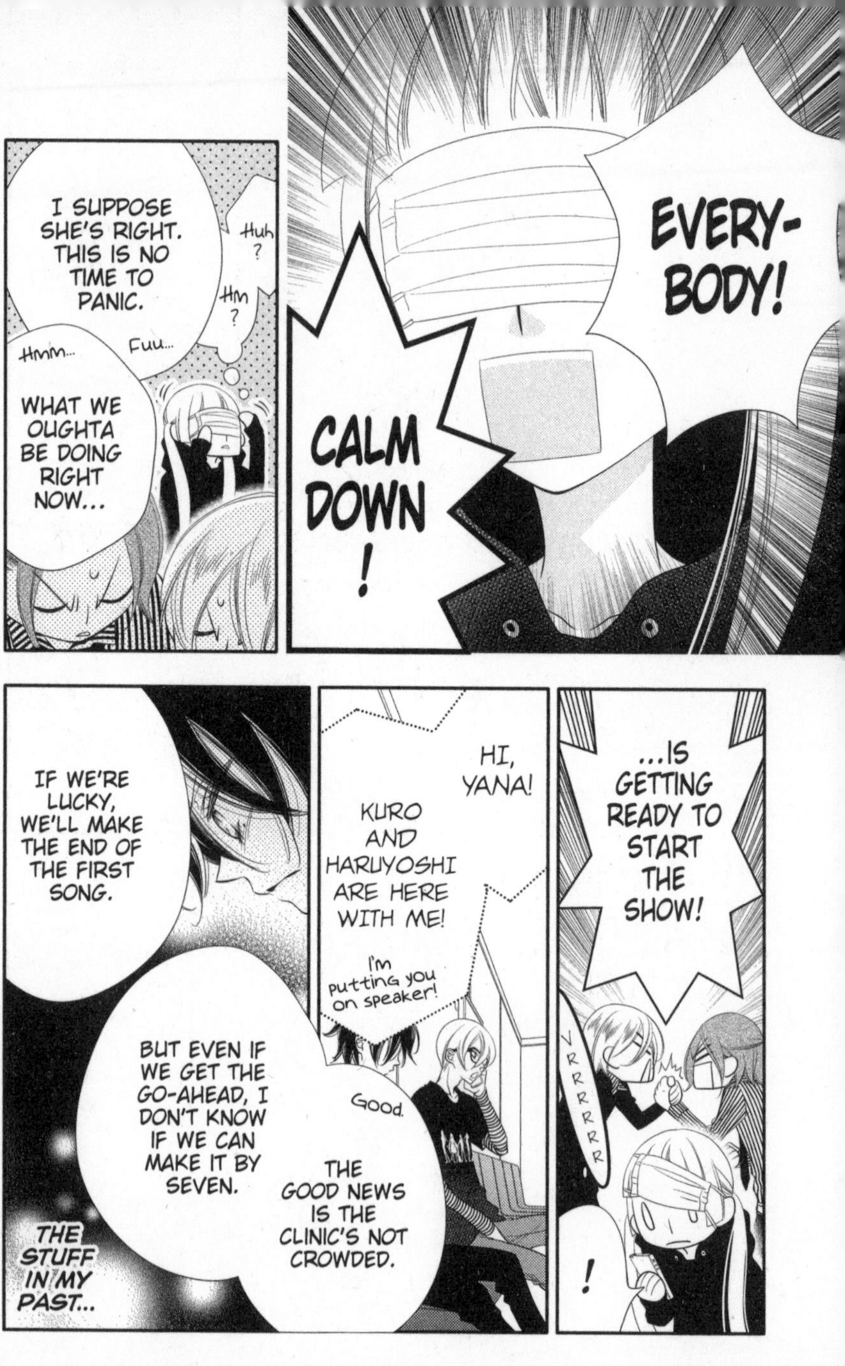
EVERY-BODY!
CALM DOWN!
Huh?
Hm?
I SUPPOSE SHE'S RIGHT. THIS IS NO TIME TO PANIC.
Fuu...
Hmm...
WHAT WE OUGHTA BE DOING RIGHT NOW...
...IS GETTING READY TO START THE SHOW!
VRRRRRR
!
HI, YANA!
KURO AND HARUYOSHI ARE HERE WITH ME!
I'm putting you on speaker!
Good.
THE GOOD NEWS IS THE CLINIC'S NOT CROWDED.
IF WE'RE LUCKY, WE'LL MAKE THE END OF THE FIRST SONG.
BUT EVEN IF WE GET THE GO-AHEAD, I DON'T KNOW IF WE CAN MAKE IT BY SEVEN.
THE STUFF IN MY PAST...

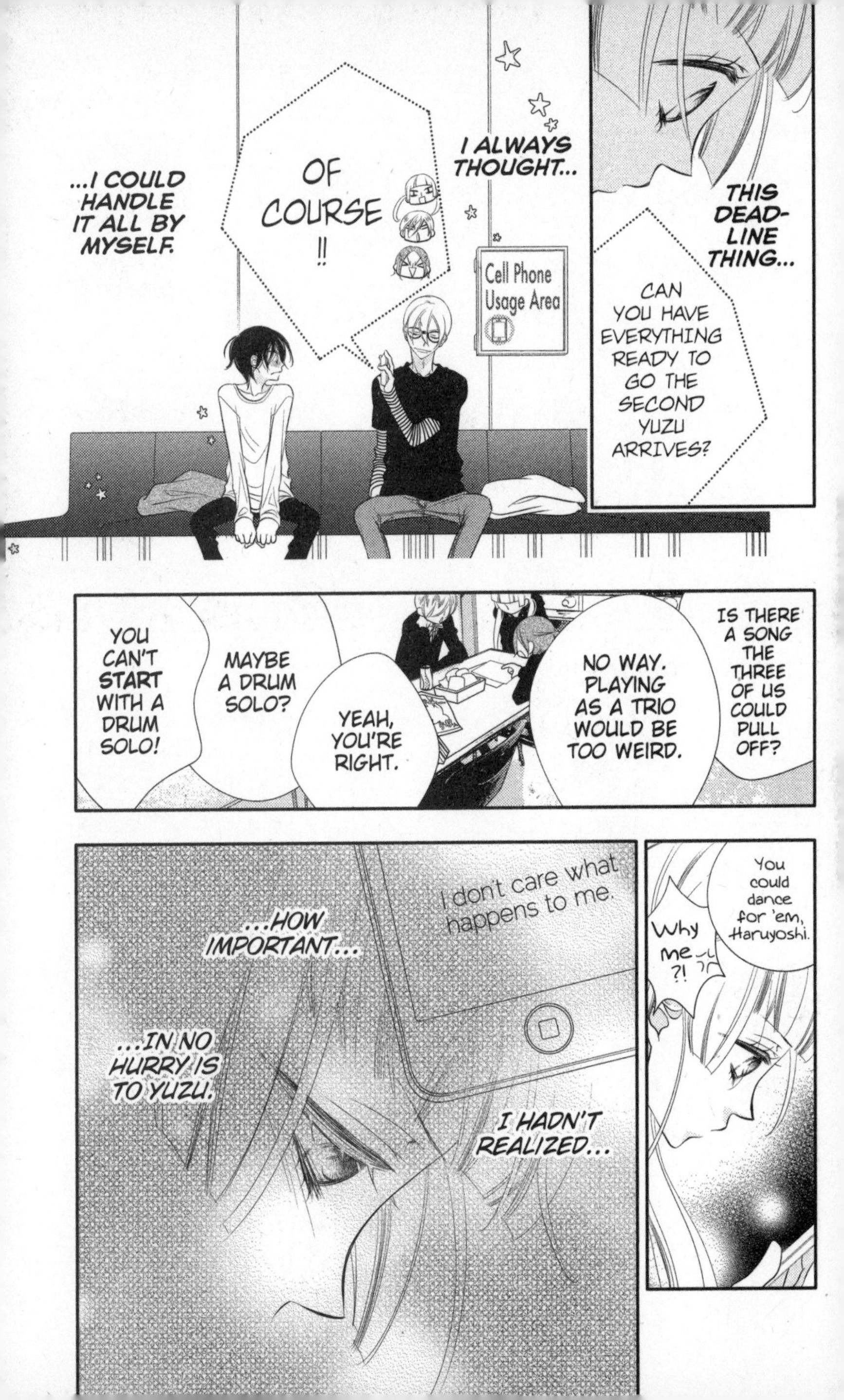
THIS DEADLINE THING...
CAN YOU HAVE EVERYTHING READY TO GO THE SECOND YUZU ARRIVES?
I ALWAYS THOUGHT...
OF COURSE!!
...I COULD HANDLE IT ALL BY MYSELF.
Cell Phone Usage Area
IS THERE A SONG THE THREE OF US COULD PULL OFF?
NO WAY. PLAYING AS A TRIO WOULD BE TOO WEIRD.
YEAH, YOU'RE RIGHT.
MAYBE A DRUM SOLO?
YOU CAN'T START WITH A DRUM SOLO!
You could dance for 'em, Haruyoshi.
Why me?!
I don't care what happens to me.
I HADN'T REALIZED...
...HOW IMPORTANT...
...IN NO HURRY IS TO YUZU.

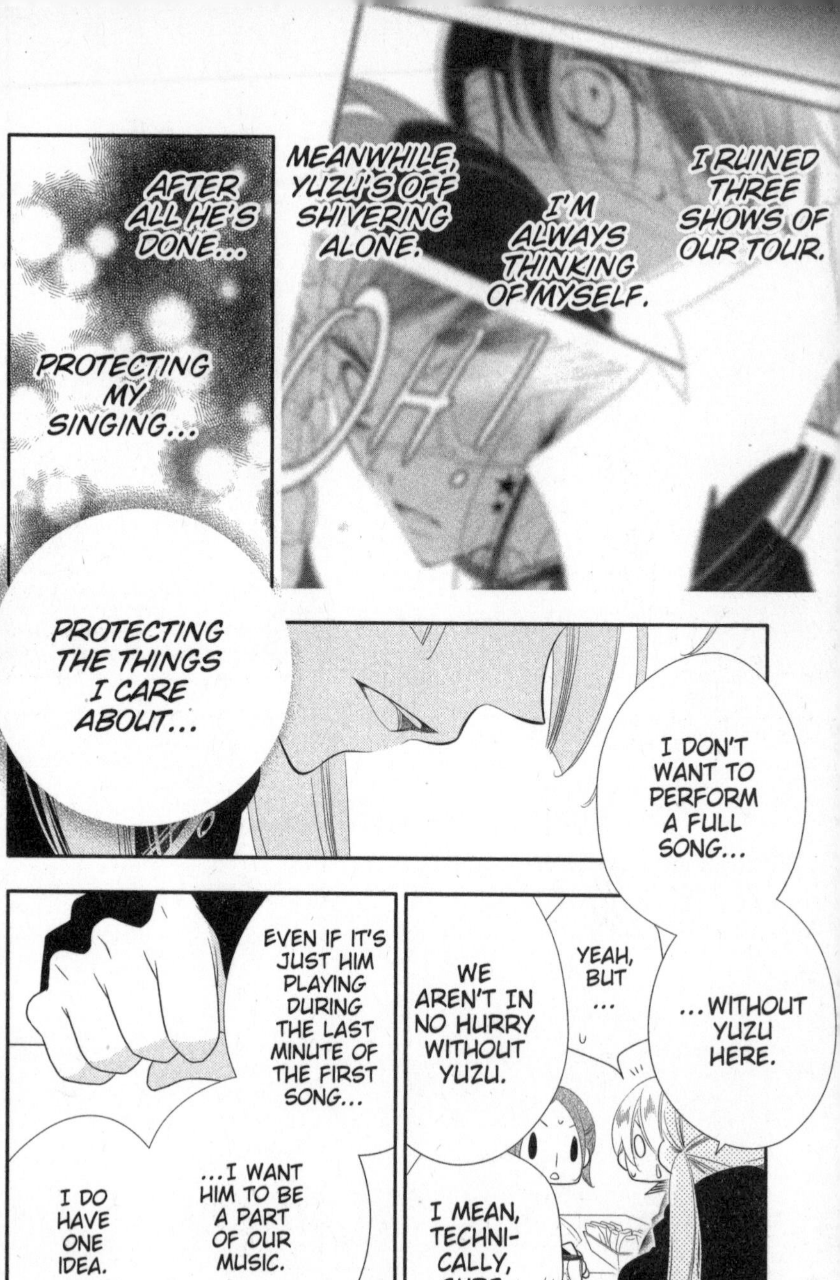
I RUINED THREE SHOWS OF OUR TOUR.
I'M ALWAYS THINKING OF MYSELF.
MEANWHILE, YUZU'S OFF SHIVERING ALONE.
AFTER ALL HE'S DONE...
PROTECTING MY SINGING...
PROTECTING THE THINGS I CARE ABOUT...
I DON'T WANT TO PERFORM A FULL SONG...
...WITHOUT YUZU HERE.
YEAH, BUT ...
WE AREN'T IN NO HURRY WITHOUT YUZU.
I MEAN, TECHNICALLY, SURE.
EVEN IF IT'S JUST HIM PLAYING DURING THE LAST MINUTE OF THE FIRST SONG...
...I WANT HIM TO BE A PART OF OUR MUSIC.
I DO HAVE ONE IDEA.

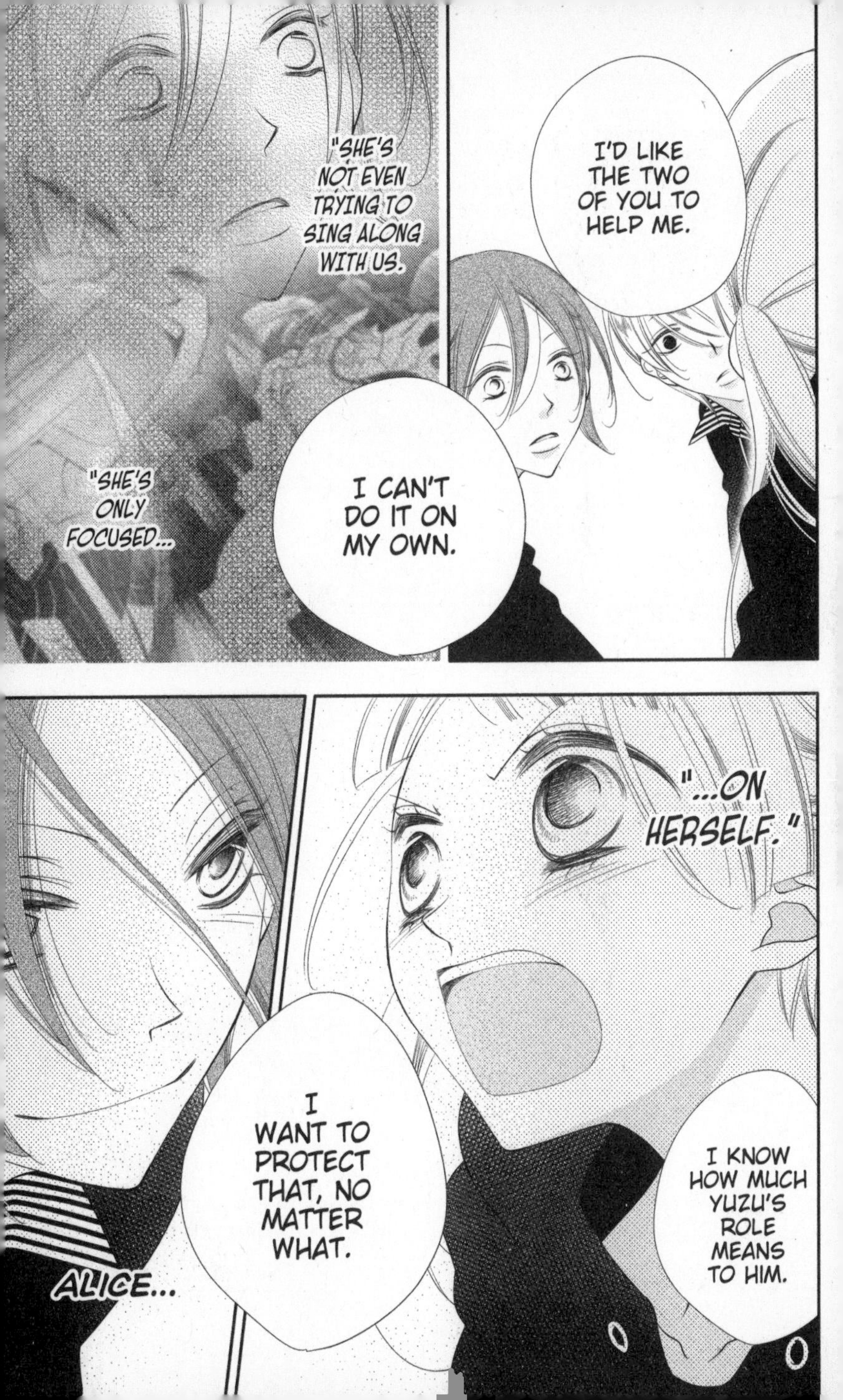
I'D LIKE THE TWO OF YOU TO HELP ME.
I CAN'T DO IT ON MY OWN.
"SHE'S NOT EVEN TRYING TO SING ALONG WITH US.
"SHE'S ONLY FOCUSED...
"...ON HERSELF."
I KNOW HOW MUCH YUZU'S ROLE MEANS TO HIM.
I WANT TO PROTECT THAT, NO MATTER WHAT.
ALICE...

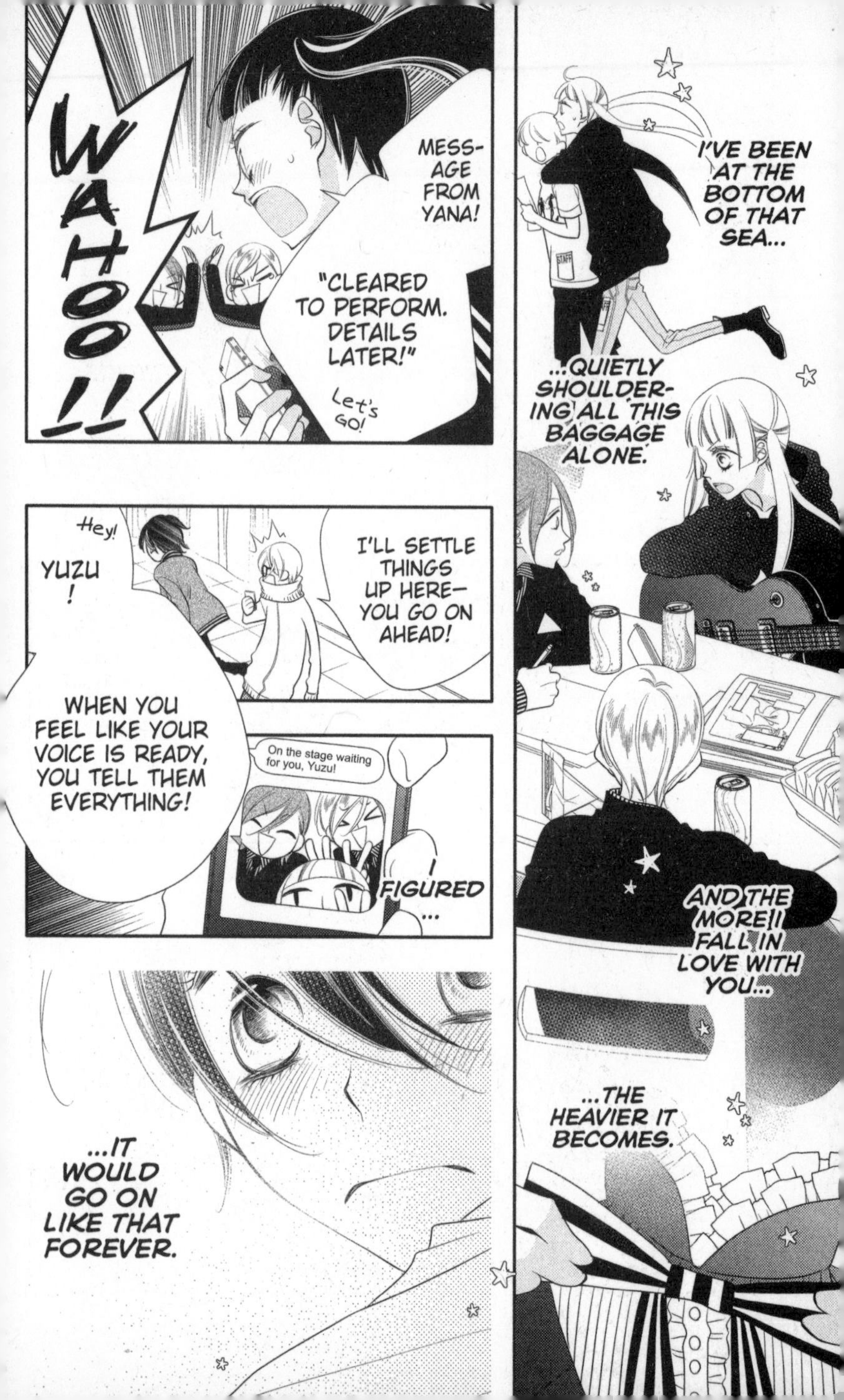
I'VE BEEN AT THE BOTTOM OF THAT SEA...
...QUIETLY SHOULDERING ALL THIS BAGGAGE ALONE.
AND THE MORE I FALL IN LOVE WITH YOU...
...THE HEAVIER IT BECOMES.
MESSAGE FROM YANA!
"CLEARED TO PERFORM. DETAILS LATER!"
Let's GO!
WAHOO!!
I'LL SETTLE THINGS UP HERE—YOU GO ON AHEAD!
Hey!
YUZU!
WHEN YOU FEEL LIKE YOUR VOICE IS READY, YOU TELL THEM EVERYTHING!
On the stage waiting for you, Yuzu!
I FIGURED...
...IT WOULD GO ON LIKE THAT FOREVER.

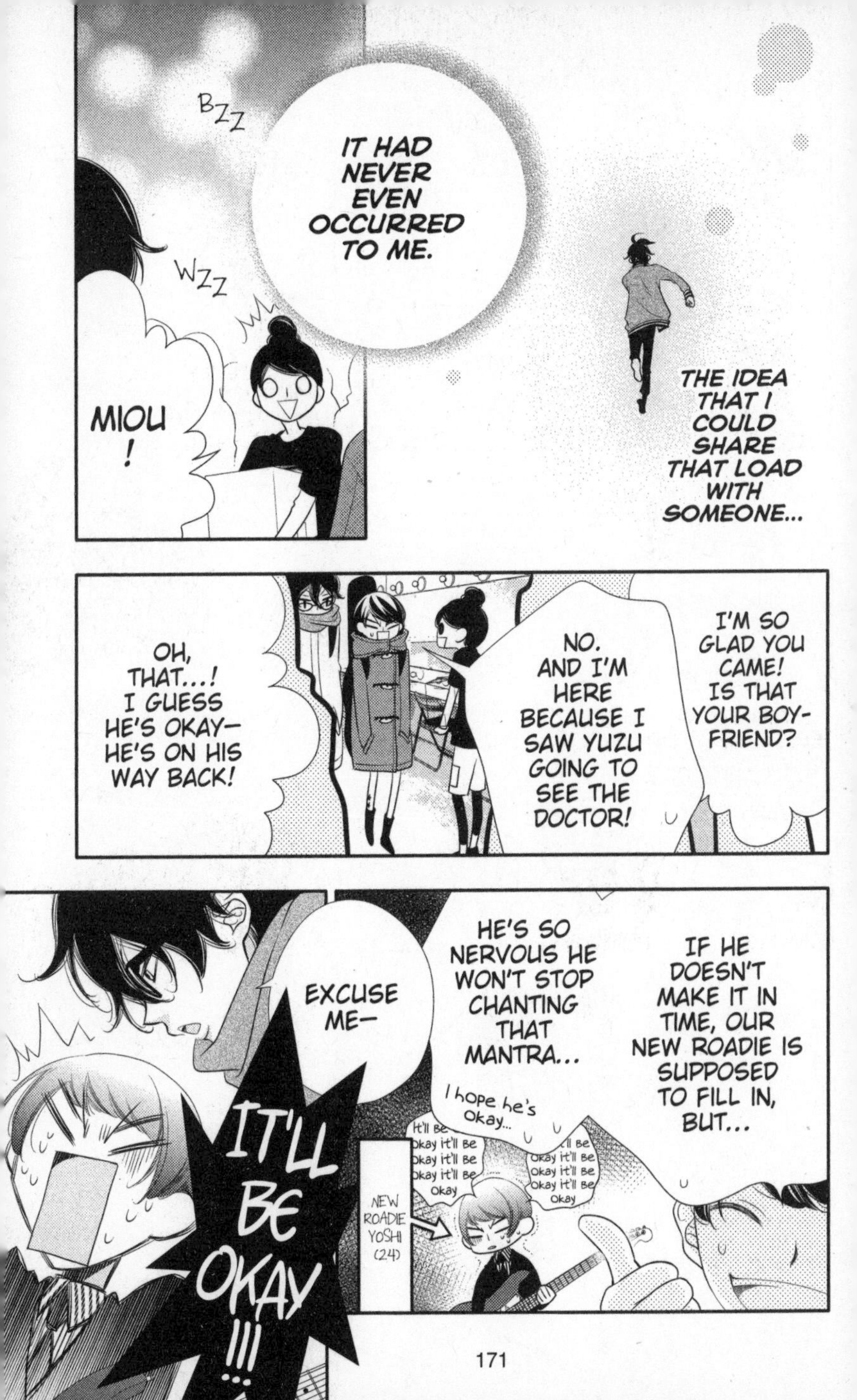
THE IDEA THAT I COULD SHARE THAT LOAD WITH SOMEONE...
IT HAD NEVER EVEN OCCURRED TO ME.
BZZ
WZZ
MIOU!
I'M SO GLAD YOU CAME! IS THAT YOUR BOY-FRIEND?
NO. AND I'M HERE BECAUSE I SAW YUZU GOING TO SEE THE DOCTOR!
OH, THAT...! I GUESS HE'S OKAY— HE'S ON HIS WAY BACK!
IF HE DOESN'T MAKE IT IN TIME, OUR NEW ROADIE IS SUPPOSED TO FILL IN, BUT...
HE'S SO NERVOUS HE WON'T STOP CHANTING THAT MANTRA...
I hope he's okay...
okay it'll be okay it'll be okay it'll be okay
It'll be okay it'll be okay it'll be okay it'll be okay
NEW ROADIE YOSHI (24)
EXCUSE ME—
IT'LL BE OKAY!!!

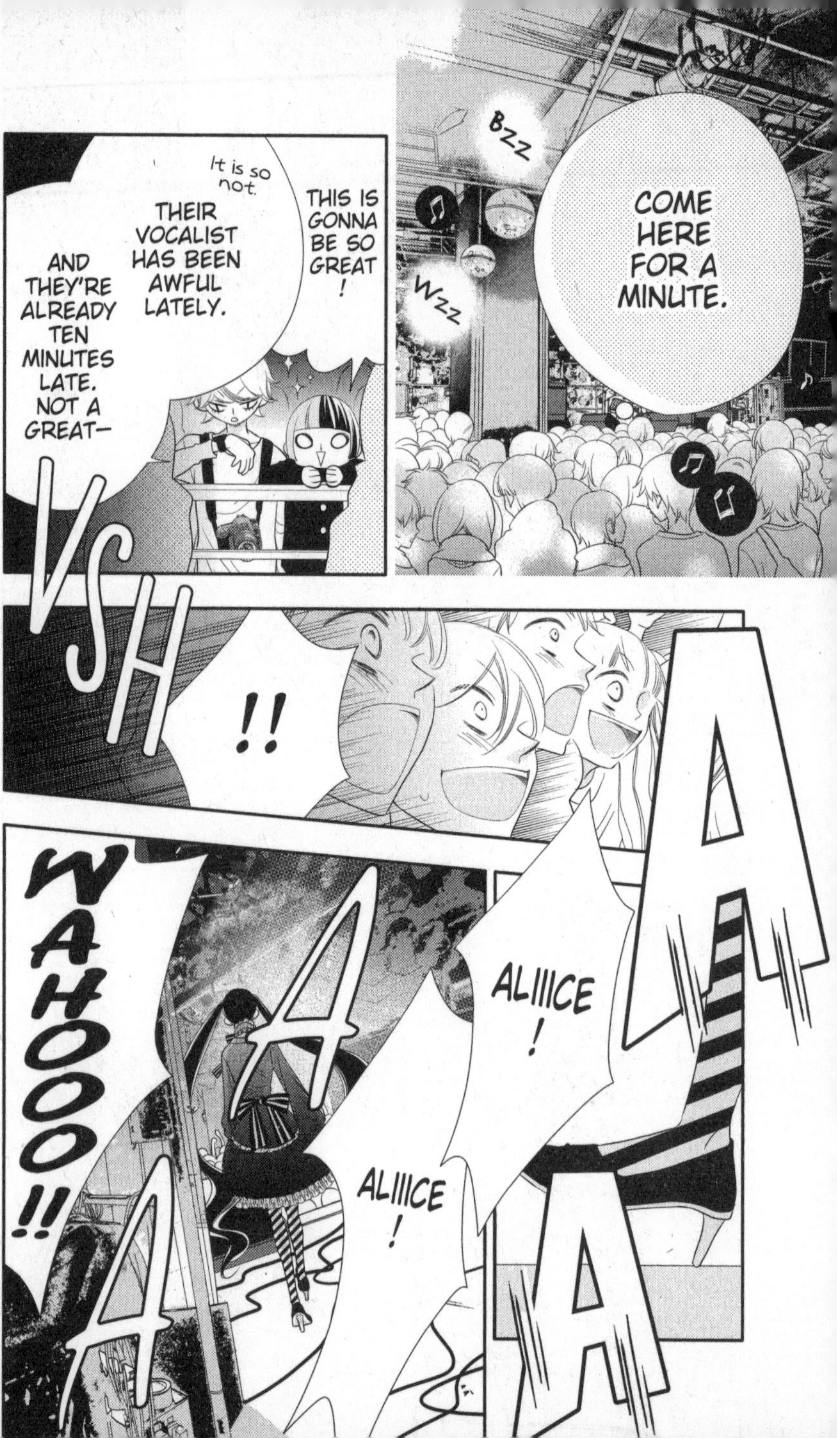
BZZ
COME HERE FOR A MINUTE.
WZZ
THIS IS GONNA BE SO GREAT!
It is so not.
THEIR VOCALIST HAS BEEN AWFUL LATELY.
AND THEY'RE ALREADY TEN MINUTES LATE. NOT A GREAT—
VSH
!!
AAAA
ALIIICE!
ALIIICE!
WAHOOO!!

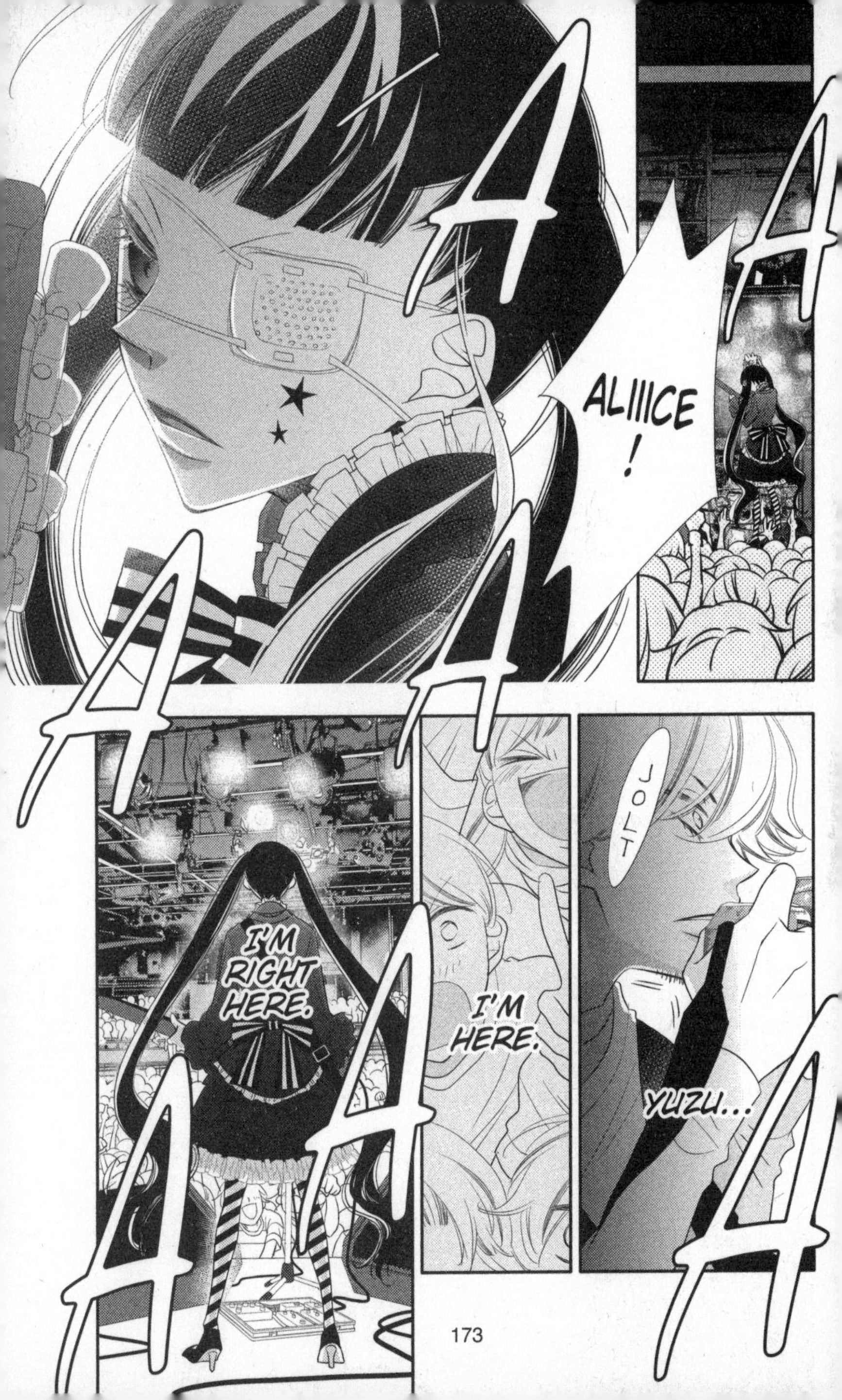
ALIIICE!
AAAAAAAAAA
JOLT
YUZU...
I'M HERE.
I'M RIGHT HERE.

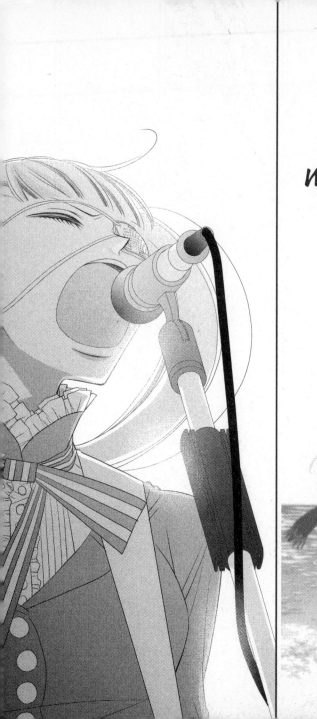

WAITING
FOR
YOU.

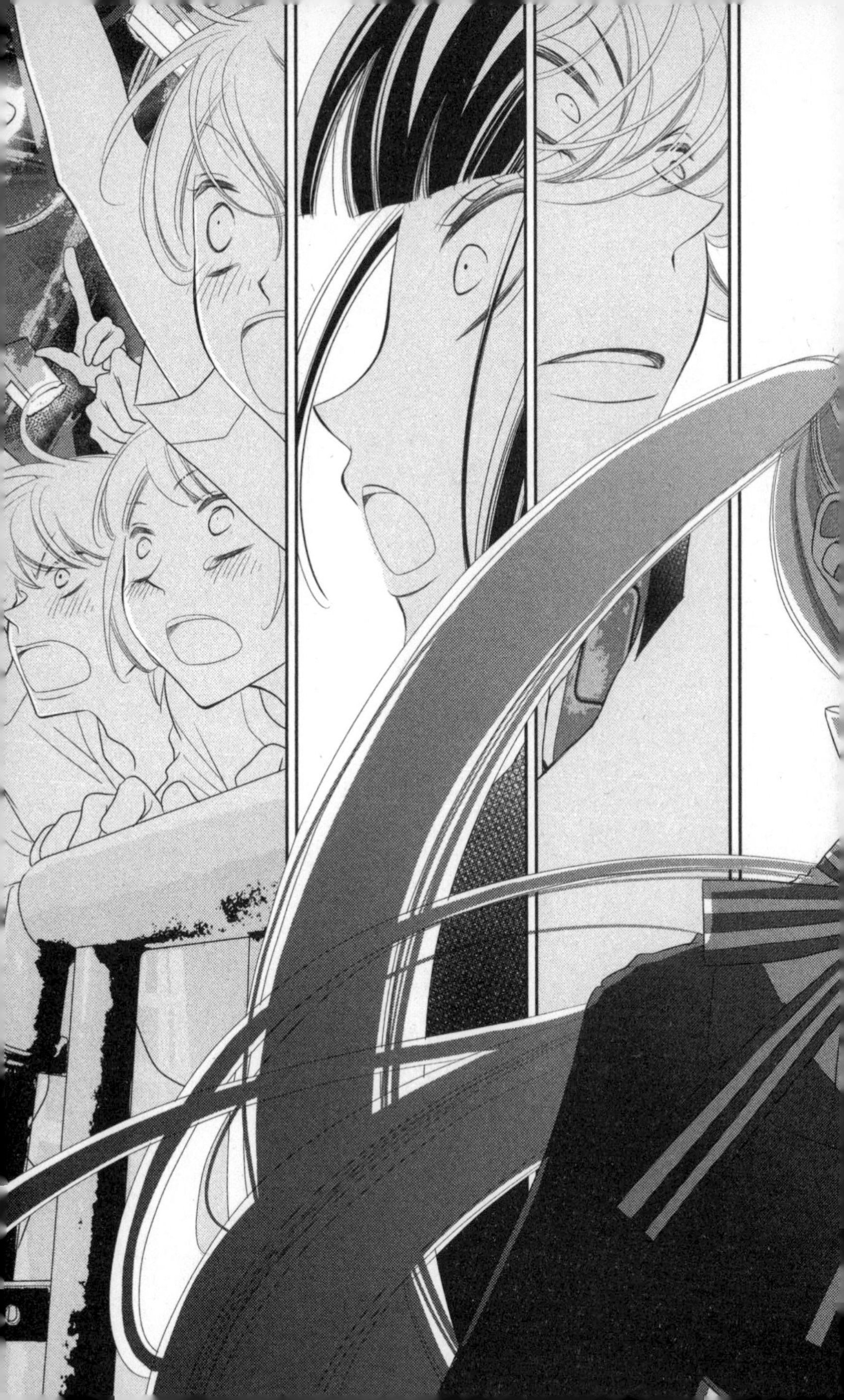

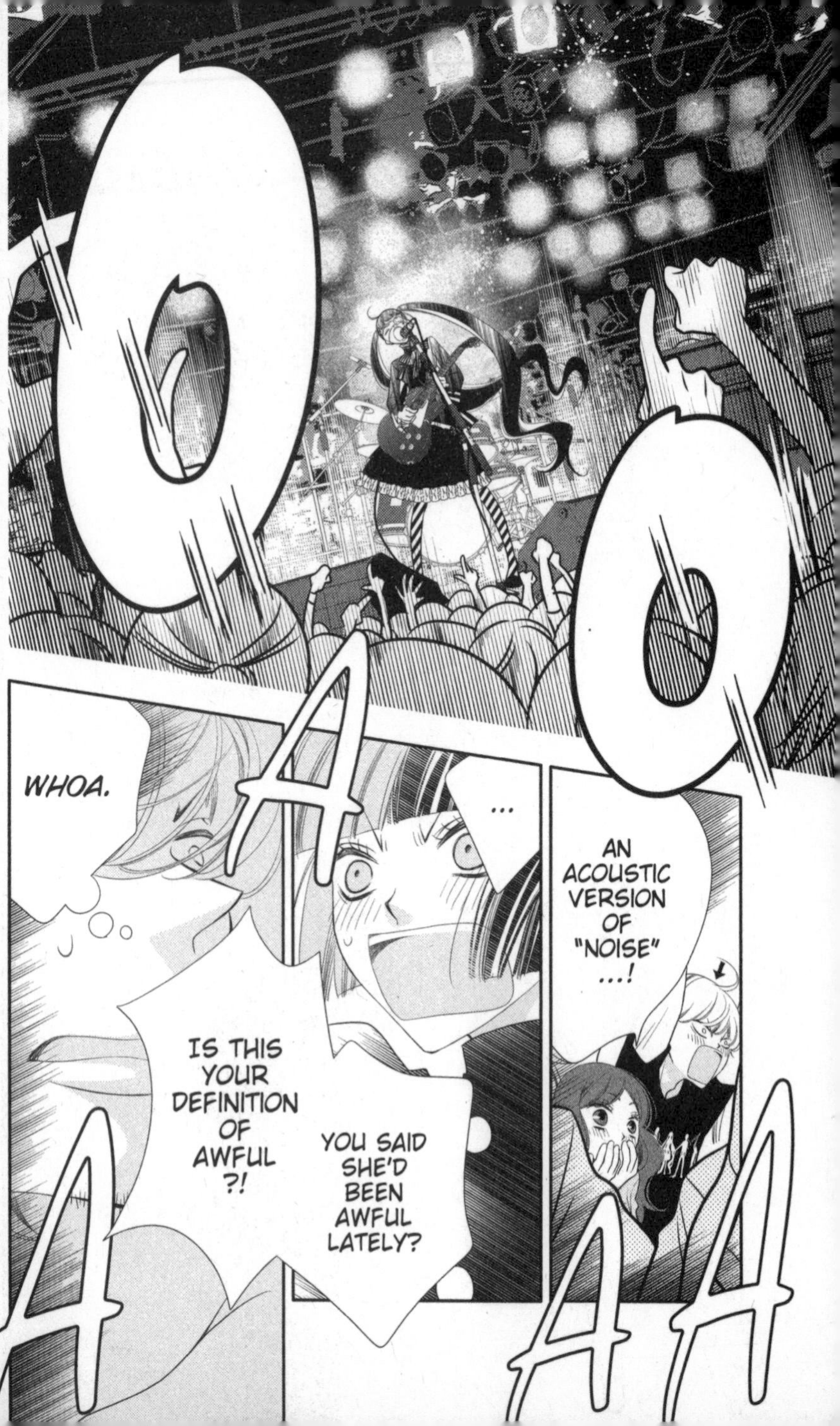
OOAAAA
AN ACOUSTIC VERSION OF "NOISE" ...!
...
YOU SAID SHE'D BEEN AWFUL LATELY?
WHOA.
IS THIS YOUR DEFINITION OF AWFUL ?!

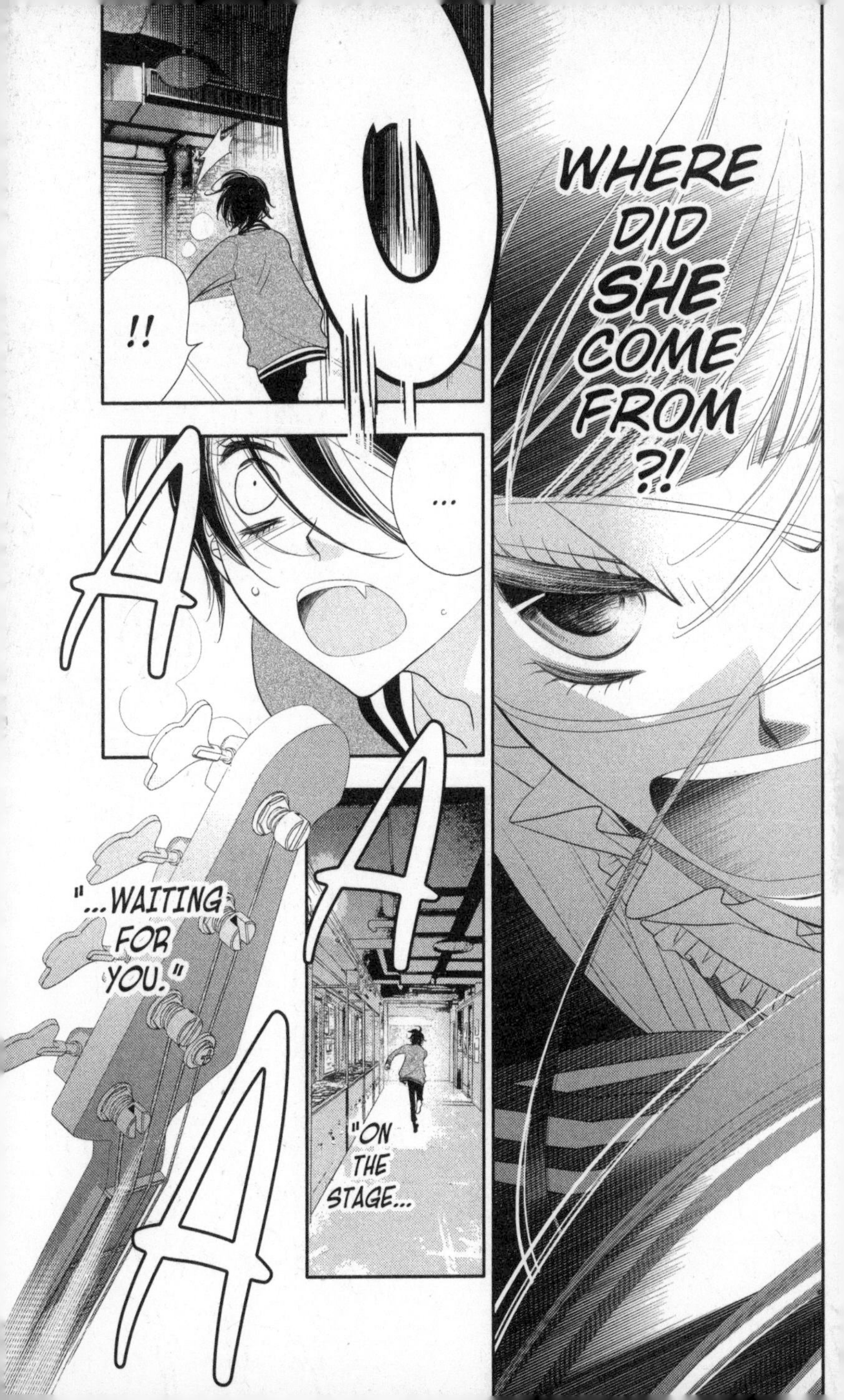

WHERE DID SHE COME FROM?!
!!
...
AAAA
"ON THE STAGE...
"...WAITING FOR YOU."

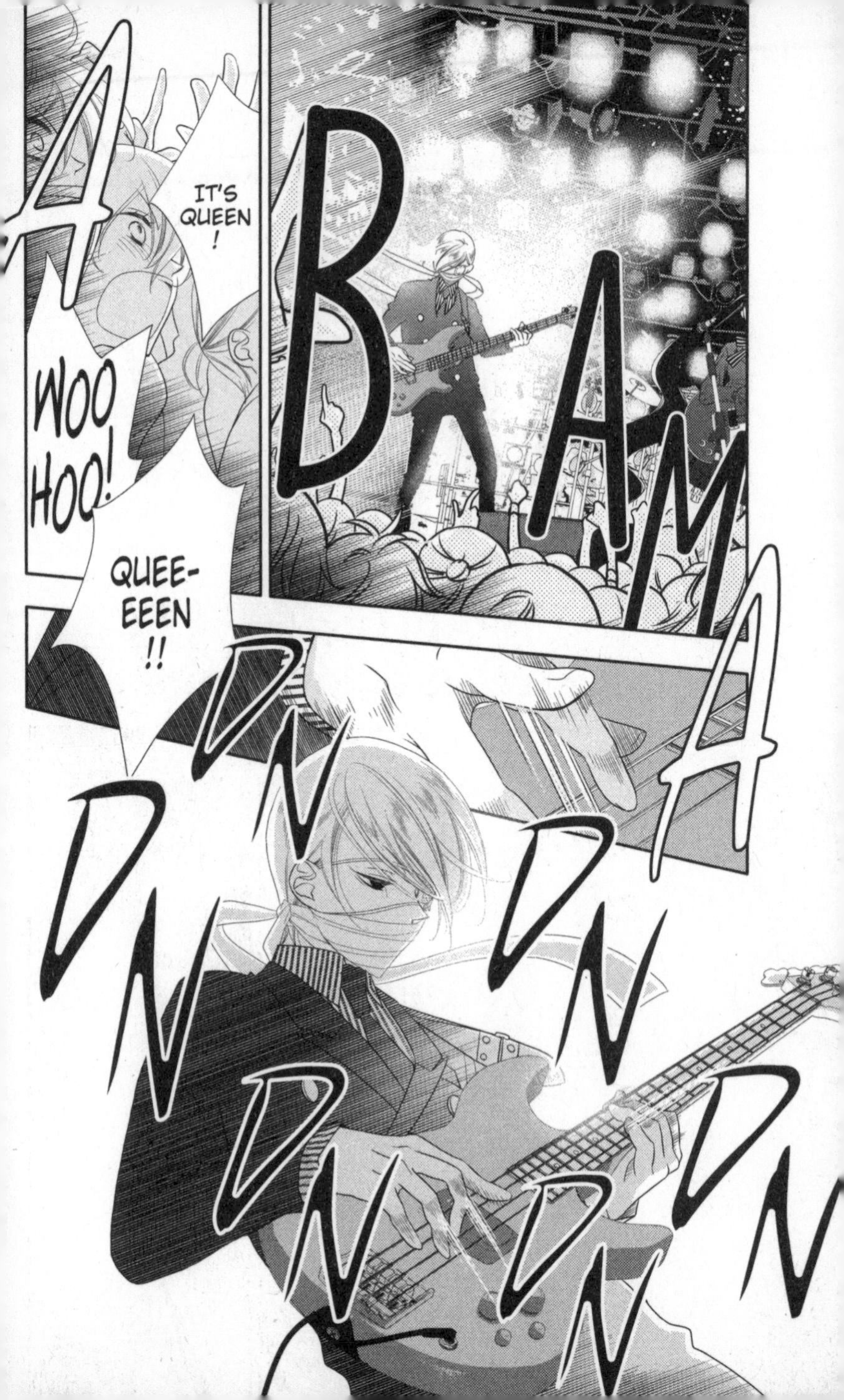
BAM
A
A
IT'S QUEEN!
WOO HOO!
QUEEE-EEEN!!
DN DN DN DN DN DN

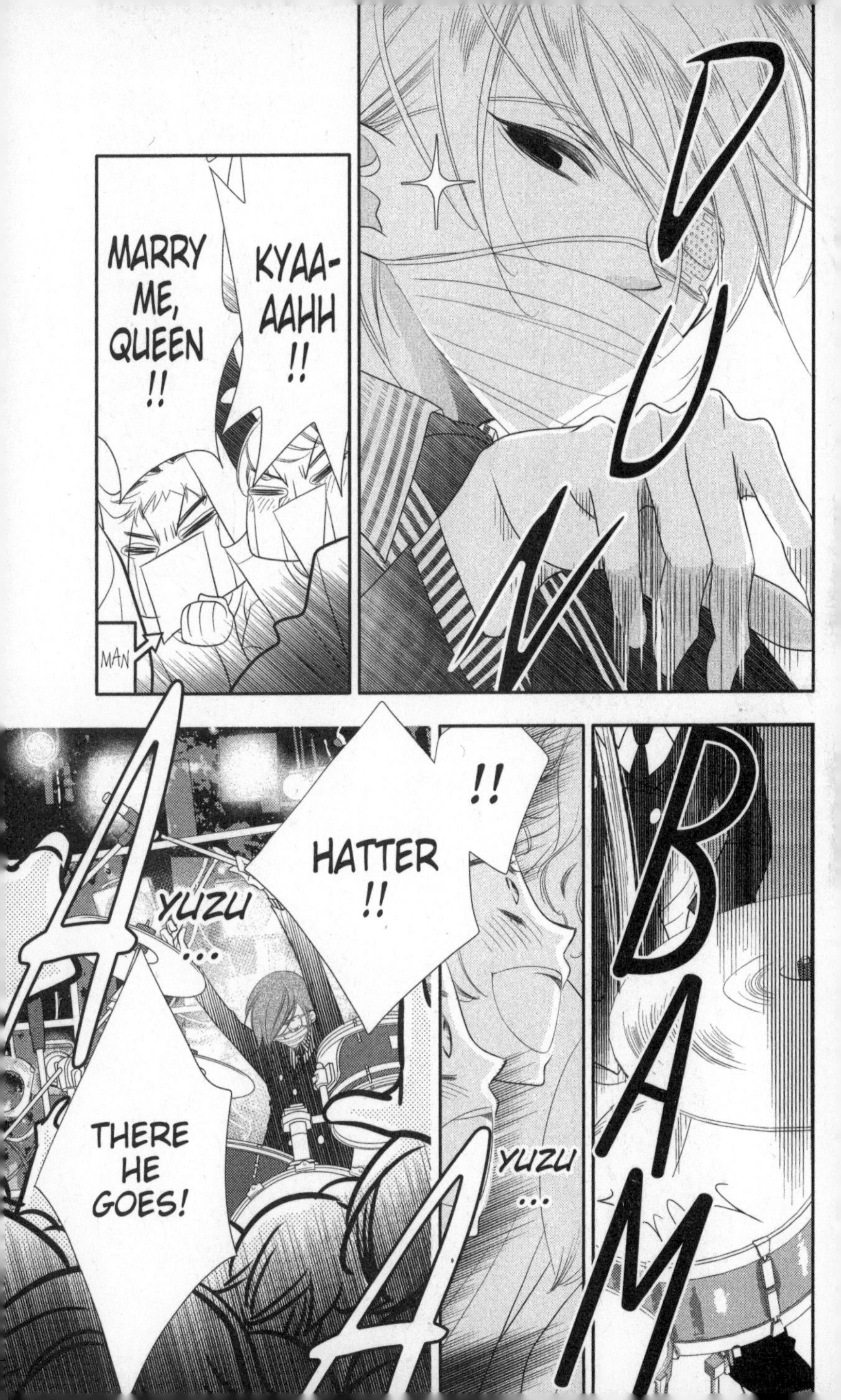
DUN
KYAA-AAHH!!
MARRY ME, QUEEN!!
MAN
BAM
YUZU...
!!
HATTER!!
YUZU...
THERE HE GOES!

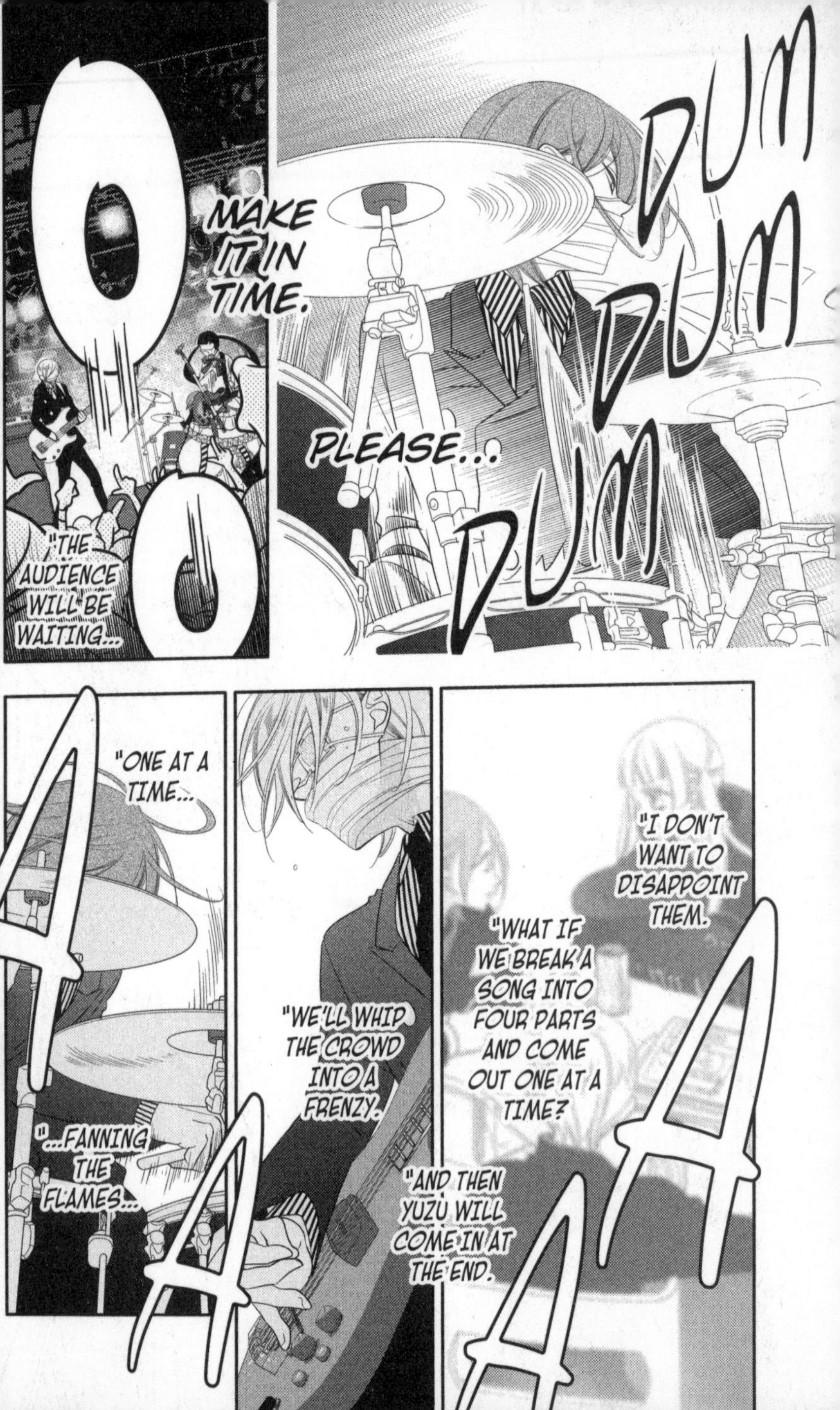
DUM DUM DUM
MAKE IT IN TIME.
PLEASE...
OO
"THE AUDIENCE WILL BE WAITING...
AAAAA
"I DON'T WANT TO DISAPPOINT THEM.
"WHAT IF WE BREAK A SONG INTO FOUR PARTS AND COME OUT ONE AT A TIME?
"AND THEN YUZU WILL COME IN AT THE END.
"WE'LL WHIP THE CROWD INTO A FRENZY.
"ONE AT A TIME...
"...FANNING THE FLAMES...

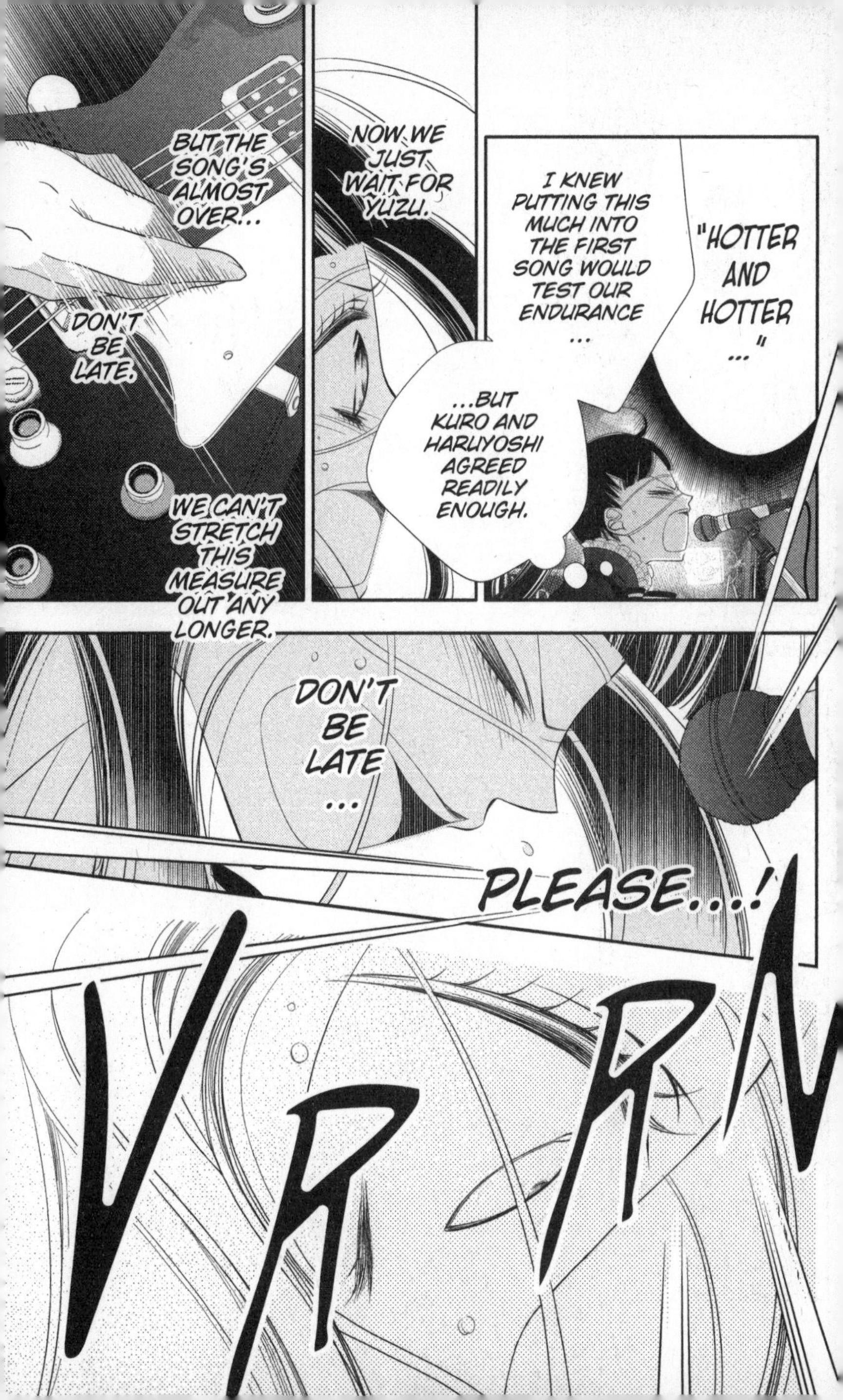
"HOTTER AND HOTTER..."
I KNEW PUTTING THIS MUCH INTO THE FIRST SONG WOULD TEST OUR ENDURANCE...
...BUT KURO AND HARUYOSHI AGREED READILY ENOUGH.
NOW WE JUST WAIT FOR YUZU.
BUT THE SONG'S ALMOST OVER...
DON'T BE LATE.
WE CAN'T STRETCH THIS MEASURE OUT ANY LONGER.
DON'T BE LATE...
PLEASE...!
VRRN

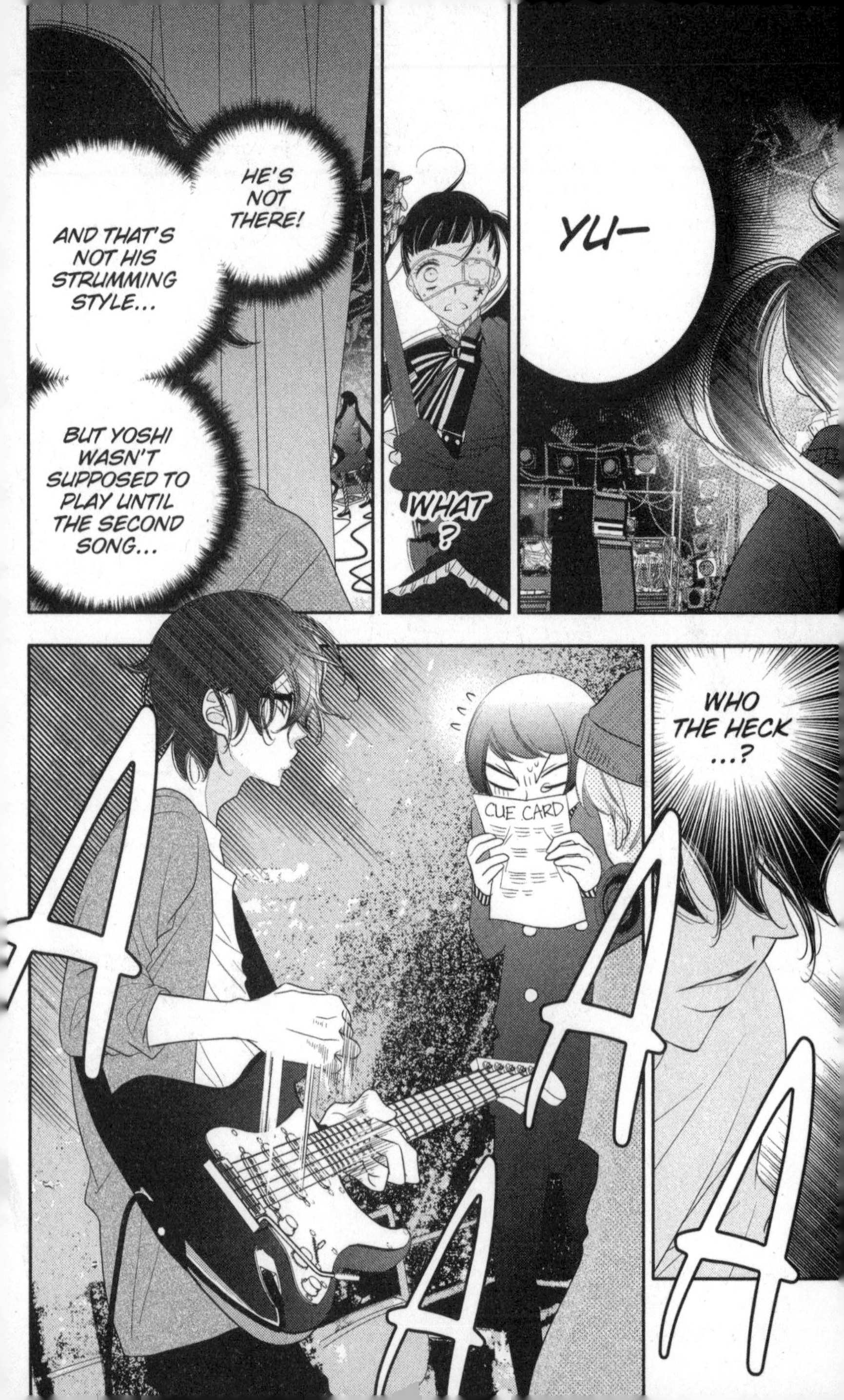
YU–
WHAT?
HE'S NOT THERE!
AND THAT'S NOT HIS STRUMMING STYLE...
BUT YOSHI WASN'T SUPPOSED TO PLAY UNTIL THE SECOND SONG...
WHO THE HECK ...?
CUE CARD

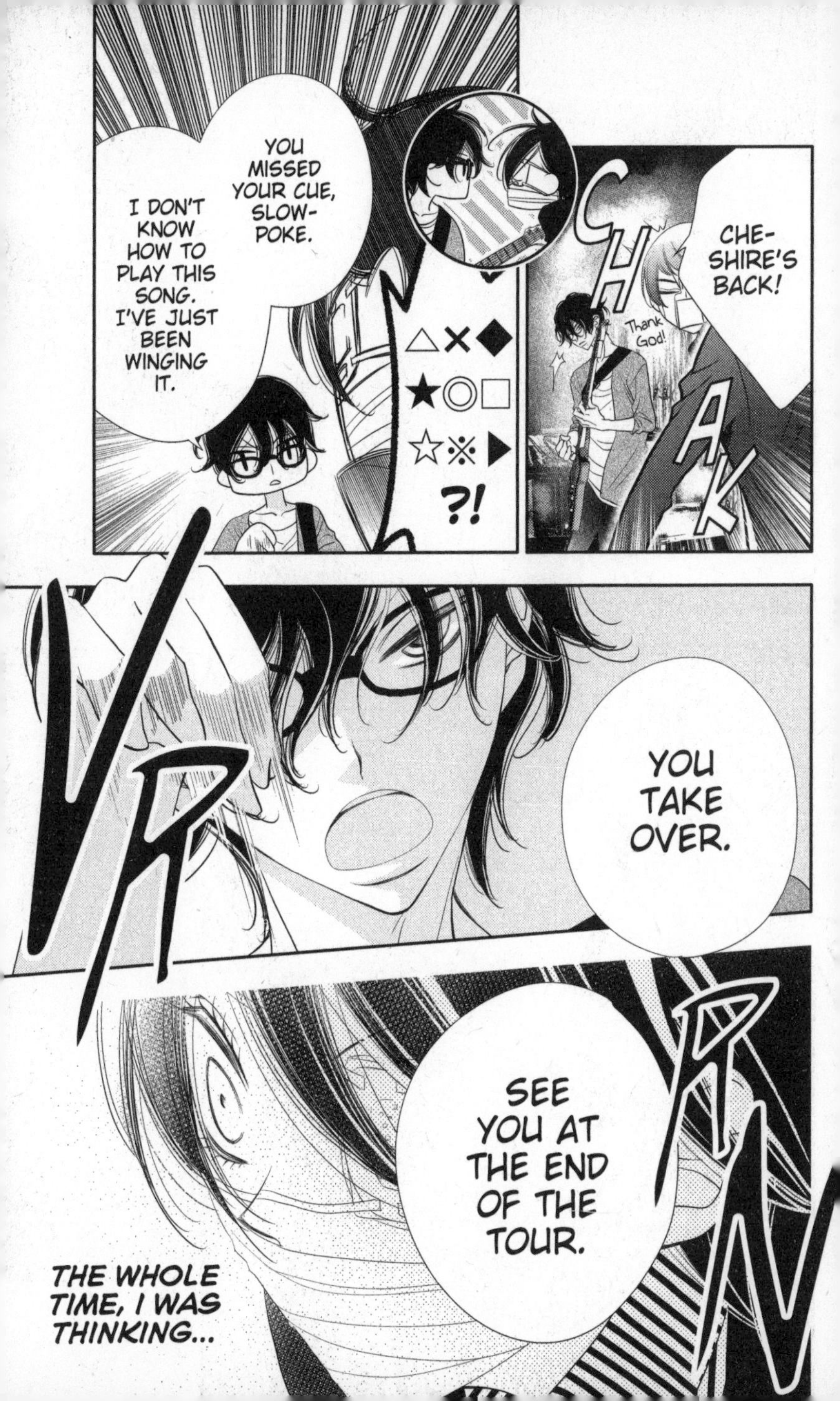
CHE-SHIRE'S BACK!
CHAK
Thank God!
YOU MISSED YOUR CUE, SLOW-POKE.
I DON'T KNOW HOW TO PLAY THIS SONG. I'VE JUST BEEN WINGING IT.
△×◆
★◎□
☆※▶
?!
YOU TAKE OVER.
SEE YOU AT THE END OF THE TOUR.
THE WHOLE TIME, I WAS THINKING...

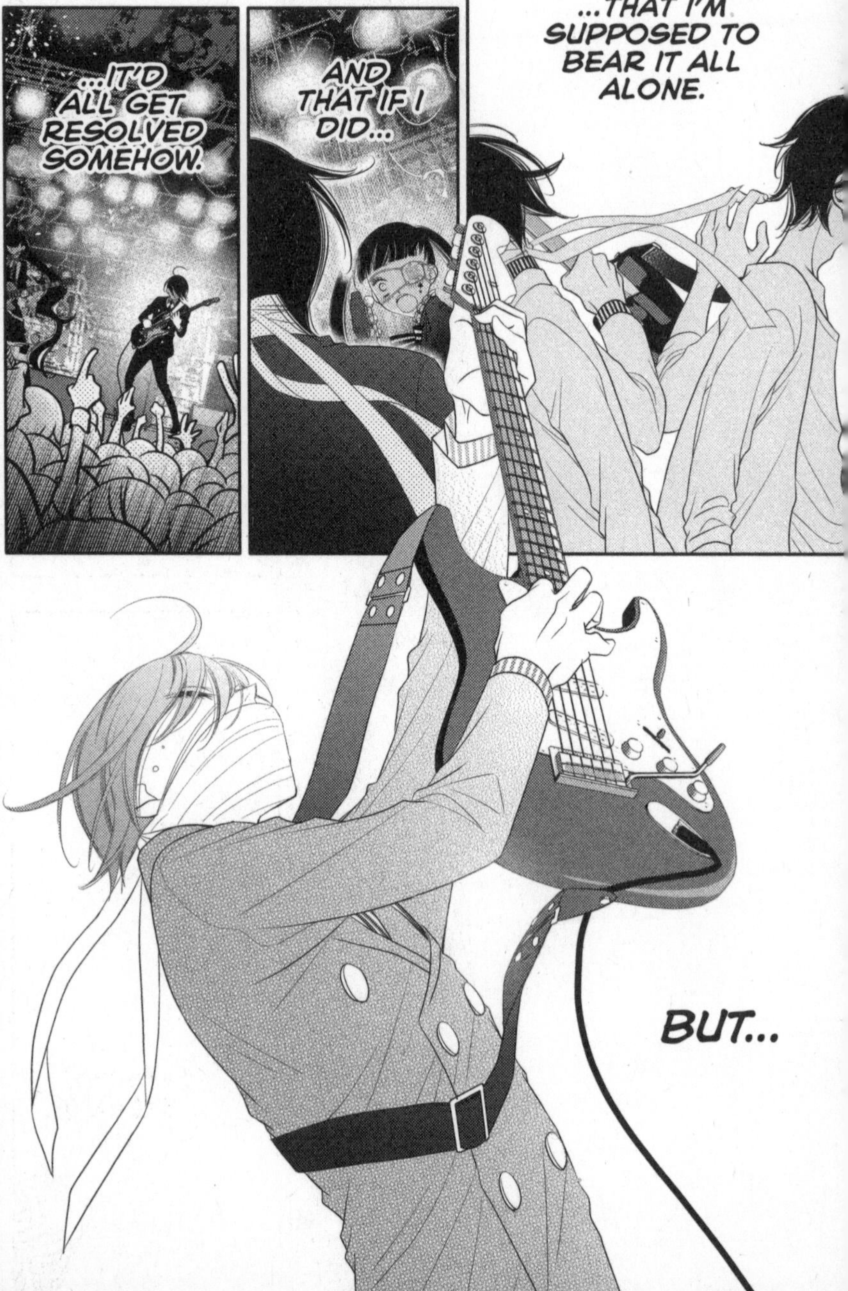
...THAT I'M SUPPOSED TO BEAR IT ALL ALONE.
AND THAT IF I DID...
...IT'D ALL GET RESOLVED SOMEHOW.
BUT...

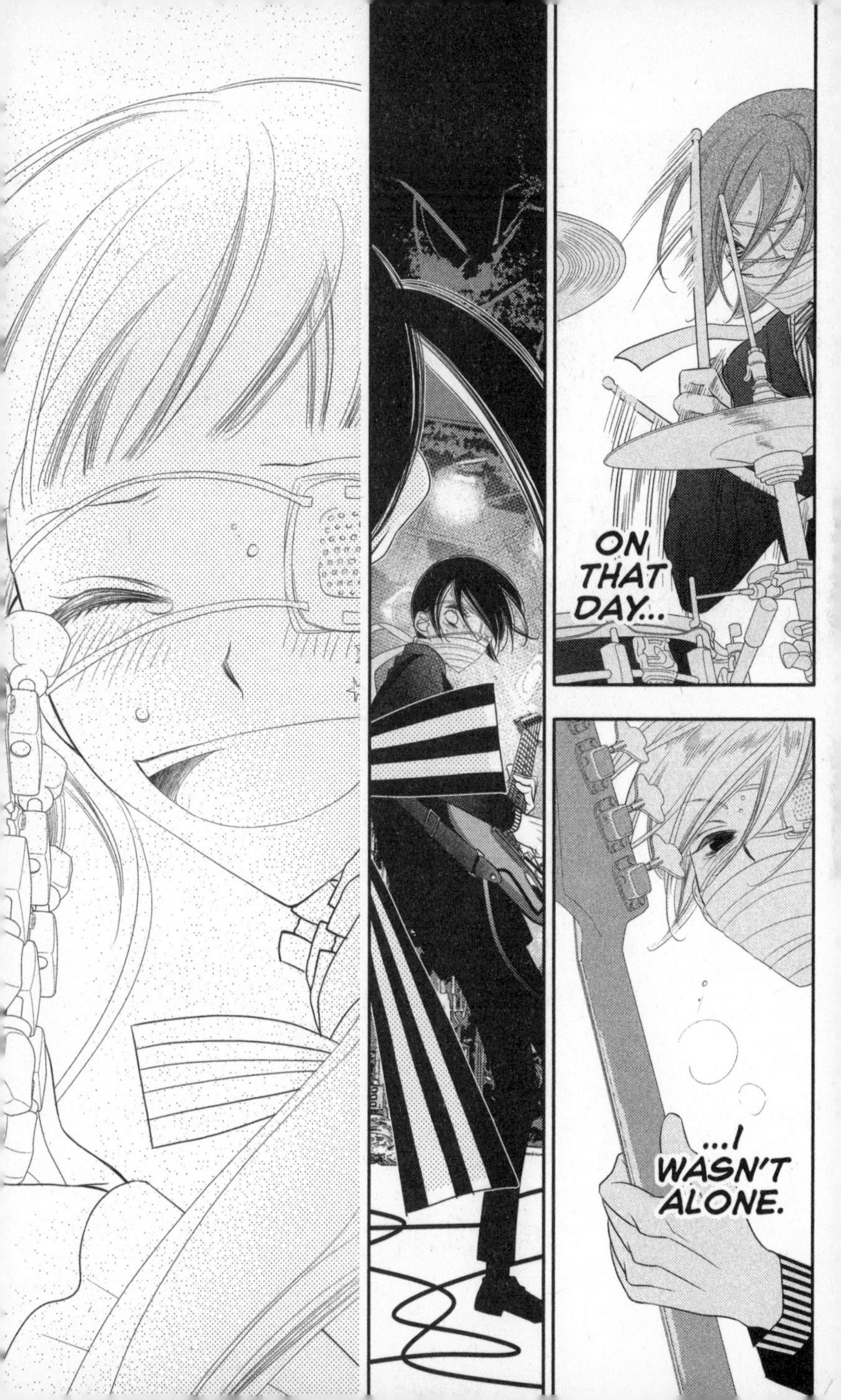
ON THAT DAY...
...I WASN'T ALONE.

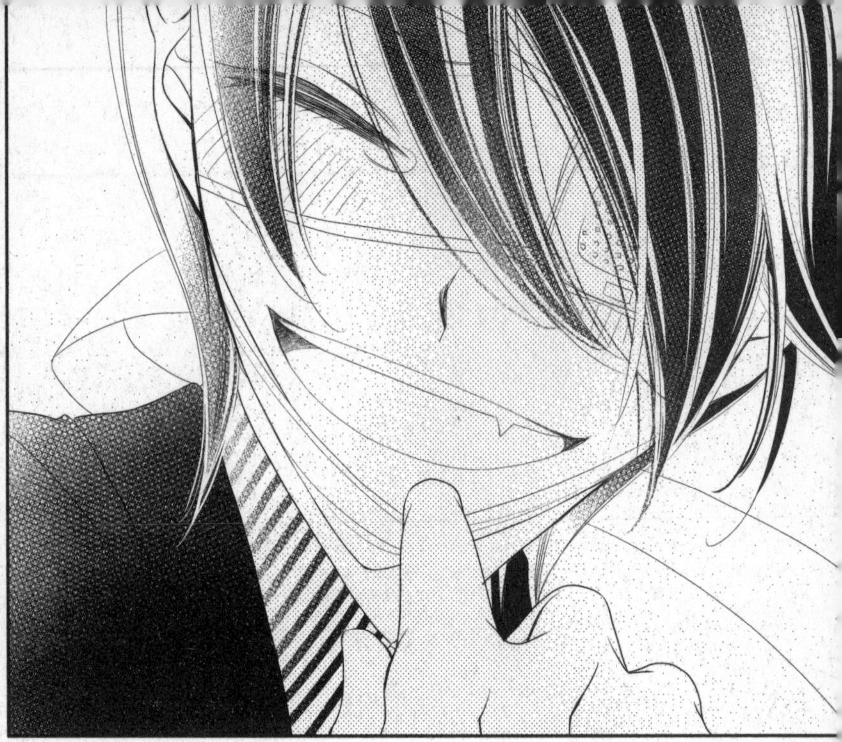

I WASN'T ALONE.

ANONYMOUS NOISE ⑨ / THE END

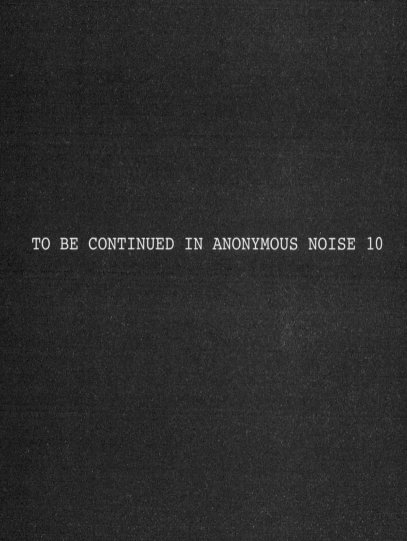

TO BE CONTINUED IN ANONYMOUS NOISE 10

AFTER SONG 52

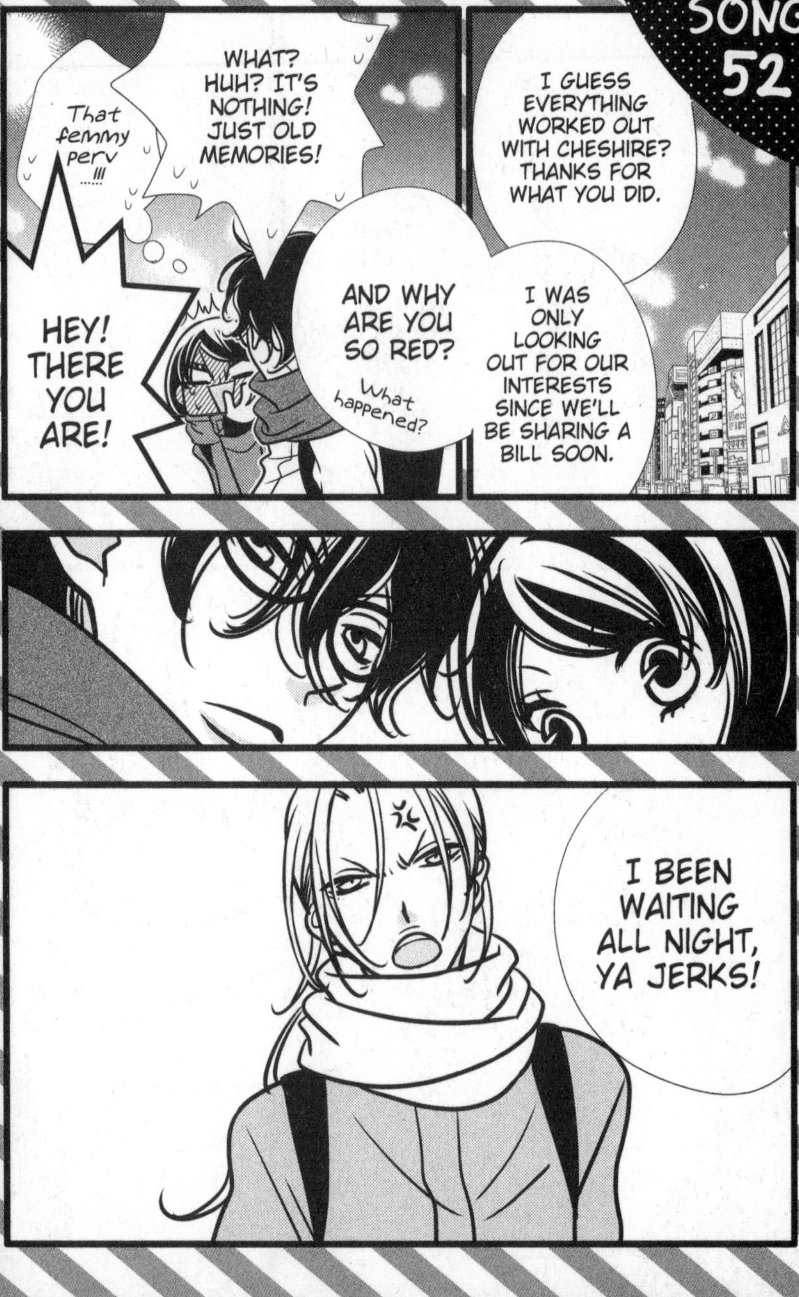

I GUESS EVERYTHING WORKED OUT WITH CHESHIRE? THANKS FOR WHAT YOU DID.
I WAS ONLY LOOKING OUT FOR OUR INTERESTS SINCE WE'LL BE SHARING A BILL SOON.
AND WHY ARE YOU SO RED?
What happened?
WHAT? HUH? IT'S NOTHING! JUST OLD MEMORIES!
That femmy perv ......!!!
HEY! THERE YOU ARE!
I BEEN WAITING ALL NIGHT, YA JERKS!

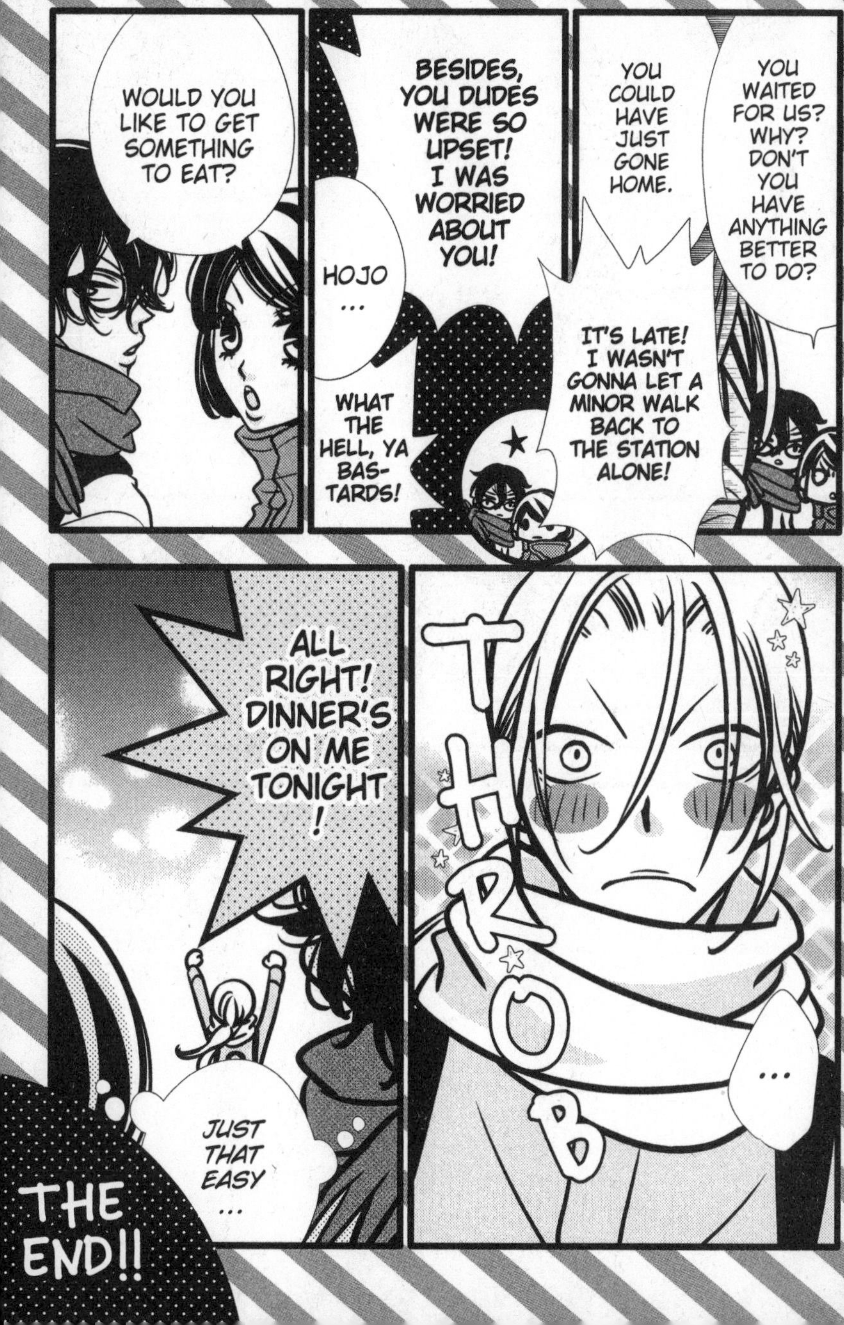
YOU WAITED FOR US? WHY? DON'T YOU HAVE ANYTHING BETTER TO DO?
YOU COULD HAVE JUST GONE HOME.
IT'S LATE! I WASN'T GONNA LET A MINOR WALK BACK TO THE STATION ALONE!
BESIDES, YOU DUDES WERE SO UPSET! I WAS WORRIED ABOUT YOU!
HOJO ...
WHAT THE HELL, YA BAS-TARDS!
WOULD YOU LIKE TO GET SOMETHING TO EAT?
THROB
...
ALL RIGHT! DINNER'S ON ME TONIGHT!
JUST THAT EASY ...
THE END!!

The joy of working with so many people to create *Anonymous Noise* is something that I expect will remain with me for the rest of my life. To you, my dear readers who have given me this opportunity, I thank you from the bottom of my heart.

- Ryoko Fukuyama

Born on January 5 in Wakayama Prefecture in Japan, Ryoko Fukuyama debuted as a manga artist after winning the Hakusensha Athena Shinjin Taisho Prize from Hakusensha's *Hana to Yume* magazine. She is also the author of *Nosatsu Junkie*. *Anonymous Noise* was adapted into an anime in 2017.